THE LAW OF NATURE CONSERVATION

The Law of Nature Conservation

Property, Environment, and the Limits of Law

CHRISTOPHER P. RODGERS
Professor of Law
Newcastle University

OXFORD
UNIVERSITY PRESS

OXFORD
UNIVERSITY PRESS

Great Clarendon Street, Oxford, OX2 6DP,
United Kingdom

Oxford University Press is a department of the University of Oxford.
It furthers the University's objective of excellence in research, scholarship,
and education by publishing worldwide. Oxford is a registered trade mark of
Oxford University Press in the UK and in certain other countries

First Edition published in 2013

Impression: 1

British Library Cataloguing in Publication Data
Data available

ISBN 978–0–19–954313–7

Printed and bound in Great Britain by
CPI Group (UK) Ltd, Croydon, CR0 4YY

Preface

This book offers a detailed consideration of nature conservation law, with a primary focus on the law of the United Kingdom. It is important to note at the outset that there is no commonly accepted definition of the precise scope and extent of 'nature conservation law'. Indeed, much of the discussion in Chapter 1 is devoted to a consideration of the parameters and nature of the subject. The text limits itself to a consideration of the law pertaining to the protection of natural habitats and to species protection. It does not attempt to engage with the wider aspects of natural resources law, nor with the relationship and interactions between natural resources protection and nature conservation. The text considers international conservation law and European Wildlife Directives, but chiefly as a contextual setting for the implementation of their requirements in domestic English law. Devolution has meant that the devolved administrations in Scotland, Wales, and Northern Ireland have started to develop distinctive approaches to wildlife conservation, and the relevant legislation has also become more fragmented. While focusing on English Law, I have endeavoured to cover differences of approach in Scotland, Northern Ireland, and Wales where relevant, although the complexity in environmental governance to which devolution has given rise sometimes makes this difficult.

Two features of the approach taken in the text merit explanation: (i) its interdisciplinary and contextual approach, and (ii) its use of property rights theory as a medium for the examination of key themes in nature conservation law. A study of nature conservation 'law' in isolation will not give the reader a full appreciation of how the law operates in practice. The text therefore draws, where appropriate, on interdisciplinary scholarship to examine the economic and policy factors which affect land management and the degradation of the natural environment, and to consider their interaction with legal mechanisms for the protection of habitats and endangered species. Where relevant, I have attempted to offer a contextual examination of English law. The protection of wildlife habitats is heavily conditioned by economic and policy factors affecting land management practices and the marine environment. The operation of both consensual and regulatory controls on land management cannot be understood without an appreciation of the economic instruments—such as, for example, farm subsidy under the common agricultural policy—that condition property management choices. And the integration of economic and legal policy instruments should be a key facet of an *effective* law of habitat protection.

Secondly, the book considers property theory and its interface with legal and economic instruments for promoting nature conservation. Environmental law deploys a very wide range of legal and economic instruments to further the protection of natural habitats, and the conservation of endangered species of animal bird and plant. These include elements of command and control regulation, management agreements, development control, and a wide range of 'soft' law instruments. Their common feature is that they all impact upon property rights, and upon the use of the resources to which property rights give access. The text offers a re-examination of nature conservation law using a resource allocation model of property rights, in order to examine the effect of legal and economic instruments for promoting nature conservation, and to examine the relationship between environmental regulation and the distribution of resources reflected in property rights. Most disputes about nature conservation are really disputes about access to economic or other resources; who, for example, should bear the cost of conservation measures, the relevant public bodies or individual landowners or commercial enterprises? These are ultimately the questions at issue in much of the litigation that has found its way into the case law discussed in the following chapters. These are questions that are mediated by property rights, and the primary functions of the legal instruments deployed in nature conservation law involve the variation and adjustment of property rights, and the consequent variation in the resources to which they allow access.

I must acknowledge the assistance of a number of colleagues in the preparation of this work. Thanks are due to Maria Lee and Michael Cardwell for reading and offering comments on Chapter 1, and on the context for a property rights analysis of the subject offered in this chapter. Anne Michelle Slater kindly read and commented on Chapter 7, and I am grateful in particular for her assistance with the final section on the designation of marine protected areas in Scotland. Margherita Pieraccini commented on Chapter 7 and offered a number of helpful insights, especially on common-pool resource management issues and the wider context of the MCZ project in England. My Newcastle colleague Ole Pedersen must be thanked for reading several chapters and offering helpful suggestions. I am also grateful to Dr Ann Sinclair for her contribution as research assistant, especially in connection with wildlife licensing and species protection issues (Chapter 5). Gemma Hayton turned some of my wilder flights of fancy into the diagrams now included in the text as Boxes 1.3, 4.4, 8.1, and 8.2, and Emilia Mickiewicz assisted with the Table of Cases. The property rights analysis of environmental liability mechanisms offered in Box 4.4 had its first airing at a research symposium at McGill Law School, and I am grateful to Professor Jane Glenn and her colleagues at McGill University for their comments and feedback, which helped me to refine my thinking on this difficult topic. Finally, the text draws in places on fieldwork undertaken between 2007 and 2010 and funded by the AHRC under project grant AH/E510310/1 (the Contested Common Land project). The financial and other support from the AHRC, and in particular its Landscape and Environment Programme team, of which the project was part, is gratefully acknowledged.

Nature conservation law is a rapidly developing subject. The text includes discussion of a number of very recent developments, including the National Planning Policy Framework for England, and the Marine and Coastal Access Act 2009. Chapter 7 includes a detailed examination of the 2009 Act and the process for the identification of candidate Marine Conservation Zones. At the time of writing, the final recommendations of the MCZ project in England were awaiting public consultation, with a view to the designation of the first MCZs under the 2009 Act in 2013. Chapter 7 should be read with this in view. Finally, as the script went to press the Law Commission published an important consultation paper on Wildlife Law reform.[1] The Commission's work programme for wildlife law reform is discussed in the following chapters, but the detailed proposals set out in their subsequent consultation paper were published after the book had gone to press. If implemented, the Law Commission's proposals will impact primarily upon species protection law (covered in Chapters 5 and 6 in this book).

The text states the law at 31 August 2012.

Chris Rodgers

Northumberland
August 2012

[1] *Wildlife Law: A Consultation Paper*, Law Commission Consulatation Paper No. 206 (August 2012).

Contents

Table of Cases

Table of Legislation

UNITED KINGDOM

Statutes

Statutory Instruments

EUROPEAN

Treaties and Conventions

Regulations

Directives

Abbreviations

AONB	Area of Outstanding Natural Beauty
CAP	Common Agricultural Policy
CCW	Countryside Council for Wales
CROW	Countryside and Right of Way Act 2000
DEFRA	Department for the Environment Food and Rural Affairs
EIA	Environmental Impact Assessment
ELS	Entry Level Stewardship Scheme (England)
Env L Rev	Environmental Law Review
ESA	Environmentally Sensitive Area
ESS	Environmental Stewardship Scheme (England)
HLS	Higher Level Stewardship Scheme (England)
JEL	Journal of Environmental Law
JNCC	Joint Nature Conservation Committee
JPL	Journal of Planning and Environmental Law
MCZ	Marine Conservation Zone
MNR	Marine Nature Reserve
MPA	Marine Protected Area
NNR	National Nature Reserve
RSPB	Royal Society for the Protection of Birds
SAC	Special Area of Conservation
SNH	Scottish Natural Heritage
SPA	Special Protection Area
SSSI	Site of Special Scientific Interest
TCPA	Town and Country planning Act 1990
WCA	Wildlife and Countryside Act 1981
WES	Wildlife Enhancement Scheme (England)
WWF	World Wide Fund for Nature

1

Nature Conservation in Legal Context

Introduction

There is no body of 'nature conservation law' that is recognized as a separate discipline in its own right, although there is a substantial (and growing) volume of legislation and case law devoted to the protection of natural habitats, wildlife species, and individual animals, plants, and birds. The law of nature conservation is largely the creation of international conventions and European law, and of their implementation in English and Scots Law by means of statute. There is also a growing focus in the modern law on the promotion of biodiversity. Statutory intervention to promote the protection of wildlife and wildlife habitats has taken place against the background of common law rules, many of which fail to confer protection on wildlife and habitats in the manner sought by modern public policy. Common law rules on ownership and property rights, as applied both to wildlife and to the land on which natural habitats are to be found, have nevertheless both shaped many of the legal instruments that will be discussed in the following pages, and continue to have important impacts upon their effectiveness in practice. The importance of common law property concepts to an understanding both of how nature conservation law works in practice, and its shortcomings, is a central theme of this work.

Species Protection and Habitat Protection—A Dual Approach

Environmental legislation has, in the United Kingdom, adopted a dual approach to promoting nature conservation. The law grants individual protection on species of Bird, Animal, and Plant ('species protection'). The principal measures here are those found in the Wildlife and Countryside Act 1981 (hereafter WCA 1981) Part 1, which will be considered in Chapter 5,[1] At the same time, the law confers protection on wildlife habitats ('habitat protection') with a view to ensuring the long-term

[1] As we will see in Chapter 5, although Part 1 of the Wildlife and Countryside Act 1981 applies in Scotland, a different text of the Act has been developed post-devolution in order to introduce provisions on wildlife protection specific to Scotland. The law therefore differs in Scotland, and in England and Wales, in some respects, and is to be found in parallel versions of the 1981 Act. This is highly unsatisfactory from the point of view of statutory drafting and the organization of the legal source texts. See Chapter 5, pp. 161 and 162.

survival of endangered and rare species by ensuring the maintenance of sufficient habitat to ensure the genetic exchange, migration, and breeding conditions for the species remaining at a 'favourable conservation status'.[2] The law on habitat protection is considered in Chapters 3 and 4. In the longer term, habitat protection is of vital importance in ensuring the successful promotion of nature conservation. Species protection and habitat protection are mutually interdependent; there is little point in granting legal protection to individual birds, animals, and plants through the law on species protection if the habitats on which they depend are unprotected. Loss of habitat is the primary cause of the decline of breeding numbers of rare and endangered bird and animal species in England and Wales.[3] The law on habitat protection in England and Wales is contained principally in the Wildlife and Countryside Act 1981, Part 2. This has been substantially amended and strengthened by the Countryside and Rights of Way Act 2000 and the Natural Environment and Rural Communities Act 2006. The 2006 Act established a new body, 'Natural England', which has assumed the statutory roles in England of the former English Nature, the Countryside Agency, and the Rural Development Service for habitat protection and related advisory matters, including the principal regulatory role in relation to protected nature conservation sites in England. A similar role is performed in Wales by the Countryside Council for Wales, and in Scotland by Scottish Natural Heritage. The statutory role and functions of the Councils are considered in more detail in Chapter 2.

The law on Habitat Protection in Scotland is now contained in Part 2 of the Nature Conservation (Scotland) Act 2004. The law in Scotland is very similar to that in England and Wales, but there are some differences that will be highlighted as relevant in the following chapters. The declared intention of the 2004 Act was to introduce a regime for Scotland that removed some of the well-known deficiencies of the law on habitat protection that have become apparent since the Wildlife and Countryside Act was first introduced in 1981.

Nature Conservation Legislation: Origins, Scope, and Policy

(a) The origins of statutory intervention

Animal plants and birds enjoy little direct protection at common law. Neither do the habitats on which they depend for their long-term survival. The focus of common law remedies is on private interests, and in particular on the protection of private property rights in animals birds and plants, and on the property rights of the owners and occupiers of the land on which their habitats are to be found. The protection of the *special attributes* of an area of land as a valuable natural habitat is a

[2] This is a term with technical legal meaning; see Chapter 3, p. 239 and Box 6.4.

[3] See *Lost Life—England's Lost and Threatened Species* (Natural England research report NE233, 2010) at 50 where the impact of habitat loss on endangered species is stressed. It is there noted that 412 of the priority species identified in the England Biodiversity Action Plan are known from fewer than five sites. Their preservation, therefore, urgently requires an expansion of the habitat available to them.

public interest consideration unrecognized by the common law, which also fails in most cases to impose a duty on the landowner to promote the environmental stewardship of his land. In those cases where the common law protects property rights in land, it protects the owner or occupier's use and enjoyment of the land and its produce, and not those attributes or features that make it valuable as a habitat for wildlife. In other words, common law remedies are neutral as to the environmental characteristics (or otherwise) of property interests unless they have a quantifiable value that can be reflected in an award of damages. This may be considered anachronistic given that the common law does, through the calculation of compensatory damages, protect the inherent *commercial* value of property; for example, against trespass or nuisance. The inherent difficulties of developing a methodology to attribute a quantifiable financial measurement to damage caused to wildlife, to wildlife habitats, and to biodiversity have led, as we shall see in Chapter 4, to the development of new environmental liability mechanisms by the Environmental Liability Directive of 2004, and its subsequent implementation in the UK. This has been created using statutory powers,[4] like much of the other nature conservation law applicable in Scotland, England, and Wales.

The limitations of the common law for protecting wildlife habitats are largely attributable to a narrow approach to notions of 'property' and to property rights in land. The theoretical basis of title to land is an intention to control the land and exclude others. This finds its ultimate expression in the fundamental rule of English property law that title to property depends solely upon a claim to prior possession, evidenced in practice by title documents or, in the case of registered land, by the registered title at HM Land Registry to the land in question. This is also the basis of the law of adverse possession, which enables someone to acquire title to unregistered land by factual possession for a period in excess of 12 years,[5] provided the claimant can show the necessary intention to exclude others from its possession and enjoyment.[6] Where the title to land is registered, a claimant can apply to be entered on the title register as registered proprietor after a period of 10 years adverse possession, but the rightful owner has the right to object by counter notice under the terms of the Land Registration Act 2002.[7] The exploitation of the land's resources can be evidence of 'possession' for these purposes, but it is the occupation of land, and not its stewardship, that is the hallmark of possessory title.

The possessory basis for notions of ownership is, similarly, evident in the rules governing the exploitation of birds, animals, and plants in English Law. Plants growing in the soil are regarded as the property of the owner of the soil. The

[4] See the Environmental Damage (Prevention and Remediation) Regulations 2009, SI 2009/153, made under s. 2 (2) and Schedule 2 para. 1A, the European Communities Act 1972.

[5] S. 15(1) Limitation Act 1980.

[6] As to which, see *Buckingham CC v Moran* [1990] Ch 623; *J A Pye (Oxford) Ltd v Graham* [2003] AC 419.

[7] See s. 97 and Schedule 6 para. 1; s. 73 and Schedule 6 para. 5, Land Registration Act 2002, for the procedures for objection by the registered owner. The procedure in the 2002 Act makes it very difficult for a squatter to claim adverse possession as the owner will be given notice and an opportunity to 'warn off' any claim to title: this was not the case prior to the 2002 Act, and is not the case where land remains unregistered.

common law also gives the owner the right to exploit wild animals (animals *ferae naturae*) that come onto his land. While they are alive, wild animals and birds are not subject to absolute ownership in English law.[8] The landowner has a right to hunt and catch wild creatures, however, and to reduce them into his possession. This is sometimes referred to as a right of 'qualified property' in those wild animals present on the owner's land,[9] and interference with this right (for example, by interfering with the owner's hunting activities) is actionable.[10] Once a wild creature has been killed or captured it becomes personal property, however, and is the property of the owner of the land on which it was found.[11] This will be the case in English law even if it is killed and reduced into possession by a trespasser; for example, a poacher, who thereby commits theft. In Scotland, on the other hand, the possessory rationale for property rights is taken to its logical conclusion, and a wild animal taken by a poacher or trespasser will become the property of the latter, and not of the owner of the land on which it was taken, although the landowner may have a right to compensation from the trespasser in these circumstances.[12]

(b) Legislation on species and habitats

Because wild animals and birds are not 'property', they have not, historically, been recognized as worthy of protection by the common law, unless, of course, they have been reduced into possession. In the absence of special statutory provision, therefore, it follows that the killing or destruction of wild animals is not in itself a wrong against anyone and, unless a recognized property right is incidentally affected,[13] it cannot be remedied in a civil action for damages or an injunction. This fundamental proposition explains the development of extensive statutory protection for wild animals birds and plants since the Second World War, and in particular, the introduction by statute of criminal liability for the protection of many endangered and vulnerable species of bird, animal, and plant; for example, by Part 1 of the Wildlife and Countryside Act 1981 and by species-specific legislation such as the Protection of Badgers Act 1992 and the Conservation of Seals Act 1970.[14]

The protection of wildlife habitats, on the other hand, raises different questions. Wildlife habitats may be found on land (terrestrial habitats), or they may be aquatic (for example, rivers, lakes, and coastal habitats). The key challenge for terrestrial

[8] Blackstone's *Commentaries on the Laws of England*, Vol. II, 391. See also *The Case of Swans* (1592) 7 Co Rep 15b at 7b; *Blades v Higgs* (1865) 11 HL Cas 621.

[9] See Blackstone *Commentaries*, Vol. II, 393; Gray and Gray, *Elements of Land Law* 5th edn (2009) at 1.2.84, 1.2.85.

[10] *Kearry v Pattinson* [1939] 1 KB 471.

[11] Blackstone *Commentaries* II 389–92. See *Blades v Higgs* (1865) 11 HL Cas 621. Merely setting traps for wild animals does not in itself create a right of property in the animals hunted, however: *Cresswell v DPP* [2006] EWHC 3379 (Admin).

[12] See Reid, *Nature Conservation Law* 3rd edn (2009) at 1.3.5.

[13] Eg in *Pride of Derby Angling and Derbyshire Angling Association Ltd v British Celanese Ltd* [1952] Ch. 149—pollution causing fish kill restrained by an injunction awarded to protect riparian rights owned by the angling association.

[14] See further Chapter 5, pp. 161 ff.

habitats is to ensure that the land on which they are found is managed by landowners in a manner that protects and promotes the special conservation features that are to be found there, and this involves reconciling the property rights of the landowner with the public interest considerations represented by the conservation needs of the site's natural features. The exploitative land use rights conferred by property rights in English law are the starting point for this exercise, and underpin much of the legislation on habitat conservation in English law. In the case of aquatic habitats property rights are also in many cases relevant, but differently expressed through, for example, the recognition of riparian rights as a separate category of property right, the rights of landowners to abstract water for domestic or industrial use, and the need to consider the rules concerning the ownership of the riverbed by landowners with property adjacent to the river. The owner of land does not 'own' water passing though it in percolating or defined channels: he has, rather, the right to the 'reasonable use' of water flowing through defined channels onto or through his land,[15] but must respect the rights of other riparian owners lower down the stream to receive an undiminished flow of water in its natural state of purity,[16] The rules governing the ownership of the foreshore are also complex. In all these cases, however, the essential nature of the role played by the law is the same: to reconcile the property rights of those with a land interest in the site on which the habitat is to be found with the public interest in conservation. How this function has been performed has changed several times since legislation on habitat conservation was first introduced in 1949.

The principal measures on habitat protection in England and Wales are now contained in Part 2 of the Wildlife and Countryside Act 1981, and are discussed in more detail in Chapter 3. It provides for the notification and protection of Sites of Special Scientific Interest (hereafter SSSIs) by the Conservation Bodies. The 1981 Act was heavily conditioned by the emphasis in UK nature conservation policy of the so-called 'voluntary principle', by virtue of which legislative intervention was aimed primarily at securing the voluntary participation of property owners in conservation measures. This was an approach that dated back to the immediate post-war years and the publication in 1947 of the Huxley Committee report on Nature Conservation in England and Wales.[17] Following the Huxley report, measures were introduced in the National Parks and Access to the Countryside Act 1949 providing for the notification of Areas of Special Scientific Interest. The law at this stage avoided any direct interference with property rights, however, and was focused instead on the introduction of a requirement for consultation with the Nature Conservancy Council on planning applications in designated areas.

[15] See *Swindon Waterworks Co Ltd v Wilts and Berks Canal Navigation Co Ltd* (1859) 11 ER 140.

[16] *Scott-Whitehead v National Coal Board* (1985) 53 P&CR 263; *Thames Heliports Plc v London Borough of Tower Hamlets* (1997) 74 P&CR 164. In practice, discharges to water will be subject to control through water discharge permits issued by the Environment Agency, and if so licensed—and provided the discharged substances are within the terms and parameters of the discharge licence—they will not be actionable.

[17] *Conservation of Nature in England and Wales*, Wildlife Conservation Special Committee Cmnd. 7122 (the 'Huxley Committee').

The Wildlife and Countryside Act 1981 greatly strengthened the environmental regulation of land use, but remained firmly rooted in the voluntary principle. The 1981 Act was premised on a protectionist philosophy aimed at preventing damaging land use proposals in areas notified as SSSIs by 'buying out' harmful development.[18] The underlying assumption of these provisions was that property entitlements give an absolute right to resource use and exploitation,[19] even if the owner's land use is environmentally damaging. The legal mechanisms introduced in the 1981 Act were therefore a curious compromise between direct intervention to restrict property rights and the need to maintain the voluntary principle on which public policy was based. Section 28 of the 1981 Act imposed restrictions on a landowner's right to carry out operations in an SSSI where they have been notified in the site notification as 'operations likely to damage' the conservation (that is, scientific) interest of the site (referred to for brevity hereafter as OLDSIs). It required a landowner to serve notice on the Conservation Body of his intention to carry out an OLDSI, and then to enter into a statutory consultation with them before carrying it out. The Act specified a consultation period of four months, during which it remained a criminal office to carry out notified OLDSIs,[20] but on conclusion of the consultation period the owner could lawfully carry them out without redress.[21] Protection of the site would ultimately depend upon the landowner trading his unfettered property entitlement in a management agreement with the Conservation Body,[22] or on the Secretary of State making a nature conservation order to protect the site.[23] Ministerial guidance provided for the payment of compensation under management agreements—either on the basis of a lump-sum payment representing loss of land value or an annual payment representing the

[18] See G. Cox and P. Lowe, 'A Battle Not the War: the Politics of the Wildlife and Countryside Act', (1983) 4 *Countryside Planning Yearbook* 48–77 and 'Countryside Politics: goodbye to goodwill?' (1983) 54 *Politics Quarterly* 268; P. Lowe, G. Cox, M. MacEwan, T. O'Riordan and M. Winter, *Countryside Conflicts: the politics of farming, forestry and conservation* (Temple Smith/Gower, 1986), Ch. 6; M. Winter, *Rural Politics: policies for agriculture, forestry and the environment* (Routledge, 1996), Ch. 8, esp. pp. 205 ff.; W. M. Adams, *Nature's Place: conservation sites and countryside change* (Allen & Unwin, 1986), Ch. 4 and *Future, Nature; a vision for conservation* (Earthscan, 1997) at pp. 37–50.

[19] Subject, of course, to planning constraints, which have a limited application to agriculture and forestry in any event: section 55(2)(e)(f) Town and Country Planning Act 1990 (exemption of use of land or buildings for agriculture or forestry purposes from definition of 'development' necessitating planning permission), Schedule 2 Part 6 Town and Country Planning (General Permitted Development) Order 1995, SI 1995/418 (permitted development rights for agricultural buildings and operations).

[20] S. 28(5) Wildlife and Countryside Act 1981.

[21] This procedure was subjected to judicial criticism by the House of Lords in *Southern Water Authority v Nature Conservancy Council* [1992] 3 All ER 481. Lord Mustill referred to the statutory consultation procedure as 'toothless' ([1992] 3 All ER 481 at 484 g).

[22] See eg S. Ball, 'Reforming the Law of Habitat Protection', Ch. 4 in C. Rodgers (ed.), *Nature Conservation and Countryside Law* (University of Wales Press, 1996) at p. 92; C. Rodgers, 'Reforming Property Rights for Nature Conservation' in P. Jackson and D. C. Wilde (eds), *Property Law: Current Issues and Debates* (Ashgate, 1998), 48; L. Livingstone, J. Rowan-Robinson and R. Cunningham, *Management Agreements for Nature Conservation in Scotland* (University of Aberdeen, 1990); C. Rodgers and J. Bishop, *Management Agreements for Promoting Nature Conservation* (RICS Research Reports, 1998), Ch. 2.

[23] Under s. 29 Wildlife and Countryside Act 1981. This power was repealed in England and Wales by Schedule 10 para. 7, and Schedule 16, the Countryside and Rights of Way Act 2000.

'profits foregone' by the landowner as a consequence of complying with the terms of the agreement.[24]

The Countryside and Rights of Way Act 2000 further strengthened the law by empowering the Conservation Bodies to refuse operational consent indefinitely to OLDSIs,[25] subject to a right of appeal to the Secretary of State.[26] The 2000 Act was strongly focused on encouraging positive conservation management by landowners. It now requires the Conservation Body to serve a site management statement when notifying an SSSI, containing a statement of their views about the management of the land and the conservation and enhancement of its natural features, flora, and/or fauna.[27] In Scotland, all SSSI notifications must also now include a site management statement that 'provides guidance to owners and occupiers of land within an SSSI as to how the natural feature [of the site] should be managed *or enhanced*'.[28] The objectives in the site management statement will provide the operational context within which decisions will be made on applications for consent to carry out OLDSIs. These provisions are discussed more fully in Chapters 3 and 4. The approach represented by the 2000 Act, and by the 2004 Act in Scotland, illustrates a movement away from an approach focused primarily on the voluntary participation landowners in the management of their land for nature conservation and towards encouraging a 'partnership' between the Conservation Bodies and landowners in delivering positive conservation management.

Another decisive factor in the move away from an approach based solely upon the voluntary principle has been the need to implement the requirements of European Union environmental law. In particular, the Habitats and Species Directive of 1992[29] required the member states to designate 'European sites' that will form part of the Europe-wide *Natura 2000* network of protected sites under the scheme established by the Directive. All sites designated under the Directive in England and Wales will also have been notified as SSSIs under the Wildlife and Countryside Act 1981 (as amended), and will therefore be subject to the habitat protection measures outlined earlier. Where a site is also designated under *Natura 2000*, however,

[24] Department of the Environment Circular 4/83, 'Wildlife and Countryside Act 1981—Financial Guidelines for Management Agreements', esp. para. 14 (lump-sum payments) and paras. 16–18 (annual payments). The guidelines were generously interpreted by the courts and gave rise to very large (and controversial) payment entitlements: see for example *Thomas v Countryside Council for Wales* [1994] 4 All ER 853; *Cameron v Nature Conservancy Council* 1991 SLT (Lands Tribunal) 85.

[25] S. 28E(3) (5) Wildlife and Countryside Act 1981, introduced by Schedule 9 Countryside and Rights of Way Act 2000.

[26] S. 28F Countryside and Rights of Way Act 2000. Operational consent granted by the Conservation Bodies for potentially damaging operations can also now be subject to conditions or time-limited.

[27] See s. 28(4) Wildlife and Countryside Act 1981, as amended by Schedule 9 Countryside and Rights of Way Act 2000.

[28] See s. 4 Nature Conservation (Scotland) Act 2004 (emphasis added). Provision is also made for the review of the site management statement and its amendment by Scottish Natural Heritage: s. 4(4) Nature Conservation (Scotland) Act 2004.

[29] Council Directive 92/43/EEC on the Conservation of Natural Habitats and of Wild Flora and Fauna, [1992] OJ L206/7.

the Directive requires the member states to provide a level of enhanced protection. In particular, it requires the member states to 'take appropriate steps to avoid, in the special areas of conservation, the deterioration of natural habitats and the habitats of species as well as disturbance of the species for which the areas have been designated, in so far as such disturbance could be significant in relation to the objectives of the Directive'.[30] Any plan or project not necessary to the management of a protected site must be subjected to an environmental assessment of its implications for the conservation objectives of the site designation and can only be permitted if it will not adversely affect the site's integrity, or if there are 'imperative reasons of overriding public interest' for permitting it. These can include public interest considerations of an economic or social nature (provided, of course, that they are of overriding importance,), but if the site hosts a *priority* species or habitat type identified by the Directive, the development can only be permitted if there are overriding considerations connected with human health or public safety, or what the Directive terms 'beneficial consequences of primary importance for the environment'.[31] The need to guarantee the protection of sites meant that an approach based purely on voluntary measures by landowners had to be abandoned, leading to the introduction of powers for the Conservation Bodies to compel appropriate management as a last resort, by, for example, the use of management orders and management schemes in protected sites.[32]

The Scope of Modern 'Conservation' Law

Contemporary nature conservation law covers a wide field of legal regulation. It is about much more than the *preservation*[33] of wildlife and habitats, and the biological diversity they exhibit. The law also promotes the recreation and improvement in habitats and populations of wildlife species. It also has a major role in conserving and promoting biodiversity, and this includes, for example, 'in relation to a living organism or type of habitat, restoring or enhancing a population or habitat'.[34] The different Acts of Parliament and subordinate legislation that will be discussed in the following chapters fall into two broad groups—those concerned with the protection of individual animals birds and plants (legislation on species protection), and those concerned with the protection of the wildlife habitats on which those species

[30] Art. 6.2 Council Directive 92/43/EEC on the Conservation of Natural Habitats and of Wild Flora and Fauna, [1992] OJ L206/7.

[31] See arts. 6.3 and 6.4 of the Council Directive 92/43/EEC on the Conservation of Natural Habitats and of Wild Flora and Fauna, [1992] OJ L206/7.

[32] The 1992 Directive was initially transposed into English law by the Conservation (Natural Habitats & Co.) regs. 1994 SI 1994/2716. This has now been replaced, after successive revisions since 1994, by the Conservation of Habitats and Species Regulations 2010, SI 2010/490. These are considered in detail in Chapter 3.

[33] 'Conservation'—the act of conserving or keeping from change loss injury, etc. (noun)(New Collins English Dictionary). In its adjectival form the phrase 'conservation' also has the attribute of describing the protection, preservation, and *careful management* of resources (italics added).

[34] S. 40(3) Natural Environment and Rural Communities Act 2006.

depend for their long-term survival (legislation on habitat protection). They are not distinct, self-contained, legal domains however, and there are close interactions between the two areas of law.

(a) Conservation of biological diversity

To these primary foci must be added a related, but distinct, focus in the modern legislation on the protection and promotion of 'biodiversity'. The use of biodiversity as an organizing legal principle[35] originates in the Convention on Biological Diversity (CBD) signed at the Earth Summit in Rio in 1992. The concept is defined in the CBD as 'the variability among living organisms from all sources including inter alia terrestrial, marine, and other aquatic ecosystems and the ecological complexes of which they are part; this includes diversity within species, between species and of ecosystems'.[36] This is a complex definition, and one that captures a number of differing (but related) interactions. The need to ensure diversity between ecosystems, for example, is the basis for the conservation of natural habitats of different kinds. 'Conservation' law is therefore not solely concerned with protecting sensitive wildlife habitats, but with protecting and encouraging the restoration of a range of *different types* of a particular habitat or habitats. On the other hand, the reference to diversity within ecosystems captures the fact that the presence of this type of diversity is often a barometer of the health of a natural habitat. Diversity *within species* reflects the fact that there are often genetic variations between different populations of bird or animal within the same species.

An important element of the approach to the protection and promotion of biodiversity endorsed by the CBD is the adoption of the 'ecosystem approach' to the management of land water and living resources.[37] The CBD's ecosystem approach is enlarged upon in 12 principles that are intended to provide the primary framework for action to preserve biodiversity, with the aim of providing for 'the integrated management of land water and living resources [to] promote conservation and sustainable use in an equitable way'.[38] These are supplemented by operational guidance agreed by the conference of the parties to the CBD and additional guidelines for its implementation.[39] The ecosystem approach is premised on the recognition that natural resources and well-functioning natural systems, such as clean water and healthy soils, are vital to our well-being and are themselves dependent upon a healthy biodiversity. It therefore seeks to take into account all the economic and non-economic benefits these services provide and to enable

35 The concept predates the 1992 CBD, and originated in the 1980s in the writings of the biologist Edward Wilson: see further Nicolas de Sadeleer, 'EC Law and Biodiversity' in R. Macrory (ed.) *Reflections on 30 Years of EU Environmental Law: A High Level of Protection?* (Europa, 2006), esp. at pp. 351–2.

36 Art. 2.1 Convention on Biological Diversity 1992.

37 The ecosystem approach was endorsed by the fifth Conference of the Parties to the CBD in 2000: COP 5 (Nairobi 15–26 May 2000), Decision V/6.

38 COP5 (Nairobi 15–26 May 2000). Decision V/6 at para. A.1.

39 COP5 (Nairobi 15–26 May 2000). Decision V/6 s. C, and Decision VII/11.

Box 1.1 Ecosystem Services Defined

The ecosystem services approach was adopted by the 1992 Convention for Biological Diversity (CBD). Ecosystems were defined in the CBD as:[40]

'a dynamic complex of plant animal and micro organism communities and their non-living environment interacting as a functional unit'.

Ecosystem 'services', on the other hand, have been defined by DEFRA as '*the products of natural systems from which people derive benefits, including goods and services, some of which can be valued economically, and others which have a non-economic value*'.[41]

The Millennium Ecosystem Assessment identified four different types of ecosystem service that can provide benefits,[42] and this analysis forms the basis of the approach adopted in, for example, the 2011 Natural Environment White Paper (England) and the National Environment Framework (Wales). Ecosystems services comprise the following:

- *Provisioning services:* we obtain products from ecosystems such as food, fibre, and medicines. Examples here would include crops, dairy produce, and meat, timber, and clean water.
- *Regulating services:* we benefit from the results of ecosystem processes such as water purification, air quality maintenance, and climate regulation. Examples here would include carbon sequestration (storage) by forests and upland peat mires, the ability of wetlands and urban drainage systems to purify water supplies for use in agriculture or for drinking water supply after treatment, and flood hazard reduction through natural or urban drainage.
- *Cultural services:* we gain non-material benefits from our interaction with the natural environment such as education and well-being. Recreation from the use of open green spaces, and cultural heritage benefits, spiritual and/or religious enrichment, aesthetic services (for example, valued landscapes).
- *Supporting services:* these are functions that are necessary for the production of all the other ecosystem services from which we benefit. Examples here would include soil formation in woodlands or through land management on farms or allotments, and natural nutrient cycling, such as soil breaking down animal or vegetative waste.

decision-makers to exercise judgment about how we use our environment based on the widest relevant range of evidence as to the impacts, costs, and benefits of their actions (see Box 1.1).

Many of the obligations agreed at Rio, and set out in the CBD, have been implemented in English law. The Natural Environment and Rural Communities Act 2006[43]

[40] See <http://www.cbd.int/decision/cop/?id=7148>.

[41] See *The Natural Choice: securing the value of nature,* Cm 8082, June 2011, at p. 12. Available at: <http://www.defra.gov.uk/environment/natural/whitepaper/>.

[42] See <http://www.maweb.org/en/index.aspx>.

[43] S. 40(1) Natural Environment and Rural Communities Act 2006. This replaced obligations introduced in s. 74 the Countryside and Rights of Way Act 2000.The latter required public bodies to 'have regard to' the purpose of conserving biological diversity 'so far as is consistent with the proper exercise of [the body's public] functions' (s. 74(1) Countryside and Rights of Way Act 2000). The duty in s. 74 of the 2000 Act only extended to ministers, government departments, and the Welsh

imposes a duty on every public authority[44] to 'have regard to'[45] the purpose of conserving biodiversity when exercising its functions, and also requires every minister of the Crown, government department, or the Welsh Assembly Government to have regard to the Convention on Biological Diversity when doing so. The Convention required the signatories (including the UK) to develop national strategies plans or programmes for the conservation and sustainable use of biological diversity.[46] This requirement was implemented by the Natural Environment and Rural Communities Act 2006, which requires the Secretary of State (in England) to consult with Natural England and to publish a list of the living organisms and types of habitat which in his opinion are of principal importance for the purpose of conserving biodiversity.[47] A similar duty is imposed on the Welsh Assembly Government.[48]

The duties set out in the Convention initially led to the production of the UK Biodiversity Action Plan in 1994.[49] The 1994 Plan drew together the various instruments and plans for nature conservation across the UK into a single integrated plan with a time horizon of activities stretching over 20 years, and recognizing the need for specific biologically determined targets for habitat and species renewal. The 1994 Plan has now been superseded by a new strategic framework *Conserving Biodiversity—The UK Approach*[50] (hereafter UKBAP) published in 2007. Implementation of the UKBAP is overseen by the UK Biodiversity Partnership (UKBP), a widely based body representing the governmental Conservation Bodies with responsibility for implementing conservation law, private individuals and bodies, funding bodies and non-governmental organizations (NGOs).[51] The work of the Partnership is coordinated by the UK Biodiversity Partnership Standing Committee (UKBPSC), which is chaired by the Department for the Environment, Farming and Agriculture (DEFRA) and includes representatives of each country's governmental and statutory Conservation Bodies, and of the conservation NGOs.[52]

The revised UKBAP lays down a framework within which individual Species and Habitat Plans, and Local Biodiversity Action Plans are situated. It adopts as a guiding principle the 'ecosystem approach' developed under the aegis of the CBD,

Assembly Government. The duty in the 2006 Act is more widely applicable to a large range of different public bodies.

44 This includes ministers of the Crown, the Welsh Assembly government, local authorities and local planning authorities, statutory undertakers, and office holders under the Crown: s. 40(4) 2006 Act.

45 The duty on public bodies in Scotland is framed in more directive terms; they must 'further' the conservation of biodiversity, insofar as this is consistent with the proper exercise of those functions: s. 1 Nature Conservation (Scotland) Act 2004.

46 Art. 6 Convention on Biological Diversity.

47 S. 41 2006 Act.

48 S. 42 2006 Act.

49 Biodiversity: the UK Action Plan (Cm.2428) 1994.

50 DEFRA, 2007. Available at: <http://jncc.defra.gov.uk/_ukbap/UKBAP_ConBio-UKApproach-2007.pdf>.

51 See generally <http://jncc.defra.gov.uk/page-5155>.

52 Membership comprises; DEFRA (chair), Countryside Council for Wales, Welsh Assembly Government, Natural England, Joint Nature Conservation Committee, Scottish Natural Heritage, Scottish Government, Department of Environment Northern Ireland, and Wildlife and Countryside Link. For further information, working papers, and minutes of meetings, see: <http://jncc.defra.gov.uk/page-5699>.

seeking to facilitate an integrated approach to the management of land, air, water, and living resources that produces conservation and sustainable resource use that is both equitable and effective.[53] A good example of the need for (and potential benefits of) an integrated ecosystem-based approach to protecting biodiversity is provided by the close connections between climate change and habitat protection. Biodiversity will potentially be impacted by climate change in myriad ways. The role of upland peat bogs in carbon sequestration has been recognized, as has the need to ensure their appropriate management as a key element of the UK's policy for climate change adaptation.[54] Many upland peat bogs and semi-natural areas are currently farmed for livestock production, as well as providing valuable areas for open air recreation (for example, in the national parks). Semi-natural grassland can sequester up to 0.6 tonnes of carbon per hectare per year, and woodland soils even more.[55] Climate change is likely to have an effect upon the ability of peat-based moorland soils to retain carbon, principally because of changes in vegetation caused by aerial pollution and projected changes in temperature and rainfall as climate change progresses, all of which will lead to soil and peat-mire degradation, which will, in turn, release large volumes of carbon into the atmosphere. An approach to protecting wildlife habitats in the uplands that seeks to minimize the impact of climate change on carbon sequestration can therefore have major benefits not only for wildlife but for the UK's strategy for combating climate change.[56] Climate change adaptation will therefore necessitate changes in the way in which agriculture is funded through, for example, the rural development programme of the EU Common Agricultural Policy, as well as the integration of management priorities for carbon sequestration into the way in which legal instruments for promoting nature conservation (for example, management agreements in SSSIs) are targeted and used.

There are 65 priority habitats and 1149 species identified in revised targets for the UK BAP adopted by the UK Biodiversity Partnership in 2007.[57] The implementation of the individual habitat and species action plans is the responsibility of the devolved administrations in Scotland, Wales, and Northern Ireland, and in England, of Natural England. The UK list of priority habitats and species is an important reference source. It will, for example, inform the lists of priority species given legal protection under domestic legislation (for example under the Wildlife

[53] Conserving Biodiversity—the UK Approach (DEFRA 2007) at p. 9 ('guiding principles').

[54] DEFRA research estimates, for example, that England's peat lands store 580 million tonnes of carbon and that the value of carbon sequestration by UK woodlands is £770 pa: see <http://www.defra.gov.uk/environment/natural/ecosystems-services/>.

[55] Conserving Biodiversity—the UK Approach (DEFRA 2007) at p. 8 and Box 3 'Climate Change and Biodiversity'.

[56] This is recognized, for instance, in draft Strategic Goal D of the CBD Strategic Plan for post-2010, and in the UK response to its implementation. Target 15 of the draft plan for the CBD requires that 'By 2020, the contribution of biodiversity to ecosystem resilience and to carbon storage and sequestration are enhanced, through conservation and restoration, including restoration of at least 15 per cent of degraded lands, thereby contributing to climate change mitigation and adaptation and to combating desertification'. See UK Biodiversity Partnership Standing Committee: UK Biodiversity Indicators, Progress Update (6 May 2010) Annex B (Draft targets and Goals for CBD Strategic Plan), available at: </http://www.ukbap.org.uk/partnership.aspx>.

[57] See <http://www.ukbap.org.uk/>.

and Countryside Act 1981, Part 1).[58] The list of priority habitats and the measures set out in *Conserving Biodiversity—The UK Approach*[59] are also important in shaping and informing the measures adopted to give legal protection to wildlife habitats. They are, for example, relevant to determining the type of land use requirements for habitat conservation that are imposed using the formal legal mechanisms in the relevant legislation; for example, site management statements, and the criteria used by the Conservation Bodies for determining requests for operational development by landowners in protected sites. The Wildlife and Countryside Act 1981[60] lays down the formal legal requirements for habitat protection in protected sites that are notified as SSSIs, including the control by the Conservation Bodies of damaging land uses and the legal mechanisms for giving operational consents for operations that may have damaging implications. The terms of the land use strategy promoted by Natural England or the Countryside Council for Wales for each protected site[61] will be informed by the nature of the habitat and the identity of the protected species found there, and this will in turn depend upon whether it is a priority habitat or species, the nature of the threat, and the action needed to reverse its decline, set by the relevant Biodiversity Action Plan.

Although the use of BAPs informs and underpins the content of legal policy for protected areas, it is also important to understand that the increasing focus on biodiversity emphasizes the need for a wider strategy requiring both (i) a recognition of the importance of protecting biodiversity outside protected areas, in, for example, the wider countryside, and (ii) the integration of conservation into a wide spectrum of policy areas, such as transport, agriculture, and land use planning. The move to a greater integration of conservation into all areas of public policy can also be seen in the adoption of a methodology to assess movement towards targets in the UKBAP using *biodiversity indicators*. The UK Biodiversity Indicators were first published by the UK Biodiversity Partnership in 2007, and are periodically reviewed and republished.[62] The Indicators are intended to display in measurable form a variety of changes in different aspects of biodiversity, including not only population sizes of protected species and habitats, but other factors such as the number of land management agreements for promoting conservation management that have been concluded for each habitat type. They also provide a tool for measuring performance towards achieving the targets set in the UKBAP,[63] and as a benchmark for the performance of a wide range of governmental policies in

[58] As to which, see Chapter 5, p. 161.

[59] Conserving Biodiversity—the UK Approach (DEFRA 2007). Available at: <http://jncc.defra.gov.uk/_ukbap/UKBAP_ConBio-UKApproach-2007.pdf>.

[60] Part 2 Wildlife and Countryside Act 1981, as amended by Countryside and Rights of Way Act 2000, as to which see further Chapter 3, 69 ff.

[61] In the case of an SSSI this will be set out in the site management statement served by the Conservation Body when designating the site—s. 28 Wildlife and Countryside Act 1981. See Chapter 3, p. 69.

[62] See now *UK Biodiversity Indicators in Your Pocket 2012* (DEFRA) available at: <http://jncc.defra.gov.uk/pdf/BIYP_2012.pdf>.

[63] See <http://jncc.defra.gov.uk/page-4229>. The initial publication in 2007 included 14 completed indicators and four in draft form. A revised full text was published on the JNCC website in 2009, with 16 completed indicators and two remaining in draft form. The final two indicators were published in May 2010.

protecting and improving biodiversity (see Box 1.2). Of the 24 measures set out in the revised 2012 Biodiversity Indicators, 17 showed an improvement since 2000, and are coded green, including bat populations, UKBAP priority species, and biological river quality. Those measures showing long-term deterioration, and therefore coded red, include populations of farmland birds, woodland birds, and wintering waterbirds, and plant diversity. Between 1970 and 2010, for example, populations of breeding farmland birds fell by 50 per cent, and that of woodland birds by 19 per cent. Since 2000 alone, populations of breeding farmland birds have declined by 14 per cent.[64] On the other hand, the proportion of agricultural land being managed for biodiversity under land management agreements increased to a point where, in 2011, over 2.9 million hectares was under targeted agreements—or 16 per cent of all agricultural land; 25 per cent in Wales, 13 per cent in Scotland, and 44 per cent in Northern Ireland.[65] Similarly, the overall total extent of land and sea in designated protected areas has progressively increased from 0.2 million hectares in 1980, to 3.5 million hectares in 2000, and to 7.5 million hectares in 2011. The increase between 2000 and 2011 is attributable in large measure to the designation of marine sites under the European Habitats Directive.[66]

The action plan adopted by the conference of the parties to the CBD at Nagoya in October 2010[67] will place a greater stress on incorporating biodiversity into other sectors and on securing other benefits, including carbon capture, from biodiversity. The development of a new set of priorities, focusing on a more 'holistic' approach to promoting biodiversity, can be seen in recent initiatives in England and Wales that signal an intention to move towards the integration of biodiversity into a wide range of policy instruments. Both the 2011 Natural Environment White Paper[68] (in England) and the new Natural Environment Framework[69] (in Wales) recognize the need to move to an 'ecosystem approach', based on the design and implementation of regulatory and management regimes that both (i) recognize the importance of ecosystem services, and (ii) are targeted at protecting the health of ecosystems as a whole. These are discussed in Chapter 9, in the context of new initiatives and the future direction of nature conservation law.[70]

(b) Defining the protected 'natural' environment

Biodiversity action plans stress the wider perspective targeted by legal and policy instruments—the need to improve and protect the diversity of species—and not

[64] See *UK Biodiversity Indicators in Your Pocket 2012* (DEFRA) at p. 30. Available at: <http://jncc.defra.gov.uk/pdf/BIYP_2012.pdf>.

[65] *UK Biodiversity Indicators in Your Pocket 2012*, p. 15.

[66] See *UK Biodiversity Indicators in Your Pocket 2012*, p. 25. For the designation of marine sites under the EC Habitats Directive, see Chapter 7, pp. 251–7.

[67] For which, see <http://www.cbd.int/decisions/cop/?m=cop-10>.

[68] *The Natural Choice: securing the value of nature*, Cm 8082, June 2011, available at: <http://www.defra.gov.uk/environment/natural/whitepaper/>.

[69] *A Living Wales—a new framework for our environment, our countryside, our seas* (2010) available at: <http://wales.gov.uk/topics/environmentcountryside/consmanagement/nef/?land=eng>.

[70] See pp. 295 ff.

Box 1.2 The UK Biodiversity Indicators*

Biodiversity indicators for the UK were first published in 2007. A revised suite of 18 indicators was published in 2010 and updated to 2012. These show changes in aspects of biodiversity (for example, the size of populations of important species, or the areas of land managed for wildlife). They provide an evidence base against which progress towards the targets set by the EU and the conference of the parties to the CBD can be measured. The 18 indicators are grouped under six focal areas, following the structure of the CBD, as follows:

Indicator	Measures
Focal Area 1 Status and trends in components of biological diversity	
1a. Population of key species (birds)	Breeding farmland birds Breeding woodland birds Breeding water and wetland birds Breeding seabirds Wintering waterbirds
1b. Population of key species (butterflies)	Semi-natural habitat specialists Generalist butterflies
1c. Population of key species (bats)	
2. Plant diversity	Arable and horticulture Woodland and grassland Boundary habitats
3. Priority species	
4. Priority habitats	
5. Genetic diversity	Native sheep breeds Native cattle breeds
6. Protected sites	Area of protected sites Condition of features
Focal Area 2 Sustainable use	
7. Woodland management	
8. Agri-environment land	Higher-type schemes Entry-type schemes
9. Sustainable fisheries	
Focal Area 3 Threats to biodiversity	
10. Impact of air pollution	Acidity Nitrogen
11. Invasive species	Freshwater ecosystems Marine ecosystems Terrestrial ecosystems
12. Spring index	

(*Continued*)

Box 1.2 Continued

Focal Area 4 Ecosystem integrity and ecosystem goods and services
13. Marine ecosystem integrity
14. Habitat connectivity
15. Biological river quality
Focal Area 5 Status of resource transfers and use
16. UK biodiversity expenditure
17. Global biodiversity expenditure
Focal Area 6 Public awareness and participation
18. Volunteer time

Each indicator is given a red, green, or amber 'traffic light' assessment based on (i) long-term change (if data preceding 1996 is available), and (ii) change since 2000.
**Source*: *UK Biodiversity Indicators in Your Pocket 2012* (DEFRA) available at: <http://jncc.defra.gov.uk/pdf/BIYP_2012.pdf>.

just give legal protection to existing plants, birds, and animals, and pre-existing natural habitats. Nevertheless, much of the legislation discussed in Chapters 3–5 is concerned with protecting species and natural habitats through a policy based on conferring legal protection on scientifically identified endangered species, and on controlling damaging activities in legally protected areas. In this area, just as much as in relation to biodiversity, legislators and judges are faced with difficult problems in giving legal effect to what are, essentially, complex and mobile scientific concepts. The judges have not yet been called upon to interpret the meaning of the statutory duty to promote 'biodiversity'. They have, however, had to consider the extent and identity of the 'natural' environment granted legal protection by the designation of protected areas such as sites of special scientific interest.

There are very few statutory definitions of 'nature conservation' of relevance in this context. The Environmental Protection Act 1990[71] states, rather unhelpfully, that it means 'the conservation of flora, fauna, or geological or physiographical features'. A more expansive definition is to be found in the Marine and Coastal Access Act 2009, which states that 'references . . . to conserving marine flora or fauna or habitat include references to conserving the diversity of such flora, fauna or habitat, whether or not any or all of them are rare or threatened'.[72] Both definitions are of limited scope and application, and there is no overarching statutory definition in domestic law of what is meant by the 'conservation' of habitats and species. The European Habitats Directive of 1992 states that for the purposes of the Directive, 'conservation means a series of measures required to maintain or restore the natural habitats and the populations of species of wild flora and fauna at a favourable status'.[73]

[71] See s. 131(6) Environmental Protection Act 1990.

[72] See s. 117(5) Marine and Coastal Access Act 2009. This is supplemented by s. 117(6) of the Act, which states that conserving a thing include not only assisting in its conservation but also enabling or facilitating its recovery or increase.

[73] Art 1(a) Council Directive 92/43/EC of 21 May 1992 on the Conservation of Natural Habitats and of Wild Flora and Fauna, [1992] OJ L206, 22/07/1992, p. 7.

'Favourable' conservation status is a key concept with a technical definition, and has been of considerable importance in the development of domestic law in order to transpose the Directive's requirements.[74] Although this definition captures the dynamic nature of 'conservation' and clearly distinguishes it from 'preservation', it nevertheless has a specific legislative context and is of specific application and scope, viz. it only applies to measures introduced to implement the protection of natural habitats and rare species protected under the terms of the Directive.

A rare opportunity to explore the wider meaning of 'conservation' and its implications arose in *Boggis v Natural England and Waveney District Council*.[75] The Court of Appeal was required to rule upon the validity of the notification as an SSSI by Natural England of an area of cliff top on the east coast of England that was subject to progressive and ongoing erosion by the sea. The cliffs were an important site for fossil deposits, and it was held that the process of erosion, exposing fossil deposits for future study, could itself be a natural feature deserving of protection. A dynamic definition of 'conservation' was adopted both at first instance and in the Court of Appeal, one that recognized that nature conservation law is not concerned solely with the protection of land or objects as they currently are. It can encompass the preservation of dynamic processes, such as, in this case, projected future soil erosion by the natural and unimpeded action of the sea, which would reveal important natural features for future study.[76] The erosion of the cliffs, a process, was itself an 'interest' meriting protection by notification as a protected area, and it was this (the exposure, itself a dynamic and inherently unstable process) that the law could seek to conserve.[77]

Similarly, the fact that a valuable conservation feature has been created by human intervention in the natural environment will not prevent the application of legal protection under the contemporary law on habitat protection; what matters is its current 'special' interest by virtue of its physiographical or geological features, flora, and fauna.[78] As the *Boggis* case graphically illustrates, however, the scope of 'conservation' law is more expansive than this. It is concerned not only with protecting ('conserving') natural habitats, species, and geological features of the natural environment as they now exist; it can also encompass the protection of natural processes, including those that will unfold in the future. The dividing line between the speculative application of legal controls on land use, on the one hand,

[74] As to which, see Chapter 6, p. 239 and Box 6.4.

[75] [2009] EWCA Civ 1061; [2008] EWHC 2954 (Admin).

[76] The notification of the site in this case was based upon a 50-year prediction of erosion of the cliff face contained in a scientific report prepared for Natural England.

[77] See [2009] EWCA Civ 1061 at paras. 16–18 (Sullivan LJ.); 'Whatever may be the meaning of conservation in other contexts one would have thought that allowing natural processes to take their course, and not preventing or impeding them by artificial means from doing so, would be a well recognised conservation technique in the field of nature conservation. "Conservation" is not necessarily the same as "preservation", although in some, perhaps many, circumstances preservation may be the best way to conserve' [2009] EWCA Civ 1061 at para. 18. See also [2008] EWHC 2954 (Admin) at para. 52 (Blair J.).

[78] There are many examples drawn from the case law on the notification of protected areas, for example as SSSIs: see for example *Fisher v English Nature* [2004] EWCA Civ 663 (creation of breeding grounds for stone curlews by arable farming practices), *Newsum v National Assembly for Wales* [2004] EWCA Civ 1565—creation of habitat for great crested newts by quarrying. See further Chapter 3, pp. 70 ff.

and legitimately conferring protection on natural processes, on the other, is a fine one, however, and heavily dependent on the application of sound scientific research to identify those natural processes qualifying for legal protection.

(c) Legal and economic instruments

The move over the last 30 years away from reliance on a voluntary approach to nature conservation, and towards one based on 'partnership' between the public agencies, landowners, land managers, and the wider public, has witnessed a gradual evolution in the range of legal and economic instruments that are used to confer protection on wildlife and wildlife habitats, as well as the development of new approaches to nature conservation. The policy of designating geographically discrete protected areas remains the keystone of the law on habitat protection. But the measures in the nature conservation law 'toolkit' now encompass a much wider range of techniques and legal instruments:

a) *Criminal Law.* The law uses criminal liability to impose sanctions for harming wildlife in some circumstances. The criminal law is used, in particular, to enforce the law on species protection—by, for example, making it a criminal offence to kill, injure, or trap protected species of bird or animal, or to damage protected plants.[79] Natural England also has power to prosecute offenders under its enforcement powers in relation to offences in SSSIs and European sites, however, and in relation to the application of environmental impact assessment to land use changes in agriculture.[80] The use of the criminal law as an enforcement tool for preventing and rectifying wildlife crime faces two problems: the difficulties inherent in proving beyond reasonable doubt in many cases that the offence has been committed, and the relatively low level of penalties available to the courts as a deterrent when sentencing offenders. These problems have been partially addressed by the adoption of new criminal offences that penalize the possession of live or dead specimens in some cases, and the creation of specific offences of possessing some proscribed poisons[81] frequently used, for example, to bait carcasses in order to kill protected animals and birds that feed on carrion. These offences will be discussed in Chapter 5.
b) *Civil Sanctions.* The use of the criminal law is a step of last resort to ensure compliance with the law. Until comparatively recently, regulators such as Natural England had little flexibility in the range of sanctions at their disposal—they could either prosecute wildlife crime or merely issue warning notices and cautions.[82] They had no scope for action between these two extremes. This was addressed by Part 3 of the Regulatory Enforcement and

[79] See Part 1 Wildlife and Countryside Act 1981, discussed in Chapter 5, pp. 163 ff.
[80] See further Chapter 3, pp. 92 ff.
[81] Ss. 43 and 44 Natural Environment and Rural Communities Act 2006. See pp. 174–5.
[82] See Natural England, *Enforcement Policy* (March 2009), especially paras. 27–30 ('alternatives to prosecution') available at: <http://www.naturalengland.org.uk>. These are discussed more fully at pp. 40 ff. and Box 2.1.

Sanctions Act 2008, which gives regulators, including Natural England and the Environment Agency, wide powers to issue civil sanctions for non-compliance with environmental law. The regulator can be empowered to issue a fixed money penalty, a discretionary monetary penalty, stop notices, and to take enforcement undertakings from 'offenders'. Fixed monetary penalties can be issued by the regulator without having to go to court, provided that 'it is satisfied beyond reasonable doubt' that the recipient has committed an offence.[83] A notice of intent must first be served by the regulator, and where a fixed penalty is imposed, no criminal proceedings can be brought in respect of the offence for which it was imposed.[84] Fixed penalties are intended for use in relation to minor infringements of environmental law, but in more serious cases the regulators can also impose 'variable monetary penalties' up to, but not exceeding, the amount that could be imposed by a fine if the matter were prosecuted in the courts, and/or take undertakings from the offender as to his future conduct and the restoration of any damage that has occurred.[85] Variable penalties are subject to similar safeguards against double jeopardy that prevent a prosecution from being commenced unless a non-monetary undertaking has not been complied with.[86] Stop notices can be served to prevent activities being carried out that either cause, or present a risk of, serious damage to the environment, including the health of animals and plants.[87] Regulators are under a duty to publish guidance about their use if civil sanctions, including the circumstances in which a penalty is likely to be imposed, its likely amount, and how liability for the penalty may be discharged.[88] The powers conferred by the 2008 Act have been extended to Natural England and now apply in its enforcement of a wide range of offences under nature conservation law[89] from 2010. It can, for example, impose fixed monetary penalties of £100, variable monetary penalties, compliance stop and restoration notices, and accept enforcement undertakings in relation to offences against animals birds and plants under Part 1 of the Wildlife and Countryside Act 1981, and in relation to damage caused to SSSIs contrary to Part 2 of the 1981 Act (as amended).[90]

[83] S. 39 Regulatory Enforcement and Sanctions Act 2008.

[84] S. 41 Regulatory Enforcement and Sanctions Act 2008.

[85] See s. 42 Regulatory Enforcement and Sanctions Act 2008. These are referred to in the Act as 'discretionary requirements'.

[86] See s. 44(2) and (3) Regulatory Enforcement and Sanctions Act 2008.

[87] S. 46(4) and (6)(b) Regulatory Enforcement and Sanctions Act 2008.

[88] S. 63 Regulatory Enforcement and Sanctions Act 2008.

[89] Environmental Civil Sanctions (England) Order 2010, SI 2010/1157. The 2010 Order came into force on 6 April 2010. The offences in relation to which civil sanctions are applicable are set out in Schedule 5 of the 2010 Order. Civil penalties can also be made available to the enforcement authorities in relation to criminal offences in Marine Conservation Zones to be designated under the Marine and Coastal Access Act 2009: see ss. 142–144 Marine and Coastal Access Act 2009, and Chapter 7, pp. 282–3.

[90] Regulatory Enforcement and Sanctions Act 2008 art. 3 and Schedule 1 para. 1 (fixed penalties), Schedule 2 (variable monetary penalties, compliance notices, restoration notices, and undertakings), Schedule 3 (stop notices), and the Table of Offences to which these powers apply in Schedule 5.

c) *Powers to Enforce Positive Management.* Many types of natural habitat require positive management to retain their conservation status, and, of course, improving the condition of degraded habitats will require positive steps and active management. For example, hedgerows, hay meadows, and many other common habitats that provide valuable feeding, cover, and breeding sites for birds and animals require active management to retain and/or improve their conservation value. When the Wildlife and Countryside Act 1981 was introduced, most of the legal powers that it conferred on the Conservation Bodies to oversee habitat protection were negative in nature, that is, they enabled the regulators to prevent damaging land use in protected sites such as SSSIs,[91] but did not give them power to require the proactive management by landowners that would be needed to improve or restore damaged habitats. Rectifying this weakness in the legal powers of the statutory Conservation Bodies was a primary objective of the Countryside and Rights of Way Act 2000. The 2000 Act gave the Conservation Bodies the power to make management schemes for the conservation and restoration of habitats in SSSIs in England and Wales.[92] If the terms of a management scheme are not being complied with by a landowner or occupier of land in an SSSI, and it appears to the Conservation Body that its special conservation features are suffering as a result of this, they have power to serve a management notice requiring landowners to carry out work on their land to ensure that it is managed in accordance with the scheme for the SSSI.[93] Similar powers were introduced in Scotland by the Nature Conservation (Scotland) Act 2004. The 2004 Act empowers Scottish Natural Heritage to request land management orders for the purpose of 'conserving, restoring or otherwise enhancing' the natural features of an SSSI.[94] The order will be made by the Scottish ministers[95] and can include positive land management obligations requiring the recipient to carry out operations for the conservation, enhancement, or restoration of the site, as well as stipulating when and how those operations are to be carried out.[96] Adherence to the partnership principle is retained however, in that this power can only be exercised where SNH have first sought to enter into a management agreement with the owner or occupier of the land, where the terms of an existing management agreement are being broken, or where it has proved impossible to trace the owner or occupier of the land in question.[97]

[91] Eg, the power to prevent landowners carrying out operations likely to damage the conservation interest of an SSSI without prior consultation with the Conservation Body—now s. 28E Wildlife and Countryside Act 1981 (as amended).

[92] See s. 28J Wildlife and Countryside Act 1981, as amended by Schedule 9 Countryside and Rights of Way Act 2000.

[93] S. 28K Wildlife and Countryside Act 1981.

[94] S. 29 Nature Conservation (Scotland) Act 2004. The power also applies on land 'contiguous to, or which SNH considers to be otherwise associated with', an SSSI: s. 29(1)(b) Nature Conservation (Scotland) Act 2004.

[95] S. 30 Nature Conservation (Scotland) Act 2004.

[96] S. 3(d) Nature Conservation (Scotland) Act 2004.

[97] See s. 29(3)(4) and (5) Nature Conservation (Scotland) Act 2004.

d) *Management Agreements.* Notwithstanding the extensive powers of the Conservation Bodies to impose civil sanctions and positive land management obligations, their primary approach remains that of seeking consensual conservation management in partnership with landowners and occupiers. The public agencies have enjoyed power to enter into land management agreements with landowners and occupiers of protected sites since the introduction of protected areas policy by the National Parks and Access to the Countryside Act 1949. These powers have been extended in the intervening years, and the Conservation Bodies now enjoy power to offer management agreements to landowners both in protected sites (such as SSSIs[98] and European sites)[99] and to landowners outside protected areas where they are necessary to promote sustainable development, including the promotion of nature conservation and protecting biodiversity.[100] The use made of these powers has changed significantly, however, since 1981. Management agreements in SSSIs were, under the 1981 Act, primarily used to 'buy out' damaging development proposals, and landowners were entitled to receive the prospective net profit they lost as a result of being prevented from carrying out environmentally damaging, but otherwise lawful, operations on their land.[101] Following the changes to the law on SSSIs introduced by the Countryside and Rights of Way Act 2000, new guidance was adopted that now stresses that management agreements must only be used in SSSIs to reward landowners for adopting positive conservation management of wildlife and conservation features on their land, and not simply to prevent damage.[102]

e) *Economic Instruments.* The use of management agreements in protected sites, such as SSSIs, is supplemented by the use of economic incentives to encourage conservation management. Incentives introduced under the aegis of the Common Agricultural Policy of the EU are especially important in securing the protection of wildlife and habitats, both in protected sites and in the wider countryside, by ensuring that agricultural methods are as environmentally friendly as possible and tailored to the protection of farmland biodiversity. Incentives take broadly two forms: the use of agreements to encourage conservation-friendly farm management under 'agri-environment' schemes, and the incorporation of environmental conditions into the agricultural subsidies paid to farmers under the Common Agricultural Policy. The rural development policy (pillar 2 of the CAP) allows the member states to establish agri-environment schemes for the payment of incentives to adopt sustainable agricultural practices. Several schemes have been adopted in

[98] See s. 15 Countryside Act 1968.

[99] Art. 16 Conservation of Habitats and Species Regulations 2010, SI 2010/490.

[100] See s. 7 Natural Environment and Rural Communities Act 2006 (Natural England's powers).

[101] See the Financial Guidelines for Payments under Management Agreements DOE Circular 04/1983.

[102] See para. 1.2 of the *Guidelines on Management Agreement Payments and other related matters* (DETR Circular 01/2001; Welsh Office 2001), made under s. 50(1) of the Wildlife and Countryside Act 1981, discussed further at pp. 116–21.

England, Wales, and Scotland under these provisions, starting with the Environmentally Sensitive Areas (ESA) programme in 1986. The Agriculture Act 1986[103] empowered the Minister of Agriculture to designate geographically discrete ESAs within which farmers could be paid for adopting environmentally friendly farming practices along the lines specified in the designating order for each ESA. This power was widely used, and by 2000 no fewer than 22 ESAs had been established, within which agreements could be offered with incentive payments for farmers willing to manage their land in accordance with prescriptions set out in standard ESA agreements for each area. ESA has since been superseded by more sophisticated schemes that target payments and management agreement prescriptions at the individual farm level, using a 'whole-farm' approach by which payments are made for the preservation, restoration, and improvement of farmland environmental features. This approach is exemplified in England by Environmental Stewardship, a scheme introduced in 2005 under which farmers can bid for the award of an agreement under the higher level or organic streams of the scheme.[104] Entry is dependent on a farm scoring sufficient points determined by the wildlife and other environmental features it presents, and the level of management offered. Similar schemes operate in Wales, notably Tir Gofal and, from 2012, Glas Tir. Agri-environment agreements under these schemes are frequently used to deliver basic conservation management in protected sites, and their operation is coordinated with the use of additional agreements (for example, in SSSIs) in order to confer additional protection on specific features as necessary.[105] The other land management tool deployed under the Common Agricultural Policy is 'cross compliance', by which environmental conditions are attached to the receipt by agricultural producers of farm subsidy payments. The 2004 reform of the CAP introduced a new subsidy—the single farm payment—for all agricultural producers. This is 'decoupled' from production so that payments were initially based on the historic subsidy claims made under the previous subsidy arrangements by each producer in 2000/2002. It is a condition of the receipt of the single payment that a farmer complies with cross-compliance conditions that supply a basic level of environmental protection for farmland wildlife features—including, for example, undertakings to avoid over grazing by livestock, and to observe the protection of SSSIs and other protected sites.[106] This is primarily a 'soft law' instrument. The public authorities have power to demand the repayment of subsidies in

[103] See s. 18(1) Agriculture Act 1986.

[104] An Uplands Environment Stewardship funding stream was added to the scheme in 2010. Participation in the Entry Level stream of the Environmental Stewardship scheme is open to all farmers.

[105] See 131 ff. And generally C. Rodgers and J. Bishop, *Management Agreements for Promoting Nature Conservation* (RICS, London, 1998); C. P. Rodgers, *Agricultural Law*, 3rd edn (Tottel Publishing, 2008) at para. 13.93 ff.

[106] See the Common Agricultural Policy Single Payment and Support Schemes Regulations 2010, SI 2010/540 (England); and the Common Agricultural Policy Single Payment and Support Schemes (Wales) Regulations 2010, SI 2010/1892 (W 185); and passim Rodgers, *Agricultural Law* (2008), Ch. 15.

the event of breaches of the cross-compliance conditions, and can impose land management notices in cases where serious environmental damage is caused in breach of the rules.

The Role of Law in Nature Conservation—Key Themes

Environmental disputes are typically disputes about access to an economic resource. This is certainly true in the law of nature conservation, where disputes will commonly involve a conflict between the desire of a landowner to use land for optimal economic purposes (for example, for development or intensive farming) and the imposition of land use restrictions by public bodies in order to protect wildlife and to preserve natural habitats. The key themes that will be addressed in this book therefore chiefly concern the different ways in which environmental regulation, economic instruments, and property rights address and resolve these tensions, how they in some cases interact, and how they can be used to promote biodiversity and conserve the natural environment.

(a) Resolving conflicting interests in nature conservation

The imposition of legal controls on the killing or exploitation of wildlife, and the restriction of land use rights in order to protect wildlife habitats, both highlight a number of conflicting interests inherent in promoting nature conservation in a legal system premised upon the private ownership of land. The relationship between the protection of *private* property rights and the promotion of the *public* interest in environmental protection is problematic. The application of nature conservation law sometimes raises tensions between *human* rights (of which the right to property is one) and the public interest in restricting property rights in order to promote environmental protection. There are also difficult issues in reconciling recreational public access to land with the conservation management of sensitive wildlife habitats. Also, much land of high nature value is subject to multiple land use rights that give access to the land resource for very different purposes; in the case of common land, for example, there will often be public access for recreation, agricultural land use by stakeholders, and conservation interests pursued by the owner of the soil and public bodies.[107] Achieving satisfactory conservation management will require that these be reconciled in a management scheme capturing the different interests involved. In practice this is often done through a publicly funded management agreement for the site, such as a Higher Level Stewardship agreement (in England) or Tir Gofal agreement (in Wales),[108] but the implementation of schemes of this kind is often hampered by the complex property rights subsisting over the land.

[107] As to which, see Rodgers, Straughton, Winchester, and Pieraccini, *Contested Common Land: Environmental Governance Past and Present* (Earthscan, 2010), and especially Ch. 4 and Ch. 5 ('Contemporary Governance of the Commons: the Quest for Sustainability').

[108] As to which, see Chapter 4, pp. 135–7.

Reconciling these competing, and often conflicting, interests is a key objective of many of the legal instruments deployed in the law of nature conservation. Whether these tensions are satisfactorily resolved will be touched upon at relevant points throughout this work.

(b) Resource allocation

These conflicts are ultimately about access to, the protection of, and the use of contested natural resources—land, its natural products, and the wildlife to be found on it. Nature conservation legislation confers protected legal status on some of these resources, by designating certain species of animal bird and plant as legally protected (for example, through Part 1 WCA 1981), and by conferring protected status on sensitive wildlife habitats (Part II WCA 1981). One of the principal functions of nature conservation law is to resolve disputes about access to contested natural resources, and in particular to reallocate decision making about *protected resources,* that is, protected species and habitats, to the state—represented in this case by the 'statutory Conservation Bodies'.[109] The primary function of the law is therefore to regulate access to the protected resource, and to control the ways in which it can be exploited by the landowner or by others. The manner in which the law reallocates access to protected natural resources differs in the case of species protection and habitat protection, with significant legal implications.

- *Species Protection.* The Wildlife and Countryside Act 1981, and other species protection legislation, makes it illegal to kill, injure, or disturb individual wild animals birds or plants of species that have been scheduled for protection.[110] The law's role here is to prevent landowners from reducing into possession, by killing or capture, a naturally occurring resource (wildlife) on their land. Although, as we have seen, the law recognizes the landowner's right to reduce animals and birds into possession by capture or killing, thereby assuming property rights over them, it prevents their exploitation if they are of a protected species. The special status of 'game' species is recognized in the legislation, and animals and birds in this category can be lawfully hunted at certain times of the year, specified by statute, reduced into possession, and used or sold in the normal way. The law of species protection does not raise human rights issues directly, because it prevents the landowner from lawfully acquiring 'property' in protected birds and animals and does not otherwise impact upon or restrict his land use rights. It does not, in other words, lead directly to a potential conflict between the pre-existing property rights of the landowner, who has no ownership of wild animals and birds, and the public interest in nature conservation.

[109] Ie Natural England, the Countryside Council for Wales or Scottish Natural Heritage—see further Chapter 2, pp. 35 ff.

[110] See further Chapter 5.

- *Habitat Protection.* In the case of habitat protection the state reallocates resource utility to itself by subjecting certain land use operations—operations likely to damage the special conservation interest, or OLDSIs—to a requirement of prior consultation and operational consent from the appropriate Conservation Bodies.[111] The legislation therefore impacts directly upon the human rights of the landowner (his right to property)[112] and can in some cases trigger a conflict between human rights law and the law of nature conservation. We will see a number of instances of this in the case law discussed in Chapter 3 concerning the notification of protected sites such as SSSIs. In this respect it is important to note that the environment is not 'un-owned'. Land is, of course, owned and may well be subject to numerous property interests—the freehold of the 'owner', tenancies granted to various categories of users, and third-party rights such as easements and covenants. Although the land itself may be owned, its special attributes (for example, as a valuable wildlife habitat) are not 'owned' as such, and neither is the wildlife to be found there, and it is these that the law of nature conservation seeks to protect. What is 'un-owned', therefore, is not necessarily the environment itself; rather, it is those *positive attributes of the environment* that the law deems worthy of protection for public interest reasons. The key question here, therefore, is different to that in species protection law (p. 24); how can the law reconcile the legal values represented by private property rights with public interest values in the protection of natural habitats?

(c) The role of property rights

Property rights play a key role in nature conservation law, and are important to an understanding both of the legal instruments that it uses (especially, but not exclusively, in relation to habitat protection) and to the way in which it is implemented in practice. Property rights are themselves an important tool for allocating access to disputed land resources,[113] such as minerals and the land's produce, and they initially define the terms on which access to that resource will be permitted by law. Historically, the common law recognized very few restrictions on the exploitative rights conferred by property ownership. This is sometimes encapsulated in the maxim *Cuius est solum eius est usque ad coelum et ad inferos*: 'he who owns the land owns everything reaching up to the very heavens and down to the depths of the earth'.[114] Although the maxim is a spectacularly inaccurate description of the land use rights conferred by property ownership in the modern law,[115] it

[111] Ie Natural England, Scottish Natural Heritage, or the Countryside Council for Wales, n. 109.

[112] The right to property is protected under art. 1 Protocol 1 to the European Convention of Human Rights and Fundamental Freedoms; see further Chapter 3, 82–4.

[113] Before the introduction of statutory measures to protect habitats and wildlife they were, indeed, the primary allocative tools used by the common law.

[114] For a detailed analysis of this concept and its application (or otherwise) in modern English Land Law see Gray and Gray, *Elements of Land Law* 5th edn (Oxford University Press, 2009) at 1.2.15 ff.

[115] The Town and Country Planning Act 1947, for example, nationalized all development rights in land. Its successor the Town and Country Planning Act 1990 requires planning permission from the local planning authority before 'development' on or under land can take place; ss. 55, 57 1990 Act.

is nevertheless the logical starting point for any discussion of property rights and land use, for it encapsulates the essential principle that, unless restricted by statute, property rights convey potentially limitless rights of exploitation of the land resource over which they are held. This explains why the legal and economic instruments applied by nature conservation law are primarily concerned with adjusting the property rights of the landowner by reallocating to public bodies (such as Natural England and the local planning authorities) important decisions on access to, and the use and exploitation of, protected natural resources.

The way in which the common law structures the constituent elements of property rights is also an important issue for environmental governance. It will, for example, determine the design of publicly funded conservation schemes and shapes the legal controls on land use imposed by statute. Also, the interaction of property concepts with environmental regulation has important human rights implications. The Human Rights Act 1998 provides that it is unlawful for any public authority to act in a manner that is incompatible with a person's human rights, as articulated in the European Convention on Human Rights and Fundamental Freedoms.[116] The Convention rights include the protection of property rights from arbitrary state appropriation.[117] This has important implications for the manner in which the public authorities implement protected areas policy by designating protected sites such as SSSIs. The courts have held, for example, that the confirmation of an SSSI site notification[118] is determinative of a landowner's civil right to use and enjoy property, and therefore potentially engages the convention rights. In human rights cases, the key issue is often the extent to which land use controls imposed by the state are proportionate to the public policy interest that is being pursued.[119] Even in a human rights context, however, the central issue is one of resource allocation; it is about who should bear the cost of nature conservation measures, and not about the desirability or statutory competence of environmental regulation.[120] The true question is the extent to which the cost of implementing public policy on environmental protection should be borne by individual property owners whose land use rights have been restricted, and the extent to which it should be borne by the public. These issues are explored further in Chapter 3.

It follows that studying the implementation of nature conservation law in England and Wales requires an appreciation of the impact on environmental governance of the central tenets of English property law. Common law notions

[116] The Convention rights are set out in Schedule 1 Human Rights Act 1998.

[117] Art. 1 of the Protocol to the European Convention on Human Rights guarantees the peaceful enjoyment of possessions, but subject to the important caveat that the state has the right to enforce such laws as it deems necessary 'to control the use of property in accordance with the general interest or to secure the payment of taxes or other contributions or penalties'.

[118] See *Aggregate Industries UK Ltd v English Nature* [2003] Env LR 3, 83. Notification is under s. 28(1) Wildlife and Countryside Act 1981, as amended by Schedule 9 Countryside and Rights of Way Act 2000. See Chapter 3, 80 ff.

[119] See *Trailer and Marina (Leven) Ltd v Secretary of State and English Nature* [2004] EWHC 153 (Admin). [2004] EWCA Civ 1580.

[120] See P. A. Joseph, 'The Environment, Property Rights and Public Choice Theory' (2003) 20 NZULR 408.

of private property right and freedom of contract heavily condition land use rights, and are key to an understanding of their potential to either harm, or alternatively to promote the protection of, wildlife species and their natural habitats. This is usually seen as a constraint on the introduction of notions of environmental stewardship into English property law. Although scholarship in the wider domain of environmental law has shown that the courts have not always ignored stewardship as an inherent attribute of property rights,[121] little attention has been paid to the particular importance of differing conceptions of property right in relation to the protection of the 'natural' environment.

The adoption of the 'voluntary' principle in the immediate post-war period recognized the importance of property rights in nature conservation law, but in a form that gave prominence to the exploitative rights of the landowner and failed to recognize stewardship obligations as a constituent element of his property rights. Starting with the National Parks and Access to the Countryside Act 1949, landowners were encouraged to participate in nature conservation management through the use of contractual measures with compensation, and with minimal direct regulation. As we have seen, the Countryside and Rights of Way Act 2000 gave wider regulatory powers to the Conservation Bodies and repositioned public policy towards the 'partnership principle', but without diminishing the central importance of property rights in achieving conservation management.

The extensive controls over land use introduced since 1981 through planning and environmental law mean that it is now arguably possible to characterize 'property' as a socially derived set of land use privileges and obligations, in which obligations of environmental stewardship are an inherent attribute of property rights.[122] The extent to which this analysis can be sustained will be another theme that will be discussed at various points in the following text. The protection of the 'un-owned' natural environment[123] is undoubtedly an area of environmental policy that presents unique challenges to a legal system based on notions of private property rights, and in which rights of exploitation and land use are commodified as 'property' rights. Common law concepts of property right have a key impact, for

[121] See eg S. Coyle and K. Morrow, *Philosophical Foundations of Environmental Law* (Hart Publishing, 2004).

[122] See eg Gray and Gray (2009) at 1.5.51–1.5.57 ('Property becomes not a summation of individualized power over scarce resources, but an allocative mechanism for promoting the efficient or ecologically prudent utilisation of... resources. So analysed, this community-oriented approach to 'property' in land plays a pivotal role in the advancement of environmental welfare. Property becomes a form of stewardship and resonates with the obligations of a civic or environmental trust' (Gray and Gray 2009 1.5.57). See also K. Gray and S. F. Gray, 'Private Property and Public propriety', Ch. 2 in McLean (ed.), *Property and the Constitution* (Hart, 1999); J. Waldron, 'What is Private Property?' (1985) 5 OJLS 313; W. N. R. Lucy and C. Mitchell, 'Replacing Private Property: the Case for Stewardship' (1996) 55 *Cambridge LJ* 566; M. Raff, 'Environmental Obligations and the Western Liberal Property Concept' (1998) 22 *Melbourne University Law Review* 657; T. W. Frazier, 'The Green Alternative to Classical Liberal Property Theory', (1995) *Vermont LR* 299; M. B. Metzger, 'Private Property and Environment Sanity' (1976) 5 *Ecology LQ* 792; E. T. Freygoyle, 'Land Ownership and the Level of Regulation: The Particulars of Owning' (1999) 25 *Ecology LQ* 574.

[123] Eg wild animals, birds, fish, plants. Not all attributes or components of the 'environment' are 'un-owned'—see pp. 24–5.

example, in relation to: (i) the designation and protection of high nature value sites such as SSSIs; (ii) the implementation of land management agreements to protect wildlife habitats; and (iii) to the implementation of economic instruments to promote environmental land management through the Common Agricultural Policy of the EU. These are all areas where the tension between the traditional common law analysis of property rights as a 'bundle' of exploitative rights, on the one hand, and property models based on viewing property as a social usufruct carrying obligations of environmental stewardship, on the other, is very evident. Property rights are also important with regard to the law of species protection: they provide, for example, the organizational nexus around which defences are made available to the owner of land (and those licensed by him) for killing or disturbing birds, plants or animals, and in other cases are imposed on those acting without the permission of the owner.[124]

Property Paradigms and Nature Conservation Law

'Property' is a multifaceted concept, capable of different interpretations that capture the different functions that property rights perform, and the differing facets of the relationship of the property holder with land. This renders attempts to analyse the relationship between property rights and environmental regulation both difficult and complex. Two closely related, but different, property models are fundamental to an understanding of the relationship between property rights and nature conservation law:

(i) an entitlements—based model that stresses the role of property rules in defining the legitimacy of land use and ownership entitlements, and
(ii) a resource allocation model that focuses on the role of property rights in allocating and defining access to the resources that land represents.

Entitlements-based models of property focus on whether there is a legally protected right to the exploitation and use of land.[125] This approach characteristically sees 'property' as constituting a 'bundle of rights' and emphasizes the power to exclude others and the right of the owner to the beneficial use and enjoyment of the land and personal property over which ownership is claimed.[126] Whether the rights are actually utilized (and if so, in what manner) is of little relevance to an entitlements-based analysis. It has been claimed, therefore, that it fails to encompass the functional relationship of property with the environment and is of limited utility for the study of environmental regulation.[127] Resource allocation models, on the

[124] See eg s. 27 Wildlife and Countryside Act 1981.

[125] See eg A. Honore, 'Ownership' in Guest (ed.), *Oxford Essays in Jurisprudence* (Oxford University Press, 1961), Ch. V p. 107 ff., and J. W. Harris, *Property and Justice* (Oxford University Press, 1996) at 140–2.

[126] This is considered by some to be a characteristic of Western liberal jurisprudence: see eg M. Raff, 'Environmental Obligations and the Western Liberal Property Concept' (1998) 22 *Melbourne University Law Review* 657; J. Penner, 'The 'Bundle of Rights' Picture of Property' (1996) *UCLA Law Review* 711.

[127] C. P. Rodgers, 'Nature's Place? Property Rights, Property Rules and Environmental Stewardship' (2009) 68 CLJ 550.

other hand, stress that property rights represent the elements of resource utility that, taken together, make up a land interest. The focus here is on the role of property rights as defining the relationship between the 'owner', the land over which property rights are asserted, and the resources to which those rights give access.[128] The bundle of property 'rights' over land that the law recognizes will define, distribute, and reflect different elements of resource utility that accrue to the 'owner' of the right in question.[129] This approach therefore captures more fully the dynamic interrelationship between property and instruments of environmental governance.[130] It also reflects economic models for property that stress the dynamic nature of property rights,[131] and emphasize their role in providing incentives to internalize the environmental externalities that have emerged from the growing technical potential of agricultural and industrial production to generate pollution and damage biodiversity.[132] This is linked to the role of property rights in promoting an economically efficient distribution and use of resources, often measured by reference to 'pareto optimality', the idea that an optimum allocation of resources, represented by property rights, will enlarge one person's rights and wealth while making a corresponding diminution in the rights and wealth of another.[133] Resource allocation models also facilitate the identification of interactions between the *form* which legal controls on land use take and the *content* of the land use responsibilities that they introduce. Viewed from this perspective, it becomes clear that much modern environmental legislation[134] effects an extensive reallocation of property rights in land, while leaving the core content of the owner's property entitlements largely intact. These interactions are described in diagrammatic form in Box 1.3 and the accompanying text.

In practice, the two models are closely related, and reflect the differing functions that property rights perform—on the one hand in defining legally sanctioned rights to land and its produce, and on the other as an allocative tool for defining the access to the land resource that the entitlement confers. Neither are they mutually exclusive. A property entitlement rule will often fulfil an initial resource allocation function; for example, in the case of leasehold land, the law of landlord and tenant will define the terms on which the tenant has access to the land resource. The landlord will commonly reserve minerals and game rights to himself when letting land, thereby

[128] See eg K. Gray and S. F. Gray, 'The Idea of Property in Land', in Bright and Dewar (eds), *Land Law: New Perspectives* (1998) at p. 15.

[129] See Gray and Gray (1998), 15 at 39 ff.

[130] See eg C. P. Rodgers, 'Nature's Place? Property Rights, Property Rules and Environmental Stewardship' (2009) 68 CLJ 550.

[131] See eg D. W. Bromley, *Environment and Economy: property rights and public policy* (Oxford University Press, 1991). See H. Demsetz, 'Towards a Theory of Property Rights' [1967] 57 *American Economic Review*, 347–59, at 373; B. Colby,'Bargaining over Agricultural Property Rights' (1995) 77 *American Journal of Agricultural Economics* 1186 (adopting a bargaining model).

[132] See Demsetz, [1967] at 348 ff.

[133] See Bromley (1991), n. 131; Demsetz [1967] at 347; R. Coase, 'The Problem of Social Costs' (1960) 3 *Journal of Law and Economics* 1; R. Barnes, *Property Rights and Natural Resources* (Hart Publishing, 2009), especially Ch. 2 pp. 41 ff.

[134] Eg Part 2 Wildlife and Countryside Act 1981 (SSSIs); Part 2 Conservation of Habitats and Species Regulations 2010, SI 2010/490 (European Sites).

Box 1.3 Property Rights and Nature Conservation—Commentary

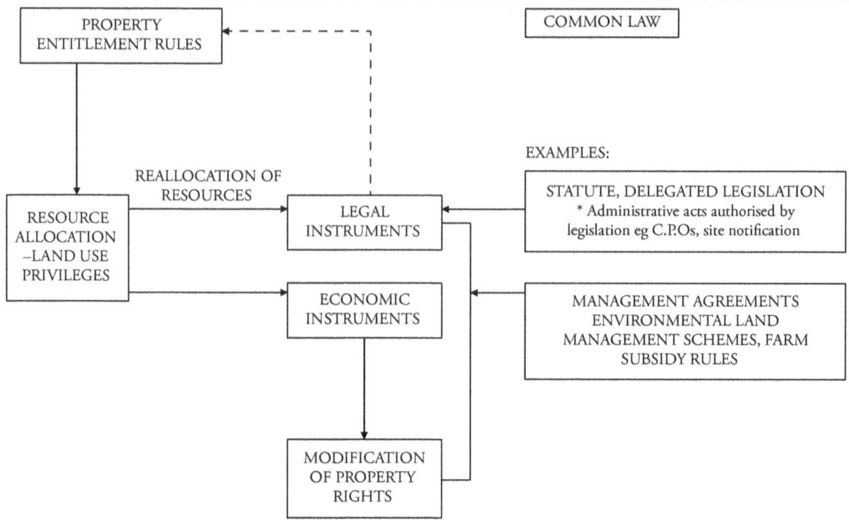

restricting the land resource available to the tenant for economic exploitation. A reallocation of resource entitlements can also be effected, however, by legal and economic instruments external to the property entitlement rules defining the land-holders interest in the land—for example, by environmental legislation restricting potentially damaging land uses, by 'soft law' instruments such as codes of practice, and by economic instruments to encourage land management for nature conservation. It is this *reallocation* of the resource entitlements initially determined by the general law that is one of the principal objectives of nature conservation law.

Finally, another way of capturing the relationship between notions of 'property' and instruments of nature conservation law would require us to see property as a web of interests, involving complex nuanced relationships (between persons and between persons and objects) represented by notions of public trust, natural use, and the law of nuisance.[135] Proponents of the resource allocation model of property rights would argue that the 'bundle of rights' approach to property entitlements arguably confuses the two central functions of property institutions; to legitimize land use entitlements, and to allocate land-based resources. The web of interests approach, on the other hand, reconciles them by attempting to capture the relationship between the owner and objects (such as land) and between the owner and wildlife. It is also useful to explain the interconnections between multiple interests in land and the different exploitative rights that they confer on their owners.[136]

Without legally protected rights in wildlife, anyone wishing to protect or promote the interests of wildlife species or their habitats (such as wildlife trusts or NGOs) will

[135] See C. A. Arnold, 'The Reconstitution of Property: Property as a Web of Interests' (2002) 26 *Harvard Environmental Law Review* 281.

[136] See eg Box 8.1 in Chapter 8 below.

Box 1.3 Property Rights and Nature Conservation—Commentary

1. Property entitlement rules determine issues of ownership and the right to use land. They also make an initial presumptive allocation of the resources that land presents (to the 'owner', tenant, commoner, etc.). Property entitlements are determined by rules of the common law and by statute; examples include the *cuius est* maxim (see p. 25), the Law of Property Act 1925, the Landlord and Tenant legislation (for example, Landlord and Tenant Act 1954 or Agricultural Holdings Act 1986).

2. The presumptive allocation of resources conferred by property entitlement rules (land use privileges) can be reallocated by either legal instruments or economic instruments.

2.1 *Legal instruments* that reallocate property rights in this sense (as rights of access to land-based resources) include *Statutes, delegated legislation,* and *administrative actions* authorized by either of the former. The Town and Country Planning Act 1990, for example, reallocates to the local planning authority decisions on the 'development' of land by requiring planning permission before development can be lawfully undertaken. The Wildlife and Countryside Act 1981 performs a similar function in restricting a landowner's ability to lawfully carry out operations likely to damage the conservation interest of an SSSI (see Chapter 3 pp. 84 ff). A similar role can be played by *delegated legislation*, and by *administrative acts* that are authorized by primary or delegated legislation; for example, compulsory purchase orders, land management orders and site notifications, such as the notification of SSSIs or European Sites.

2.2 *Economic instruments* that adjust property rights to effect a reallocation of resources include land management agreements, management schemes, agri-environment schemes, incentive payments, and farm subsidies. The economic incentive for environmental management that they provide may be clothed with legal enforceability, for example, through the law of contract (management agreements) or public law (subsidies).

3. Economic instruments cannot alter the beneficiary's property entitlements, which are predetermined by statute or common law (point 1). They can simply reallocate the land use privileges that they represent—typically for a predetermined period, such as the duration of a land management agreement, following which they will revert to the *status quo ante* indicated by the property entitlement of the holder. Property entitlements can, however, be altered or modified by some legal instruments; for example, statutes, delegated legislation, and compulsory purchase orders. Other legal instruments have more limited effect and solely effect a reallocation of the land resource, and not property entitlements; for example, site notifications and land-management schemes.

have no property-based right of action to prevent damage to wildlife or the ecosystems on which they rely. The absence of property-based remedies in the common law for ecosystem damage means that much greater responsibility for the enforcement of nature conservation law falls to governmental regulatory agencies. The web-of-interests approach would, instead, require us to consider wildlife as being dependent upon, and integrally connected to, the land that it inhabits.[137] As will become evident from the discussion in the following chapters, there is also a complex web of individuals and organizations that have different legal responsibilities and interests in wildlife, their ecosystems, and the land on which they are to be found. Indeed, the 'partnership principle' that underpins modern environmental policy[138] stresses the central role that these different actors can, and should, play in delivering the effective conservation management of protected habitats and species. The web-of-interests analysis captures this complex set of interactions more fully than entitlement theories of property rights. It also defines property rights with regard to good stewardship and not simply consumptive entitlements, and facilitates an analysis of the quasi fiduciary role of property ownership in which the owner has duties of care not only in respect of the land itself but also in respect of the natural environment to which the land, or water, is integrally connected.[139]

Conclusion—Defining 'Conservation' Law

It will be clear from this introductory overview of the scope of the subject, and of the key themes of this work, that the parameters of 'nature conservation law' are potentially very wide, and inherently difficult to define with precision. The most meaningful definition that can be offered of conservation law as a discrete subject is therefore a purposive one. The subject matter of conservation law is not just the protection of pre-existing natural habitats, species, or important landscape features. The law has a positive role to play in devising suitable legal mechanisms to integrate environmental policy for the protection of species and habitats, and for the promotion of biodiversity, into a wide range of laws that currently govern the use and exploitation of land and other resources in the countryside and in the marine environment. The law plays a proactive role, both in relation to the protection of natural habitats (for example, in protected areas) but also in relation to biodiversity. The law also sits (perhaps uncomfortably) at the interface between conservation *science* and environmental management. The content of biodiversity action plans, the site management requirements for protected areas, and the assessment of the vulnerability or otherwise of endangered species, are all matters for the environmental scientist, not the lawyer. Once appropriate strategies have been devised, based on sound scientific evaluation of the needs and requirements of ecosystems and species, however, it is for the law to clothe them in legal enforceability in order to ensure that wildlife is appropriately protected and biodiversity promoted. The legal tools in the conservation lawyer's 'toolkit', and by which this task must be carried out, are various and cut across traditional legal disciplinary boundaries. 'Nature conservation law' encompasses areas of legal scholarship ranging from the law of torts, public law, the law of contract, and property law. The multifaceted nature of the modern law of nature conservation makes it a fascinating, but challenging, subject to study and master.

[137] Arnold (2002) at 351, 356. [138] pp. 6–7. [139] Arnold (2002) at 352.

2

The Governance of Nature Conservation

Introduction—Governance and the Partnership Principle

The governance arrangements for the creation and management of protected areas in the UK, for the protection of species of plant, animal, and bird, and for the development of national and regional conservation strategies, are complex. They are characterized by the statutory imposition of responsibility for a large variety of matters affecting the natural environment on public bodies. The achievement of conservation objectives for the management of the land resource, and perhaps to a lesser extent aquatic resources, is largely state-mediated. A miscellany of public bodies, from central and local government to the statutory Conservation Bodies, have direct responsibility for the administration and implementation of nature conservation law and policy. To these can be added other public bodies whose activities impact directly upon biodiversity and nature conservation, such as those government departments responsible for agriculture and forestry: the Environment Agency, the Marine Management Organisation, and the public utilities. The coordination of their policies and activities with public policy for promoting nature conservation is important, as is the development of an integrated approach to marine and terrestrial resource use that targets conservation objectives effectively.

Although the setting and monitoring of conservation objectives, of targets for biodiversity, and objectives for habitat and species protection, is largely state mediated, in practice a wide range of private sector bodies, charitable, and non-governmental organizations play a major role in managing land and aquatic resources for nature conservation. These include many large landowning bodies, such as the National Trust and the RSPB, and a wide range of local wildlife trusts, local biodiversity action partnerships, and other local and national organizations. The Natural Environment white paper of 2011[1] signalled a major shift in the governance of nature conservation towards a greater emphasis on local partnerships to deliver nature conservation objectives at local level. In particular, it posited the establishment of local nature partnerships bringing together NGOs, local charities, wildlife groups, local authorities, and local businesses to 'work in a joined up and strategic way [in local areas] to help manage the natural environment to produce

[1] *The Natural Choice—securing the value of nature*, (DEFRA 2011) available at: <http://www.defra.gov.uk/environment/natural/whitepaper/>.

multiple benefits for people, the economy and the environment'.[2] We will consider the role of local partnerships, and how they will integrate into the legal framework for conservation governance, in the concluding section of this chapter.[3]

The public bodies, and especially the statutory Conservation Bodies, will retain a key role in identifying protected areas and endangered species, in undertaking the scientific monitoring and research that underpins nature conservation and its implementation, and in enforcing, where necessary, legal measures to protect habitats and species. To a certain extent, the development of the local nature partnerships proposed in the Natural Environment white paper represents an extension and deepening of the 'partnership principle' that underpins modern nature conservation law.[4] It also emphasizes, and may in the future accentuate, a key tension that runs throughout the governance of nature conservation between:

(i) The need for scientifically researched and defined conservation objectives, monitoring, and appraisal of the status of protected species and natural habitats. This is essential to comply with legal obligations to protect habitats and species under international and European law, and must therefore be state mediated. Similarly, the enforcement of land use and other controls in protected areas, and the enforcement of the criminal law on species and habitat protection, must be transparent and adhere to rule of law standards of impartiality and probity. This must also, therefore, be state mediated. The adoption of a technocratic and state mediated 'top-down' approach to these aspects of environmental governance is inescapable.

(ii) On the other hand, effective environmental governance must recognize the need to develop integrated strategies if we are to *manage* the natural environment effectively. These are often best developed at a local level, using local expertise and local knowledge, and the partnership principle emphasizes that to achieve the best results the active cooperation of local actors, include landowners, local communities and organizations, is necessary. At the same time, however, local strategies must adhere to ecological criteria that are set by governmental bodies. Where, for example, land that is to be managed by a local partnership includes a protected habitat within a protected area, such as an SSSI or SAC, this must be appropriate to deliver the legal obligations for site protection applied by EC or national law.[5]

One of the key problems for environmental governance is therefore to secure a balance between achieving the necessary ecological coherence in conservation management on the one hand, and promoting the engagement of local actors in

[2] See *An Overview of the Local Nature Partnership Role* (DEFRA April 2012) at p. 1. Available at: <http://www.archive.defra.gov.uk/environment/natural/documents/local-nature-partnerships-overview120402.pdf>.

[3] See p. 61.

[4] See Chapter 1, p. 7.

[5] As to which, see Chapter 3 pp. 84 ff. (SSSIs) and Chapter 6 pp. 216 ff. (SACs and SPAs).

conservation management on the other. This requires a careful balancing of the 'top-down' application of state-mediated management criteria with a 'bottom-up' approach to conservation management that engages local actors, organizations, business, and landowners.[6] The essential nature of this problem has not been changed by the Natural Environment white paper or by the Localism Act 2011, but there has been a shift in the balance within the 'partnership' towards a greater emphasis on a bottom-up approach engaging local actors in conservation management.

The Statutory Conservation Bodies

Until the Environmental Protection Act 1990, a fundamental functional distinction was maintained in conservation governance between (i) the protection of landscape features and recreational access to the countryside, and (ii) nature conservation. This was reflected in a division of responsibility in the public bodies charged with overseeing and implementing public policy in each area. The central role in providing a comprehensive framework for promoting nature conservation was originally played by the Nature Conservancy Council, first established in 1949.[7] Policy on landscapes and recreation was dealt with by two separate bodies, the Countryside Commission for Scotland,[8] and the Countryside Commission,which covered England and Wales.[9]

The Environmental Protection Act 1990 divided the former Nature Conservancy Council into three separate bodies: the Nature Conservancy Council for England (now Natural England),[10] the Nature Conservancy Council for Scotland (Scottish Natural Heritage),[11] and the Countryside Council for Wales. The work of the three regional bodies is coordinated by the Joint Nature Conservation Committee (JNCC), another body established under the 1990 Act.[12] The roles of the Countryside Commissions and the Conservation Bodies were merged in Wales and Scotland, with Scottish Natural Heritage and the Countryside Council for Wales assuming statutory responsibility for both landscape and nature conservation. This was intended to facilitate a more integrated approach to conservation and related countryside issues. In England the division of responsibilities persisted

[6] The same problem is evident in the designation process under the Marine and Coastal Access Act 2009. Balancing the outcomes of a wide stakeholder consultation exercise in identifying Marine Conservation Zones with the ecological criteria determined by the statutory Conservation Bodies for marine protected areas has been problematic—see Chapter 7, pp. 262 ff.

[7] By the National Parks and Access to the Countryside Act 1949; in its seminal form prior to abolition in 1990, it operated under the Nature Conservancy Council Act 1973.

[8] Countryside Scotland Act 1967.

[9] Countryside Act 1968. The Countryside Commission replaced the National Parks Commission created by the 1949 Act.

[10] Established under Part 1 Natural Environment and Rural Communities Act 2006, in succession to, inter alia, English Nature (the former Nature Conservancy Council for England).

[11] Established under Part 1 the Natural Heritage (Scotland) Act 1990.

[12] S. 133 Environmental Protection Act 1990.

until 2006, when the Natural Environment and Rural Communities Act 2006 introduced further reform to the administration of nature conservation law. The 2006 Act created a new public agency with responsibility inter alia for nature conservation in England—Natural England.[13] The latter assumed the functions and role of English Nature, the (dissolved) Countryside Agency, and the Rural Development Service in relation to England, and enjoys a considerably wider and more integrated countryside role than its predecessor, English Nature.

The regional nature Conservation Bodies are collectively referred to in the Natural Environment and Rural Communities Act 2006 as 'the UK Conservation Bodies'[14] and comprise:

1. *Natural England* (combining the roles of the former English Nature, Countryside Agency, and Rural Development Service),
2. *Scottish Natural Heritage* (formerly the Nature Conservancy Council for Scotland),
3. *Countryside Council for Wales* (exercising powers of the former Nature Conservancy Council in Wales, and additionally powers of the former Countryside Commission in Wales), and
4. *Council for Nature Conservation and the Countryside* (in Northern Ireland).

For brevity, references in this and the following chapters to 'the Conservation Body' in the singular should be taken as references to one of the following: Scottish Natural Heritage, Natural England, the Council for Nature Conservation and the Countryside, or the Countryside Council for Wales, as the context requires. The Conservation Bodies have many functions in common. Since the devolution of responsibility for nature conservation policy, and related areas of public policy (for example, agriculture and forestry) to the devolved assemblies in Scotland, Wales, and Northern Ireland, the powers and duties of the Conservation Bodies have developed in ways that in some respects differentiate their roles. In these cases, when discussing distinct provisions applicable to one of the Conservation Bodies (but not the others), the Conservation Body will be referred to by name in the following text and in the other chapters of this work.

The Conservation Bodies have the duty of advising on the implementation of conservation policies in the UK, and additionally have a specific statutory role in several areas. Natural England, for example, has a wide-ranging and multifaceted countryside role. Its general purpose is to 'ensure that the natural environment is conserved, enhanced and managed for the benefit of future generations, thereby contributing to sustainable development'.[15] This general purpose includes: (a) promoting nature conservation and protecting biodiversity; (b) conserving and enhancing the landscape; (c) securing the provision and improvement of facilities for the study, understanding, and enjoyment of the natural environment; promoting

[13] S. 1 Natural Environment and Rural Communities Act 2006.
[14] See s. 32 Natural Environment and Rural Communities Act 2006.
[15] S. 2(1) Natural Environment and Rural Communities Act 2006.

access to the countryside and open spaces and encouraging open air recreation; and (e) contributing in other ways to social and economic well-being through the management of the natural environment.[16]

The statutory Conservation Bodies are 'non-departmental public bodies', and while they are not regulators in the same sense as, for example, the Environment Agency, they do nevertheless have a wide range of regulatory and licensing powers and functions. The powers enjoyed by the Conservation Bodies to pursue their statutory objectives are wide ranging. The Environmental Protection Act 1990 reallocated many of the nature conservation functions of the former Nature Conservancy Council to the new Conservation Bodies, and they have subsequently been further widened by statute.[17] The most important of relevance to this work are the following:

(i) They are responsible for notifying Sites of Special Scientific Interest (SSSIs) under the Wildlife and Countryside Act 1981, for the establishment and management of National Nature Reserves under the National Parks and Access to the Countryside Act 1949 and for giving support for education on conservation.[18] They also have ancillary powers in relation to protected sites; for example, to offer, and make payments under, management agreements.[19]

(ii) They can give a wide range of advice to public bodies on conservation issues, including the Secretary of State or other Ministers, and on the development and implementation of nature conservation policy.[20] If a public authority rejects advice given by Natural England, the latter must inform them in writing of that fact and explain why the advice was not accepted.[21] They can also give advice to private individuals.

(iii) Natural England has wide power to provide advice and disseminate knowledge to any other person about nature conservation in their area, and to give financial assistance, for example, in the form of grants, or guarantees, to support to further its general purpose in promoting sustainable development.[22]

(iv) They can commission or support research relevant to the exercise of the Conservation Body's conservation functions.[23]

[16] S. 2(2) Natural Environment and Rural Communities Act 2006.

[17] S. 132 and Schedule 9 Environmental Protection Act 1990. The powers of Natural England are set out in, and considerably widened by, ss. 3–13 Natural Environment and Rural Communities Act 2006. Those of Scottish Natural Heritage are set out in ss. 2 and 4 Natural Heritage (Scotland) Act 1991.

[18] See Schedule 9 Environmental Protection Act 1990. The changes made by Schedule 9 to legislation applicable to Scotland continues to apply to Scotland: s. 4(5) Natural Heritage (Scotland) Act 1991.

[19] See e.g. s. 7 Natural Environment and Rural Communities Act 2006 (Natural England's management agreement powers).

[20] S. 4 Natural Environment and Rural Communities Act 2006.

[21] S. 4(3) Natural Environment and Rural Communities Act 2006.

[22] See s. 6 Natural Environment and Rural Communities Act 2006.

[23] S. 3 Natural Environment and Rural Communities Act 2006.

(v) The Conservation Bodies also have power under the 1981 Act[24] to make financial grants and loans for the purpose of fostering the understanding of nature conservation, and to cover expenditure by an individual in doing anything conducive to nature conservation.

In exercising these functions, the statutory Conservation Bodies are directed to 'take appropriate account of actual or possible ecological changes'.[25] The Secretary of State must give Natural England guidance in relation to the exercise of any of its functions that relate to or affect regional planning and associated matters.[26] The Secretary of State also has power to give Natural England directions of a general or specific character as to the exercise of its functions.[27] Natural England must have regard to guidance so issued by government, and must comply with directions issued by the Secretary of State.[28] This power, however, does not extend to those functions of Natural England that are exercised through the Joint Nature Conservation Committee (pp. 41–3).[29] This includes providing advice on nature conservation matters that relate to the whole UK, or which arise outside the UK.[30] Neither does the power to give directions apply to the operational exercise of the bodies' powers to designate areas for special protection; for example, as sites of special scientific interest.[31]

The Conservation Bodies also have an enforcement role. Their principal regulatory roles are in relation to wildlife management and licensing, and in relation to protected areas. These are wide ranging and extend to offences relating to SSSIs, heather and grassland burning, the conversion of uncultivated and semi-natural areas to intensive farming, breaches of wildlife licences, and offences connected with the poisoning of animals and with injurious weeds.[32] As non-departmental governmental bodies, the Conservation Bodies are subject to the regulators' statutory compliance code,[33] which requires regulatory functions to be carried out in a balanced, proportionate, consistent, and transparent manner, and one that uses risk assessment to target resources to areas where they are needed most.[34] These

[24] S. 38 Wildlife and Countryside Act 1981.

[25] S. 131(2) Environmental Protection Act 1990.

[26] S. 15 Natural Environment and Rural Communities Act 2006.

[27] S. 16 Natural Environment and Rural Communities Act 2006. The Secretary of State also has power to give directions to Scottish Natural Heritage under s. 11 Natural Heritage (Scotland) Act 1991.

[28] S. 15(6) Natural Environment and Rural Communities Act 2006 (guidance); s. 16(5) Natural Environment and Rural Communities Act 2006. (directions).

[29] S. 16(2) Natural Environment and Rural Communities Act 2006.

[30] See s. 34(2) Natural Environment and Rural Communities Act 2006.

[31] S. 131(4) Environmental Protection Act 1990.

[32] For a review of the regulatory powers exercised by Natural England, and the degree to which they comply with the Hampton report principles, see: *Natural England, A Hampton Implementation Review Report* (Department for Business Innovation and Skills and the Better Regulation Executive, July 2009) available at: <http://www.naturalengland.org.uk/images/natural-england-regulatorystrategy_0tcm6-20560.pdf>.

[33] The *Code of Practice on Guidance on Regulation* (Department of Business Innovation and Skills, 2009), available at: <http://www.bis.gov.uk/files/file53268.pdf>.

[34] See eg *Natural England's Regulatory Strategy* (2008), available at: <http://www.naturalengland.org.uk/images/natural-england-regulatorystrategy_tcm6-20560.pdf>.

principles can be seen in Natural England's enforcement strategy, which targets resources to enforcement in cases where there is greatest risk of environmental damage, and implements the outcomes of the 2005 Hampton review and the principles of the better regulation initiative.[35] This is summarized in Box 2.1.

Natural England have the power to bring criminal proceedings,[36] but will consider the full range of enforcement mechanisms in each case to deal with breaches of conservation legislation; this might include issuing cautions, warnings, civil penalties, or in serious cases criminal prosecution. In each case, it will consider and apply proportionate enforcement mechanisms to achieve one or more of a number of outcomes: to achieve full restoration of environmental harm (the most important outcome of enforcement), to prevent further harm to the natural environment, to eliminate any illicit financial gain or benefit that has been obtained through non-compliance, to deter future reoffending and non-compliance, and where necessary, to secure the punishment of serious or persistent offenders.[37] The priority in all cases is to change the behaviour of offenders.[38] Prosecution will be reserved for serious offences. Where an offence is categorized as technical or minor, then a proportionate response is likely to involve issuing a warning letter or fixed money penalty (civil sanction); if it is classified as medium or significant, then a variable monetary penalty or simple caution may be used to deliver a proportionate deterrent.

Natural England will only use its power to prosecute in closely defined circumstances: where there is enough evidence to provide a realistic prospect of conviction against each defendant, and (if this is established) only where it is in the public interest to do so.[39] The sort of public interest factors that Natural England will consider include the impact of the offence on the natural environment, the forseeability of the offence, the likelihood of repetition or continuation of the offence (for example, illustrated by a history of recurring conduct) whether the offence is widespread in the area where it was committed, whether a prosecution would have a positive impact maintaining community confidence, the deterrent effect of prosecution in each case, and the intent and attitude of the offender.[40] In general, its primary stance is to work with other stakeholders to encourage compliance, reduce the need for enforcement action, and to protect the natural environment. This accords with the 'partnership' approach to nature conservation on which public policy is ultimately now founded,[41] and means that the use of prosecution

[35] See the *Code of Practice on Guidance on Regulation* (Department of Business Innovation and Skills, 2009), available at: <http://www.bis.gov.uk/files/file53268.pdf>.

[36] S. 12 Natural Environment and Rural Communities Act 2006. Note that it has a discretionary power, not a duty, to prosecute offences.

[37] See Natural England, *Enforcement Guidance* (2011) at para. 5.6 et seq. Available at: <http://www.naturalengland.org.uk/Images/enforcement-guidance_tcm6-29091.pdf>.

[38] See para. 1.2 Natural England, *Enforcement Guidance* (2011).

[39] See para. 5.20 Natural England, *Enforcement Guidance* (2011). Public interest factors are set out in the Code for Crown Prosecutors. See: <http://www.cps.gov.uk/publications/code_for_crown_prosecutors/codetest.html>.

[40] Para. 5.22 Natural England, *Enforcement Guidance* (2011).

[41] See Chapter 1, p. 7.

Box 2.1 Natural England's Enforcement Guidance[42]

The primary focus is on working in partnership with stakeholders. In deciding which enforcement mechanisms to apply, Natural England will follow five 'principles of regulation' as set out in its published *Compliance and Enforcement Position:*[43]

1. Enforcement action will be *consistent:* although each incident will be unique, similar approaches will be taken in similar cases to achieve similar outcomes, taking into account the severity of the damage or disturbance, history of non-compliance, and the attitude of the offender.
2. Enforcement action will be *proportionate* to the nature of the offence, and will take account of the risk to the environment, seriousness of breach, likely environmental outcomes, and whether it is in the public interest to pursue it.
3. Enforcement action will be *transparent.* It will be carried out in an open and transparent way so that those regulated and others know what they can expect of Natural England in its enforcement role.
4. Enforcement action will be *targeted.* Enforcement efforts and resources will be aimed where they will be most likely to achieve outcomes.
5. Enforcement action will be *accountable.* Enforcement outcomes will be measured and published annually to evaluate performance and instill confidence in those who are regulated, the public, and the Conservation Body's partners.

The statistics for enforcement in relation to criminal damage to SSSI features in England[44] reveal that in 2009–10 113 warning letters were issued three cautions and in only two cases were prosecutions instituted. In 2010–11 there were 100 recorded offences of damage to SSSIs in England: in 92 cases a warning letter was issued, and in eight a formal caution. No prosecutions were brought. No civil sanctions were served by Natural England under the Regulatory Sanctions and Enforcement Act 2008 or the Environmental Civil Sanctions (England) Order 2010.[45]

and other means of regulatory enforcement are a measure of last resort to secure compliance with statutory standards of habitat and wildlife protection.[46]

[42] See Natural England, *Enforcement Guidance* (December 2011) available at: <http://www.naturalengland.org.uk/Images/enforcement-guidance_tcm6-29091.pdf>.

[43] Natural England *Compliance and Enforcement Position* (December 2011) p. 5, available at: <www.naturalengland.org.uk/Images/compliance-enforcement-position_tcm6-29090.pdf>.

[44] Natural England, *Annual Report on Natural England's Enforcement Activity 1 April 2010 to 31 March 2011*, available at: <http://www.naturalengland.org.uk/Images/annual-report2010-11_tcm6-27479.pdf>.

[45] Public Register—civil sanctions and prosecutions (Natural England) available at: <http://www.naturalengland.org.uk/freedom_of_information/class6.aspx>.

[46] See also the Countryside Council for Wales' statement on enforcement, which makes it clear that the Council will seek wherever possible to work with landowners and managers to secure positive conservation measures, in preference to prosecution. In 2005 out of 62 infringements of the SSSI legislation in Wales, none resulted in prosecution; 20 were dealt with by the issuing of advice, 12 with a warning, and seven with a caution: <http://www.ccw.gov.uk/landscape–wildlife/protecting-our-landscape/special-landscapes–sites/protected-landscapes/sssis/sssi–report/enforcement-on-sssis.aspx?lang=en>. Scottish Natural Heritage's enforcement policy also prioritizes voluntary action by perpetrators of wildlife crime in preference to prosecution: see *SNH Guidance: Policy Guidance—Wildlife Crime* (March 2008) available at: <http://www.snh.gov.uk/docs/A328657.pdf>.

The Conservation Bodies' regulatory and enforcement powers are considered in more detail as appropriate in the following chapters:

(i) Regulatory powers in relation to the management of SSSIs and other terrestrial protected areas are considered in Chapter 3,[47]

(ii) Licensing and offences in connection with the protection of individual plants, animals, and birds are considered in Chapter 5,[48]

(iii) Regulatory powers in relating to European sites and also species of animal plant and bird protected under the European Habitats and Wild Birds Directives are considered in Chapter 6,[49] and

(iv) The regulatory powers exercised in relation to marine protected areas and marine licensing by the Marine Management Organisation, by the Secretary of State and by the Scottish and Welsh ministers are considered in Chapter 7.[50]

The Joint Nature Conservation Committee

The implementation of international conventions to which the UK is a signatory, and of European Union environmental directives, is a key aspect of the role of the statutory Conservation Bodies in overseeing the implementation of nature conservation law in the UK. These require the coordination of certain aspects of policy and practice at a national level where it is implemented by the regional bodies, and in some cases, the development of 'national'-level policy and practice to be applied by the statutory Conservation Bodies. Accordingly 'special' functions of the statutory Conservation Bodies can only be exercised by a joint committee; the Joint Nature Conservation Committee (JNCC).[51] The JNCC has 14 members, including a chairman and five members appointed by the Secretary of State, and the chairman, or deputy chairman, and one other member of each Conservation Body.[52] The JNCC was established by the Environmental Protection Act 1990 to coordinate the operation of the (then) new regional Conservation Bodies, and to implement UK-wide conservation policy. It was reconstituted with widened powers to undertake conservation functions of national or international significance by the Natural Environment and Rural Communities Act 2006. The chief import of the 2006 Act was to extend its remit to Northern Ireland by incorporating representation from the province's Council for Nature Conservation and the Countryside.

[47] See Chapter 3, pp. 69 ff.
[48] See Chapter 5, pp. 170 ff.
[49] See Chapter 6, at pp. 220 ff.
[50] See Chapter 7, at pp. 279 ff.
[51] Ss. 31 and 34 Natural Environment and Rural Communities Act 2006. These powers were previously defined in s. 133 Environmental Protection Act 1990 (repealed by Schedule 12 Natural Environment and Rural Communities Act 2006). The JNCC's constitution and procedural rules for its meetings are set out in Schedule 4 Natural Environment and Rural Communities Act 2006.
[52] Schedule 4 para. 1 Natural Environment and Rural Communities Act 2006.

The statutory Conservation Bodies have a number of functions of national and international significance that can only be exercised through the JNCC.[53] These include the following:[54]

(i) the provision of advice to the Secretary of State, Scottish ministers, or National Assembly of Wales on the development and implementation of nature conservation policy or conservation matters that arise throughout the UK or raise issues common to England, Wales, Scotland, or Northern Ireland, or issues that arise in one or more of them but affect the interests of the UK as a whole, or arise outside the UK,

(ii) the provision of advice, etc. and dissemination of knowledge about nature conservation in Great Britain or elsewhere,

(iii) the establishment of common standards for monitoring nature conservation, and the conducting of research relevant to conservation matters,

(iv) commissioning research that the JNCC thinks is relevant to its coordinating role in nature conservation.

The joint committee also has responsibility for implementing certain national functions in relation to wildlife protection that require coordination and a national level approach. The most important is the periodic review and revision of the lists of protected animals and plants set out in the Wildlife and Countryside Act 1981.[55] The Secretary of State can give the joint committee general or specific directions as to the discharge of any of its functions, but cannot give it directions in relation to its power to revise and review the lists of protected animal and plants under the 1981 Act.[56]

The scientific research commissioned and carried out by the joint committee is important in underpinning the coordination and delivery of nature conservation across the UK. The joint committee can give advice and/or information to any of the regional Conservation Bodies on any matter which, in the joint committee's opinion, arises throughout the UK and raises issues common to England, Wales, Scotland, and Northern Ireland, or which arises in one or more of the regions and affects the interests of the UK as a whole, or which arises outside the UK.[57] Importantly, the Conservation Bodies must have regard to any advice given by the joint committee when discharging their functions relating to nature conservation.[58]

The joint committee produces a wealth of research and evidence that can be accessed through its website.[59] Among its key outputs are the Guidelines for the

[53] S. 33 Natural Environment and Rural Communities Act 2006.

[54] S. 34(2) Natural Environment and Rural Communities Act 2006.

[55] S. 36 Natural Environment and Rural Communities Act 2006; ss. 22 (3) and 24 (1) Wildlife and Countryside Act 1981 (as to which, see Chapter 5, p. 162).

[56] See s. 38(1) Natural Environment and Rural Communities Act 2006.

[57] S. 35(1) Natural Environment and Rural Communities Act 2006.

[58] S. 35(2) Natural Environment and Rural Communities Act 2006.

[59] See <http://www.jncc.org.uk>.

Selection of Biological SSSIs,[60] and the Geological Conservation Review,[61] which are used by the Conservation Bodies and ensure that a consistent approach is applied to the identification and notification of Sites of Special Scientific Interest across the UK. Another important output is the common standards monitoring framework,[62] which underpins the assessment of the condition and conservation status of protected areas designated for legal protection; for example, SSSIs and SACs. This is important for the purpose of assessing the impact of conservation management on the protected features of sites and reporting to government and the European Commission.[63] The joint committee has partnerships with a wide range of non-government conservation groups[64] to implement surveillance of key species under the aegis of the UK terrestrial biodiversity surveillance scheme. It also carries out the reporting function for the UK under a range of multilateral environmental agreements, such as CITES and the Ramsar Convention on Wetlands of International Importance, as well as reporting on national implementation and other issues arising under European Community environmental law. The joint committee collates and maintains, for example, the data on Special Areas of Conservation designated under the 1992 Habitats Directive, and on their conservation status, and is responsible for the submission of reports to the European Commission.

Governmental Bodies

(a) Central government

Most of the important governance functions in relation to the conservation of habitats and species are performed by the statutory Conservation Bodies: Natural England, the Countryside Council for Wales, Scottish Natural Heritage, and the Conservation Service in Northern Ireland. Nevertheless, central government also plays a central role, not only in shaping the environmental policy and legislation on nature conservation that is implemented by the Conservation Bodies, but also indirectly through the issuance of guidance and directions to the Conservation Bodies on the application of these powers in practice. In most primary legislation, the role of the central government is expressed through the conferment of powers and responsibilities on the 'Secretary of State'. In practice, this means the Secretary of State for the Environment, Food and Rural Affairs, as DEFRA is the Westminster governmental department with responsibility for the environment and countryside affairs, although since devolution some of these functions are carried out in

[60] *Guidelines for the Selection of Biological SSSIs* (JNCC, Peterborough) available on the JNCC website at: <http://www.jncc.gov.uk/page-1457>.

[61] *Geological Conservation Review*, (JNCC, Peterborough) available at: <http://jncc.defra.gov.uk/default.aspx?page = 2947>.

[62] For which, see <http://jncc.defra.gov.uk/page-2217>.

[63] As to which, see Chapter 6, p. 239 and Box 6.4.

[64] Eg the Bat Conservation Trust, the British Trust for Ornithology, the Game and Wildlife Conservation Trust, and the Wildfowl and Wetlands Trust.

Scotland and Wales by, respectively, the Scottish Government and Welsh Assembly Government.

The most obvious illustration of power residing ultimately with central government is reflected in the fact that the chairman and board members—to a maximum of 15—of Natural England are appointed by the Secretary of State.[65] The Board members of the Countryside Council for Wales are appointed post-devolution by the Welsh Assembly Government, and those of Scottish Natural Heritage by the Scottish ministers.[66] The Secretary of State (in England), Scottish ministers, and Welsh Assembly Government, also all have power to exercise indirect control of the Conservation Bodies. The Secretary of State must give Natural England guidance on any of its functions that relate to regional planning, and has discretion to give it guidance as to any of its other functions.[67] The Secretary of State can also give Natural England general or specific *directions* 'as to the exercise of its functions', with which the latter is obliged to comply.[68] This power is necessary to ensure that international or European treaty obligations for which the Secretary of State retains responsibility are reflected in and implemented through the operational practices of the Conservation Bodies; for example, in relation to the selection and protection of protected areas.[69] It clearly gives the Secretary of State power to issue guidance as to the *manner in which* the Conservation Bodies exercise their statutory functions. There is a query as to whether the power extends to issuing directions to the Conservation Body as to the exercise of its operational powers in relation to the notification and protection of specific SSSIs or other protected sites.[70] And of course, Natural England is funded through grant funding from the Secretary of State.[71]

Central government also retains a number of important operational roles. It is the Secretary of State who must propose the list of Sites of Community Importance eligible for notification to the European Commission,[72] the first stage in notifying Special Areas of Conservation under the Habitats Directive.[73] And it is the Secretary of State (or Welsh Assembly Government in Wales, or Scottish ministers in Scotland) who must then designate the site as a Special Area of Conservation once it has been adopted as a site of community importance under the Directive.[74] The implementation of devolution for Scotland and Wales has added a further layer of complexity to the governance arrangements for administering nature conser-

65 Schedule 1 para. 3 Natural Environment and Rural Communities Act 2006.

66 EPA 1990, Schedule 9; Schedule 1 para. 3 Natural Heritage (Scotland) Act 1991.

67 S. 15(2) and (3) Natural Environment and Rural Communities Act 2006.

68 See s. 16(1) and (5) Natural Environment and Rural Communities Act 2006.

69 See Chapter 3, pp. 68 ff. and Chapter 6, pp. 216 ff.

70 The power to issue directions was contained originally in s. 131(4) Environmental Protection Act 1990, which established the regional Conservation Bodies, but did not extend to giving them directions as to SSSIs or their notification. The formulation in s. 16 Natural Environment and Rural Communities Act 2006 would appear somewhat wider, and to have extended the power into their operational decision making.

71 S. 14 Natural Environment and Rural Communities Act 2006.

72 See Conservation of Habitats and Species Regulations 2010, SI 2010/490, regs. 10 and 3(1) (definition of 'appropriate authority').

73 As to which, see Chapter 6, p. 210 and Box 6.1.

74 See Conservation of Habitats and Species Regulations 2010, SI 2010/490 reg. 11.

vation law. The Scotland Act 1998 transferred full legislative and ministerial powers to the new Scottish Government and Scottish Parliament for all matters relevant to the subject matter of this work (nature conservation and related issues concerning land use, such as agriculture policy and legislation).[75] In Wales, the devolution of powers to the Welsh Assembly and Welsh Assembly Government has been more limited under the Government of Wales Acts 1998 and 2006. The Assembly has no power to introduce primary legislation, but can make secondary legislation on a range of specified transferred matters, including agriculture. Ministerial powers have also been transferred to the Welsh Assembly Government under a large number of pre-existing legislative measures, for example, power to notify Special Areas of Conservation under the Conservation of Habitats and Species Regulations 2010, licensing powers under the Wildlife and Countryside Act 1981 permitting the killing of protected species in certain circumstances by specified individuals, and various powers under other conservation statutes such as the Conservation of Seals Act 1970 and Protection of Badgers Act 1992. The transfer of these powers in Wales has not produced any significant difference in approach to that obtaining in England.

The central UK government retains responsibility for the assumption of, and adherence to, treaty obligations. This is of importance in relation to obligations under the various European Directives on conservation, principally the Habitats Directive. The UK government remains liable for the transposition of Directives into England, Welsh, and Scottish law, and for their subsequent implementation. Infringement proceedings brought by the European Commission for the incomplete or ineffective implementation of wildlife protection under the European Habitats Directive will be brought against the UK government.[76] Nevertheless the administration and protection of European wildlife sites rests with the devolved governments. Under the constitutional settlement reached in 1998 to structure the relations between the central and devolved governments, set out in several constitutional 'concordats', the devolved administrations undertook to implement national obligations, and while the UK government would be liable to pay any fines levied by the European Court of Justice in infringement proceedings for breaches or non-implementation of European environmental directives, the sums so paid will be deducted from the grant aid distributed to the devolved administrations by central government.[77]

[75] Certain 'reserved' matters are retained by the Westminster Parliament, but these do not touch on the subject matter of this work: Schedule 5 Scotland Act 1998. The Westminster government retains the power to legislate on any matter or subject matter however: s. 28(7). For a detailed survey of the impact of devolution, see C. T. Reid, 'Devolution and the Environment' in A. Ross (ed.), *Environment and Regulation* (Edinburgh University Press, 2000).

[76] For examples see *Commission v United Kingdom* (2005) Case C 06/04, [2005] ECR I–9017 (failure to transpose EC Habitats Directive provisions fully, see Chapter 6, p. 219); *Commission v United Kingdom* (2005) Case C 06/04, [2005] ECR I–9017 (failure to designate offshore marine SACs, see Chapter 7, p. 252).

[77] See <http://webarchive.nationalarchives.gov.uk/+/http://www.dca.gov.uk/concordat/concord_scot.htm#e> (Scottish concordat) and <http://webarchive.nationalarchives.gov.uk/+/http://www.dca.gov.uk/concordat/concord_wales.htm> (Welsh concordat).

(b) Local government

A detailed consideration of the structure of local government in Scotland, England, and Wales is beyond the scope of this work. There is a single tier of local government based on unitary authorities in Scotland and Wales. In England the position is a little more prosaic, with unitary authorities in most areas, some metropolitan authorities, and in London a two tier structure based upon the London Boroughs, City of London Corporation, and the Greater London Authority[78] in which the London boroughs act as principal planning authorities in each area, while the Greater London Authority has overarching planning powers enabling it, for example, to call in and require changes to local development plans.[79]

The local authorities exercise a wide range of functions, many of which have relevance to the promotion of nature conservation. The most directly relevant are their functions as local planning authorities, both in formulating development plans for their areas and in relation to development control. As a consequence of the implementation of the Habitats and Species Directive,[80] development plans for any area in England[81] must include 'policies encouraging the management of features of the landscape which are of major importance for wild fauna and flora'.[82] The objective is to encourage, through the land use planning system, the maintenance of habitat features which by virtue of their linear or continuous structure, are necessary for genetic exchange, breeding, and migration of wild animal and bird species.[83] The features to be accommodated in plans are those which 'by virtue of their linear or continuous structure' are essential for the migration, dispersal, and genetic exchange of wild species; for example, traditional field boundaries and hedge systems, riverbanks and other features (such as ponds) used as stepping stones by wildlife species.[84]

Direction over the content of development plans and the manner in which development control applies is maintained through planning policy guidance issued (in England)[85] by the Department of Communities and Local Government—until 2012 through PPS 9 on Biological and Geological Conservation and now the *National Planning Policy Framework.*[86] PPS 9 required that plans should offer

[78] Greater London Authority Act 2007.

[79] For a more detailed account, see V. Moore and M. Purdue, *A Practical Approach to Planning Law* 12th edn (Oxford University Press, 2012), Ch. 2.

[80] Dir. 92/43/EEC on the Conservation of Habitats and Species, [1992] OJ L206/7.

[81] As to which, see Planning and Compulsory Purchase Act 2004, ss. 17 and 62, (local development plans and local development documents).

[82] Reg. 39(1) Conservation of Habitats and Species Regulations 2010, SI 2010/490. Similar provision is made in relation to Scotland by reg. 37 of the Conservation (Natural Habitats etc.) Regulations, 1994 SI 1994/2716.

[83] See art. 10 Directive 92/43/EEC on the Conservation of Habitats and Species, [1992] OJ L206/7.

[84] Reg. 39(3) Conservation of Habitats and Species Regulations 2010, SI 2010/490.

[85] In Wales Technical Advice Notes ('TANS') issued by the Welsh Assembly Government and in Scotland planning guidance issued by the Scottish ministers.

[86] Planning Policy Statement 9, *Biological and Geological Conservation* (revised 2005) and ODPM Circular 06/2005, DEFRA Circular 01/2005: *Biodiversity and Geological Conservation—Statutory Obligations and their Impact within the Planning System* (August 2005). Now Ch. 11 paras. 109 ff. of

reasonable certainty to developers and landowners about the weight to be given to nature conservation interests in reaching planning decisions.[87] Local plans should include planning policies to be applied to nature conservation sites, such as SSSIs, and include policies to minimize impacts on biodiversity.[88] These principles are complemented by policies in other relevant planning guidance issued to local planning authorities; for example, in relation to sustainable development in the countryside the National Planning Policy Framework encourages the targeting of building and other development on farms away from sites that may have a high nature conservation interest and towards land of poorer agricultural quality and/or versatility.[89]

Development control decision-making by local planning authorities is 'plan led', and a decision to grant or refuse planning permission for development 'must be made in accordance with the plan unless material considerations indicate otherwise'.[90] Spatial policies for promoting nature conservation that are included in the development plan for an area will therefore have considerable weight in development control determinations. The Town and Country Planning Act 1990[91] requires that a local planning authority 'shall have regard to the provisions of the development plan, in so far as material to the application, and to any other material considerations'. Where development is to take place in a protected area, such as an SSSI, the conservation interest will be a 'material consideration' that must be taken into account by the local planning authority in its determination, as will the planning guidance set out in the National Planning Policy Framework. The weight to be attached to the differing 'material' considerations relevant in each case is for the planning committee to determine, however, and nature conservation considerations may be outweighed by other relevant considerations (including those relating to social and economic development) even if this is contrary to the conservation interest in a particular case.[92] Where development is proposed in a site designated for protection as a European site under the Habitats or Wild Birds Directives, on the other hand, the regulations transposing the Directives into English Law[93] impose restrictions on the circumstances in which a local planning authority can authorize development that is damaging to the site or will produce disturbance of a protected species contrary to the requirements of the Directives. The manner in which development controls decision making is applied

the *National Planning Policy Framework* (2012), available at: <http://www.communities.gov.uk/documents/planningandbuilding/pdf/2116950.pdf>.

[87] PPS 9 *Biological and Geological Conservation* (2005) para. 1 principle (ii).

[88] Para. 117 of the *National Planning Policy Framework* (2012) (see earlier n.83).

[89] See *National Planning Policy Framework* (2012) paras. 111 ff. These policies were formerly in PPS7 *Sustainable Development in Rural Areas* (2004) at para. 28.

[90] S. 38(6) Planning and Compulsory Purchase Act 2004, replacing s. 54A Town and Country Planning Act 1990.

[91] See s. 70(2) Town and Country Planning Act 1990.

[92] For an example where this occurred, see *R v Poole Borough Council ex parte BeeBee* [1991] JPL 643 (Schiemann J.)

[93] See reg. 68 Conservation of Habitats and Species Regulations 2010, SI 2010/490, and more generally, Part 6 Ch. 2 (Planning) of SI 2010/490.

in protected areas is considered more fully in Chapter 3 and, in relation to European sites, in Chapter 6.[94]

Local authorities also have power to designate local nature reserves.[95] More generally, they also have power to enter in to management agreements with the owners and occupiers of land in their area for the purpose of preserving and/or enhancing the natural beauty of the countryside, or for promoting its enjoyment by the public.[96] The exercise of their other powers as, for example, highways authorities and coast protection authorities, can also have major implications for the promotion of nature conservation and the environment more widely.

(c) National Park Authorities

The National Parks and Access to the Countryside Act 1949 provided for two types of landscape designation, National Parks, and Areas of Outstanding Natural Beauty ('AONB'). The 1949 Act (as amended) gives Natural England and CCW the power to designate as a National Park, in England and Wales respectively, those 'extensive tracts' of countryside which, by reason of their natural beauty and the opportunities they offer for open-air recreation, necessitate measures being taken to preserve and enhance their natural beauty.[97] They must also take account of the area's wildlife and cultural heritage, and the extent to which it is possible to promote opportunities for the understanding and enjoyment of its special qualities by the public.[98] Where there is a conflict between these principles, the duty to conserve and enhance the natural beauty of the area takes precedence.[99]

Both national parks and AONBs are administered by representative public bodies, and the exercise of their functions are important for the furtherance of nature conservation within the designation park or AONB, as the case may be. In the case of a national park, each park is administered by a National Park Authority established for this purpose. The National Park Authority acts as the planning authority for the purpose of deciding all development control matters within its area. It holds full planning and development control powers within the park, and has power to take all actions that are expedient to attain the objectives for which the park was established.[100] The membership of the park authority will include a specified number of local authority and parish members, plus a number

[94] See Chapter 4, pp. 140 ff. (SSSIs) and Chapter 6 (European sites), pp. 225 ff.

[95] See s. 21 National Parks and Access to the Countryside Act 1949, and further Chapter 3, p. 102.

[96] S. 39 Wildlife and Countryside Act 1981; Countryside Scotland Act 1967 as amended (latterly by Natural Heritage Scotland Act 1991 Schedule 10 para. 4).

[97] S. 5(1) National Parks and Access to the Countryside Act 1949, amended by s. 62 Environment Act 1995: in Scotland similar powers are now exercised by the Scottish ministers under s. 1 National Parks (Scotland) Act 2000.

[98] S. 5(2) and (2A), amended by s. 59 Natural Environment and Rural Communities Act 2006. In Wales the Countryside Council for Wales' powers are exercised under s. 130(1) and Schedule 8 Environmental Protection Act 1990.

[99] S. 11A National Parks and Access to the Countryside Act 1949, inserted by s. 62 Environment Act 1995: s. 9(6) National Parks Scotland Act 2000.

[100] S. 63 Environment Act 1995.

of additional members appointed by the Secretary of State. The local authority and parish members must, however, provide the majority of park authority members.[101] The principal means by which the parks' objectives are pursued is through the establishment of a development plan in each case, and the imposition of special development control rules in national parks.[102]

(d) Conservation boards

In Areas of Outstanding Natural Beauty, the minister has power to establish conservation boards to oversee management of the Area.[103] Proposals for the establishment of a conservation board for an AONB must be made by the minister, who must consult Natural England or CCW, and all local authorities with land in the area, before formulating a proposal. The Secretary of State's power to establish conservation boards is exercisable by statutory instrument, subject to annulment by resolution of either House of Parliament, and can only be made if the majority of local authorities consent to the proposal.[104] The order must make provision for any local authority powers which are to be transferred to the conservation board (for instance, planning powers and powers in relation to public health legislation) and can make provision for the transfer of property rights or liabilities, including supplementary provision for the management and custody of transferred property, and for any liabilities transferred to include liabilities under any enactment, and for the transfer of staff, compensation for loss of office pensions, and other staffing matters.[105]

(a) Where a conservation board is established it must, in exercising its functions, have regard to[106] the purpose of conserving and enhancing the natural beauty of the Area of Outstanding Natural Beauty, and to

(b) The purpose of increasing the understanding and enjoyment by the public of the special qualities of the AONB. If there is a conflict between these two purposes, they must attach greater weight to purpose (a); that is, conserving and enhancing the natural beauty of the area. The conservation board must also seek to foster the economic and social well-being of local communities within the AONB, but without incurring significant expenditure in doing so, and must to that end cooperate with local authorities and public bodies whose functions include economic or social development within the relevant

[101] See Schedule 7 paras. 1(2)-(6) Environment Act 1995, amended by s. 61 Natural Environment and Rural Communities Act 2006. In Wales two-thirds of members are appointed by the local authorities.

[102] See further Chapter 3, pp. 107–8.

[103] Under provisions in s. 86 the Countryside and Rights of Way Act 2000 conservation boards can be established by the Secretary of State (in England) and the National Assembly for Wales (in Wales). Conservation Boards can be established in relation to existing AONBs, or in relation to new AONBs upon designation.

[104] See s. 86 Countryside and Rights of Way Act 2000.

[105] See generally s. 88(8) Countryside and Rights of Way Act 2000.

[106] S. 87(1) Countryside and Rights of Way Act 2000.

area.[107] Conservation boards have a general power[108] to do anything which in their opinion is calculated to facilitate, or is conducive or incidental to the accomplishment of, their statutory purposes, or the carrying out of any functions conferred on them by statute. Importantly, however, development control and planning functions must remain with the local planning authority.[109] Conservation boards will also have the right to acquire land, and also to dispose of land where necessary.[110] Furthermore, where the Secretary of State or the Welsh Assembly Government, whichever applies, considers it expedient for the fulfilment of the statutory purposes for which a conservation board has been established, it may provide for the transfer to the board of local authority functions insofar as they relate to the AONB in question, or provide for any function of a local authority to be exercisable concurrently by the local authority and the conservation board.[111]

The exercise of these powers is important in relation to nature conservation within each AONB, and is considered in more detail in Chapter 3 in the context of protected areas policy.[112]

(e) Other public bodies

A number of other public bodies exercise regulatory roles that can impinge in important ways on nature conservation and biodiversity. Principal among these are the functions of the Environment Agency and of the Scottish Environment Protection Agency, and of the Marine Management Organisation (MMO) in relation to the marine environment.

The Environment Agency exercises a wide range of regulatory functions in relation to all three environmental media—land, water, and air. It is the lead regulator for environmental permitting[113] and as such is responsible for issuing permits for discharges to water, to air, and for waste disposal, including those for installations under the integrated pollution prevention and control (IPPC) regime. The way in which it exercises these functions, and the terms on which, for example, environmental permits are granted for discharges of effluent or other noxious substances to the environment all have major implications for nature conservation and biodiversity. When exercising its statutory functions the Agency's principal aim must be 'to protect or enhance the environment, taken as a whole, [so] as to make the contribution towards achieving sustainable development' set out in Ministerial guidance to the Agency.[114]

107 S. 87(2) Countryside and Rights of Way Act 2000.

108 See s. 87(4) Countryside and Rights of Way Act 2000.

109 S. 86(3), (4) Countryside and Rights of Way Act 2000. Cf. National Parks (pp. 104–108) where these powers are transferred to the National Parks Authority.

110 Schedule 14 Countryside and Rights of Way Act 2000.

111 S. 86(3) of the 2000 Act.

112 See Chapter 3, pp. 108 ff.

113 Under the Environmental Permitting (England and Wales) Regulations 2010 SI 2010/675, amended SI 2010/676, SI 2010/2172.

114 S. 4(1), (3) Environment Act 1995.

Its powers in relation to the control of water pollution are especially important in the context of nature conservation. It is responsible for implementing, through its permitting and other regulatory powers, the requirements of the European Water Framework Directive,[115] which places the achievement of good ecological status for water by 2015 at the centre of European environmental policy. The ministers and other public authorities must exercise their powers so as to secure compliance with the Directive.[116] The Directive requires river basin management planning, with a management plan established for each river basin district containing objectives which are based largely on ecological criteria.[117] The Directive's requirements as to ecological quality will be implemented through the setting of water quality objectives for each body of water within a river basin management plan, and their use in the exercise of all regulatory functions in relation to those waters, including the fixing of the terms of discharge consents to the aquatic environment.[118] A full description of these regulatory powers is beyond the scope of this work.[119] It is important to note, however, that the Agency is under a duty generally to promote the conservation and enhancement of the natural beauty and amenity of inland and coastal waters and of land associated with such waters, and to promote the conservation of flora and fauna which are dependent on the aquatic environment.[120]

The MMO was established under Part 1 of the Marine and Coastal Access Act 2009 and exercises a number of functions in the governance of the marine environment which are directly relevant to nature conservation. In England, the Secretary of State's powers to grant licences under the Conservation of Seals Act 1970 have been transferred to the MMO,[121] as has the power to issue licences in the English inshore region under the Wildlife and Countryside Act 1981; for example, to authorize the killing or taking of specified species of animal or bird.[122] One novel feature of the 2009 Act is the provision made for the further transfer of powers from the Secretary of State to the MMO by agreement, in relation to either the whole UK marine area or specified parts of it.[123] The MMO may, in turn, enter into an agreement granting an 'eligible body' power to exercise MMO functions in relation to the UK Marine Area or specified parts of it, with the Secretary of State's consent.[124] The eligible bodies to which it can transfer functions in this way include the Environment Agency, Natural England, any inshore fisheries and

[115] Council Directive 2000/60/EC on framework in water policy, [2000] OJ L327/1.

[116] Water Environment (Water Framework Directive) (England and Wales) Regulations 2003, SI 2003/3242; s. 2(1) Water Environment and Water Services (Scotland) Act 2003.

[117] These are set out in Annex V of Directive 2000/60/EC.

[118] See eg the Surface Waters (River Ecosystems) (Classification) Regulations 1994, SI 1994/1057.

[119] See W. Howarth and D. McGillivray, *Water Pollution and Water Quality Law* (Shaw & Sons, 2001).

[120] See s. 6(1) Environment Act 1995. This is not an absolute statutory duty: it only applies 'to such extent as [the Agency] considers desirable'.

[121] S. 9 Marine and Coastal Access Act 2009. See <http://www.marinemanagement.org.uk/index.htm>.

[122] See s. 10 Marine and Coastal Access Act 2009, and for the relevant powers under s. 16 Wildlife and Countryside Act 1981, see Chapter 5, p. 170 ff.

[123] Under powers in s. 14 Marine and Coastal Access Act 2009.

[124] See s. 15 Marine and Coastal Access Act 2009.

conservation authority, and a local fisheries committee or harbour authority.[125] The MMO has responsibility for managing Marine Protected Areas in England out to the limits of the continental shelf, and will as part of this remit have responsibility for the management of Marine Conservation Zones designated under the 2009 Act once these are established.[126] It also has responsibility for the marine licensing system established under the 2009 Act, which applies to a wide range of activities in the marine environment, including the licensing of the use of vehicles, boats, aircraft, marine structures, and containers, and the licensing of extraction and deposit in the UK marine area.[127] The exercise of these powers for the conservation of the marine environment is considered in more detail in Chapter 7.

Non-Governmental Conservation Bodies

A large number of voluntary organizations exist to promote nature conservation, at both local and national level, and in relation to specific geographical areas and specific species of animal, plant, and bird. The advancement of environment protection and improvement is a charitable purpose under charities legislation in both England and Wales,[128] and in Scotland,[129] and many of these bodies have the status of charitable trusts. Many of these non-government bodies, such as the National Trusts and the RSPB, own and manage large areas of land for conservation purposes. In addition, they manage many areas of land that have been declared as National Nature Reserves[130] or local nature reserves.[131] Many also play an important partnership role in monitoring and implementing biodiversity action plans, in developing local biodiversity action partnerships,[132] and in the surveillance of the conservation status of target species in partnership with the joint nature conservation committee.

(a) The National Trusts

The National Trust was founded in 1894, and the separate National Trust for Scotland in 1935.[133] The National Trust occupies a unique legal position as a charitable trust incorporated by statute; the powers and duties of the Trustees, and

[125] S. 16(1) Marine and Coastal Access Act 2009. The Secretary of State has power by order to add to the list of eligible bodies to whom powers can be transferred; see s. 16(2) Marine and Coastal Access Act 2009 Marine and Coastal Access Act 2009.

[126] As to which, see Chapter 7, pp. 257 ff.

[127] For marine licensing see Chapter 7, pp. 273 ff.

[128] S. 2(2)(i) Charities Act 2006.

[129] S. 7(2) Charities and Trustee Investment (Scotland) Act 2005.

[130] For designation, see Chapter 3, pp. 99 ff.

[131] See Chapter 3, p. 102.

[132] Between 2000 and 2010, 119 local biodiversity partnerships were established in England, and a further nine regional biodiversity fora. See <http://www.naturalengland.org.uk/ourwork/conservation/biodiversity/protectandmanage/default.aspx>.

[133] National Trust for Scotland Confirmation Act 1935, and subsequent Acts in 1938, 1947, 1952, 1961, and 1973.

of the Trust as to the management of its properties, are set out in no fewer than six Acts of Parliament.[134] The management and administration of the Trust is now dealt with in accordance with a Parliamentary scheme implemented in 2005.[135] The Trust was initially formed as a not-for-profit association limited by guarantee by Victorian philanthropists in 1894, and reincorporated by Act of Parliament in 1907 with the following statutorily defined objectives:

> The National Trust shall be established for the purposes of promoting the permanent preservation for the benefit of the nation of lands and tenements (including buildings) of beauty or historic interest and as regards lands for the preservation (so far as practicable) of their natural aspect features and animal and plant life.[136]

Some land owned by the Trust is inalienable, and must be held by it for the benefit of the nation, thus guaranteeing its preservation for public benefit in the future.[137] When acquiring new land, the Trustees can also resolve that if the land is 'proper to be held for the benefit of the nation' it can be declared inalienable for the future.[138] The National Trust Act 1937 gave the Trust enhanced powers to bind land by entering into covenants or agreements with the owner restricting its development or use so as to further the Trust's objectives.[139] This enables the Trust to further its nature conservation objectives by taking conservation easements and management agreements from another landowner, and more importantly, enabling it to enforce the agreement or covenant against a successor if the owner sells or transfers the land to someone else. The enforcement of such arrangements normally requires the retention by the claimant of adjacent land that the agreement will benefit. This restriction does not apply to the Trust, which can take conservation easements and covenants from a landowner even though it has no land of its own in the immediate vicinity. The Trust also has power to make by-laws on its land so as to prevent damage, to preserve and protect public access for recreation, to protect plants or natural features, and to prevent the disturbance of animals and birds.[140]

The Trust has over 4 million members in England and Wales, and plays a very significant and important role in implementing land management for nature conservation on its estate. It owns approximately 248,000 hectares of land in England and Wales, much of which is of environmental significance and sensitivity. It owns significant amounts of land that host a variety of semi natural habitats, for example:[141] 7940 ha of parkland (up to 40 per cent of the total area of this habitat

[134] The National Trust Acts 1907, 1919, 1937, 1939, 1953, and 1971.

[135] Charities (National Trust) Order 2005.

[136] S. 4(1) National Trust Act 1907.

[137] See s. 21(1) National Trust Act 1907. The land to be held on this basis was initially set out in Schedule 1 to the 1907 Act.

[138] S. 21(2) National Trust Act 1907.

[139] S. 8 National Trust Act 1937.

[140] S. 24 National Trust Act 1971; and see s. 12 National Trust Act 1937. The powers set out in s.24(1)(a)–(s) of the 1971 Act are very wide ranging. Many have direct relevance to the protection of natural habitats, eg the prevention of the cutting of peat or taking of soil, cutting or burning of gorse, heather, timber, or shrubs (s. 24(1)(a) National Trust Act 1971).

[141] See data available on the National Trust website at: <http://www.nationaltrust.org.uk/main/w-chl/w-countryside_environment/w-nature/w-nature-wildlife.htm>.

found in England and Wales); 28,060 ha of acid grassland (2 per cent of the total area); 18,840 ha of upland heath (1 per cent); 4324 ha of lowland heath (7.5 per cent); 9710 ha of blanket peat bogs; and 1485 ha of salt marsh (3 per cent). In addition to owning significant proportions of the land hosting semi-natural habitats in England and Wales, the Trust also owns 141,800 ha of farmland—a significant proportion of which is designated for its high nature value; for example, as Sites of Special Scientific Interest (SSSIs) or nature reserves.[142] In total, 90,670 ha of National Trust land is included in notified SSSIs,[143] 7 per cent of the total SSSI area in England and Wales. No less than 500 SSSIs include land owned or managed by the Trust—over 10 per cent of the SSSIs in England and Wales. It also owns 57 National Nature Reserves, encompassing 10,946 ha of Trust land—over half of the total number of National Nature Reserves. Many of these sites are of European level significance—360 in England, Wales, and Northern Ireland are Special Areas of Conservation, and 117 are Special Protection Areas.

Restoring and protecting habitat types that have been lost in the post-war period—such as hedgerows, semi-natural grassland, and hay meadows—is a major objective of the Trust's policy for its managed estate. The Trust is able, therefore, to directly affect the promotion of nature conservation objectives through the positive use of property ownership and the adoption of conservation policies in its acquisition and management of land. Unlike most public bodies, however, the decisions of its Trustees are not subject to judicial review, and attempts to challenge their policy decisions in the courts must be authorized by the Charity Commissioners. An example of the constructive use of property rights to promote conservation objectives, and of the limitations on the scope of available legal challenge to the Trust's policy decisions, was provided by the controversial adoption in the 1990s of a ban on hunting across land owned by the Trust.[144]

(b) The Wildlife Trusts

There are 47 local Wildlife Trusts covering most of the UK, organized under an umbrella organization, the Royal Society of Wildlife Trusts.[145] The Trusts are voluntary organizations, but have a significant impact on the recreation and management of important habitats at local level. The Trusts collectively manage over 2000 local nature reserves across the UK, and in 2009 adopted an overarching set of policy objectives to create a 'living landscape'.[146] Their activities, although organized at a local level—often on a county basis—and voluntary, come into contact with the legal regime for promoting nature conservation in several ways.

[142] See <http://www.nationaltrust.org.uk/main/w-chl/w-countryside_environment/w-nature/w-nature-wildlife-designated_sites.htm#stats>.

[143] As to which, see Chapter 3, pp. 68 ff.

[144] See *Scott v National Trust* [1998] 2 All ER 705 and *R v Council of the National Trust for Places of Historic Interest or Natural Beauty ex parte Scott* [1998] 1 WLR 236.

[145] See <http://www.wildlifetrusts.org/>.

[146] See <http://www.wildlifetrusts.org/sites/wt-main.live.drupal.precedenthost.co.uk/files/A%20Living%20Landscape%20report%202009%20update.pdf>.

They can, for example, be charged with the management of local nature reserves, and the Conservation Bodies can use their statutory powers to make by-laws in order to facilitate the protection of nature reserves managed by voluntary bodies such as the Trusts.[147] Even if they do not have the funds to purchase land for conservation management (for example, to create nature reserves) they can deliver conservation management on land owned by other bodies. They also act as partners in biodiversity action plans in many areas, and can have a role in habitat and species monitoring; for example, that undertaken by the Joint Nature Conservation Committee.[148]

In addition to the local wildlife trusts, which are regionally organized, there are also a number of conservation trusts devoted to the study and conservation of specific species of animal plant and bird; for example, the Bat Conservation Trust,[149] the Game and Wildlife Conservation Trust,[150] Butterfly Conservation,[151] and the Whale and Dolphin Conservation Society.[152]

General Duties on Public Bodies

(a) Promoting biodiversity

The recognition of the need to promote and protect biodiversity, as an objective distinct from promoting the protection of specific habitats and species, is of fairly recent provenance, and has been introduced into domestic law following the adoption of the UN Convention on Biological Diversity in 1992. A duty in these terms was introduced in 2000, and replaced by a more widely based statutory duty in the Natural Environment and Rural Communities Act 2006. Every public authority must, when exercising its functions, have regard 'so far as consistent with the proper exercise of those functions' to the purpose of conserving biodiversity. Conserving biodiversity is, in this context, defined to include restoring or enhancing a population of a living organism, or restoring or enhancing a particular type of habitat.[153] The public authorities to which this duty applies are widely defined. They include all ministers of the Crown, the National Assembly of Wales, any public body (including a government department, local authority, or local planning authority), a statutory undertaker, and any person holding office under the Crown or whose position is publicly funded.[154] Ministers, government departments, and the National Assembly of Wales are, additionally, placed under a more specific duty to have regard to the UN Convention on Biological Diversity 1992 when exercising

147 See s. 35 Wildlife and Countryside Act 1981.

148 See pp. 42–3.

149 See <http://www.bats.org.uk/>.

150 See <http://www.gwct.org.uk/>.

151 See <http://www.butterfly-conservation.org/>.

152 See <http://www.wdcs.org.uk/>.

153 See s. 40(1) and (3) Natural Environment and Rural Communities Act 2006. This provision replaced s. 74 Countryside and Rights of Way Act 2000.

154 See s. 40(4) Natural Environment and Rural Communities Act 2006.

their functions.[155] This general duty is supplemented by a duty imposed on the Secretary of State (and in Wales on the Welsh Assembly Government) to publish a list of the living organisms and types of habitat which are, in their opinion, of principal importance for the purpose of conserving biodiversity.[156] A further general duty is then imposed on them to take such steps 'as appear to be reasonably practicable'[157] to further the conservation of the living organisms and types of habitat included in the list published in accordance with the principal duty.[158]

(b) General conservation duties

A number of public bodies have statutory powers and functions whose exercise potentially impact upon the conservation of wildlife and natural habitats. The exercise by local and central government bodies of development control powers under the Town and Country Planning legislation is of central importance in protecting natural habitats from the inappropriate and potentially damaging development of land. The powers of the agriculture ministers to make financial subventions to landowners and farmers, for example, to fund agricultural improvements may impact upon natural habitats if they encourage intensive farming or operational work on farm land that has high nature value. The exercise of similar powers by the Forestry Commission in relation to afforestation projects can have similar effects on forest habitats and wildlife, and the Environment Agency and MMO have wide powers in relation to the protection of the aquatic environment, the exercise of which may have major implications for nature conservation in individual cases. Many of these public bodies are subject to general statutory duties to promote the conservation of nature and wildlife, although these are expressed in different terms in the relevant legislation.

An exhaustive analysis of these powers is beyond the scope of this work.[159] The principal statutory duties with direct relevance to the protection of natural habitats and wild flora and fauna include the following. The agriculture ministers are required,[160] when discharging any functions connected with agriculture in relation to any land, to have regard to, and 'endeavour to achieve', a reasonable balance between the promotion and maintenance of a stable and efficient agriculture industry, the economic and social interests of rural areas, the conservation and enhancement of the natural beauty and amenity of the countryside, and the

[155] See s. 40(2) Natural Environment and Rural Communities Act 2006.

[156] See Natural Environment and Rural Communities Act 2006, s. 41 (England), s. 42 (Wales).

[157] For a consideration of the enforcement of statutory duties phrased in this manner see *Friends of the Earth v Sec of State* [2008] EWHC 2518 Admin (see later in this chapter p. 59).

[158] In practice, this obligation will be discharged principally through the specification of operations likely to damage the conservation interest in protected sites, and the requirement for a statutory consultation with the Conservation Bodies before a landowner can lawfully carry these out—see Chapter 3, pp. 84 ff.

[159] See S. A. De Smith, J. Jowell and Lord Woolff, *Judicial Control of Administrative Action*, 6th edn (Sweet & Maxwell, 2007), paras. 11.01 et seq. C. Reid, *Nature Conservation Law*, 3rd edn (Sweet & Maxwell, 2009) at 2.2.2–2.3.1.

[160] S. 17(1) of the Agriculture Act 1986.

promotion of its enjoyment by the public. This involves balancing the conservation interest with a range of other relevant countryside issues. It clearly means, however, that the environmental impact of operations or works for which grants are sought will be relevant to the resolution of applications for grant aid.[161] A similar balancing function is imposed on the Forestry commissioners to 'endeavour to achieve a sustainable balance between' the development and maintenance of forest and timber production on the one hand, and the conservation and enhancement of natural beauty, and the conservation of flora and fauna and geological or physiographical features of special interest on the other.[162]

The Environment Agency is under a duty 'to such extent as it considers desirable' to promote the conservation and enhancement of the natural beauty and amenity of inland and coastal waters and land associated with those waters, and to promote the conservation of flora and fauna that are dependent on those waters.[163] This duty will be relevant, for example, when the Agency is exercising its statutory functions in relation to water pollution control, including the issue of environmental permits for the discharge of potentially noxious or polluting matter to rivers or other controlled waters,[164] and decision making on enforcement in cases of breaches of pollution control legislation. It will also be relevant in the exercise of its other powers; for example, in cases of flood prevention work and to ensure sustainable water supply.

In some cases there is a duty to balance conservation interests against other policy or operational interests when exercising statutory functions. This is the case, for example, where statutory undertakers exercise their statutory powers to enter land to carry out work for the supply of water or electricity. It also applies to the powers of the agriculture ministers when making public grants for improvements to land or other purposes, and also in the sphere of forestry administration (by the Forestry Commission). In some cases statutory powers that appear to impose a direct conservation duty in fact impose a duty that is, essentially, a duty to *balance* the conservation interest with other competing objectives. A good example of this phenomenon is the duty of the Environment Agency to promote nature conservation and the conservation of flora and fauna.[165] Although this is expressed as a clear duty, it is also expressed to be without prejudice to the other duties of the Agency under section 7 of the Environment Act 1995, and the latter requires the Agency to consider a wide range of factors when formulating proposals relating to its functions, including inter alia promoting public recreation, conservation of buildings and archaeological sites, and 'to have regard to the effect which the proposals would have on the economic and social well-being of local communities in rural

[161] Grant aid for agricultural improvements is available under, eg, s. 29 of the Agriculture Act 1970 or under the Farmland and Rural Development Act 1988.

[162] See s. 1(3A) Forestry Act 1967, added by s. 4 Wildlife and Countryside (Amendment) Act 1981. This balancing duty applies to the exercise of any of their functions under the Forestry Acts 1967–79.

[163] S. 6(1) Environment Act 1995.

[164] See the Environmental Permitting (England and Wales) Regulations 2010, SI 2010/675, as amended.

[165] S. 6(1) Environment Act 1995.

areas'.[166] Although there is a clear duty on the Environment Agency to consider nature conservation interests when exercising its functions, therefore, this must be balanced against a number of other competing objectives, some (but not all) of which may be compatible with promoting the conservation of flora and fauna.

In other cases, many public bodies must exercise what is essentially a balancing function when making decisions on land use. This is most obviously the case in relation to development control. A local planning authority must take into account all material considerations when making a decision on an application for planning permission to develop land.[167] Where development is proposed for land that has been notified as an SSSI or Special Area of Conservation because of its high nature value, then the nature conservation interest will be a material consideration to be taken into account before a decision can be made. In such cases the local planning authority will also have to conduct an environmental impact assessment and must consider all relevant 'environmental information' before making a decision.[168] This will include the environmental impact statement supplied by the developer with the application for planning permission, a range of other information provided by statutory consultees (such as the Environment Agency and the Conservation Body) and representations made by members of the public and/or NGOs. Planning guidance issued by central government, both on impact assessment and on biodiversity and nature conservation, must also be considered before a decision can be made.[169] The conservation interest is, however, only one of the material factors that must be considered when making a decision on development consent.[170] The conservation interest is one factor that *must* be taken into account before a decision is made, but it does not have precedence; other relevant factors must be taken into account and the weight accorded to them is for the planning authority to decide when drawing the necessary balance. As we shall see, when we consider the implementation of EU environmental law, the weight to be attached to the conservation interest is given much greater prominence in relation to habitats and species that are protected under the Habitats and Species Directive of 1992.[171]

Judicial scrutiny of the exercise of 'balancing' duties is weak, and statutory duties of the kind described earlier are rarely directly enforceable in the courts. The courts will only intervene to strike down a decision of this type by a public body if it

[166] S. 7(1)(c) Environment Act 1995.

[167] S. 70 Town and Country Planning Act 1990.

[168] Town and Country Planning (Environmental Impact Assessment) Regulations 2011 SI 2011/1824, esp. reg. 2(1) definitions of 'Schedule 2 development' and 'sensitive areas'. An EIA will be required if any part of a proposed development is within inter alia an SSSI or SAC.

[169] See the *National Planning Policy Framework* (2012); former PPS 9 *Biological and Geological Conservation* (2005); Circular 02/1999 *Environmental Impact Assessment* (Department for Communities and Local Government).

[170] S. 70(2) Town and Country Planning Act 1990 simply requires the development control committee to 'have regard to the provisions of the development plan, so far as material to the application, and to any other material factors' when making a decision to grant or refuse planning permission. See generally Moore and Purdue (2012) at paras. 12.25 ff.

[171] See Chapter 6, pp. 228–230.

appears 'so unreasonable that no reasonable authority could ever come to it'.[172] This will usually be because either the decision was carried out following an unreasonable process, in violation of common law principles, or is oppressive in some way.[173] The court will rarely intervene to dictate the weight to be given to different factors in the statutory balancing process required of a public body exercising a statutory duty. In planning law cases, the courts will leave the balancing of the various material factors in a development control decision to the local planning authority, which must make a judgment as to the weight to be attached to each of them, including the weight to be attached to the conservation interest if the land has high nature value because it hosts a protected habitat or species.[174] The courts will rarely intervene to adjudicate on the weight attached to particular 'material' considerations, but they may do so in rare cases if there is evidence that excessive weight has been attached to one consideration at the expense of others.[175] In cases involving potential development in sites hosting protected nature conservation features, the result is often that the legal protection afforded to the conservation interest from allegedly inappropriate development is weak.[176]

Where legislation creates public duties to further conservation and/or biodiversity of a non-balancing nature, the statutory language creating the duty usually qualifies it by reference to external factors or by reference to the financial or other imperatives that must be taken into account when deciding upon actions to be taken in pursuance of the duty. Phrases such as 'as far as practicable', and 'to such extent as it consider desirable', therefore qualify the statutory duty they impose, and permit public bodies to take into account a wide range of other factors, including the financial resources at their disposal to implement measures to promote the aims in view, such as nature conservation.[177]

> This is the language of 'effort' to achieve targets, rather than of guarantee that targets will be reached. However, the obligation remains to take the steps considered necessary to make these efforts as far 'as reasonably practicable'. To this extent, the language of policy has been translated into the language of statutory duty and the court can be guided by the use of similar language in relation to other statutory duties, and in particular duties imposed upon government.[178]

The principal benefit of imposing such statutory duties upon public bodies is that—although not directly enforceable in many cases—they do ensure that the

[172] See Lord Greene MR in *Associated Provincial Picture Houses Ltd v Wednesbury Corporation* [1948] 1 KB 223 at 229.

[173] See Lord Woolf, J. Jowell, and A. Le Sueur, *De Smith's Judicial Review*, 6th edn (Blackwell, 2007) at 11.018 ff.

[174] See *Tesco Stores v Secretary of State for the Environment* [1995] 1 WLR 759, HL.

[175] See Woolf, Jowell, and Le Sueur (2007) at 11.034.

[176] See eg *R v Poole B.C. ex parte BeeBee* [1991] 3 JEL 293.

[177] See eg *Friends of the Earth v Sec of State* [2008] EWHC 2518 Admin (judicial consideration of a duty to produce, and then implement, a programme to eradicate 'as far as reasonably practicable' fuel poverty under ss. 2(5) and (6) of the Warm Homes and Energy Conservation Act 2000).

[178] *Friends of the Earth v Secretary of State* [2008] EWHC 2518 Admin, judgment at para. 19 per McCombe J.

matrix of 'relevant' considerations to which the decision maker must have regard, when exercising the functions conferred by statute, includes the interests of furthering biodiversity and nature conservation. Public authorities are created by statute—including those, such as Natural England or Scottish National Heritage, that are directly involved in conservation governance, and their power to prosecute objectives that include promoting biodiversity and nature conservation depend upon the considerations they are entitled to take into account when exercising their statutory functions. However weak, therefore, the imposition of statutory duties on various public bodies to further conservation and/or biodiversity, or to consider doing so alongside the pursuit of other objectives, means that actions taken to further these objectives cannot be challenged as ultra vires. It also means that conservation interests must be considered before a decision can be made in many cases, even if the ultimate decision is then taken to authorize or undertake actions that have an adverse impact on the natural environment. The nature of many of the obligations on public bodies and statutory undertakers (to balance different considerations alongside nature conservation) means that their primary statutory functions may necessitate discounting nature conservation in practice. But the fact that they must consider the needs of promoting biodiversity and conservation at least means that the impact of their actions on the natural environment must be considered in each case as part of the decision-making process. It also means that a decision made without demonstrably having done so may be open to challenge on judicial review for irrationality.[179]

(c) Duties to promote sustainable development

A number of statutes impose a duty on public bodies to further sustainable development. We saw earlier[180] for example, that the principal objective of the Environment Agency when exercising its statutory powers is to discharge them so as to make a contribution towards achieving sustainable development.[181] Promoting sustainable development has been a key public policy goal since the early 1990s.[182] It has been woven into the framework of obligations imposed upon public bodies and regulators in the last 20 years in many environmental statutes, policy documents and circulars, including, for example, planning policy guidance issued by central government,[183] and now the *National Planning Policy Framework* for England issued in 2012.[184] The concept is multifaceted and variable, but

[179] *Associated Provincial Picture Houses Ltd v Wednesbury Corporation* [1948] 1 KB 223. And see further Woolf, Jowell, and Le Sueur (2007) at 11.036 ff.

[180] See p. 50.

[181] S. 4(1) Environment Act 1995.

[182] See *Sustainable Development—the UK Strategy*, Cm. 2426 (1994), and latterly *Securing the Future: Delivering the UK Sustainable Development Strategy*, Cm. 6467 (2005).

[183] Eg PPS 1 *Delivering Sustainable Development* (ODPM 2005).

[184] Available at: <http://www.communities.gov.uk/documents/planningandbuilding/pdf/2116950.pdf>. See especially para. 14 (presumption in favour of sustainable development).

unquestionably includes the promotion of biodiversity and the protection of the natural environment.

The concept of sustainable development is dynamic in nature with mobile elements, and is therefore subject to change—unsurprisingly, there has been no attempt to define it in the various statutes in which it has been used to impose duties on public bodies. Some statutes impose the achievement of sustainable development as an aim or objective to be pursued by public bodies when exercising their statutory functions. Others impose a duty on public bodies to use their powers to further sustainable development. In both cases, there is a problem of definition. The concept is inherently vague, but essentially imposes a duty to balance the interests of economic development, environmental protection, and social sustainability (the equitable distribution of resources) in policy development and, where statutory duties are imposed on public bodies to take it into account, in the implementation of that policy by public bodies. A large number of statutes now impose requirements on public bodies to further sustainable development, either as aims and objectives of the use of statutory powers, or as discrete duties, and these vary enormously in the manner in which they are drafted, and in the nature and specificity of the duties they impose.[185] Commentators have argued that in the modern context, ecological sustainability is the dominant paradigm of the three.[186] It follows, therefore, that when statutes impose *duties* to pursue sustainable development on public bodies, this will require a consideration of biodiversity, the protection of natural resources, and a duty to further nature conservation when they are exercising their legal functions.

A New Approach—Local Partnerships?

We noted at the beginning of this chapter that the Natural Environment white paper of 2011[187] signalled a major shift in the governance of nature conservation towards a greater emphasis on local partnerships to deliver nature conservation objectives at local level. We will therefore conclude this review of the governance arrangements for nature conservation by examining in more detail how this will work, and how it will change the manner in which nature conservation in England is promoted and administered. The implications of this for the future direction of nature conservation law and policy more broadly will be examined in the concluding chapter.[188]

[185] For a comprehensive review see A. Ross, 'Why legislate for Sustainable Development? An Examination of Sustainable Development Provisions in UK and Scottish Statutes' (2008) 20 JEL 35–68.

[186] See A. Ross, 'Modern interpretations of sustainable development' (2009) 36 *Journal of Law and Society* 32–54; K. Bosselmann, *The Principle of Sustainability—Transforming Law and Governance* (Ashgate, 2008).

[187] *The Natural Choice—securing the value of nature*, (DEFRA 2011) available at: <http://www.defra.gov.uk/environment/natural/whitepaper/>.

[188] Chapter 8, pp. 295 ff.

The white paper proposed the establishment of local nature partnerships,[189] and envisaged that they would comprise members from local government, statutory agencies, business, local 'civil society organizations', and members of the public. These will operate using an ecosystems services approach to nature conservation at a local level. The concept is modelled upon, and will be complementary to, Local Enterprise Partnerships, with the emphasis firmly on development of the green economy and sustainable resource use. Another key feature of the new partnerships will be the adoption of an integrated landscape-scale approach, enabling their work to cross existing administrative boundaries, such as local authority boundaries. Local nature partnerships will be recognized by the statutory Conservation Bodies and by government. DEFRA will host an annual ministerial event at which they can share experience problems and successes.

In 2011/12, £1 million was provided to establish the first partnerships and criteria against which applications will in future be judged were established.[190] The first local nature partnerships (41 in England) were established in 2012.[191] The partnerships will not supplant the role of public and governmental bodies in the administration of nature conservation law. They are, however, intended to signal a move away from a purely state-mediated approach to the administration of nature reserves, protected areas, and other aspects of the natural environment, and towards an approach that engages as wide a range of local actors (public, private, and charitable) as possible in delivering the effective management of natural resources.

The other challenge addressed by the white paper was that presented by the Lawton review,[192] viz. to prevent the further fragmentation of biodiversity and provide a more holistic and comprehensive approach to protecting the natural environment. The Natural Environment white paper envisaged the creation of Nature Improvement Areas.[193] These will bring together partnerships of local authorities, local communities and landowners, the private sector, and conservation organizations. The Nature Improvement Areas will be based on a local assessment of opportunities for restoring and connecting nature on a larger and more geographically significant scale. This is intended to address the need for Ecological Restoration Zones on a large scale, as identified by the Lawton report. The government sponsored a competition to identify areas that could qualify as Nature Improvement Areas, and provided £7.5 million in initial funding to establish them. The first 12 Nature Improvement Areas were announced in February 2012.[194] The role of the new improvement areas is intended to provide a larger-scale planning

[189] *The Natural Choice—securing the value of nature*, (DEFRA 2011) paras. 2.15–26.

[190] See *Local Nature Partnership Application Assessment Criteria* (DEFRA, April 2012) available at: <http://www.archive.defra.gov.uk/environment/natural/documents/lnp-assessment-criteria120402.pdf>.

[191] See *List of Current Local Nature Partnerships* (DEFRA, July 2012). Available at: <http://archive.defra.gov.uk/environment/natural/documents/lnp-list-20120717.pdf>.

[192] J. H. Lawton, P. N. M. Brotherton, V. K. Brown, et al. (2010), *Making Space for nature: a review of England's wildlife sites and ecological network,* available at: <http://www.defra.gov.uk/pubications/files/pb13428-newp-discussion-239710.pdf>. This is discussed further in Chapter 8, pp. 296 ff.

[193] See Lawton et al. (2010) at para. 2.27.

[194] See <http://www.defra.gov.uk/environment/natural/whitepaper/nia/>.

framework for nature conservation. This is linked to and supported by policies in the new National Planning Policy Framework, and local partnerships in the nature improvement areas will be able to influence land use development through the planning reforms it implements.

Significantly, although the new partnerships will be important in delivering conservation management at a local scale, and developing new and more diverse governance arrangements for nature conservation, the statutory roles and duties of the various public bodies with responsibility for the development and implementation of nature conservation policy remain unchanged. The initiatives signalled by the 2011 Natural Environment white paper therefore signal a shift in the *balance* between central government direction of policy and its implementation, and local management of high nature value sites and improvement areas. They have not, however, changed the fundamental nature of the legal framework for environmental governance in the administration of nature conservation.

3

Natural Habitats: Designation and Protection

Introduction—Protected Areas Policy

The protection of the natural habitats of wild species of flora and fauna is fundamental to ensure their survival. Degradation of habitat is a primary cause of biodiversity loss, both in the UK and internationally. The introduction of laws protecting individual species from exploitation will not arrest this without a complementary approach focused to ensuring the continued availability of a healthy range of natural habitat for protected species. We saw in Chapter 1[1] that the implementation of nature conservation policy in the UK has focused on a dual approach—the law grants individual protection to endangered species of bird animal and plant (species protection), while at the same time providing for the designation of protected areas to ensure the maintenance of a sufficient natural habitat for those species to ensure the genetic exchange, migration, and breeding conditions necessary to their survival (habitat protection). Species protection will be considered in Chapter 5. This chapter will focus on the identification and designation of protected areas under the domestic law of England, Wales, and Scotland. Chapter 4 will then consider the different legal and economic instruments deployed in protected areas to ensure appropriate habitat management.

In some countries habitat management is achieved principally through state ownership of sensitive protected areas. This is partly the case, for example, in the USA and Canada, where federal and state parks fulfil some of the functions that protected areas perform in the UK. In a densely populated island like the UK, however, setting aside large tracts of land for the exclusive protection of wildlife is not a feasible option. We also have a highly developed system of private property ownership that has evolved over many centuries, and under which all land is subject to private property rights—conferring rights to ownership, exploitation, and control of the land and its resources. The approach that has been pursued in the UK focuses instead, therefore, on working in partnership with landowners and other stakeholders to achieve the desired protection of natural habitats.[2] In the case of terrestrial habitats, this has meant the adoption of legal measures to manipulate the property rights of landowners and land managers in order to redistribute access to the land resource in ways that benefit natural habitats—and seek to ensure their protection. The efficacy of the extant statutory provisions for terrestrial habitat

[1] See Chapter 1, pp. 1–2. [2] See Chapter 1, p. 7.

conservation depends upon their impact on property rights and the effectiveness with which they can be enforced, for example, against landowners and third parties. The protection of the marine environment has proved more problematic, largely because there is no property rights regime underpinning the exploitation of marine living resources, and therefore no focal point for the enforcement of controls aimed at ensuring the conservation of the marine environment. The approach here has focused, instead, on the development of integrated planning in the use of marine protected areas and their resources, involving both stakeholders and regulatory and public bodies. This approach is seen most clearly in the Marine and Coastal Access Act 2009, and is examined in more detail in Chapter 7.

The manipulation of property rights by legal and economic instruments, and focused on delivering terrestrial habitat management, is therefore a key theme that will be explored in Chapters 3 and 4. This will involve a consideration of the *extent to which* property rights are manipulated to deliver the protection and restoration of natural habitats, the *manner in which* this is achieved by different legal and economic instruments, and the *nature of the property rules* that the law deploys to achieve the desired policy objectives for nature conservation. The difficulties inherent in developing a legal framework for marine habitat protection, where an absence of property rights is a key factor for policy implementation, are discussed in Chapter 7 and will provide a contrast and counterpoint to the property rights analysis underpinning the description of terrestrial habitat protection that follows in this chapter.

The development of the modern network of protected areas has proceeded in an ad hoc manner, resulting in a complex mosaic of site designations with differing objectives and foci. There are now at least 19 different categories of protected area that are underpinned in the UK (or parts of the UK) by statutory designations. The number is greater if non-statutory protected areas are included, such as Biosphere reserves and GeoParks notified for protection to UNESCO. Box 3.1 gives an overview of those protected areas that have a statutory basis for designation in English Law.[3]

There is a fundamental differentiation in UK protected areas policy between (i) designations focused on ensuring landscape protection and recreational access to the countryside by the public, and (ii) designations focused exclusively on promoting nature conservation. This binary approach goes back to the National Parks and Access to the Countryside Act 1949, which made provision in the immediate post-war years for the designation of the first national parks, and also for what were then known as Areas of Special Scientific Interest. Although national parks are designated primarily for the opportunities they offer for open air recreation, and for the

[3] For an earlier review see K. Bishop, A. Phillips, and L. Warren, 'Protected Areas for the Future; Models from the Past' (1997) 40 *Journal of Environmental Planning and Management* 81–110. The authors identify 29 protected designations of relevance to the conservation of nature—but this does not, of course, include designations introduced since 1997 (such as Marine Conservation Zones introduced under the Marine and Coastal Access Act 2009). The methodology used in this study included areas that are given protection under administrative arrangements, such as agri-environmental schemes (Environmentally Sensitive Areas and Tir Cymen are included, for example). This is somewhat wider than the parameters of the analysis in Box 3.1, which is limited to those protected areas designated under statutory provision.

Box 3.1 Protected Areas in Great Britain[4]

Protected Area Designation	*Geographical scope*	*Statutory or other legal authority*
Areas of Outstanding Natural Beauty (AONB)	England, Wales, Northern Ireland	National Parks and Access to the Countryside Act 1949, Environment Act 1995
National Scenic Areas	Scotland	Planning (Scotland) Act 2006; Town and Country Planning (Scotland) Act 1997 s. 262A
Areas of Special Protection	England, Scotland, Wales	Protection of Birds Act 1954
		Wildlife and Countryside Act 1981
(Wildlife Refuges)	(Northern Ireland)	Wildlife (Northern Ireland) Order 1985
Country Parks	England, Scotland, Wales	Countryside Act 1968; Countryside (Scotland) Act 1967
Historic Gardens and Designated Landscapes	Scotland	Town and Country Planning General Development Procedure (Scotland) Order 1992
Limestone Pavement Orders	England Wales Scotland	Wildlife and Countryside Act 1981
Local Nature Reserves	England, Wales, Scotland	National Parks and Access to the Countryside Act 1949,
Marine Conservation Zones	England, Wales, UK Offshore	Marine and Coastal Access Act 2009
Scottish Marine Protected Areas	Scotland	Marine (Scotland) Act 2009
Marine Nature Reserves	England, Wales, Northern Ireland	Wildlife and Countryside Act 1981
(now Marine Conservation Zones in England and Wales)		Nature Conservation and Amenity Lands (Northern Ireland) Order 1985
National Nature Reserves	England, Wales, Scotland, Northern Ireland	National Parks and Access to the Countryside Act 1949, Wildlife and Countryside Act 1981

4 See the Directory at <http://jncc.defra.gov.uk/page-1527> maintained by the Joint Nature Conservation Committee.

National Parks	England, Wales, Scotland	National Parks and Access to the Countryside Act 1949 National Parks (Scotland) Act 2000
Natural Heritage Areas	Scotland	Natural Heritage (Scotland) Act 1991
Ramsar sites (also designated as SPAs and SSSIs under domestic legislation)	United Kingdom	Convention on Wetlands of International Importance 1971
Regional parks	Scotland	Wildlife and Countryside (Scotland) Act 1981
Sites of Special Scientific Interest (SSSIs)	England, Wales, Scotland	Wildlife and Countryside Act 1981; Nature Conservation (Scotland) Act 2004
Areas of Special Scientific Interest	Northern Ireland	Wildlife and Countryside Act 1981
Special Areas of Conservation (SACs)	England, Wales, Scotland, Northern Ireland, UK territorial waters beyond 12 nautical miles	Conservation of Habitats and Species Regulations 2010;
Sites of Community Importance (SCIs)		Offshore Marine Conservation (Natural Habitats etc.) Regulations 2007
Special Protection Areas (SPAs)	England, Wales, Scotland, Northern Ireland, UK territorial waters beyond 12 nautical miles	Wildlife and Countryside Act 1981; Offshore Marine Conservation (Natural Habitats etc.) Regulations 2007
World Heritage Sites	United Kingdom (25 sites, including five natural heritage sites)	World Heritage Convention 1972 (UNESCO) (ratified by UK 1984)

protection of their sensitive landscape features, they nevertheless also include high nature value areas, and the promotion of nature conservation is an objective that they also encompass. Areas of Special Scientific Interest are now known as Sites of Special Scientific Interest (SSSI), and have an exclusive focus to nature conservation. There is, therefore, no 'bright line' distinction between nature conservation and landscape designations. Neither are they mutually exclusive—designations are often overlapping, and one area of land may have multiple designations subsisting over it at any one time.

The history of nature conservation policy in the UK has, since 1949, moved from one largely based on a policy of voluntarism, to one where the statutory Conservation Bodies pursue a partnership approach with landowners and managers—albeit with important regulatory powers to compel appropriate land management should a voluntary approach fail. The 1949 Act provided for the designating of Areas of Special Scientific Interest, but did not even require the landowner to be notified of this; it was intended as a notification to the local authority of the land's importance; for example for the purposes of deciding planning applications for development in the area concerned. The Wildlife and Countryside Act 1981 introduced an element of compulsion by requiring landowners to notify the statutory Conservation Bodies of their intention to carry out potentially damaging operations likely to harm the sites conservation interest. But this did not implement a regulatory prohibition on land use changes, which could be carried out after a four-month consultation period had elapsed. The increased protection that these powers conferred on sites only applied, however, to sites re-notified after 1981 under the Wildlife and Countryside Act. This gave rise to a major task for the Conservation Bodies during the 1980s and 1990s in re-notifying sites previously notified under the earlier legislation. The Countryside and Rights of Way Act 2000 further strengthened the regulatory controls potentially available to the Conservation Bodies in SSSIs by giving them power to indefinitely refuse consent to potentially damaging operations.

The powers of the Conservation Bodies under the Wildlife and Countryside Act 1981 (as amended) are important in protecting SSSIs from damage by activities that do not require planning permission from the local authority. Where development requiring planning consent is proposed, on the other hand, the protection of SSSIs is delivered through planning law and planning guidance, and the decision-making body in this case will be the local planning authority. There is therefore a fundamental division in responsibility for decision making on land use proposals in protected sites, between (i) the local authorities in the case of land use proposals requiring development consent, and (ii) the statutory Conservation Bodies in the case of non-development issues. This further complicates the structure of the relevant law on land use in protected areas.

Sites of Special Scientific Interest (SSSIs)

SSSIs are the primary nature conservation designation in England, Wales, and Scotland. The notification of land as an SSSI has been used to implement a number of international and European wildlife treaty obligations, and sites protected under, for instance, the Habitats and Species Directive and the Ramsar Convention on Wetlands are also notified as SSSI under the domestic legislation. This confers the basic legal protection required to satisfy the UKs obligations to protect internationally important habitats. There were 4119 SSSIs in England at the end of 2010, over 70 per cent of which have also been designated for protection under the Habitats Directive or the Ramsar Convention.[5] SSSIs vary enormously in size; the Elenydd

[5] See *Protecting England's 'Natural Treasures: Sites of Special Scientific Interest'* (Natural England, report NE306, 2011) at p. 7. Available at: <http://publications.naturalengland.org.uk/publication/47003?category=20003>.

SSSI in mid-Wales covers over 22,770 ha,[6] for example, while the River Tyne at Ovingham SSSI[7] covers a mere 3 ha. The notification of land as an SSSI is the responsibility of the Conservation Body in each region; that is Scottish Natural Heritage, the Countryside Council for Wales, and Natural England.

(a) Notifying an SSSI

The Wildlife and Countryside Act 1981[8] places a duty on the Conservation Body to notify areas as 'sites of special scientific interest' (SSSIs) if the conditions in the Act are satisfied. The key provision is section 28 of the 1981 Act, which was replaced with a remodelled section 28–28R by the Countryside and Rights of Way Act 2000.[9] This provides that where the Conservation Bodies 'are of the opinion that an area of land is of special interest by reason of any of its flora, fauna or geological or physiographical features', they have a duty to notify that fact to the local planning authority, to the owner and occupier of any of that land and to the Secretary of State. The site notification must specify the flora, fauna, geological, or physiographical features by reason of which the land is considered of special interest, and 'any operations appearing to the [Conservation Body] to be likely to damage that flora or fauna or those features'.[10] The carrying out of these operations will, following notification, require a prior consultation with the Conservation Body, and the list of operations notified as likely to damage the conservation interest is an important constituent of the site notification instrument for adjusting property rights. This is discussed further below.[11]

The site notification must also contain a statement of the Conservation Body's views about the management of the land—including any views they may have about the conservation and enhancement of the sites flora and fauna or its other notified features.[12] The applicable provisions in Scotland are more specific, requiring Scottish Natural Heritage to serve a site management statement giving guidance to owners and occupiers of land within an SSSI as to how the natural features of the site should be conserved or enhanced, and can include information that promotes the understating or enjoyment by the public of the natural features of the site.[13]

[6] See C. P. Rodgers, E. A. Straughton, A. Winchester, and M. Pieraccini, *Contested Common Land: Environmental Governance Past and Present* (Earthscan, 2010), Ch. 8, pp. 152 ff. for an account of the contemporary governance of this SSSI.

[7] Notified for its fluvial geomorphology—the site facilitates the study of flood plain sedimentation over a 200-year period: see <http://www.sssi.naturalengland.org.uk/Special/sssi/sssi_details.cfm?ssi_id=1005741>.

[8] These powers were formerly contained in s. 23 National Parks and Access to the Countryside Act 1949.

[9] S. 75 and Schedule 9 Countryside and Rights of Way Act 2000. References in the text will be to the remodelled s. 28 as replaced by Schedule 9. The provisions applicable in Scotland are set out in s. 3 Nature Conservation (Scotland) Act 2004.

[10] S. 28(4) Wildlife and Countryside Act 1981.

[11] See pp. 84 ff.

[12] S. 28(4) Wildlife and Countryside Act 1981 inserted by Schedule 9 Countryside and Rights of Way Act 2000. This requirement also satisfies the need for a management plan for the site if it has also been designated a European site under the Habitats and Species Directive: see art. 6.1 of Directive 92/43/EC and Chapter 6, pp. 217 ff.

[13] See s. 4(2) and (3) Nature Conservation (Scotland) Act 2004.

Box 3.2 Sites of Special Scientific Interest in Great Britain

	Number	Area (hectares)	Land area (of England, Wales, etc.)
England	4114	1,076,986 ha	8%
Wales	1019	235,000 ha	12%
Scotland	224	352,824 ha	
Northern Ireland	196	94,200 ha	
Total	5553	1,759,010 ha	

Sources: State of the Natural Environment Report 2008 (Natural England) available at <http://www.naturalengland.org.uk/Images/sone-section6.3_tcm6-4794.pdf>.

<http://www.snh.gov.uk/protecting-scotlands-nature/protected-areas/national-designations/sssis/>.

<http://www.ccw.gov.uk/landscape–wildlife/protecting-our-landscape/special-landscapes–sites/protected-landscapes/sssis/current-sssis-in-wales.aspx?lang=en>.

The site notification takes effect immediately, but it must specify a period of not less than three months (from the date of the giving of the notification) within which representations and objections can be made, and specify the manner in which they are to be made.[14] See Box 3.2 for the extent of the SSSI network in England, Wales, Scotland and Northern Ireland.

(i) *Potential scope of notification*

There is no formal appeal against notification in England and Wales,[15] although the notification and confirmation of land as an SSSI can be challenged on judicial review. There have been a number of judicial challenges to the notification provisions, in both their original and amended form. These have focused on the scope of the scientific judgment available to the Conservation Body when identifying land for inclusion in protected sites, the nature of the land, and the natural processes that can be the subject of notification, and the procedural requirements of the notification process itself.

The exercise of scientific judgment by the Conservation Body as to the special interest of a site, and the identification of the land to be included within it, is informed and guided by scientific research—and especially by the *Guidelines for the Selection of Biological SSSIs* formulated by the Joint Nature Conservation

[14] S. 28(3) Wildlife and Countryside Act 1981.

[15] The position in Scotland is different. An Advisory Committee on SSSIs is established by s. 21 Nature Conservation (Scotland) Act 2004. Landowners can request a reference to the advisory committee for an assessment of the special interest of the land (or any of it) included in the site notification. SNH must consider the advice given by the Advisory Committee, although its decisions are not binding upon it: see s. 21(8) Nature Conservation (Scotland) Act 2004. This procedure permits of an independent scientific review of the basis of the notification, is the land of 'special interest'? No review of the scientific and factual basis of the notification is possible, however, under the law applicable in England and Wales. The number of cases referred to the advisory committee in Scotland is small.

Committee.[16] The guidelines make it clear that the identification of 'special' interest is a matter of informed best judgment, and not one of the rigid application of objective rules.[17] The guiding principles set out in the guidelines are that for those habitats that have suffered widespread loss, degradation, and fragmentation—for example, in the lowlands as a result of intensive farming—all remaining natural and semi-natural examples of relevant habitats have special interest. But for larger expanses of undeveloped habitat (for example, in the uplands) it is considered important that a proportion of the total area is selected for SSSI status and protection. This has led to two approaches to site selection being adopted by Natural England in practice, and their notification strategy is further explained in Box 3.3:[18]

1. A minimum-standards approach to habitats that are endangered, requiring all examples above a minimum threshold to be eligible for selection. Salt marshes, rare fen types, bats, nationally rare estuarine and freshwater fish are examples of habitats and species where sites with relevant habitat types have been notified on this basis, and
2. An exemplar-representation approach in the case of habitats and species that are still widespread; for example, sand dunes, intertidal marine habitats, and woodlands.

The guidelines supply an informative and guidance role, and are not binding on the Conservation Body in the exercise of its expert judgment in individual cases. In *Fisher v English Nature,*[19] for example, the notification of an SSSI included extensive open fields because of their importance as a breeding site for the migratory stone curlew. The site included large areas of bare land resulting from spring-sown crops that mimic the curlews' preferred habitat of stony, open heathland. The birds do not nest in exactly the same place each year, however, and several attempts at establishing nesting sites may take place in different locations in any one year. English Nature had previously adopted the practice of not giving SSSI status to habitats for migratory birds that nest sporadically on the land in question. This policy was changed in February 2000. It was held that English Nature's overriding duty under section 28 is to apply their scientific expertise, and this meant that they could not accept any self-imposed constraints on the exercise of their judgment. The claimants also argued, unsuccessfully, that English Nature was not entitled to depart from the JNCC Selection Guidelines, which caution against the designation

[16] For the function and role of the JNCC see p. 41. The publication of SSSI selection criteria is central to its role in ensuring that common rules are applied across the UK by the regional agencies in identifying and notifying sites for protection. The guidelines were originally published in 1990, and have been reviewed subsequently. The latest guidance is available on the JNCC website at: <http://www.jncc.gov.uk/page-1457>. Decisions on geological SSSIs are informed by the JNCC's *Geological Conservation Review*, for which, see: <http://jncc.defra.gov.uk/default.aspx?page=2947>.

[17] *Guidelines for the Selection of Biological SSSIs* (JNCC, Peterborough) at para. 3.1.

[18] See Natural England, 2008, *Sites of Special Scientific Interest (SSSI): a notification strategy for England* at Appendix 1 and Table 1. Available at: <http://www.naturalengland.org.uk/Images/Notification%20strategy%20for%20web_tcm6-15235.pdf>.

[19] [2003] EWHC 1599. See judgment at para. 26. See also *R (Western Power Distribution Investments Ltd) v Countryside Council for Wales* [2007] EWHC Admin 50.

of arable cropland. The court held that although the guidelines are meant to fulfil an informative and guidance role, the Conservation Bodies are entitled to depart from them if they go beyond that, and place any constraint upon the exercise of their expert judgment. The availability to the Conservation Body of resources to provide appropriate management for a potential SSSI is, similarly, not a relevant consideration; the duty to notify rests solely on the exercise of their scientific judgment as to the 'special' interest of the site, not the council's ability or otherwise to resource its protection post-notification.[20]

The implementation of an ecosystem approach to habitat management would indicate that all land that is necessary for the breeding, migration, and exchange of a protected species, or which formed an integral part of a habitat mosaic, should be within the notification provision and be considered as of 'special interest'. This issue was considered in one of the early challenges to the extent of the notification power in section 28, *Sweet v Secretary of State.*[21] In this case, Schiemann J. held that an area can be of 'special interest', and hence validly subjected to notification under the 1981 Act, if it constitutes or forms part of a single environment for the flora or fauna, the protection of which is sought by the site notification. It follows that areas of land which form part of the ecosystem on which protected flora or fauna rely, or which are integral to the overall natural habitat to be protected, can be notified as well as the land actually bearing the flora and/or fauna in question.

The concept of 'special interest' is even wider than this, however, and can also encompass the notification of land in, or under which, natural processes are at work that generate the 'special' interest worthy of protection. In *Boggis v Natural England*[22] it was held that a geological exposure (in this case the exposure by erosion of sediments and fossils in a cliff face) was legitimately a feature of 'special interest' that justified the notification of the cliff face and an area up to 225 metres to the landward side of the cliffs, based on a 50-year projection of future erosion and exposure patterns. In other words, the geological exposure, in the form of the exposed cliff face, was itself a geological feature that could—if of 'special' interest—be the subject of an SSSI notification.[23] It is also clear that a site can be of 'special' interest and notifiable even if it is not the best example of the habitat type that it presents.[24]

[20] See *R (Western Power Distribution Investments Ltd) v Countryside Council for Wales* [2007] EWHC Admin 50 (CCW had adopted policy CCW P03 50(C), for the notification of sites between 2004–2007, and which stressed that sites would only be notified if they were necessary to underpin international obligations or if the site was under threat. Financial considerations were relevant to this approach, as they had decided there was little point in notifying SSSIs if there were insufficient resources to maintain them into the future, see [2007] EWHC Admin 50 at para. 25. The policy was described as 'flawed' by Collins J, [2007] EWHC Admin 50 at para. 26.)

[21] [1989] 2 PLR 14 925 (decided under the parallel designation provisions in s. 29 of the 1981 Act.

[22] [2009] EWCA Civ 1061; [2008] EWHC 2954 (Admin).

[23] [2009] EWCA Civ 1061 at para. 13 (Sullivan LJ.). And see Chapter 1 pp. 17–18 for further discussion of issues raised by this decision, including the meaning of 'conservation' in this context.

[24] See *R (Western Power Distribution Investments Ltd) v Countryside Council for Wales* [2007] EWHC Admin 50, esp. at para. 35 (waxcap fungi habitat at Lisvane and Llanishen reservoirs near Cardiff found to be the fifth most important in Wales and tenth most important in the UK, but internationally important due to paucity of sites elsewhere in the EU. Notification as SSSI upheld by Collins J.).

Box 3.3 Natural England's Notification Strategy for SSSIs in England (2008)

There is no statutory purpose laid down for the SSSI network of protected sites—either in the Wildlife and Countryside Act 1981 or elsewhere. DEFRA Guidance states that: '*The purpose of SSSIs is to safeguard, for present and future generations, the diversity and geographic range of habitats, species, and geological and physiographical features, including the full range of natural and semi-natural ecosystems and of important geological and physiographical phenomena throughout England. The sites included within the series of SSSIs are intended collectively to comprise the full range of natural and semi-natural habitats and the most important geological and physiographical sites.*'[25] In 2008 Natural England adopted a Notification Strategy setting out strategic objectives for the notification of SSSIs in England, and implemented from 2009/10 a review of existing notifications to evaluate the suite of protected sites against a set of strategic priorities. This adopted three strategic principles for the future review of the network:[26]

1. It should comprise the full diversity and range of habitats species and geological and physiographical features throughout England.
2. It should contain our most valuable nature conservation and earth heritage sites. Value (and thus 'special interest') should be seen as both a factor of intrinsic conservation needs both now and in the future and of the value of these features to society (eg for ecosystem services such as carbon storage and flood management).
3. It should be comprised of individual SSSIs that include entire management units, whole systems that are (if possible) able to respond dynamically to natural processes and the predicted effects of climate change. It should also contribute to ecological networks to increase habitat connectivity and reduce habitat fragmentation.

The Biodiversity Action Plan process[27] will be used as a driver to inform the future implementation of this new strategic approach to SSSI notifications. From 2009 a review of the overall coverage of the SSSI network has been undertaken at national level, so that the contribution that each site makes to the national network can be identified and evaluated, and any gaps in the coverage of the network identified. This has been complemented by a review undertaken by local Natural England offices of all current SSSIs to assess whether they are still of special interest, whether the features of interest are properly identified, and their ability to adapt dynamically to climate change impacts.

(ii) Procedure on notification

The notification procedure for establishing an SSSI involves two stages—notification and confirmation—and the period between the two is important for the

[25] DEFRA 2003, Sites of Special Scientific Interest: Encouraging Positive Partnerships, London: DEFRA.

[26] Sites of Special Scientific Interest: a notification strategy for England (Natural England 2008) at para. 3.1. Available at: <http://www.naturalengland.org.uk/Images/Notification%20strategy%20for%20web_tcm6-15235.pdf>.

[27] See Chapter 1, p. 11 ff.

Conservation Body to undertake further investigation, consultation, and the consideration of objections.[28] Following the initial notification, the Conservation Body must allow those affected by it a minimum of three months in which to lodge objections to the notification, or to make representations. The manner in which representations can be made, and the time within which this must be done, must be specified in the site notification.[29] The Conservation Body must make the basis for the notification sufficiently clear to enable an affected landowner to make a full objection, should he wish to do so.[30] If the notification is insufficiently clear as to the reasons for which the site is being notified as an SSSI, it may be quashed on judicial review.[31]

The second stage involves the confirmation or withdrawal of the notification. Following the initial site notification the Conservation Body has nine months, beginning on the date it was served on the Secretary of State, in which to give notice to those persons on whom the notification was served either withdrawing or confirming the notification.[32] The SSSI notification will cease to have effect upon notice of withdrawal being given, or upon the expiry of the nine-month period if no notice of withdrawal or confirmation is given within that time.[33] The Conservation Body has power to confirm the notification with or without modifications—but cannot add to the list of operations likely to damage the conservation interest that were specified in the initial site notification, or extend the area to which the SSSI applies.[34] If they confirm the notification with modifications, it takes effect from the date of service of their notice of confirmation, and has effect in its modified form to so much of the land originally notified which remains subject to it.[35]

In *R v Nature Conservancy Council ex parte London Brick Co Ltd*,[36] it was suggested that at the confirmation stage the Conservation Body has a wider discretion whether to confirm the SSSI notification with or without modifications. This was subsequently held in *Fisher v English Nature*[37] to be wrong as a matter of statutory construction, even though the language of the 1981 Act is permissive when describing the Conservation Body's confirmatory powers.[38] The role of the

[28] *R v Nature Conservancy Council ex parte London Brick Co. Ltd* [1996] Env LR 1 (May J.); *Fisher v English Nature* [2004] EWCA Civ 663.

[29] S. 28(3) Wildlife and Countryside Act 1981, as amended.

[30] *R v Nature Conservancy Council ex parte Bolton Metropolitan District Conservation Body* [1995] Env LR 237 (Popplewell J.).

[31] In *R v Nature Conservancy Council ex parte Bolton MBC* [1995] Env LR 237. English Nature had considered the site both on its current state of conservation interest, and its possible potential for future restoration. Bolton MBC (the recipients of the notification) had only made representations on its potential for restoration when objecting to the notification of the site. This was held to be a breach of natural justice in that the Conservation Body had not made the basis of the notification (ie the sites current conservation interest, as well as its potential) sufficiently clear to enable Bolton MBC to make a full response and objection. English Nature's confirmation of the notification was accordingly quashed.

[32] S. 28(5) Wildlife and Countryside Act 1981.

[33] S. 28(6) Wildlife and Countryside Act 1981.

[34] S. 28(7) Wildlife and Countryside Act 1981.

[35] S. 28(4C) Wildlife and Countryside Act 1981.

[36] [1996] Env LR 1 (May J.).

[37] [2003] EWHC 1599, see esp. judgment paras. 18 ff.

[38] See s. 28(5)—'the Council *may*... give notice... confirming the notification' (italics added).

Conservation Body in the notification process is one of exercising expert judgment, not discretion. The legislation requires them to apply expert judgment at each of the two stages in order to determine whether the statutory criteria are satisfied, to specify the flora, fauna, physiographical, or geological features by reason of which the site is of special interest, and to specify the operations likely to damage that special interest. If, having considered the objections and representations made by affected parties, and any other evidence that has emerged in the interim, their judgment is that the site remains of special interest within the meaning of the 1981 Act then they have no residual discretion to refuse to confirm the notification. Indeed, if Natural England could withdraw the notification in these circumstances, the paradoxical position would arise where they would come under an immediate duty to notify the site again, a circular exercise of their statutory powers that the legislature could not have intended.[39]

The formation of an opinion as to the 'special interest' or otherwise of a potential SSSI is clearly a partially subjective exercise, but in exercising their judgment the Conservation Body's officers must confine themselves to a consideration of scientifically relevant facts and criteria. This can give rise to difficult questions. What, for example, is the scope for their scientific judgment to change from time to time in response to developments in scientific knowledge and research? And can the Conservation Body limit the manner in which they exercise their statutory power to notify and confirm SSSIs by reference to the way in which they have interpreted scientific evidence in previous cases, or by reference to research reports on which they have based their prior notification policy?

These issues were considered in *Aggregate Industries v English Nature.*[40] English Nature had failed to confirm an earlier notification of part of an SSSI in 1993 because the habitat it created for heathland birds (such as nightjars, crossbills, and hobbies) was temporary. The conifers present on the plantation would grow within five to ten years and the foliage cover would prevent the subjacent regeneration of groundcover on which the bird populations depended. Crucially, however, their approach to notifying temporary habitats changed in 2000 when they considered a research report that supported the designation of temporary habitats as SSSIs. This was deemed necessary to make progress towards moving candidate Special Protection Areas (SPAs) under the 1979 Wild Birds Directive to full SPA status.[41] When the remainder of the site was confirmed as an SSSI in 2001 the only new feature was the fact that the rotationally felled conifers provided a breeding habitat for three bird species protected under Annex 1 of the Wild Birds Directive (nightjar, woodlark, and the Dartford warbler). It was held that English Nature's original refusal to confirm the whole of the plantation as an SSSI did not create a legitimate expectation of non-notification for the remainder of the site, neither did it prevent them from changing their policy towards the notification of temporary habitats. Adapting their policy response was a legitimate facet of the exercise of the specialist

[39] *Fisher v English Nature* [2004] EWCA Civ 663.
[40] [2003] Env LR 3, 83.
[41] As to which, see Chapter 6, pp. 203 ff.

scientific judgment that the 1981 Act requires them to bring to bear in the identification and notification of protected sites. The net result of judicial interpretation of the notification provisions, therefore, is that although the Conservation Bodies have no discretion whether to confirm a notification if they are still of the opinion that a site is of special interest, they do have a very considerable latitude in the exercise of their expert judgment in the process leading to the formation (or otherwise) of that opinion.

(iii) Factors that can be taken into account

The cases confirm that the Conservation Bodies have wide power to apply scientific expertise to the assessment of potential SSSIs, but other factors will clearly also have relevance. The role of governmental policy on aspects of conservation and environmental protection is of particular relevance, and one question that arises is the weight to be attached to factors of policy orientation in the decision-making process when sites are selected for designation. For example, the policy followed by the Conservation Bodies is that all sites selected for inclusion in the list of SPAs established under the Wild Birds Directive, or terrestrial SACs under the Habitats Directive, should also be notified as SSSIs under the 1981 Act. For the purposes of judicial control of decision making by the relevant public bodies, the question is one of the extent to which these factors can be considered 'material' to the decision in hand, or whether they are irrelevant and therefore render any decision in which they are instrumental open to judicial review on grounds of irrationality or Wednesbury unreasonableness.

In both *Aggregate Industries* and *Fisher v English Nature* (above) the SSSI notification that was challenged was linked to the designation of a wider geographical area as an SPA under the Wild Birds Directive. This raised the question of the relevance of policy considerations connected with the completion of the SPA site network to the notification of individual SSSIs under the 1981 Act. In *Aggregate Industries* the fact that the site was to become an SPA under the Birds Directive, following notification as an SSSI, was held to be a relevant consideration provided the primary reason for the notification was that the Conservation Body had formed the opinion that the site met the criteria for notification in section 28. In *Fisher* the court went somewhat further, holding that it was permissible to take into account the site's role as part of a larger geographical area of European habitat significance when considering it for notification. In *Fisher*, ironically, the landowners would have been content to have an SPA designation on the land, but were opposed to the SSSI notification because of the additional land use restrictions that this would impose on them.

Perhaps the most important point in the court's ruling on this aspect of the *Fisher* litigation was that English Nature were not entitled to refuse to notify the SSSI because they considered that the fauna to be protected—in this case stone curlews—could be protected better in some other way which interfered less with the landowners prerogative to manage the land as they saw fit; for example, by securing a voluntary management agreement or by simply classifying the site as an

SPA, but not as an SSSI under the 1981 Act. A related issue arose in *Boyd v English Nature*.[42] This case concerned the notification as an SSSI of several meadows that support nationally important examples of rare fen meadow and species-rich neutral grassland communities. English Nature were alleged to have taken irrelevant considerations into account when notifying the site, in that they excluded from the SSSI a further area of land which their scientific survey showed also supported the habitats involved (West Swainford farm). The West Swainford site was excluded because it was already being managed within the Countryside Stewardship Scheme and was not therefore prioritized for SSSI notification. Essentially, the issue here was English Nature's right to prioritize sites and target its resources at those that were not already being protected in some other way. The court agreed with English Nature's submission that it was entitled to take into account its own set of priorities, and that the inclusion of the West Swainford site in the Countryside Stewardship Scheme was not an irrelevant consideration in the setting of those priorities.

(iv) Variation of the notification

The Countryside and Rights of Way Act 2000 introduced flexibility into the notification process by making provision for the subsequent designation of additional land and the variation of an SSSI notification. This may be important to adjust the site's boundaries and review its protected status from time to time; for example, to reflect changing ecological circumstances or new scientific evidence as to the protected habitat's health and status. The 1981 Act now provides that an SSSI notification can be varied by the Conservation Body in a number of different situations:

- the matters specified or stated in the notification can be varied[43] at any time once the SSSI notification has been confirmed (but not before confirmation). This enables the Conservation Body to change, for example, the list of operations stipulated in the notification as likely to damage the conservation interest (OLDSI), or the terms of the site management statements served with the notification. Notice must be given in the same manner as for the initial SSSI notification, and the amendments are subject to the same procedure for objections and confirmation (within a period of nine months) as applies on notification.
- Additional land can be added to the notification, but only if it is adjacent to the SSSI and the Conservation Body considers that when added to the SSSI, 'the combined area of land would be of special interest by reason of its flora, fauna, geological, or physiographical features'.[44] The additional land may not, viewed on its own, be of special interest, but the combined area is. The

[42] [2003] EWHC 1105.
[43] S. 28A Wildlife and Countryside Act 1981.
[44] S. 28B(1) Wildlife and Countryside Act 1981.

notification is subject to the same procedures for objections and confirmation as the initial SSSI notification.[45] An SSSI can also be enlarged[46] by the Conservation Body notifying additional land outside an existing SSSI, where that additional land itself has special interest. The same procedure applies as for site notification and the notification of additional land.

- An SSSI can be denotified if the Conservation Body is of the opinion that all or part of the site is no longer of special interest.[47] In this case, the Conservation Body must give notice of its intention to denotify to the local planning authority, the Secretary of State, every owner or occupier of any of the land included in the SSSI, the Environment Agency, and any relevant statutory water undertaker and internal drainage board.[48] These powers were amended by the Natural Environment and Rural Communities Act 2006 to make it clear that the power can be used to denotify land that has been included in an SSSI in error, as opposed to simply facilitating the denotification of land that was once of special interest (but is no longer so).[49] The denotification must be confirmed nine months after notice to denotify has been given. Similar consultation provisions apply as for notification, and variation of the SSSI notification (p. 73).

(v) Service of notices

The site notification must be given to the local planning authority in whose area the land is situated, to 'every owner or occupier of any of that land' and to the Secretary of State,[50] as must its subsequent withdrawal or confirmation. Similarly, notice of the Conservation Body's decision to denotify land that is within an SSSI must be given to the same classes of person,[51] as must the subsequent withdrawal or confirmation of denotification. Service of a site notification may in some cases be problematic if the land appears to be unoccupied, or if the identity of the current occupiers is difficult to determine. The Natural Environment and Rural Communities Act 2006 introduced new provisions[52] by virtue of which the validity of an SSSI notification will not be affected by failure to serve it on every owner and occupier, provided 'all reasonable steps' have been taken to ensure that notice is served on every owner and occupier of land to which the notice relates. The notice

[45] See s. 28B(2)–(9) Wildlife and Countryside Act 1981.
[46] S. 28C Wildlife and Countryside Act 1981.
[47] See s. 28D(1) Wildlife and Countryside Act 1981.
[48] Ss. 28D(2) Wildlife and Countryside Act 1981.
[49] S. 56 Natural Environment and Rural Communities Act 2006, amending s. 28D(1) Wildlife and Countryside Act 1981. The amendment replaced the words 'no longer' of special interest with 'not' of special interest. It is not necessary that the land to be denotified must have previously been of special interest.
[50] S. 28(1) Wildlife and Countryside Act 1981.
[51] See s. 28D(2) Wildlife and Countryside Act 1981. In this case, notice must also be given to the Environment Agency and statutory undertakers.
[52] S. 57 Natural Environment and Rural Communities Act 2006, introducing a new s. 70B Wildlife and Countryside Act 1981.

is deemed to be served at the time when the Conservation Body took the last of the steps in its attempted service of the notices.[53] This will be relevant to the calculation of the time limits for the subsequent confirmation of notification/denotification by the Conservation Body under the 1981 Act. It will also facilitate the notification of sites where the identity or whereabouts of the current occupiers is unknown. In these circumstances, however, the owner or occupier will not be liable for carrying out unauthorized operations likely to damage the site's conservation interest unless and until they are served with a copy of the site notification.[54]

Natural England has power to put up and maintain notices or signs relating to the site on any land included in an SSSI.[55] It is an offence for 'any other person'—including not only the owner or occupier but also third parties—to intentionally or recklessly and without reasonable excuse take down, damage, or obscure any notice placed on the land under this statutory power.[56] Natural England's officers have statutory powers of entry for the purpose of putting up and maintaining notices or signs erected pursuant to these provisions.[57] These powers will be useful where the identity of the owner or occupier is uncertain or unknown, and are also relevant in making third parties aware of the present of an SSSI on the land—knowledge that the land is an SSSI is, for instance, a necessary ingredient to some of the criminal offences applicable for damaging protected sites.[58]

The SSSI notification requires service on those to be bound by it. There will be no redress against a new owner or occupier who is unaware of the site's designated status, and who has not received notification from the Conservation Body, if s/he subsequently damages the conservation features of the SSSI. The 2000 Act amended the law,[59] which now places the owner of land included in an SSSI under a duty to notify the Conservation Body when s/he disposes of any interest or 'becomes aware that [the notified land] is occupied by an additional or a different occupier'.[60] This will apply where there is a sale of freehold land by the owner, and, for instance, where there is a change of tenant if the SSSI land is tenanted. The owner must send a notice to the Conservation Body within a 28-day period after disposing of his legal interest or becoming aware of a change of occupation of the land; for example, a change of tenant or licensee). The Conservation Body must be notified of the date on which the owner disposed of his interest in the land and the name and address of the person to whom it was disposed. Alternatively the

[53] S. 70B(4) Wildlife and Countryside Act 1981, inserted by s. 57 2006 Act.

[54] S. 70B(6) Wildlife and Countryside Act 1981. For the criminal offences applicable to SSSIs see p. 92 ff.

[55] S. 28S Wildlife and Countryside Act 1981. Inserted by S. 58 Natural Environment and Rural Communities Act 2006.

[56] S. 28S(3) Wildlife and Countryside Act 1981, as inserted by the 2006 Act.

[57] S. 51(1)(ka) Wildlife and Countryside Act 1981, inserted by s. 58 Natural Environment and Rural Communities Act 2006.

[58] See p. 92–4.

[59] See now s. 28Q Wildlife and Countryside Act 1981, inserted by Schedule 9 of the Countryside and Rights of Way Act 2000.

[60] S. 28Q(1) Wildlife and Countryside Act 1981.

notice must inform them of the date on which the change of occupation took place and, as far as the owner knows them, the name and address of the new occupier. Failure to give notice, without reasonable excuse, is a criminal offence.[61] The duty to notify is triggered by any 'disposal' of an interest in, or possession of, the land, and this is widely defined to include not only its sale but also an exchange or lease of land, or the creation of an easement right or privilege or any other disposal, except by way of mortgage.[62]

(vi) Site notification—the human rights implications

The Conservation Body's power to notify SSSIs, and the manner in which they are exercised, have been challenged under the Human Rights Act 1998 in several cases. The cases have focused on the 'procedural' right to a determination by an impartial tribunal when civil rights are affected by state action,[63] and the 'substantive' right to the protection of property.[64]

Article 6 of the European Convention of Human Rights and Fundamental Freedoms (ECHR) provides that 'in the determination of his civil rights . . . everyone is entitled to a fair and public hearing . . . by an independent impartial tribunal established by law'. In both *Aggregate Industries UK Ltd v English Nature*[65] and *Boyd v English Nature*[66] the courts ruled that the confirmation of an SSSI notification engages the civil rights of the landowner. The additional question is therefore whether the procedure laid down in the 1981 Act for the notification and confirmation of SSSIs confers the required level of impartiality and objectivity to comply with the procedural safeguards of the ECHR.

It was held in *William Sinclair Holdings v English Nature*[67] that the procedure for confirming SSSI notifications was not 'impartial' because the decision to confirm the notification was made by English Nature's Council—the same body that had made the initial notification. There was therefore no independent review of the objections and representations made by objectors. In this case, Turner J held that the decision would also fall foul of the requirement for a fair and public hearing if it was reached by way of written submissions without any opportunity for the evidence upon which the submission of objectors was based to be challenged. An interim injunction was granted to prevent English Nature proceeding to confirmation of the SSSI. Although the case did not subsequently proceed to a full hearing of the human rights issues, it signalled a number of potential problems. These duly materialized in a later case—*Aggregate Industries v English Nature*—where it was confirmed that there was a sufficient want of the necessary objective appearance of impartiality and independence on the part of English Nature's Council when

[61] S. 28Q(4) Wildlife and Countryside Act 1981. This is punishable with a fine not exceeding level 1 on the standard scale.
[62] S. 28Q(5) Wildlife and Countryside Act 1981.
[63] Art. 6 European Convention of Human Rights and Fundamental Freedoms ('ECHR').
[64] Art. 1 Protocol 1 to the European Convention of Human Rights and Fundamental Freedoms.
[65] [2003] Env LR 3, 83. [66] [2003] EWHC 1105. [67] [2002] Env LR 4, QBD.

confirming the notification for it not to be an independent and impartial tribunal for the purpose of article 6.[68]

Although article 6 does not give signatory states an express 'margin of appreciation' as to the manner in which the convention right is guaranteed,[69] nevertheless a fair balance has to be struck between the competing interests of protecting the individual on the one hand, and giving sufficient freedom of action to the executive authorities on the other.[70] This balance has been struck in relation to article 6 by accepting that the necessary guarantees can be found in a 'composite' procedure within which the necessary convention rights are protected, but not by a single procedure before a discrete tribunal. In *Bryan v UK*[71] the European Court considered UK planning enforcement procedures in a case involving an appeal against an enforcement notice requiring the demolition of a mock-Tudor dwelling erected in breach of planning control.[72] It was there held that although the appeal proceedings before the planning inspector were not in themselves sufficiently impartial to satisfy the convention,[73] nevertheless the High Courts' power to review the inspector's decision, coupled with safeguards applied to the proceedings before the planning inspector themselves,[74] together ensured full compliance with the procedural standards required by the Convention.

The composite approach was also endorsed by the House of Lords in the *Alconbury case*[75] when reviewing the legitimacy of the procedures for planning appeals under article 6. In *Alconbury,* the House of Lords stressed the importance of the decision maker (in that case, planning committee members) being democratically accountable for the exercise of their town and country planning powers.[76] The administrative arrangements for decision making in the application of nature conservation law are, by contrast, more technocratic and 'closed'. There is no democratic accountability either of the Conservation Body's actions when confirming SSSI notifications, or of the actions of their officers when granting or refusing operational consent for operations likely to damage the conservation interest (OLDSIs)[77] in an SSSI. Nevertheless, in *Aggregate Industries v English Nature* the Court of Appeal took the view that it was *not* necessary to the application of the

[68] See [2003] Env LR 83 at 119. The appearance of impartiality was stressed as of particular importance in the context of art. 6: see also *LB of Tower Hamlets v Runa Begum* (2002) EWCA Civ 239.

[69] Cf. art. 1 of the Protocol to the Convention, which protects the citizen's right to property, which expressly requires and permits a balance to be struck between the interests of the individual and those of society as a whole.

[70] See generally, M. Demerieux, (2001) 21 OJLS 521, esp. at 551 ff.

[71] (1995) 21 EHRR 342.See also *LM&R v Switzerland* (1996) 22 EHRR CD 130.

[72] Allegedly with the benefit of agricultural permitted development rights for the erection of a livestock building under Part 6 of the 1995 GDO.

[73] They could be withdrawn from the Inspector at any time by the Secretary of State, thus depriving them of the necessary appearance of impartiality.

[74] Requiring, for instance, that the inspector acts in a quasi-judicial manner, exercise independent judgment and uphold the principles of openness, fairness, and impartiality.

[75] *R (on the application of Alconbury Developments Ltd) v Secretary of State for the Environment Transport and the Regions* [2003] AC 295.

[76] See the comments of Lord Hoffmann at [2003] 2 AC 295 at para. 72.

[77] As to which, see further at pp. 84 ff.

composite approach for the decision maker to be democratically elected. A key element in deciding whether the procedure in question is ECHR compliant is whether it can be relied upon to produce a 'fair and reasonable' result or decision. The court's view in *Aggregate Industries* was that the safeguards provided by the Wildlife and Countryside Act 1981 ensured that this was the case.[78] The courts have also ruled that it is not necessary to apply more intensive scrutiny by judicial review in nature conservation cases than would be required in an ordinary case in order to satisfy the composite approach.[79]

The second issue to which the SSSI notification provisions give rise in the context of the ECHR is their potential to infringe the protection of property rights by the Convention.

Article 1 of the Protocol to the ECHR (hereafter 'article 1') guarantees the peaceful enjoyment of possessions. The article 1 right is not unqualified, however, as the state has the right to enforce such laws as it deems necessary 'to control the use of property in accordance with the general interest or to secure the payment of taxes or other contributions or penalties'. The jurisprudence of the European Court of Human Rights has established that the article in fact comprises three elements; a general right to the peaceful enjoyment of possessions, a second rule covering the deprivation of possessions (which is made subject to conditions), and a third rule providing for the control of the use of property in accordance with the general interest.[80] Article 1 could potentially apply at different stages in the notification, confirmation, and subsequent management of land as an SSSI.

In *Fisher v English Nature*[81] one of the grounds on which the claimants challenged the SSSI notification was that its confirmation breached article 1, because it was a disproportionate interference with the claimant's peaceful possession of his land. This required an examination of the margin of appreciation allowed to the state by the express qualification of the convention right, and the consequent degree to which derogations from the convention right were permissible. The claimants argued that the legislative provisions were disproportionate in the absence of compensation for the loss in the value of land consequent upon its notification as an SSSI. This was argued to be a disproportionate burden because, unlike the Town and Country Planning Act 1990, the 1981 Act applies only to the approximately 5000 sites in England and Wales which had been notified as SSSIs, covering approximately 7 per cent of the land area of the country. At first instance, Lightman J held that the wide margin of appreciation allowed to the state under article 1 meant that the controls prescribed by law must be without any reasonable foundation if they are to be regarded as disproportionate.[82] The issue of proportionality

[78] The safeguards include the right to make representations, the right of appeal to the Secretary of State against the confirmation for the SSSI, and the right of judicial review in the courts on matters of law: the full list of safeguards pointed to by the court in forming this view is given in the first instance judgment at [2003] Env LR 126–7.

[79] See *Boyd v English Nature* [2003] EWHC 1105 at paras. 26–30.

[80] See *Jacobsson v Sweden* [1989] 12 EHRR 56.

[81] [2003] EWHC 1599; [2004] EWCA Civ 663.

[82] On this point see *Fredin v Sweden* [1991] 13 EHRR 784.

only arose if the statutory scheme was not itself convention-compliant. On this issue, he held that the relationship of proportionality between the measure and the social evil to be remedied does not involve a test of strict necessity. It followed that although there might be a better means of achieving the same ends,[83] this does not necessarily mean that an SSSI notification will be disproportionate within the meaning of the Convention.[84]

The Court of Appeal upheld the first instance decision in the *Fisher* litigation, but disposed of the proportionality issue on narrower grounds. As Wall LJ. put it,[85] on the facts all that SSSI status imposed was a need to consult with English Nature before particular activities were undertaken. Insofar as the notification imposed restrictions on particular farming activities, however, the claimants brought forward no evidence that could render the restrictions disproportionate. It was not therefore necessary to decide the wider issue—whether the SSSI scheme was itself convention-compliant. The court viewed the evidence in *Fisher* as 'surprisingly weak'. Little solid evidence was submitted on the effect of the SSSI on land values, and there were no objections to the list of potentially damaging operations served with the notification. The overall argument on this aspect of article 1 was also weak. The claimants chose not to challenge the legality of the legislation itself or the overall SSSI scheme, and against that background Wall LJ. observed that he 'struggled to ascertain why it was that the imposition of an SSSI on the appellants was so disproportionate as to render the decision to confirm [the notification] unlawful. A bare assertion that the SSSI serves no useful purpose is not . . . a reason of itself for refusing to confirm.'[86]

Importantly, in both cases where this issue has arisen—*Fisher v English Nature* and *Trailer and Marina (Leven) Ltd v Secretary of State and English Nature*[87]—the interference with property rights was interpreted by the courts as an interference with land use, rather than an expropriation of title. In land use infringement cases the jurisprudence of the European Court makes it clear that while the payment of compensation will generally support a finding of non-violation, it is not essential. There is an extensive case law in the ECHR, but because of the nature of the balancing exercise to be carried out, most of the decisions are fact-specific.[88] In *Trailer and Marina*, for example, the court held that the availability of compensation will be of significance only 'on rare occasions rather than as a matter of routine'[89] in land use cases, whereas it will usually be decisive of the proportionality issue in expropriation cases.

[83] The claimants in *Fisher v English Nature* argued (unsuccessfully) that the site would be better protected by the conclusion of a management agreement without its formal notification as an SSSI.

[84] The general point thus applied in *Fisher v English Nature* was established, albeit in a different statutory context, in *James v UK* [1986] 8 EHRR 123.

[85] [2004] EWCA Civ 663 at para. 147.

[86] *Fisher v English Nature* [2004] EWCA Civ 663 at paras. 142/143.

[87] [2004] EWHC 153 (Admin); [2004] EWCA Civ 1580.

[88] In addition to *Jacobsson v Sweden* (see n.80) and *Fredin v Sweden* (see n.32) see *Tre Traktorer Aktiebolag v Sweden* [1989] 13 EHRR 309, *Baner v Sweden* (1989) 60 DR 125, and *Chassagnou v France* [1999] 29 EHRR 615.

[89] [2004] EWHC 153 at para. 81 Ouseley J.

In general terms, therefore, the scheme of the 1981 Act for the notification and confirmation of SSSIs has been held to be ECHR compliant. There remains the possibility, however, that a notification might be quashed if, in an individual case, it is found to have a disproportionate effect on a landowner or occupier who is subject to it. If an SSSI notification can be shown to have a disproportionate impact on a landowner affected by it, and it can be shown that the Conservation Body—for example, Natural England—failed to take this into account when confirming the notification, then this might justify a claim for judicial review of the notification under article 1 of the Protocol.[90] This will put the onus on applicants to present clear evidence of diminution in land values consequent on the SSSI notification, and of demonstrable loss of income flowing from the restrictions to be imposed.[91] It will also require the Conservation Bodies to consider each case on its merits, taking into account the financial impact of the potential SSSI notification on the owners and occupiers of the land under consideration, and in appropriate cases to offer compensation—possibly under the terms of a management agreement—to those affected by the notification. The Court of Appeal gave no indication in *Fisher* of the manner in which these factors might impact on future cases, but the decision fell short of giving Natural England approval to proceed with SSSI notifications without considering their potential impact on individual landowners. The full impact of the proportionality issues on decision making in this area will only become clearer with further litigation.[92]

(b) Operations likely to damage the conservation interest (OLDSIs)

The key mechanism for the regulation of land use in SSSIs is the requirement of a statutory consultation with the Conservation Body before a landowner or occupier can lawfully carry out operations that have been specified in the site notification as likely to damage the flora, fauna, or other special features of the site.[93] These are often referred to as 'Operations Likely to Damage the Conservation Interest' of the site—hereafter 'OLDSIs'. Under the original scheme of the 1981 Act, a four-month delay applied when a landowner wished to carry out OLDSIs, and gave notice of his intention to the Conservation Body. The primary mechanism for achieving the protection of the site was the conclusion of a management agreement to ensure the future management of the land accorded with the conservation objectives of the site notification. The 2000 Act strengthened the protection of SSSIs by giving the Conservation Body the power to refuse consent to OLDSIs indefinitely, subject to a

[90] *Fisher v English Nature* [2004] EWCA Civ 663 at para. 141 (Wall LJ.).

[91] Not to be confused with loss of profits foregone by being unable to carry out proscribed operations once the SSSI is in place—this is not allowed for in the *Guidelines on Management Agreement Payments and other related matters* (DETR, 2001). These were considered and upheld in the *Trailer and Marina* litigation, discussed further on pp. 119 ff.

[92] For a discussion of the wider implications of the emergence of proportionality as a ground of judicial review in planning cases, see M. Purdue, 'The Human Rights Act, planning and proportionality' (2004) 6 Env L Rev 161.

[93] As to which see, s. 28(4)(b) Wildlife and Countryside Act 1981.

right of appeal against refusal to the Secretary of State. While the conclusion of a voluntary management agreement with the landowner remains centrally important to secure long-term site protection, the terms on which agreements are negotiated has fundamentally changed. Payments under a management agreement will only be available for positive management that promotes or restores the conservation interest of the site, and not simply for preventing the damaging operations that have been 'bought out' by the agreement concluded following the statutory consultation under section 28.[94]

(i) Statutory consultation

The amended 1981 Act[95] now provides that the owner or occupier of any land included in an SSSI shall not 'carry out, or cause or permit to be carried out', on the land any operation specified in the site notification as likely to damage the conservation interest unless certain closely defined conditions are satisfied. These are that:

(a) The owner or occupier has, after service of the notification, given the Conservation Body notice of their proposal to carry out the operation, specifying its nature and the land on which it is proposed to carry it out. The notice of intent does not have to be in writing, and

(b) The operation is then either carried out with the Conservation Body's written consent, or in accordance with the terms of a management agreement with the Conservation Body,[96] or that the operation is carried out in accordance with a management scheme or a management notice under the 1981 Act (as to which, see pp. 95 ff).

If a request for operational consent to carry out an OLDSI is granted, the Conservation Body can give consent subject to conditions and/or for a limited period, as specified in the consent.[97] It is a criminal offence to carry out an OLDSI other than in accordance with these provisions.[98] When considering a request for operational consent for OLDSIs in an SSSI, the Conservation Body will carry out an assessment of their implications for the protected features of the site. If the site is also a European Site designated as an SAC or SPA under the Habitats or Wild Birds Directives, it must carry out an 'appropriate assessment' before granting consent, and the terms on which it can do so are constrained by the requirements of the Directives and the regulations implementing them in England and Wales.[99]

[94] See the *Guidelines on Management Agreement Payments and Other Related Matters* (DETR 2001) paras. 1.1 and 1.2.

[95] See s. 28E(1) Wildlife and Countryside Act 1981.

[96] Ie an agreement under s. 16 National Parks and Access to the Countryside Act 1949, s. 15 Countryside Act 1968, or s. 7 Natural Environment and Rural Communities Act 2006. As to which, see Chapter 4, p. 112–116.

[97] S. 28E(4) Wildlife and Countryside Act 1981.

[98] S. 28P(1) Wildlife and Countryside Act 1981.

[99] See Chapter 6, pp. 220 ff.

Prior to the Countryside and Rights of Way Act 2000, it was only illegal to carry out notified operations for a four-month period following the giving of notice of the land owner's intent. After this period had elapsed, the OLDSIs could be lawfully carried out unless a Nature Conservation Order was granted by the Secretary of State to protect the site.[100] This was a compromise struck during the passage of the 1981 Act between the promotion of the public interest in nature conservation and the protection of property interests. It gave very limited protection against unwarranted damage to SSSIs, however, and was widely criticized.[101] The law was strengthened by the 2000 Act, and the Conservation Body can now refuse operational consent to OLDSIs without time limit. The extension of land use control that this represents was tempered, however, by the introduction of a right of appeal to the Secretary of State against a refusal of operational consent or against the conditions imposed by the Conservation Body. The Conservation Body has four months in which to give a decision on an application for operational consent for an OLDSI. When granting consent for a limited period or subject to conditions, they must give the applicant notice of their reasons for imposing the conditions, or for the limitation of the period of consent, or for refusing, withdrawing or modifying the consent as appropriate. If they neither give consent nor refuse it within four months, the applicant can treat the Conservation Body as having refused consent, and any appeal s/he subsequently makes is to be determined on that basis. The existence of a right of appeal has been held to be centrally important to the compliance of the new regime with the Human Rights Act.[102]

(ii) Impact on property rights

The primary focus of the land use restrictions in SSSIs is the protection of conservation features from damage caused by the owner or occupier of the land. The imposition of a statutory consultation procedure for carrying out OLDSIs, coupled with the more expansive powers post-2000 for the Conservation Bodes to refuse operational consent, has implications for the allocation of property rights and resource use in protected sites. Viewed through the prism of a resource allocation model of property rights,[103] the overall impact of the mechanism set out in section 28 of the 1981 Act is to transfer property rights from the landowner to the

[100] Ie under s. 29 Wildlife and Countryside Act 1981 (since repealed by Schedule 16 Part III Countryside and Rights of Way Act 2000).

[101] See eg comments in *Southern Water v Nature Conservancy Conservation Body* [1992] 3 All ER 481 (House of Lords) by Lord Mustill at 484. 'It needs only a moment to see that this regime is toothless, for it demands no more from the owner or occupier of an SSSI than a little patience. Unless the Conservation Body can convince the Secretary of State that the site is of sufficient national importance to justify an order under s. 29. . . a task rarely achieved—the owner will within months be free to disregard the notification and carry out the proscribed operations, no matter what the cost to the flora etc. on the site. In truth the Act does no more in the great majority of cases than give the Conservation Body a breathing space within which to apply moral pressure, with a view to persuading the owner or occupier to make a voluntary agreement.'

[102] See *Fisher v English Nature* [2003] EWHC 1599 at para. 46 (Lightman J.); [2004] EWCA 663 at paras. 142 ff. (Wall LJ.).

[103] Chapter 1, pp. 28–32.

state—represented in this case by the Conservation Body notifying the SSSI. The site notification does not expropriate property to the state; rather it reallocates key decisions on land use, and thereby on access to the land resource, to the Conservation Body. The extent of the rights transferred, and the nature of the decisions reallocated to the Conservation Body, will depend in each case upon the terms of the list of OLDSIs served on the landowner and/or occupiers of the site when the SSSI is notified. In practice, the list of OLDSIs included in the notification of many SSSIs is often extensive, as the examples given in Box 3.4 illustrate.

Perhaps the most important aspect of the land use regime is the wide discretion the 1981 Act gives to the Conservation Bodies when compiling the list of OLDSIs to be served in each SSSI, and thereby to modify by administrative act the property rights of site owners and occupiers. There is surprisingly little guidance on the ambit of this administrative power in the 1981 Act itself, in policy guidance or in the case law. Neither have the courts given clear guidance on the extent to which, and the principles by reference to which, they will control the use of the Conservation Body's powers when setting OLDSIs. The relative paucity of case law on this key aspect of the legal regime for protecting SSSIs reflects, perhaps, the fact that Natural England and CCW pursue a consensual approach to achieve resolution of operational land use issues in SSSIs, in accordance with the partnership approach to habitat management.[104] The formal procedure outlined in the 1981 Act for notifying an intention to carry out OLDSIs, followed by the negotiation of a management agreement with the Conservation Body, is rarely used in practice.[105]

The 1981 Act requires the Conservation Body to specify in the site notification 'any operations appearing to the Council to be likely to damage that flora or fauna or those features' by reason of which the site is of special interest.[106] Two issues are central to the scope of the body's administrative role in determining OLDSIs in each case—the identification of 'operations' that can legitimately be notified as OLDSIs, and the causal nexus that is required between them and potential damage to the site's conservation features. The term 'operations' in the original section 28 was considered in *Sweet v Secretary of State.*[107] It was given a wide meaning, and it was held that it should not be interpreted in the same manner as under the planning legislation, where the term 'operations' carries an active connotation limiting it to the carrying out of development or engineering

[104] As to which, see Chapter 1, p. 7.

[105] See eg qualitative data at <http://commons.ncl.ac.uk/casestudies> on SSSI management in Eskdale, Ingleborough, Norfolk, and the Elan Valley, with specific reference to SSSIs with common grazing and other registered common rights. Also C. Rodgers and J. Bishop, *Management Agreements for Promoting Nature Conservation* (RICS 1998), Ch. 2.

[106] S. 28(4)(b) Wildlife and Countryside Act 1981, as amended.

[107] [1989] 2 PLR 14.

Box 3.4 Operations Likely to Damage the Conservation Interest—A Case Study

The *Ingleborough SSSI* in North Yorkshire covers 5230 ha. It hosts Britain's finest karst landscape, with limestone pavements and an extensive cave system, and Ingleborough itself is one of the 'three peaks' in the Yorkshire Dales National Park. The SSSI supports a range of rare vegetation types typical of karst habitats, including calcareous grassland dominated by blue-moor grass, blanket-bog with hare's tail cotton grass Sundew, cranberry and bog asphodel. The Colt Park NNR has some of the best examples of limestone pavement in the UK and the summit plateau of Ingleborough itself supports an arctic-alpine flora with purple saxifrage, yellow mountain-saxifrage, roseroot and alpine meadow grass. The site management statement makes it clear the diverse range of habitats necessitate a flexible management regime—the limestone pavements require protection from heavy grazing to encourage the growth of flora, while for the dry upland heath elsewhere in the SSSI livestock grazing is an important management tool (but one that requires careful use). Different grazing intensities are required at different times of the year.

The *Operations Likely to Damage the Conservation Interest* list 28 operations which require prior consultation with Natural England before being undertaken. These include: cultivation (including ploughing, rotovating, harrowing, and re-seeding); changes in the grazing regime (including the type of stock grazed or intensity or seasonal pattern of grazing); stock feeding; mowing; applying manure or fertilizers; the release of any wild feral or domestic animals onto the site (except sheep and cattle); drainage; the extraction of any minerals including peat shingle and sand; construction or removal of roads, tracks, walls fences, ditches or earthworks; the erection of permanent or temporary structures; and the use of vehicles likely to damage or disturb features of interest. Ingleborough provides a case study of both the impact of the notification of OLDSIs on property rights, and their limitations as a tool of environmental management.

(i) The primary land uses in the SSSI are sheep farming, recreational walking and caving. The OLDSIs reallocate land use decisions on most aspects of sheep farming to Natural England. They also override the property rights of graziers in other respects, eg the land is common land over which several graziers have a right of turbary (the right to take peat). This is wholly negated by the prohibition on the removal of minerals and peat in the OLDSI list.

(ii) The notification of OLDSIs is a blunt instrument giving baseline protection to the habitats protected. It has no legal impact on the second major threat to habitat management—recreational walking and caving. And it cannot provide for the flexible management required by the site management statement. This can only be delivered through the use of agri-environment agreements (such as Higher Level Stewardship) with graziers, under which grazing intensity at different times of the year can be monitored and controlled in the manner sought by Natural England.[108]

References: <http://www.sssi.naturalengland.org.uk/Special/sssi/old/OLD1001537.pdf> (full list of OLDSIs).

<http://www.sssi.naturalengland.org.uk/citation/citation_photo/1001537.pdf> (SSSI notification and citation).

<http://www.sssi.naturalengland.org.uk/Special/sssi/sssi_details.cfm?ssi_id=1001537> (site management statement—'views about management').

[108] As to which, see further Rodgers et al. (2010) at 128–33.

operations on land. In *Sweet,* Schiemann J. held that in the context of the 1981 Act it had a wider meaning than this, and could legitimately encompass passive activities which have a potentially damaging effect on wildlife and habitats, including, for example, the release of chemicals or seeds, and the grazing of livestock. This therefore facilitates the notification of a potentially wide range of activities and land uses as OLDSIs under the 1981 Act.

There must be also, however, be a causal nexus between the potentially adverse impact of the operations notified and the site's conservation features—the Conservation Body can only notify operations that are 'likely' to damage the conservation interest of the site and its features. In contrast to the expansive approach in *Sweet* (see earlier), the courts have adopted a more restrictive interpretation of the necessary causal nexus required to justify the inclusion of potentially damaging operations in the list of OLDSIs. It was held in the Scottish case of *North Uist Fisheries Ltd v Secretary of State for Scotland*[109] that for an operation to be 'likely' to damage the site, and therefore notifiable, there must be a *probability* that the operations concerned would cause damage to the site's conservation features if carried out, and not a mere possibility that they might do so. This would appear to conflict with the precautionary principle of European environmental law, which would suggest a wider interpretation facilitating the inclusion as OLDSIs of *any* operations that have the potential, whether probably or otherwise, to damage a site's conservation features. Certainly, where an SSSI has also been designated an SAC or SPA under European law, such an approach would be inappropriate. Natural England and CCW have a duty to protect European sites and protected species from damage and disturbance.[110] Applications for operational consent in European sites therefore require them to carry out an 'appropriate assessment' of the operations implications for the integrity of the sites conservation features.[111] It was held by the European Court of Justice in the *Waddenzee case*[112] that a precautionary approach should apply in this context, and that operational consent can only be given following an environmental assessment if there is no reasonable scientific doubt as to the absence of adverse effects. This being the case, it would be anachronistic were anything other than a precautionary approach to be adopted at the prior stage when OLDSIs are identified and specified in the European site notification. Whether a similar precautionary approach should be applicable when notifying OLDSIs in an SSSI that is not part of the *Natura 2000* network of European protected sites, however, awaits judicial decision and guidance.

[109] *North Uist Fisheries v Secretary of State* (1992) JEL 241.

[110] See art. 6 Directive 92/43/EEC and Chapter 6, p. 213 ff.

[111] See further Chapter 6, p. 222.

[112] *Landelijke Vereneging to Behold van deer Waddenzee v Staatssecretaris van Landbouw, Natuurbeheer en Visserij* [2004] ECR I–7405, Case C 127–02.

(iii) *Implications for human rights*

The imposition of legal controls on OLDSIs has been challenged on the basis that it may impose disproportionate restrictions on ownership rights in an SSSI. In *Fisher v English Nature*[113] it was held that issuing a list of OLDSIs was not itself a breach of article 1 of the Protocol to the ECHR.[114] All the 1981 Act requires is that a statutory consultation on proposed operations is initiated and that consent be obtained before they are carried out. If and when a landowner applies for operational consent a fair balance can be struck in determining whether consent is granted in the particular case—the required balance being between the public interest in protecting the wildlife habitat for which the site was notified—stone curlews, in the *Fisher* case—and the claimant's interest in carrying out the operation. The regime is not disproportionate in as much as it includes a mechanism for affecting the required balance in individual cases.

The Court of Appeal in *Fisher* placed particular emphasis on the fact that the landowner is free at all times to apply to be absolved from the bonds imposed upon him by applying for operational consent.[115] This ignores the fact, noted earlier, that the framework of reference within which the balance must be struck was fundamentally changed by the 2000 Act. English Nature can now indefinitely refuse operational consent, subject to a right of appeal against refusal to the Secretary of State.[116] The procedure differs from that in planning cases in other key respects, notably because there is no mechanism for public consultation on applications for operational consent in wildlife sites, and there is no obligation on the Conservation Bodies to furnish detailed written reasons for a refusal of operational consent. The key to the regime's compliance with the convention right appears to have been the facility for appeals to the Secretary of State. Nevertheless, although the management regime for SSSIs was pronounced to be convention-compliant in *Fisher*, it remains the case that its application in individual cases must accord with article 1 and with, in particular, the proportionality principle. The action taken by the Conservation Bodies must in each individual case be proportionate to the public policy interest that is being pursued, and they must consider any allegedly disproportionate burden the OLDSI list is claimed to impose on the landowner or occupier in each case. The application of the proportionality principle will depend on the facts of individual cases.

(c) **Duties of public bodies and statutory undertakers**

Much SSSI land is owned by public bodies like government departments, local government, or public agencies. Additionally, much major work carried out on

113 [2003] EWHC 1599; [2004] EWCA Civ 663.

114 As to which, see p. 82.

115 See *Fisher v English Nature* [2003] EWHC 1599 at para. 46 (Lightman J.). The claimants dropped the argument based on the operational consent procedure on appeal—see [2004] EWCA 663 at paras. 142 ff. for Wall LJ.s comments (albeit obiter dicta) on this aspect of the case.

116 S. 28P Wildlife and Countryside Act 1981, inserted by Schedule 9 the 2000 Act.

SSSIs will be done by the public utilities—for example, the water or electricity companies. For this reason, special rules apply to operations carried out on SSSI land by statutory undertakers and other public authorities. They are, in the first place, under a duty to take reasonable steps, consistent with the proper exercise of their functions, to further the conservation and enhancement of the flora, fauna, or geological/physiographical features by reason of which land has been notified an SSSI.[117] This does not guarantee the protection of a site when a statutory undertaker or public body exercises statutory powers to carry out works, but it does at least mean that they must consider the conservation interest in protecting land which is notified as an SSSI against other relevant considerations when exercising their statutory powers. This duty applies to any minister, the Welsh Assembly Government, a local authority, a person holding office under the crown, any statutory undertaker, or 'any other public body of any description'.[118]

A modified version of the consultation procedure for OLDSIs (earlier) applies where a public body wishes to carry out work in an SSSI. Before carrying out any operation likely to damage an SSSI or any of its features, it must notify the Conservation Body which may either refuse consent, or give it with or without conditions. A refusal of operational consent does not, however, prevent the public body or undertaker carrying out a potentially damaging operation. It must, instead, give further notice that it intends to carry out the operations notwithstanding and, when doing so, to indicate how it has taken into account any written advice received from the Conservation Body in response to its initial notice of intent.[119] Any operations subsequently undertaken must be carried out in such a way as to give rise to as little damage as is reasonable practicable in all the circumstances to the flora, fauna, or geological/physiographical features by reason of which the site is of special interest, taking account in particular of any advice received from the Conservation Body. Finally, the public body or statutory undertaker must restore the site to its former condition so far as is reasonably practicable if any damage does occur. The provisions are complemented by similar consultation duties that apply where a pubic body or undertaker itself uses its powers to authorize a third party to carry out operations in an SSSI.[120] Of particular importance is the fact that the duty to consult applies, in both cases, even if the operations are to take place outside the boundaries of an SSSI. Even if they are to occur outside the geographical boundaries of the SSSI, the fact that they are likely to damage any of the conservation features of the site is itself sufficient to bring the consultation provisions into play. This could prove very important, for example, in the case of works by statutory water undertakers which might—in the case of flood prevention works, for example—have a major impact on the hydrology of sites within a wide radius of the works in question.

[117] S. 28G(2) Wildlife and Countryside Act 1981.
[118] See s. 28G(3) Wildlife and Countryside Act 1981.
[119] S. 28H(4) and (5) Wildlife and Countryside Act 1981.
[120] See s. 28I Wildlife and Countryside Act 1981.

(d) Potential liabilities under the 1981 Act

The penalties for damaging SSSIs in breach of the terms of the 1981 Act were considerably strengthened by the Countryside and Rights of Way Act 2000.[121] The latter also broadened the impact of the legislation by creating potential liabilities for third parties—other than the owner or occupier of the site—who damage an SSSI or its features.

(i) Liability of the owner and/or occupier

The primary focus of the legislation remains, nevertheless, the prevention of damage by the owner or occupier of land that hosts habitats of special interest. To this end, any person who, without reasonable excuse, carries out or causes or permits the carrying out of an OLDSI in contravention of the 1981 Act[122] is guilty of an offence and liable on summary conviction to a fine not exceeding £20,000 or on conviction on indictment to a fine.[123] This provision does not apply to damage to an SSSI caused by third parties—unless they acted with the owner's permission or instructions, in which event the owner or occupier may himself be principally liable for 'causing or permitting' the damage in question.

The liability extends to the acts of anyone considered to be an 'occupier' for the purposes of the Act. This was considered in *Southern Water Authority v Nature Conservancy Council*[124] where a restrictive interpretation was adopted that limits liability to acts done (i) by the owner, or (ii) by an 'occupier' with a legally recognized right of occupation or some relationship of permanence with the land. The House of Lords held that an 'occupier' is someone who, although lacking legal title to the land, nevertheless 'stands in such a comprehensive and stable relationship with the land as to be, in company with the actual owner, someone to whom the [notification procedures] could sensibly be made to apply'.[125] It does not extend, therefore, to a stranger who enters the land for a few weeks solely to carry out work on it—and an independent contractor was not, therefore, held to be liable for damage under this provision. Other categories of occupancy right may, however, give rise to uncertainty. A tenant would clearly be an 'occupier' for these purposes and potentially liable for damage. A wide range of other common occupancy types may not—what of a commoner exercising registered rights of common?[126] Or a licensee of farmland with short-term contractual rights to use the

[121] See now s. 28P Wildlife and Countryside Act 1981, as amended.

[122] Ie unless in accordance with the conditions set out in s. 28E(3) Wildlife and Countryside Act 1981, eg with operational consent or under a management agreement with Natural England or CCW.

[123] S. 28P(1) Wildlife and Countryside Act 1981.

[124] [1992] 3 All ER 481.

[125] [1992] 3 All ER 481 at 488 per Lord Mustill.

[126] A common grazier would be an 'occupier' for these purposes, as s/he would have a stable relationship with the land, and property rights recognized by the Commons Register for the land in question: see Nature Conservancy Council Press statement PPG 4/1991 (statement made to House of Lords, 17 October 1990, by Baroness Blatch); and C. P. Rodgers 'Environmental Management of Common Land: Towards a New Legal Framework?' (1999) 11 JEL 231–55.

land for grazing or cropping purposes? In such cases the possibility that the owner may retain liability for 'causing or permitting' may be important in protecting an SSSI from damage caused by temporary occupiers.

(ii) Liability of public bodies and undertakers

A public body or statutory undertaker which damages any of the special features of an SSSI without first complying with the statutory consultation requirements outlined earlier,[127] and then fails to give notice of its intention to proceed with unconsented operations without first giving notice[128] will, unless there was a 'reasonable excuse' for carrying out the operation without complying, be guilty of an offence and liable on summary conviction to a fine not exceeding £20,000 or on conviction on indictment to an unlimited fine.[129] The Natural Environment and Rural Communities Act 2006[130] further extended this liability so that a public body will also be liable for permitting the carrying out of an operation by someone else that damages any of the flora, fauna, geological, or physiographical features of an SSSI. It will be liable[131] unless it has complied with the statutory consultation requirements and waited 28 days before deciding whether to give its permission to the operation being carried out.[132] If it decides to permit the operation against the subsequent advice of the Conservation Body, it must give notice to this effect and then wait for a further 21 days before authorizing it to be carried out.[133]

This rather complex set of arrangements is intended to allow the Conservation Body sufficient notice and time to fully investigate the likely impact on the SSSI and take steps to achieve its protection if necessary; for example, through compulsory purchase or a management order. There is a defence if there was a 'reasonable excuse' for permitting the carrying out of the operation in question: it is a 'reasonable excuse' for these purposes if the operation was an emergency operation particulars of which were notified to Natural England as soon as practicable.[134]

(iii) Liability of third parties

A major weakness of the legal regime for protecting SSSIs before the 2000 Act was the restriction of its application solely to owners and occupiers of SSSI land. The 1981 Act[135] now contains a separate criminal offence for damage to SSSIs by third parties; for example, fly tippers or transient occupants. Any person who without reasonable excuse intentionally or recklessly destroys or damages any of the special

[127] Ie those in s. 28H, Wildlife and Countryside Act 1981 discussed at p. 84 ff.
[128] See s. 28H(4)(a) Wildlife and Countryside Act 1981.
[129] S. 28P(3) Wildlife and Countryside Act 1981.
[130] See s. 55 Natural Environment and Rural Communities Act 2006.
[131] See s. 28P(5A) Wildlife and Countryside Act 1981.
[132] See s. 28I Wildlife and Countryside Act 1981.
[133] S. 28I(6) Wildlife and Countryside Act 1981.
[134] S. 28P(5B) Wildlife and Countryside Act 1981.
[135] S. 28P(6) Wildlife and Countryside Act 1981.

features by reason of which the land is notified an SSSI, or intentionally or recklessly disturbs any of its fauna, with knowledge that what he destroyed, damaged, or disturbed was within an SSSI, is guilty of an offence liable on summary conviction to a fine not exceeding £20,000 or on conviction on indictment to a fine. The offence requires proof of knowledge on the part of the accused that the site was an SSSI. It is not clear whether it will suffice that the alleged perpetrator ought reasonably to have known that the land was SSSI land when he committed the damaging acts in question.

A second offence was created by the Natural Environment and Rural Communities Act 2006.[136] It is now an offence for anyone—other than a public authority acting in the exercise of its functions[137]—to intentionally or recklessly destroy or damage the nature conservation or geological features of an SSSI, or to disturb its fauna without reasonable excuse. This is a strict liability offence and does not require knowledge that what was destroyed or damaged was within an SSSI. An offender is liable on summary conviction to a fine not exceeding level 4 on the standard scale. The court has power to make restoration orders in relation to both of these offences.

(iv) Exceptions to liability

It is not an offence to carry out an operation if the occupier has a reasonable excuse for carrying it out.[138] For these purposes it is a 'reasonable excuse' for a person to carry out an operation that damages the conservation interest of an SSSI in either of two situations:[139]

- It is authorized by planning permission granted under the Town & Country Planning Act 1990,[140] or has been permitted by a statutory undertaker which has consulted the Conservation Body as required by the 1981 Act[141] or
- It is an emergency operation particulars of which, including details of the emergency, were notified to the Conservation Body as soon as practicable after the commencement of the operation. No guidance is offered by the 1981 Act, and no definition of 'emergency' is given in the Act or case law. The provision is intended to exonerate emergency operations in situations where it would be impossible or impractical to initiate and use the statutory consultation procedure for OLDSIs. The precise ambit of the defence is unclear, however. The express requirement to notify the Conservation Body 'as soon as practicable after the commencement of the operation'[142] would suggest, it is submitted,

136 S. 55 Natural Environment and Rural Communities Act 2006, inserting a new s. 28P(6A) in the Wildlife and Countryside Act 1981.

137 Ie s. 28G authority—see p. 90ff.

138 See s. 28P(1) Wildlife and Countryside Act 1981.

139 See s. 28P(4) Wildlife and Countryside Act 1981.

140 S. 28P(4)(a) Wildlife and Countryside Act 1981.

141 Under s. 28I Wildlife and Countryside Act 1981 (pp. 90–1).

142 See s. 28P(4)(b) Wildlife and Countryside Act 1981.

that for the defence to apply it must be impossible on the facts to notify the Conservation Body before undertaking the operation. Examples would include remedial action to deal with an outbreak of fire or an unforeseeable flood, requiring emergency remedial action to protect livestock or premises. If the circumstances are such that it is reasonably practicable to inform the Conservation Body before undertaking the remedial work that causes the damage, however, it is suggested that it will not constitute an 'emergency' for these purposes.

(e) Powers to achieve positive management

The 1981 Act was based on a 'preventative' approach; that is, that of preventing damaging operations and 'buying out' development with compensation payable under management agreements with landowners and occupiers of SSSIs. Many types of protected habitat require positive management in order to retain their special interest, however, and the measures in the original 1981 Act were poorly equipped to achieve this. Examples might include hay meadows and dry heathland, or the machair habitat of the Outer Hebrides, where light grazing by livestock is desirable at certain times of the year to encourage wildflowers and other vegetation, or fenland habitats where positive management to maintain optimum water levels is required to provide ideal breeding and feeding conditions for invertebrates.[143] The statutory consultation provisions which apply before OLDSIs can be carried out are aimed at preventing unwarranted damage to SSSI features. They cannot deliver positive management, or the creation or improvement of natural habitats. The Countryside and Rights of Way Act 2000 therefore introduced provisions enabling the Conservation Bodies in England and Wales to introduce management schemes on SSSI land and, in appropriate circumstances, to enforce positive management obligations by serving Management Notices on owners and occupiers.[144] Scottish Natural Heritage has similar powers in relation to SSSIs in Scotland:[145] it can propose the making of a land management order to the Scottish ministers, and this can include requirements for operations to be carried out on the land to conserve, restore or enhance habitats.[146] The discussion here will focus on the provisions for management schemes and orders in England and Wales.

(i) Management schemes

The Conservation Body can prepare a management scheme for all or part of an SSSI, either when initially notifying the SSSI or at any time thereafter. It cannot exercise its legal powers to establish the scheme without first giving notice of their proposals

143 Consider eg the habitat in *Sweet v Secretary of State* (1989) 2 PLR 14, which concerned the maintenance of appropriate water levels in the Somerset Levels for invertebrate habitats.

144 These powers are set out in s. 28J and s. 28K of the 1981 Act (as amended).

145 See ss. 29–34 Nature Conservation (Scotland) Act 2004.

146 See s. 31(d) Nature Conservation (Scotland) Act 2004.

(including a copy of the Scheme) to every owner and occupier of land to which it would relate and consulting them about the terms of the proposed Scheme.[147] Where a management scheme has been proposed, it is subject to confirmation, following consultation with affected land owner/occupiers and other relevant consultees, under provisions which mirror those for consultation on the initial notification of an SSSI (pp. 69 ff). Objections must be made within three months, and the scheme must be confirmed by the agency within nine months. If the management scheme is confirmed, it has effect from the time the notice of confirmation is served on all the relevant owners and occupiers. If it is not withdrawn or confirmed within nine months, the Conservation Body's initial notice establishing it ceases to have effect. There is no right of appeal against the making of a management scheme, although the Conservation Body's power to confirm a scheme with modifications is restricted in that it cannot be exercised so as to make complying with the scheme more onerous.[148] Once the scheme is established the Conservation Body may at any time cancel it or propose its modification, in which event the consultation provisions described earlier apply.

(ii) Management orders

The 2000 Act also conferred powers on Natural England and the Countryside Council for Wales to make management orders requiring positive management of SSSI land. A management order can be made where there is a management scheme for the SSSI, but the terms of the scheme are being ignored or broken in circumstances that mean its flora or fauna is being inadequately conserved or restored. The making of a management order is a measure of last resort, and its application hedged around with safeguards for the landowner. There is a right of appeal to the Secretary of State. And, before serving a management notice, the Conservation Body must be able to show that they have been unable to conclude, on reasonable terms, a management agreement with the owner to deliver the requirements of the management scheme.

Under the terms of a management order, the Conservation Body has wide powers to require the carrying out by the owner or occupier of such work on the land or such other things as may be specified, provided they appear to them to be reasonable in order to ensure that the land is managed in accordance with the management scheme already established for the site. Moreover, if any of the work required by it is not done—or not done within the period specified in the Notice—the Conservation Body can enter the land and carry it out themselves. If they do so they can recover from the owner or occupier upon whom the notice was served any expenses reasonably incurred. Quite apart from his potential liability for the Conservation Body's expenses in carrying out the work themselves, the owner/occupier who fails to carry out the terms of a management order, without reasonable excuse, will also be committing a criminal offence and be liable on summary

[147] See s. 28J(3) Wildlife and Countryside Act 1981 (as amended).
[148] See s. 28J(10) Wildlife and Countryside Act 1981.

conviction to a fine not exceeding the statutory maximum, or on conviction on indictment to a fine.[149]

(f) Payments by the Conservation Body

In several situations, the UK Conservation Bodies are obliged to offer payment for SSSI management, and in some others they can make payments on a discretionary basis. Where the Conservation Body uses its statutory powers to modify or withdraw an operational consent it has granted for the carrying out of OLDSIs[150] they *must* make a payment to any owner or occupier of the land who suffers loss because of the modification or withdrawal of consent.[151] Where a management scheme is established under the provisions described earlier,[152] on the other hand, the Conservation Body has discretion whether to make payments. This power applies to allow them, if they think fit, to make one or more payments to any owner or occupiers of land in relation to which the scheme applies, while it is in force.[153] This will enable the making of either lump sum or periodic payments. The quantification of the payments in both cases is governed by guidance published by the ministers.[154]

(g) Powers of entry

Prior to the 2000 Act the Conservation Bodies had limited rights of entry onto private land for the purpose of carrying out their statutory functions in relation to SSSIs. This limited their ability to enforce the law effectively. The 2000 Act conferred on them wide statutory powers to enter onto land for the purposes of identifying, notifying and supervising the management of SSSIs.[155]

(i) Scope of powers of entry

The Conservation Body's officers, and others so authorized by them for this purpose, have the right to enter private land for the following purposes:

- To determine whether the land should be notified as an SSSI, and in the case of land already notified to assess the condition of the flora fauna and/or other features by reason of which it has been notified as an SSSI.

[149] See s. 28P(8) Wildlife and Countryside Act 1981.

[150] See s. 28E(6) Wildlife and Countryside Act 1981 and pp. 84 ff.

[151] S. 28M(1) Wildlife and Countryside Act 1981.

[152] Ie under S. 28J Wildlife and Countryside Act 1981, and see p. 95.

[153] S. 28M(2) Wildlife and Countryside Act 1981.

[154] S. 28M(3) Wildlife and Countryside Act 1981. In England this is governed by DETR circular *Guidelines on Management Agreement Payments and other related matters* (February 2001), issued under s. 28M and s. 50 Wildlife and Countryside Act 1981. This also applies to management agreements in SSSIs, and is discussed in more detail in Chapter 4, pp. 119 ff.

[155] S. 51 Wildlife and Countryside Act 1981, as amended by s. 80 Countryside and Rights of Way Act 2000.

- To determine whether or not to enter into a management agreement with the owner or occupier.
- Where occupational consent has been granted for a potentially damaging operation to be carried out at the site, they can enter to assess whether any conditions attached to it are being complied with. They also have a power of enter to ascertain whether a criminal offence is being committed, either under the land management rules in the Act or under by-laws made for the site.
- To formulate a management scheme for the land, or to decide whether an existing scheme should be modified. Where a management scheme is in place, they can enter in order to prepare a management order.
- They have powers of entry for the purposes of ascertaining whether a management agreement covering the site is being adhered to, or whether a management scheme or management order is being observed.
- To determine whether to offer a payment in respect of an operational consent which has been withdrawn or modified, or where payment is proposed under a management scheme.[156]
- To determine any questions relating to the acquisition of land, either by agreement or using the UK Conservation Body's compulsory purchase powers.
- To put up, maintain or remove notices or signs erected on the land by the Conservation Body.[157]
- The powers of entry also apply for the purposes of determining whether to make a Limestone Pavement Order[158] or an order under the 1981 Act preventing agricultural operations (such as ploughing) on heath- or moorland in national parks.[159]

When exercising rights of entry the Conservation Body's officers or agents can use a vehicle or boat to enter the land and, if they reasonably believe they may be obstructed in doing so, can take a police constable with them, in addition to such material and equipment as they need for the purpose of their inspection. They are also entitled to take samples of the land and anything on it; for example, vegetation. If the land is unoccupied, or the occupier is temporarily absent, the person exercising the right of entry must leave the land as 'effectively secured' against unauthorized entry as he found it.

[156] The power to make payments is contained in s. 28M Wildlife and Countryside Act 1981. The power of entry supplements this by conferring the necessary powers to enter and carry out an assessment of whether the landowner has suffered/will suffer financial loss as a consequence of the exercise of the UK Conservation Bodies powers.

[157] S. 51(1)(ka) inserted by s. 58 the Natural Environment and Rural Communities Act 2006.

[158] Ie under s. 34 of the 1981 Act. See p. XX.

[159] As to which, see s. 42 Wildlife and Countryside Act 1981.

(ii) Compensation

The Conservation Body has a duty to compensate an owner or occupier whose land is entered in pursuit of these powers in certain circumstances. Compensation must be paid if he sustains damage as a result of the entry, except in cases where damage is attributable to the fault of the person who sustained it.[160] Compensation must also be paid if damage is sustained as consequence of the officer who enters failing to leave the site adequately secured.[161]

(h) Compulsory purchase

The Conservation Bodies have wide powers of compulsory purchase in relation to SSSI land.[162] They may compulsorily acquire all or part of any SSSI where either:

(a) they are satisfied that they are unable to conclude, on reasonable terms, an agreement with the owner or occupier as to the management of the land, or

(b) they have entered into a management agreement, but are satisfied that it has been breached in such a way that the land is not being managed satisfactorily. Where they acquire land compulsorily, the Conservation Body may either manage the land themselves, or dispose of it (or any interest in it) on terms designed to secure that the land is managed satisfactorily. If any dispute as to whether or not there has been a breach of a management agreement, for the purposes of triggering the power of compulsory purchase, it is determined by an arbitrator appointed by the Lord Chancellor.[163]

Nature Reserves

Nature reserves are protected areas in which nature conservation is the primary consideration. They therefore provide a contrast to the more extensive network of SSSIs (see earlier) in which management for nature conservation is sought alongside other land uses, including, for example, forestry or agriculture. A nature reserve is therefore defined as (i) land managed solely for a conservation purpose, or (ii) land managed not only for a conservation purpose but also a recreational purpose, if the management of the land for recreational purposes does not compromise its

[160] See s. 51(5) Wildlife and Countryside Act 1981 as amended.

[161] S. 51(5)(b) Wildlife and Countryside Act 1981. The duty, and the duty to compensate, is limited to making the premises as secure as they were prior to entry—a factor that could prove problematic in cases of dispute. A counsel of caution would dictate that a note of the condition of gates, locks, etc., be taken on entry to avoid dispute in the event of later unauthorized entry giving rise to damage.

[162] S. 28N Wildlife and Countryside Act 1981, as amended and enlarged by Countryside and Rights of Way Act 2000.

[163] S. 28N(3) Wildlife and Countryside Act 1981.

management for the conservation purpose intended.[164] They are intended to be areas where the primary focus is the conservation of nature, the study of their flora and fauna, and recreational activities that are compatible with these objectives. To this end the management of land for a 'conservation purpose' is defined to mean:

(a) providing, under suitable conditions and control, special opportunities for the study of, and research into, matters relating to the fauna and flora of Great Britain and the physical conditions in which they live, and for the study of geological and physiographical features of special interest in the area, or

(b) preserving flora, fauna, or geological or physiographical features of special interest in the area[165]

Nature reserves are designated by the Conservation Body—Scottish Natural Heritage and the Countryside Council for Wales,[166] or Natural England.[167] The power to designate arises where the Conservation Body considers it expedient in the national interest that land should be managed as a nature reserve, for the purpose set out earlier.[168] The Conservation Body must make a declaration as to the nature reserve status of the land concerned and advertise this in a manner best suited to bring it to the attention of all with a relevant interest.[169]

The management of land within nature reserves is achieved primarily through the use of management agreements, by the passing of byelaws, and in some cases by the use of compulsory acquisition to bring the site into the ownership of the Conservation Body. The Conservation Bodies have power to enter into management agreements with the owner, lessee or occupier of land that they consider should be managed as a nature reserve in the national interest.[170] Management agreements under the 1949 Act can impose restrictions on the exercise of the owner or occupier's rights over the land, and provide for its management in such manner as seems appropriate to achieve the satisfactory maintenance of the land as a nature reserve. Management agreements can also bind the Conservation Body to defray the costs of managing the land and make provision for payment of compensation to an owner or occupier in respect of agreed restrictions on the way the land is managed. The key focus here is on adjusting the existing property rights of owners and occupiers, through an economic exchange achieved by the conclusion of an agreement with the Conservation Body. The existing property rights of the occupier

[164] S. 15(1) National Parks and Access to the Countryside Act 1949, as amended by Schedule 11 para. 12 Natural Environment and Rural Communities Act 2006.

[165] S. 15(2) National Parks and Access to the Countryside Act 1949, as amended by Schedule 11 para. 12 Natural Environment and Rural Communities Act 2006.

[166] Under s. 132 Environmental Protection Act 1990, s. 4(7) Natural Heritage Scotland Act 1991.

[167] Under its general powers to promote nature conservation in s. 2 Natural Environment and Rural Communities Act 2006.

[168] S. 16 National Parks and Access to the Countryside Act 1949.

[169] S. 19 National Parks and Access to the Countryside Act 1949.

[170] For SCH and CCW this power is set out in s. 16 National Parks and Access to the Countryside Act 1949. Natural England has the power to do so under its general management agreement powers in s. 7 Natural Environment and Rural Communities Act 2006. In England these are formally termed 'nature reserve agreements', s. 15A National Parks and Access to the Countryside Act 1949, as amended by Schedule 11 para. 13 Natural Environment and Rural Communities Act 2006.

will, accordingly, determine whether payment can be made, their quantum and the other terms of the agreement. In England and Wales, a management agreement will be enforceable against subsequent owners and occupiers of the site in the same way as a restrictive covenant, the benefit of which is deemed to be vested in the Conservation Body.[171] In Scotland the same effect is achieved by registering the agreement in the Register of Sasines.[172]

The Conservation Bodies also have powers to make by-laws for the protection of nature reserves.[173] By-laws can impose restrictions on the activities of third parties, including the public, over the land—unlike management agreements, where the focus is on restricting the rights of the owner and occupier of the land itself. By-laws can, accordingly prohibit or restrict the entry to, or movement within, a nature reserve by people, animals, and vehicles, and restrict the killing of animals or destruction of vegetation.[174] By-laws cannot, however, interfere with the exercise by any person of a right vested in him as an owner, lessee or occupier of land within a nature reserve, neither can they interfere with the exercise of public rights of way. In other words, the rights of an owner or occupier must be adjusted through a management agreement—with payment in respect of the adjustments to property rights required to effect conservation management, if appropriate.

Although the use of management agreements is the chief method of protecting areas designated as nature reserves, the Conservation Bodies also enjoy powers of compulsory purchase over land in nature reserves. This power can be exercised where the Conservation Body considers that land should be managed as a nature reserve in the national interest, but has been unable to conclude a management agreement securing that the land will be satisfactorily managed for that purpose.[175] The power of compulsory purchase can also be used where there is a management agreement, but its terms have been broken. In this event, notice of the terms breached must be given and the landowner or occupier must be given a reasonable time in which to remedy the breach.[176]

The powers outlined earlier have general application to all nature reserves. Provision is made, however, for the declaration of two specific types of nature reserve—National Nature Reserves, and Local Nature Reserves.

(i) National Nature Reserves

Special provision is made by the Wildlife and Countryside Act 1981[177] for the Conservation Body to declare land a National Nature Reserve (NNR). The land must currently be subject to management as a nature reserve—either by the Conservation Body itself, by a private owner or occupier under a management agreement with the

171 S. 16(4) National Parks and Access to the Countryside Act 1949.
172 S. 29(2) Land Registration (Scotland) Act 1979.
173 S. 20 National Parks and Access to the Countryside Act 1949.
174 See s. 20(2) National Parks and Access to the Countryside Act 1949.
175 See s. 17 National Parks and Access to the Countryside Act 1949.
176 See s. 18 National Parks and Access to the Countryside Act 1949.
177 S. 35 Wildlife and Countryside Act 1981.

Conservation Body, or by another body approved for this purpose by the Conservation Body.[178] Following its declaration as an NNR, the Conservation Body can make by-laws for the management of the Reserve by an approved Body subject to the same limitations as apply to nature reserves outlined earlier.[179]

In practice, Natural England manages approximately two-thirds of the NNRs in England, while other organizations approved by Natural England manage the remaining third—including the National Trust, Wildlife Trusts, the RSPB, and local authorities. All NNRs in England are also notified SSSIs, and the legal protection afforded to SSSIs will also apply to underpin their management and protection. There are currently 224 NNRs in England, and 72 in Wales, representing the most important sites in the SSSI network.[180]

(ii) Local Nature Reserves

Local authorities[181] can also designate Local Nature Reserves ('LNR') if they think it expedient that land should be managed as a nature reserve in the interests of the locality.[182] The designation and management of land as a LNR is based on the same criteria as nature reserves designated by the Conservation Bodies, and set out earlier. So, for example, where land is declared an LNR, it must be managed primarily for conservation, with recreation permitted only as a managed subordinate use—provided it does not conflict or impede conservation management. It followed that where a LNR was declared by a local authority in circumstances where the public enjoyed statutory recreational rights over the land under a public trust, the two land uses were potentially incompatible and the LNR declaration was invalid.[183] Where land has been declared an LNR, the local authority enjoys the same powers as the Conservation Bodies set out earlier, including the power of compulsory purchase if this is in the interest of the locality. They must, however, consult the Conservation Body on the exercise of their functions in respect of local nature reserves.[184]

Limestone Pavement Orders

Limestone pavements are areas of limestone wholly or partly exposed on the surface of the ground and which have been fissured by natural erosion.[185] They are a natural

178 Eg local wildlife trust or bodies such as the RSPB or National Trust.

179 Ss. 35(3) and (4) Wildlife and Countryside Act 1981.

180 See <http://www.naturalengland.org.uk/ourwork/conservation/designatedareas/nnr/default.aspx/>.

181 In England and Wales this power can also be exercised by National Park Authorities.

182 S. 21 National Parks and Access to the Countryside Act 1949.

183 *Western Power Distribution Investments Limited v Cardiff City Council* [2011] EWHC 300 (Admin). The public enjoyed the benefit of a public trust for recreational use under the Public Health Act 1975 on land adjoining a former reservoir, which the council wished to declare a nature reserve. See also *Western Power Distribution Investments Limited v Cardiff City Council* [2010] EWHC 1802 (Admin).

184 See s. 21(6) National Parks and Access to the Countryside Act 1949.

185 See the definition in s. 34(6) Wildlife and Countryside Act 1981.

feature of certain parts of the country—for example the karst areas of the central Pennines—and are by their nature vulnerable to damage from quarrying, and sometimes from unsympathetic agricultural operations. In England and Wales, areas in which limestone pavements are present can be protected by their designation under Limestone Pavement Orders made under the Wildlife and Countryside Act 1981.[186]

The identification of limestone pavements is initially to be carried out by the Conservation Bodies. Where Natural England or CCW are of the opinion that a limestone pavement is of special interest by reason of its flora, fauna, or geological/physiological features, they must notify the planning authority in whose area the land is situated.[187] The decision as to the designation of the area under a Limestone Pavement Order is then undertaken either by the Secretary of State or the local planning authority. If either believes that the character or appearance of the land would be likely to be adversely affected by the removal or disturbance of limestone, they have power to make a Limestone Pavement Order protecting the site. The order takes effect immediately, but must be reviewed by the minister after advertisement and notification to all owners and occupiers of land affected by it. The minister will review all orders, whether made by himself or the local planning authority, and his decision to confirm an order must also be advertised and notified to relevant land owners.[188] Most areas of limestone pavement in England and Wales are now subject to orders.[189]

The principal legal effect of a Limestone Pavement Order is to prohibit the removal or disturbance of limestone on or in the land designated.[190] Since the quarrying of limestone on any substantial scale will require planning permission,[191] the making of a Limestone Pavement Order will be primarily relevant to restrain operations that do not require planning permission; for example, agricultural operations that may involve damaging or removing limestone. The only circumstances in which operations can be carried out are where they are sanctioned by planning permission obtained on application under Part III of the Town and Country Planning Act 1990.[192] In this case the legal status of the land will be considered as a material factor by the planning authority prior to granting permission, and the views of the Conservation Body will be sought as a statutory consultee on the application. Contravention of a Limestone Pavement Order is a criminal

[186] S. 34 Wildlife and Countryside Act 1981. The provisions for the designation of Limestone Pavement Orders were repealed in Scotland by Schedule 7 para. 4 Nature Conservation (Scotland) Act 2004.

[187] S. 34(1) Wildlife and Countryside Act 1981.

[188] The order cannot be challenged in legal proceedings once six weeks have elapsed from its confirmation being advertised and notified to landowners and occupiers affected by it: Schedule 11 Wildlife and Countryside Act 1981.

[189] See <http://www.limestone-pavements.org.uk/legal.html> for further information on limestone pavement conservation from the UK and Ireland Biodiversity Action Steering Group.

[190] S. 34(2) Wildlife and Countryside Act 1981.

[191] It will be operational development in on or under land within s. 55 Town and Country Planning Act 1990.

[192] S. 34(5) Wildlife and Countryside Act 1981.

offence punishable on summary conviction by a fine not exceeding the statutory maximum and on indictment by a fine.[193]

Limestone Pavement Orders provide an environmental management tool of limited utility. Their only legal effect is to prevent the removal of limestone—they prohibit the extraction and disturbance of limestone but cannot, unless used in conjunction with other management instruments, be used to achieve positive management of limestone habitats. Because of their rich and sensitive habitat features, many limestone pavements will be in areas notified as SSSIs. Limestone pavements are also a priority habitat within Annex 1 of the EC Habitats Directive.[194] In practice, in cases where a pavement is included within an SSSI notification similar management objectives can be achieved by site notification. An example is provided by Box 3.4. The Ingleborough SSSI encompasses some of the finest limestone pavement habitats in England. The list of OLDSIs served on landowners and occupiers in the SSSI prohibits the removal of minerals, expressly including limestone pavement and spoil, without prior consultation with Natural England.[195] It is a criminal offence for a landowner or occupier who has been served with the list of OLDSIs to do so. The practical importance of a Limestone Pavement Order in a case like this is, therefore, to extend protection to prohibit the removal or disturbance of limestone by third parties and the public. Ingleborough also illustrates the inherent limitations shared by both the SSSI and Limestone Pavement Order mechanisms. Neither can, used in isolation, deliver positive management. Limestone pavements often support a fragile and valuable population of flora, and conservation management of these habitat features requires positive management that can best be achieved through the use of management agreements with landowners and land managers—as has been the case in Ingleborough itself.[196] The use of Limestone Pavement Orders confers valuable protection on pavements that are situated outside the confines of notified SSSIs or SACs.

National Parks

National Parks were introduced in England and Wales following the Second World War, under the National Parks and Access to the Countryside Act 1949. They have a wider purpose and focus than SSSIs and nature reserves, with the promotion of landscape protection and open air recreation by the public sitting alongside the preservation of the 'natural beauty' of the countryside designated as a national park. The 1949 Act (as amended) now gives Natural England and CCW the power to designate as a national park, in England and Wales respectively, those 'extensive tracts' of countryside which, by reason of their natural beauty and the opportunities

193 S. 34(4) Wildlife and Countryside Act 1981.

194 See Chapter 6, pp. 213 ff.

195 Operations Likely to Damage the Conservation Interest; Ingleborough, Craven: OLD1001537, ref. No. 20. Available at: <http://www.sssi.naturalengland.org.uk/Special/sssi/old/OLD1001537.pdf>.

196 See Box 3.4 at p. 87. And for further discussion, see Rodgers et al. (2010) pp. 128 ff.

they offer for open-air recreation, necessitate measures being taken to preserve and enhance their natural beauty. They must also take account of the area's wildlife and cultural heritage, and the extent to which it is possible to promote opportunities for the understanding and enjoyment of its special qualities by the public.[197]

The International Union for the Conservation of Nature produced a simplified classification system for protected areas in 2002,[198] Category 2 of which identifies criteria for the designation of national parks.[199] The paradigm objectives of national parks should, according to the IUCN, combine the preservation of ecosystems with the promotion of tourism. The management of national parks should therefore aim at the promotion of 'inspirational, educational, cultural, and recreational purposes at a level which will maintain the area in a natural or near natural state', while also maintaining respect for the ecological attributes, or geomorphologic and aesthetic qualities for which the park was designated. The criteria for the designation of national parks in England and Wales, as set out in the 1949 Act, to some extent mirror these considerations, combining recognition of the landscape and aesthetic value of national parks with the opportunities they offer for open-air recreation for the public.[200] There is, however, a much closer focus on nature conservation in the IUCN classification than is present in English law. Nevertheless, the additional controls on development and land use in national parks—outlined on pp. 107 ff. play an important role in complementing and underpinning the protection of high nature value areas, such as SSSIs, many of which are situated in designated national parks.

The criteria for designation in England and Wales[201] require Natural England and CCW to have regard to two special characteristics of 'extensive tracts of country' when deciding whether to make a national park designation order: their 'natural beauty' and 'the opportunities they afford for open air recreation, having regard to both their character and to their position in relation to centres of population'. Both criteria are potentially problematic. The reference to the 'natural beauty' of an area under the 1949 Act was outmoded and did not, for example, permit a consideration of the cultural or natural heritage of an area. This is in marked contrast to the wider designation criteria adopted in Scotland under the National Parks (Scotland) Act 2000, which requires Scottish Natural Heritage to have regard to a range of wider environmental criteria when putting proposals to the Scottish ministers for national park designations in Scotland. These include the need to conserve and enhance the natural and cultural heritage of an area, to

[197] S. 5(2) and (2A), amended by s. 59 Natural Environment and Rural Communities Act 2006. In Wales the Countryside Council for Wales' powers are exercised under s. 130(1) and Schedule 8 Environmental Protection Act 1990.

[198] For the background to the development of the IUCN categorization principles see A. Gillespie, *Protected Areas in International Environmental Law* (Leiden, 2007) at 29–32.

[199] CBD, COP7 decision VII/28 Protected Areas. The IUCN classification organizes protected areas into six categories and was adopted at the 7th Conference of the parties to the Convention on Biological Diversity in 2004.

[200] See the objectives for National Parks set out in s. 5(1) National Parks and Access to the Countryside Act 1949, as amended by s. 59 Natural Environment and Rural Communities Act 2006.

[201] S. 5(2) Natural Environment and Rural Communities Act 2006.

promote sustainable use of natural resources in the area, and the desirability of promoting understanding and enjoyment of the area by the public.[202]

The designation criteria applicable in England and Wales were widened by the Natural Environment etc Act 2006[203] to require Natural England to take into account an area's wildlife and cultural heritage when assessing its 'natural beauty'. In relation to the second criterion—the opportunity for open air recreation afforded by the park—it had been held in litigation arising from the designation of the New Forest National Park in 2002[204] that there must be more than a 'speculative possibility' that the public would be able to enjoy rights of access to land proposed for inclusion in a national park. Land over which there were no public rights of way, in relation to which the estate owners had declared an intention not to permit more than occasional permissive access for special occasions, and which was not open access land,[205] could not therefore be included in a designation order.[206] The second criterion was also extended by the 2006 Act to require Natural England in future to take into account the extent to which 'it is possible to promote opportunities for the understanding and enjoyment of [the area's] special qualities by the public'.[207] Whether this new formulation removes the problem adverted to in the New Forest litigation—that an absence of public rights of way renders it impermissible to consider that an area presents the 'possibility' for open air recreation—has been judicially doubted.[208]

Designation orders must be confirmed by the minister before taking effect. The Conservation Body must also make recommendations to the minister[209] as to the enhancement and preservation of the area's natural beauty. Before making a designation order the Conservation Body must consult every local authority whose area includes land to be designated a national park.[210] Detailed provisions as to the making, confirmation, and variation of designation orders are set out in Schedule 1 to the 1949 Act. These provide for the publication of draft designation proposals in the Gazette, two national newspapers, and one local newspaper, and the holding of public inquiries to consider objections. Each national park is administered by a national park authority, which holds full planning and development control powers

[202] S. 1 National Parks (Scotland) Act 2000.

[203] S. 59(1) Natural Environment and Rural Communities Act 2006, adding a new s. 5(2A) to the National Parks and Access to the Countryside Act 1949.

[204] *Meyrick Estate Management Ltd v Secretary of State for the Environment Food and Rural Affairs* [2005] EWHC 2618 (Admin); [2007] EWCA Civ 53.

[205] Ie not access land under s. 2 and Schedule 4 Countryside and Rights of Way Act 2000.

[206] *Meyrick Estate Management Ltd v Secretary of State for the Environment Food and Rural Affairs* [2005] EWHC 2618 (Admin) (Sullivan J.); upheld by Court of Appeal at [2007] EWCA Civ 53.

[207] S. 5(2A)(b) National Parks and Access to the Countryside Act 1949, added by s. 59(1) NERCA 2006.

[208] See *Meyrick Estate Management Ltd v Secretary of State for the Environment Food and Rural Affairs* [2007] EWCA Civ 53, judgment at para. 57 (Chadwick LJ.): 'it is far from self evident that the lacuna would no longer exist.... the question [under the extended s. 5(2)(b)] would be whether the inspector had explained how it is possible to promote opportunities for the understanding and enjoyment of the area's special qualities by the public in the absence of public access'.

[209] Under s. 6 National Parks and Access to the Countryside Act 1949.

[210] S. 7 National Parks and Access to the Countryside Act 1949, as amended by s. 60(2) Natural Environment and Rural Communities Act 2006.

within the park, and has power to take all actions that are expedient to attain the objectives for which the park was established.[211]

The principal means by which the parks' objectives are pursued is through the establishment of a development plan in each case, and the imposition of special development control rules in national parks. Permitted development rights are restricted in national parks, necessitating an application for planning permission to the park authority for a wider range of activities than would otherwise by the case. In other cases permitted rights are not withdrawn, but must be exercised with prior consultation with the park authority; for example, before the erection, extension, and alteration of buildings, or the formation or alteration of private rights of way, in a national park.[212] Many of the authority's planning powers require consultation with the Conservation Body (Natural England or CCW) prior to being exercised. Additionally, the Wildlife and Countryside Act 1981[213] gives each park authority power to give financial assistance by way of grant or loan in order to fund expenditure which is conducive to the enhancement of the natural beauty of a national park and its enjoyment by the public. Conditions can be imposed on financial aid, including terms making provision for repayment in certain circumstances.

These powers can be used to promote nature conservation, within a national park, alongside public access and recreation. The protection of habitats can also be pursued through the use of protective orders to prevent some kinds of intensive agricultural activity. The 1981 Act[214] confers on the minister power to impose additional restrictions on the carrying out of agricultural operations on land which comprises moor and/or heath within a designated national park. This power is exercisable by order. If an order is made under this provision it will become a criminal offence to plough, or otherwise convert into agricultural land, any land which is moor and heath and which has not been agricultural land within the preceding 20 years.[215] It is also an offence under the 1981 Act to carry out, on such land, other agricultural operations 'which appear to the minister likely to affect the character or appearance of the land', and which are for that reason specified in an order. This power is intended to protect important semi-natural landscape features. The law does not apply an absolute prohibition on land conversion, however. It imposes a statutory consultation period (of 12 months) if the landowner gives notice of his wish to plough or convert land, and within this period it remains

211 S. 63 Environment Act 1995. As to which, see Chapter 2, p. 48.

212 See arts. 1(5) and 1(6) Town and Country Planning Permitted Development Order 1995, restricting permitted rights for enlargement of dwellings and industrial units. For agricultural permitted development rights in this context see C. Rodgers, *Agricultural Law* 3rd edn (Tottel Publishing, 2008) at 12.49 ff.

213 See s. 44 Wildlife and Countryside Act 1981.

214 S. 42 Wildlife and Countryside Act 1981.

215 S. 42(2) Wildlife and Countryside Act 1981. The use of land for rough grazing (a common land use in upland areas of moor and heath) is not 'agricultural land' for this purpose and does not therefore disapply the power to restrict ploughing and conversion (see s. 52(1) Wildlife and Countryside Act 1981).

unlawful to initiate the project.[216] Once 12 months have elapsed it ceases to be a criminal offence to carry out the conversion project in question, however. This is intended to give the national park authority time in which to negotiate a land management agreement with the landowner to protect its landscape and amenity value. In some respects, therefore, this power closely resembles the controls on land use imposed by the notification of OLDSIs in SSSIs (p. 84).

The power to make orders to protect moor land is of less direct utility since the introduction of general rules, applicable both within and outside national parks, that require an environmental impact assessment and permission before a project to convert semi-natural land to intensive agricultural use can be undertaken. All conversion projects will be screened, and if a screening decision suggests that it would be likely to have significant environmental effects, then an EIA must be carried out through a bespoke administrative consent procedure administered by Natural England, the Scottish Government Rural Payments and Inspections Directorate (SGRPID), and the Welsh Assembly Government.[217] Where an order to protect moor or heath has been made, as described earlier, it will also be necessary to obtain permission from the national park authority.

Areas of Outstanding Natural Beauty

Like national parks, Areas of Outstanding Natural Beauty (AONBs) are designated for reasons of landscape protection and not nature conservation per se. Nevertheless, the conservation of the natural beauty of an area designated as an AONB will include the conservation of its fauna, flora, and geological and physiographical features, and they therefore play an important role in complementing the protection given to high nature value areas such as SSSIs, many of which will be situated in AONBs.

AONBs were originally designated by the Countryside Commission under the National Parks and Access to the Countryside Act 1949.[218] Under the 1949 Act control of environmental policy in AONBs lay largely with local authorities, and was conducted through the medium of planning control. The law governing AONBs was recast by the Countryside & Rights of Way Act 2000 and considerably strengthened. Natural England and the Countryside Council for Wales[219] can designate an area of land which is of Outstanding Natural Beauty, but not in a national park, as an AONB for the purpose of conserving and enhancing the natural beauty of the area. Before making a designation order, they must consult every local authority whose area includes any part of the area to which the proposed AONB order relates, and the draft order must be published in the London Gazette

[216] See s. 42(3) and (4) Wildlife and Countryside Act 1981.

[217] The Environmental Impact Assessment (Agriculture) (England) (No. 2) Regulations 2006, SI 2006/2522; Environmental Impact Assessment (Agriculture) (Scotland) Regulations 2006, SSI/2006/582.

[218] S. 87 National Parks and Access to the Countryside Act 1949.

[219] S. 82 Countryside and Rights of Way Act 2000.

and in one or more local newspapers circulating in the area. The order must be confirmed by the Secretary of State (in the case of an AONB in England) or by the National Assembly for Wales (where the order is made by the Countryside Council for Wales in relation to land in Wales). Local authorities enjoy the same powers as national park authorities in relation to national parks, and the 1949 Act[220] gives the local planning authority power to make by-laws to protect land in an AONB. This is supplemented by the Countryside, etc. Act 2000[221] which gives any local planning authority whose area consists of or includes the whole or any part of an AONB power to take all such action as appears to them expedient for the accomplishment of the purpose of conserving and enhancing the natural beauty of the area of the AONB or so much of it as is included in their area. The Countryside and Rights of Way Act 2000[222] places a general duty on any Minister of the Crown, any public body (including local authorities), any statutory undertaker, or any person holding public office to have regard to the purpose of conserving and enhancing the natural beauty of an AONB when exercising or performing any functions in relation to land in the area.

The principal innovation introduced by the Countryside and Rights of Way Act 2000 was the introduction of powers to establish Conservation Boards for AONBs.[223] Where a conservation board is established, it must within two years prepare and publish a management plan formulating its policy for the management of the AONB and for the carrying out of its functions in relation to it. Where no conservation board has been established, the management plan must be prepared by all relevant local authorities in respect of each AONB[224] and set out its policy for the management of the AONB and for the carrying out of its functions in relation to it. Where a management plan is already in existence, a conservation board or relevant local authority can review it and adopt the plan as reviewed as their AONB management plan. A statutory duty of consultation is applied,[225] requiring the local authority and/or conservation board to take into consideration any observations made by statutory consultees. Where they are proposing to publish, adopt, or review an AONB management plan under these provisions, the conservation board or local authority must give notice to the statutory Conservation Body; that is, either Natural England or the Countryside Council for Wales. They must also give notice to every local authority whose area is wholly or partly contained within the AONB of its intention to review and adopt the management plan. The Secretary of State (as respects England) and the

220 S. 90 National Parks and Access to the Countryside Act 1949.

221 S. 84(4) Countryside and Rights of Way Act 2000.

222 S. 85 Countryside and Rights of Way Act 2000.

223 Under provisions in s. 86 of the 2000 Act conservation boards can be established by the Secretary of State (in England) and the National Assembly for Wales (in Wales). Conservation Boards can be established in relation to existing AONBs, or in relation to new AONBs upon designation. The constitution and establishment of Conservation Boards is considered in Chapter 2, pp. 49–50.

224 See s. 89 Countryside and Rights of Way Act 2000. This must have been done before the end of three years following the commencement of the 2000 Act or within three years of the date on which the area is designated an AONB.

225 See s. 90 Countryside and Rights of Way Act 2000.

National Assembly for Wales (as respects Wales) have power to make grants to a conservation board on such terms as they think fit.[226]

The principal impact on land use of an AONB is through tighter planning controls, and in this sense they bear similarities with national parks (pp. 107–8). A range of permitted development rights are withdrawn in AONBs, principally for industrial and residential development.[227] This means that the exercise of these development rights will necessitate an application for planning permission to the local planning authority, and the AONB management plan will be a material factor in considering whether or not permission should be granted. There are however, fewer restrictions on agricultural and forestry operations than there are in national parks.

[226] S. 91 Countryside and Rights of Way Act 2000.

[227] AONBs are 'Art. 1(5) land' within the meaning of the Town and Country Planning Permitted Development Order 1995.

4

Natural Habitats: Management

Introduction

It was noted in Chapter 1 that environmental policy on nature conservation has moved since 1981 from a position of almost exclusive reliance on the voluntary principle, by which landowners were encouraged to participate in conservation work by financial and other incentives, to a 'partnership' approach, where the delivery of nature conservation is viewed as a joint enterprise between the Conservation Bodies, landowners, and the public.[1] The continuing tension between voluntarism and partnership approaches is most clearly seen in the law governing habitat management. The law seeks to maintain a balance between the public interest in promoting nature conservation and protecting the private property rights of landowners. The way in which this balance is drawn has changed markedly since the Wildlife and Countryside Act 1981.

The overall approach to habitat management remains primarily one of voluntarism, but the balance drawn in the law has shifted since 1981 towards the protection of biodiversity and paying landowners for positive conservation work—for recreating and restoring habitats, and not just protecting existing natural features from destruction and damage. This can be seen in the way that the legal and economic instruments available to govern and shape habitat management have changed—often subtly—as a consequence of legislation enacted since the Wildlife and Countryside Act 1981, especially in the Countryside and Rights of Way Act 2000 and the Natural Environment and Rural Communities Act 2006. The emphasis in the modern law is still on the voluntary participation of landowners in conservation management, and the use of land management agreements with landowners remains the primary mechanism deployed to achieve this. But the regulatory framework within which the negotiation of management agreements takes place has fundamentally changed. Natural England and the other Conservation Bodies now enjoy extensive powers to protect the natural features of protected areas such as SSSIs and SACs. These stem primarily from the notification of OLDSIs that cannot be carried out in protected sites without prior consultation with the Conservation Bodies.[2] But the Conservation Bodies rarely use their regulatory powers, and their significance lies primarily in the parameters they establish for the negotiation of consensual management by landowners. If a satisfactory management agreement

[1] See Chapter 1, p. 7. [2] See Chapter 3, pp. 84 ff.

cannot be obtained for the protection of a high nature-value site, then the Conservation Body has sufficient regulatory powers to protect the site from damage and neglect, but securing its positive management is an altogether more challenging proposition. This cannot be achieved through regulatory means alone. It requires an approach based on the modification of the landowner's property rights under a management agreement, in which property rights are traded for economic benefit in return for obligations as to positive land management, or under a management scheme established under the 1981 Act (as amended) if a suitable land management agreement cannot be concluded. Similarly, the economic framework within which landowners make decisions on land management with environmental implications has shifted markedly. This can be seen, especially, in the 2003 reforms to the Common Agricultural Policy of the EU, and the introduction of 'cross-compliance' attaching environmental protection conditions to the subsidies paid to farmers.

Many of the instruments available to the Conservation Bodies and other public agencies today are the same as those in place in 1981—the use of criminal sanctions, land management agreements, planning law, and economic instruments such as farm subsidies and rural development schemes. But their objectives, design, and application have changed radically in the last 20 years as environmental policy has moved strongly in favour of encouraging positive habitat management, and away from the 'protectionist' stance of the Wildlife and Countryside Act 1981 as originally conceived.[3]

Management Agreements

(a) Sites of special scientific interest (SSSIs)

Natural England and the other Conservation Bodies have power to enter into management agreements on land in a notified SSSI.[4] A management agreement will commonly be offered, for example, where the owner has notified the Conservation Body of his intention to carry out an operation likely to damage the site's conservation interest, contrary to the site notification.[5] In practice, the formal procedures for the notification by landowners of their intention to carry out OLDSIs are rarely used. Negotiations over operations in SSSIs that do not require planning consent are usually conducted informally, and will frequently result in a negotiated settlement, whereby the operation may be carried out in modified form agreed with the Conservation Body, or under a management agreement with them that also preserves the site's natural features.[6] The power to offer a management

[3] For an interesting review of the development of legal instruments for habitat management up to the passage of the Countryside and Rights of Way Act 2000 see K. Last, 'Mechanism for Environmental Regulation—Study of Habitat Conservation', in A. Ross (ed.), *Environment and Regulation* (Hulme Papers on Public Policy, vol. 8, Edinburgh, 2000), pp. 38–61.

[4] S. 15 Countryside Act 1968.

[5] See Chapter 3, pp. 84 ff.

[6] See C. Rodgers and J. Bishop, *Management Agreements for Promoting Nature Conservation* (RICS, 1998), esp. Ch. 2; L. Livingstone, J. Rowan-Robinson and R. Cunningham, *Management Agreements*

agreement is not, however, confined to this situation, and the Conservation Body may offer an agreement (and the owner may seek one) at any time. When concluded, a management agreement in England and Wales will be a local land charge, and in Scotland may be lodged in the Register of Sasines.

The power to offer management agreements was widened by the 2000 Act to enable the Conservation Bodies to offer agreements to the owner or occupier of other land, whether or not adjacent to the SSSI, if this is necessary for the protection of the conservation features of the site.[7] This power might be useful, for example, where conservation management is needed on farmland near, but not adjacent to, a notified SSSI in order to fully protect the wildlife habitat on the notified site. Indeed, treating SSSIs as isolated pockets of special interest will not necessarily address all the factors that may impair the achievement or maintenance of their favourable conservation status. Guidance from DEFRA to the Conservation Bodies has therefore suggested that they should use their enhanced powers to offer management agreements outside the confines of an SSSI to address with landowners not only activities within an SSSI itself but on their adjoining land. This can be used to develop a 'whole farm' approach to the management of both SSSI and non-SSSI land within an agricultural holding, for example, and in the case of wetland habitats can be used to address the management of the whole hydrology unit[8] so as to maximize the benefits to the protected area.

Natural England and the Countryside Council for Wales use these powers to operate environmental land management schemes in SSSIs aimed at fostering positive land management to improve and restore the rural environment. In England this is exemplified by the Wildlife Enhancement Scheme (WES) operated by Natural England, under which grant payments for a variety of positive management obligations are made. WES is based on a 'whole farm plan' management strategy and is available on SSSI land in England. Payments are made for a variety of positive management obligations, including for example restoring drystone walls and vernacular buildings, and for targeting specific conservation objectives that cannot be achieved through other means. Agreements under WES are often used to 'cushion' specific conservation interests in an SSSI, in addition to agri-environment agreements with farmers that deliver more general conservation management of the land and habitat. An example of the combined use of management agreements entered into under SSSI legislation and agri-environment schemes to deliver an integrated approach to conservation management is given in Box 4.2 (heather regeneration in Eskdale Cumbria) on p. 135.

for Nature Conservation in Scotland (Aberdeen, 1990); and generally, A. Ross and J. Rowan-Robinson, 'Behind Closed Doors: the use of agreements in the UK to protect the environment' (1999) 1 Env L Rev 82.

[7] S. 15(2) Countryside Act 1968, amended by s. 75(3) Countryside and Rights of Way Act 2000. This power was previously limited to land adjacent to the SSSI in question.

[8] See *Sites of Special Scientific interest: Encouraging Positive Partnerships* (code of guidance) (DEFRA, 2003) at para. 28. Made under s. 33 Wildlife and Countryside Act 1981. Available at: <http://archive.defra.gov.uk/rural/documents/protected/sssi-code.pdf>.

(b) Refusal of capital grant

Where a landowner applies for a capital grant[9] he can in some circumstances compel the offer of an agreement if the application is refused on conservation grounds after objections by the Conservation Body or a National Park Authority.[10] When considering an application for capital grant for agricultural operations on land within an SSSI, the minister has a duty to further the conservation of flora, fauna, geological, and physiographical features of the site.[11] If the Conservation Body objects to the making of a grant, the minister cannot make financial aid available without first considering the terms of their objection. Similarly, where land is within a national park, the National Park Authority has power to object to the making of a capital grant for improvements, in which event the minister will have to consider their objections before making a decision.[12] If the application is refused as a consequence of these objections, the relevant Conservation Body (or National Park Authority, as the case may be) must, within three months of receiving notice of refusal, offer the landowner a management agreement. This must make provision for restrictions on the activities in respect of which the grant was refused on conservation grounds, and make payments to the applicant(s).[13]

(c) European sites

Where land is in a 'European site' (for example, a special area of conservation or special protection area) the Conservation Body may enter into a management agreement with a person who has an interest in land forming part of, or adjacent to, the site.[14] This can be for the management, conservation, restoration, or protection of the site (or any part of it) and can impose obligations in respect of the use of the land, restrictions on the exercise of rights over it, and require the carrying out of such work as is expedient for the purposes of the agreement.[15] The management agreement will, in practice, be closely focused to the achievement and maintenance of the favourable conservation status of the site's natural features, and this will be reflected in the site management statement served when the site was originally notified.

Management agreements in 'European sites' may therefore contain land management obligations of both a restrictive and positive nature. Indeed, it is envisaged that agreements should make provision for the *restoration*, and not merely for the protection, of European wildlife sites. Where the ownership of the land affected subsequently changes, covenants of a positive nature would not normally run

[9] Under s. 29 Agriculture Act 1970, eg to carry out land improvements.
[10] S. 32(2) Wildlife and Countryside Act 1981.
[11] S. 32(1) Wildlife and Countryside Act 1981.
[12] See ss. 39(5) and 41 Wildlife and Countryside Act 1981.
[13] Ss. 32(2) and 41(4) Wildlife and Countryside Act 1981.
[14] Reg. 16 Conservation of Habitats and Species Regulations 2010, SI 2010/490. On European sites see Chapter 6, p. 217.
[15] Reg. 16(2) Conservation of Habitats and Species Regulations 2010, SI 2010/490.

with the land and be binding on successive owners.[16] It is expressly provided, however, that a management agreement is binding on persons deriving title under or from the person with whom the Conservation Body made the agreement, and that it will be enforceable by them against those persons.[17] The effect of this is to annex the benefit of the agreement to the Conservation Body, enabling them to enforce both its positive and restrictive terms against a subsequent owner of the site or any part of it.

(d) Nature reserves

Where the Conservation Bodies consider it would be in the national interest that land should be managed as a nature reserve, they have power to conclude management agreements with the owner, lessee, or occupier of the land to secure this objective.[18] The property nexus is very evident in the use of management agreements in nature reserves; management agreements are intended to limit the exercise of legal rights over the land, whether of land use or otherwise, and the agreement can, therefore, impose such conditions as seem expedient on the exercise of rights over the land by the landowner or other occupier. The conditions which may be included in a management agreement include provision for the management of the land in such manner, and the doing of such work, etc. as seem expedient for the purposes of the agreement, and it can provide for the cost of performing the agreement to be defrayed by the Conservation Body or the owner or occupier, or partly by each party.[19] Similarly, the agreement may make other provision as to the making of payments by the Conservation Body, and the payment of compensation for the effect of restrictions, as may be specified in the agreement. The management agreement provisions are supplemented by powers of compulsory purchase exercisable where the Conservation Body cannot conclude a satisfactory agreement, or where a landowner is in breach of the terms of a management agreement into which it had previously entered.[20] The use of management agreements with landowners is supplemented by the ability of the Conservation Bodies to make by-laws, which can restrict the activities of third parties other than the landowner or occupier of the land in question.[21]

(e) General powers—Natural England

The Natural Environment and Rural Communities Act 2006[22] gave Natural England a general power to enter into management agreements with any person 'who has an interest in land about the management of that land'. It can exercise this

[16] The rule in *Tulk v Moxhay* (1848) 2 Ph 774.
[17] See reg. 16(4) Conservation of Habitats and Species Regulations 2010, SI 2010/490.
[18] S. 16 National Parks and Access to the Countryside Act 1949.
[19] See s. 16(3) National Parks and Access to the Countryside Act 1949.
[20] Ss. 17 and 18 National Parks and Access to the Countryside Act 1949.
[21] As to which, see Chapter 3, p. 101.
[22] S. 7 Natural Environment and Rural Communities Act 2006.

power in any situation where it appears to it to further its general purpose to further sustainable development.[23] This general power is not limited to land in SSSIs or other protected areas. It could be used to secure a management agreement on land contiguous to an SSSI in order to protect natural features on the protected site from activities that may impact upon the protected habitat; for example, to prevent water drainage which may have an impact upon the water level in a wetland habitat. Or it may be used to secure agreement in cases where no implications for protected sites are involved.

(f) General powers—local authorities

Local authorities enjoy a general power to enter into management agreements for the purpose of conserving and enhancing the natural beauty or amenity of land which is in the countryside and within their area, or for promoting its enjoyment by the public.[24] This power enables them to conclude an agreement with 'any person having an interest in the land' concerned (for example, a tenant or a freehold owner) and is exercisable irrespective of whether the land is within an SSSI or any other area given protection by statutory designation. Local authorities also have a general duty[25] to have regard in the exercise of their functions to the desirability of conserving the natural beauty and amenity of the countryside. A management agreement concluded under these powers can impose restrictions on the methods used to cultivate the land, on its use for agricultural purposes, or the exercise of rights over the land. It may also impose obligations on the owner or other occupier to carry out works or land management operations. Additionally, a management agreement can also give the planning authority itself power to carry out the works necessary to the performance of its functions under the National Parks and Access to the Countryside Act 1949 and the Countryside Act 1968. It may also contain such incidental and consequential provisions as appear necessary or expedient for the purposes of a management agreement; for example, making provision for payments to the owner or occupier of the land.[26] These powers are used to underpin the management of local nature reserves.

Payments under Management Agreements

The basis on which payments to landowners under management agreements was calculated was, until 2001, governed by a Department of the Environment circular issued shortly after the passage of the Wildlife and Countryside Act 1981.[27] Following the introduction of new rules for the protection of SSSIs by the

[23] As set out in s. 1 Natural Environment and Rural Communities Act 2006.
[24] S. 39 Wildlife and Countryside Act 1981.
[25] Under s. 11 Countryside Act 1968.
[26] See s. 39(2) Wildlife and Countryside Act 1981.
[27] *Financial Guidelines for Management Agreements under the Wildlife and Countryside Act 1981.* DETR Circular 4/83.

Countryside and Rights of Way Act 2000 this was replaced by new guidance, the *Guidelines on Management Agreement Payments and related matters* (DETR 2001) ('the 2001 Financial Guidelines'). The 2001 Financial Guidelines were a key element in changing the 'protectionist' philosophy of the Wildlife and Countryside Act 1981, and are strongly premised on the need to move away from 'buying out' damaging land use proposals, and towards paying landowners for positive conservation work on SSSIs. The development of a public conservation-goods model for management agreements in protected sites is one of the most important legacies of the 2000 Act and the 2001 Guidelines.

The 2001 Financial Guidelines have statutory effect in relation to management agreements entered into in three situations:[28]

(i) In an SSSI where the Conservation Body has been notified of an intention to carry out an OLDSI[29] and offers a management agreement to prevent damage to the site;

(ii) In an SSSI, national park, or other designated area, where farm capital grant has been refused because of an objection on conservation grounds, and

(iii) Where the Conservation Body has undertaken to voluntarily apply the guidelines whenever other types of capital grant have been refused.[30]

Additionally, payments made to landowners in European sites will be governed by the guidance, where they are offered an agreement having given notice of their intention to carry out a potentially damaging operation, or where they have been refused a capital grant because of objections from the Conservation Body.[31]

(a) 'Net Profits Foregone'—the 1983 Guidelines

Under the arrangements originally introduced for management agreements in 1983 (the 1983 Financial Guidelines)[32] payments under an agreement could take two forms—either annual payments based on the net profit foregone by the landowner as a consequence of being unable to proceed with operations notified as damaging to the conservation interest of the site,[33] or a lump-sum payment reflecting the loss in capital value of the land subject to the SSSI restrictions in return for an agreement extending over a 20-year period.[34] Annual payments were the norm under management agreements concluded under the 1983 Guidelines, and agree-

[28] See s. 50(1) Wildlife and Countryside Act 1981.

[29] As to which, see Chapter 3, p. 84.

[30] See s. 32(2) Wildlife and Countryside Act 1981.

[31] See reg.18 Conservation of Habitats and Species Regulations 2010, SI 2010/490.

[32] 'Wildlife and Countryside Act 1981—Financial Guidelines for Management Agreements', Department of the Environment Circular 04/83.

[33] 'Wildlife and Countryside Act 1981—Financial Guidelines for Management Agreements', Department of the Environment Circular 04/83, paras. 16–18.

[34] 'Wildlife and Countryside Act 1981—Financial Guidelines for Management Agreements', Department of the Environment Circular 04/83, para. 14.

ments were individually negotiated by the Conservation Body and landowner in each case. If agreement could not be reached it was referable to arbitration by a single arbitrator. The transaction costs involved in securing an agreement were therefore high, especially as the Conservation Body was obliged to pay the reasonable professional costs incurred by the landowner in negotiating the agreement.[35]

The 1983 Financial Guidelines gave a considerable amount of guidance as to how the 'net profit foregone' as a consequence of a proposed management agreement was to be calculated, but were judicially criticized as overly prescriptive in matters of valuation detail, unfocused, and poorly drafted.[36] They were also controversial, as they were premised on the notion that landowners were entitled to undertake unrestricted land use operations and activities, however environmentally damaging these might be, unless their property rights were 'bought out' by the public Conservation Bodies in return for payment.[37] The net result, often, was that management agreements were offered to preserve the *status quo ante*, an approach that involved committing considerable public resources to fund the preservation of the natural features of SSSIs, but without any tangible gain in terms of the restoration, improvement, or creation of natural habitats as a result of the public investment made over the period of the agreement.[38] It was also alleged that the level of compensation that could be obtained under management agreements was so high that it was forcing up the value of SSSI land over which agreements might be made, thereby making it more expensive for the Conservation Bodies to ultimately use their compulsory purchase powers to acquire sites on which agreements could not be concluded.[39]

The model of property rights reflected in the 1983 Financial Guidelines was one which stressed the absolute prerogative of the property owner to determine how the land resource was to be used, and in which no implicit restraint based on a duty of environmental stewardship was recognized. The absence of any element of environmental stewardship as an attribute of property rights was, furthermore, reinforced by judicial interpretation of the guidelines, which explicitly recognized and reinforced the landowner's prerogative in matters of land use. This can be seen most clearly in *Thomas v Countryside Council for Wales*,[40] discussed in Box 4.1 on p. 120 below.

[35] 'Wildlife and Countryside Act 1981—Financial Guidelines for Management Agreements', Department of the Environment Circular 04/83, para. 29.

[36] See *Thomas v Countryside Council for Wales* (1994) 4 All ER 853, in which Rougier J. criticized the drafting of para. 11 of the 1983 Guidelines ('Minimising Losses') as 'earning few prizes for drafting'.

[37] See eg M. Shoard, 'The Wildlife and Countryside Act and the Development of a Conservation Protection Racket' in *This Land is Our Land* (Gaia, 1997) at pp. 364 ff.

[38] See *Cameron v Nature Conservancy Council* 1991 SLT (Lands Tribunal) 85 and *Thomas v Countryside Council for Wales* (above n.36) for examples of large awards under management agreements conclude under the 1983 Guidelines. In the *Cameron* case, the Scottish Lands Tribunal awarded £555,000.

[39] See M. Shoard, *This Land is Our Land* (Gaia, 1997) at 374, and the examples given at 374–7.

[40] [1994] 4 All ER 853.

(b) Reform—the 2001 Financial Guidelines

Revised Financial Guidelines were introduced in 2001 following the reforms to the SSSI legislation introduced by the Countryside and Rights of Way Act 2000.[41] The 2001 Guidelines provide that where the conservation interest of an SSSI or European site is not being maintained, or where it is subject to inappropriate management, the Conservation Bodies can offer a management agreement with payments in return for positive conservation measures; that is, operations or measures that the land manager would not normally undertake for economic reasons.[42] The agreement offered by Natural England will normally be a Wildlife Enhancement Scheme agreement with a standard payment menu for positive capital works and annual payments. However, the 2001 Guidelines also require that, when calculating payments, reference will be made to the income foregone by the owner/occupier, as well as the costs incurred by him in implementing positive management.

The chief difference between this approach and the 'net profit foregone' calculation under of the 1983 Guidelines is that the income foregone is now used to calculate the standard annual payment regime to be offered by the Conservation Body under a Wildlife Enhancement Scheme agreement, rather than as the basis of an individual management agreement negotiation in each case. The change of emphasis in the role of 'income foregone' reflects the fact that the incentive payment offered under a positive agreement is often derived by looking at the net profit foregone by the owner as a consequence of the changes in land management agreed, although other factors may also be present; for example, additional payments for capital works.[43] Where a positive agreement is concluded under a scheme such as the Wildlife Enhancement Scheme, with a standard payment menu for positive capital works and annual payments, the distinction is more clearly drawn, although here, also, it is to some extent artificial, as the 'menu' of standard incentive payments will initially be calculated by taking account of participants' potential losses of income. Under the 2001 Financial Guidelines, positive agreements under schemes such as the Wildlife Enhancement agreements are the norm.

The 2001 Guidelines, together with the enhanced powers of the Conservation Body to refuse consent to OLDSIs,[44] represented a fundamental shift in the underlying attributes of property rights in SSSIs. The notion that a landowner has an unrestricted *right* to exploit property—irrespective of the environmental damage that this might cause—has been replaced by a regulatory approach that stresses environmental responsibility as an integral component of property rights. This has also been reflected in a marked shift in judicial attitudes to property rights in SSSIs (see Box 4.1).

[41] See *Guidelines on Management Agreement Payments and other related matters* (DEFRA 2001). Available at: <http://archive.defra.gov.uk/rural/documents/protected/sssi-payments.pdf>.

[42] *Guidelines on Management Agreement Payments and other related matters* (DEFRA 2001), paras. 1.2 and 2.1.

[43] See Rodgers and Bishop (1998), Chs. 2 and 3.

[44] See Chapter 3, pp. 84 ff.

Box 4.1 Management Agreements—Shifting Judicial Interpretations of Property Rights and Environmental Stewardship

The basis for calculating the 'net profit foregone' to be compensated by a management agreement was considered in 1994 in *Thomas v Countryside Council for Wales*. CCW sought a reduction in Thomas' sheep flock grazing a sensitive clifftop habitat, and refused to give their consent to an increase in his flock. They produced a management plan and draft agreement, in which payments were calculated by reference to an optimum farm management plan that maximized its income taking into account the SSSI conditions and OLDSIs. Instead of implementing the optimum management plan, Thomas drastically reduced his sheep flock and converted much of his farm to arable crops. This resulted in a greater loss of profit, and consequently a much larger claim for 'net profits foregone' under the 1983 Financial Guidelines. The High Court quashed an arbitrator's decision that calculated the compensation on the basis of CCW's optimum farm management plan. In doing so, Rougier J. gave an expansive interpretation of the property owner's right to manage his land without interference. He accepted that landowners must mitigate their losses, and could therefore only claim compensation if they acted reasonably. But he gave a wide interpretation to what would be considered 'reasonable', and stressed the right of the property owner to manage his land as he wished.

'Was the claimants' decision to adopt the farming system which they did a reasonable one? That question is not to be answered solely in terms of the commercial optimum. Profitability is a factor... but any test of reasonableness should take account of other circumstances including personal factors of amenity, even of aesthetic preference.'

Compare this with the following statement by Neuberger LJ. in 2004 *in R (Trailer and Marina (Leven) Ltd) v Secretary of State and English Nature.*

'the consequence of... the 2000 Act [has] been to... reduce, sometimes substantially, the income which could be obtained from activities on an SSSI, and consequently its market value.... The public benefit enjoyed as a result of the 2000 Act will, in the absence of any compensation provisions, have been at the expense of the owners and occupiers of SSSIs. However, given the purpose and genesis of the legislation... that cannot... justify an argument that there has been an infringement of the rights of the owner of an SSSI whose value has been substantially diminished as a result of the amendments effected by the 2000 Act.'

In *Thomas*, CCW had to pay enhanced compensation under the 1983 Guidelines to reflect the additional losses generated by the 'aesthetic' preference of the farmer in adopting an unprofitable farming system. Under the 2001 Guidelines, he would have received nothing, unless he undertook positive management of the habitat protected by the SSSI notification. Can it be claimed, therefore, that the judges have, in the human rights cases since 2001, recognized a responsibility of environmental stewardship as an attribute of property rights?

The way in which the 2001 Guidelines have been implemented by the Conservation Bodies has been challenged under the Human Rights Act 1998 on the basis that they infringe the protection of property rights from arbitrary and disproportionate state interference guaranteed by article 1 of the Protocol to the ECHR. In

R (Trailer and Marina (Leven) Ltd) v Secretary of State and English Nature[45] the owners of an SSSI challenged the manner in which the 2001 Guidelines had been applied, and in particular the way in which the formula under which compensation was payable on the basis of net profits foregone had been replaced under the transitional provisions in the 2000 Act. The SSSI in this case was a shallow, slow-moving canal with a number of aquatic plant species of international importance. The site notification restricted dredging operations and the owners were unable to reopen the canal for commercial use. They had previously negotiated a five-year management agreement with English Nature in 1997, under which they were paid £19,000 a year for managing the canal in accordance with a management plan which envisaged a limited number of fishing pegs and restricted boating to the occupants of a trailer park adjacent to the canal. English Nature subsequently withdrew the payment of annual compensation from the negotiations for a new agreement, and offered terms with greatly reduced payments for the conservation management of the canal. It was alleged by the claimants that the combined effect of the 2000 Act and the 2001 Financial Guidelines had reduced the value of their interest in the canal to virtually nil.

The Court of Appeal rejected the claim, holding that the amended 1981 Act was not vulnerable to the accusation of inherent incompatibility with article 1, and that the statutory management provisions in SSSIs did not amount to a disguised appropriation of ownership. Having reviewed the case law of the European Court of Human Rights, the court concluded that this was a control of land use situation—and not disguised expropriation—and that the test to be applied was essentially subjective. Provided the state *could properly take the view* that the benefit to the community outweighed detriment to the individual, a fair balance would be struck without the requirement to compensate the landowner.[46] Having regard to the purpose of the legislation, and to the safeguards applied by the Act to protect landowners where operational consent for OLDSIs was sought, the benefit to be achieved by the amendments made by the 2000 Act—although achieved at the expense of the owners and occupiers of SSSIs—could not justify the argument that they were inherently incompatible with the right to property protected by article 1 of the Protocol to the Convention.[47] Although the scheme of the 2000 Act was held to be Convention compliant, however, the Court of Appeal indicated that there could be individual cases in which, if the 2001 Guidelines were construed so as to exclude compensation for restrictions on property rights, this could amount to an unlawful act by the Conservation Body.[48] In other words, the Conservation Body must consider each case on its merits, and in particular consider whether the land use controls imposed by the SSSI notification and list of OLDSIs are such that compensation is required to render the impact on property rights proportionate to the public interest to be achieved.

[45] [2004] EWHC 153 (Admin); [2004] EWCA Civ 1580.
[46] [2004] EWCA Civ 1580 judgment at para. 62 (Neuberger LJ.).
[47] [2004] EWCA Civ 1580 judgment at para. 71 (Neuberger LJ.).
[48] [2004] EWCA Civ 1580 judgment at para. 70 (Neuberger LJ.).

Economic Instruments for Conservation Management

(a) The Common Agricultural Policy

The British countryside is extensively farmed, and the types of agricultural practice used to produce food have an important impact on farmland biodiversity, and on the conservation of habitats and wild species of bird, animal, and plant. The close relationship between agriculture and the state of our natural heritage can be seen in, for example, the proportion of protected sites in which damage is attributable to unsuitable agricultural practices, such as overgrazing by livestock and the draining of wetland habitats. Farming—and the manner in which it is conducted—is heavily conditioned by the complex system of financial subsidies and subventions that are paid to producers under the EUs Common Agricultural Policy (CAP), and changes in agricultural support therefore have a potentially major impact on nature conservation.

The CAP has been responsible for increasing food production in Europe, but this has been achieved by the use of ever more intensive farming methods, and by the use of large volumes of pesticides herbicides and fertilizers—with damaging impacts on water quality, increased soil and air pollution, and damage to farmland biodiversity. The need to reorientate agricultural policy away from a focus on intensive production, and towards integrating environmental protection considerations, was increasingly recognized from the early 1980s, and the emerging changes in CAP policy thereafter were shaped by two factors: (i) the 1987 Single European Act, which added new articles to the EC Treaty to give environmental protection a legal basis as one of the objectives of the Community, and made the integration of environmental protection requirements into the operation of all European policies, including agriculture, obligatory, and (ii) the need to reconfigure subsidy arrangements in the negotiations for a new WTO Agreement on Agriculture.[49]

The first stage in bringing environmental concerns into the operation of the CAP came with the 1992 CAP reform. This included the introduction of the 'Agri Environment Regulation',[50] which required the member states to draw up national schemes to promote farming methods that reduced the polluting impacts of agriculture and addressed land uses that are compatible with the protection of the environment and natural resources. The 1992 regulation also made co-financing for agri-environment schemes available from Community funds. The environmental reforms were closely associated at this stage with market and supply-side management, and environmental requirements were also introduced into some of the common market organizations for agricultural products within the CAP. The payment of arable subsidies was reformed, for example, to require the compulsory

[49] See C. P. Rodgers, 'Environmental Policy and the Reform of European Agricultural Law', Chapter 11 in M. N. Cardwell, M. R. Grossman, and C. P. Rodgers (eds), *Agriculture and International Trade: Law, Policy and the WTO* (CAB International, 2003), Ch. 11.

[50] Council Regulation 2078/92, [1992] OJ L21585.

set aside of land from production, and its management for environmentally beneficial purposes. This involved introducing a new technique of environmental regulation into the CAP ('cross compliance') making the receipt of arable and some livestock subsidies conditional upon the observance of basic environmental safeguards. The set aside scheme required farmers to put 10 per cent of their arable land aside from production and, in addition to basic environmental conditions, manage it in accordance with one of several management options that targeted, for example, the, production of wildbird cover or field margins.[51] Until its abolition following the CAP 'Health Check' in 2008, the set aside scheme delivered significant environmental benefits,[52] and its abolition has led to a significant reduction in the proportion of land not under cultivation for arable crops. Cross-compliance conditions were also attached to payments to sheep and beef producers to tackle damage arising from overgrazing and the use of unsuitable supplementary feeding techniques to feed animals.[53]

The second stage in realigning European agricultural policy with environmental protection concerns came with the Agenda 2000 reform programme. The Agenda 2000 reform was agreed in Berlin in March 1999 and ushered in a period of fundamental change in CAP support regimes, signalling a shift in financial support away from production subsidies and towards producers. The reforms were extended by the Mid-term Review of Agenda 2000, agreed in June 2003.[54] Farm subsidy payments were substantially 'decoupled' from production under the Mid Term Review proposals, and switched decisively towards providing income support for producers. Following the Mid Term Review, most direct payments to farmers were reconfigured under the 'single farm payment' (SFP) implemented from 1 January 2005, explicitly as a form of 'income support'.[55] The transfer of farm support from product to producer had started with the 1992 reforms, and Agenda 2000 represented a 'deepening and extending [of] the 1992

[51] Council Regulation 1765/92 [1992] OJ L181/12, and Arable Area Payment Regulations 1995, SI 1995/1738 (esp. Schedules 1 and 2). See generally C. Rodgers, 'Environmental Gain, Set-aside and the Implementation of EU Agricultural Reform in the United Kingdom', in Rodgers (ed.), *Nature Conservation and Countryside Law* (University of Wales Press, 1996), Ch. 5.

[52] See *Farming and the Environment: Final Report of Sir Don Curry's High Level Set Aside Group* (DEFRA 2008). Available at: <http://archive.defra.gov.uk/foodfarm/policy/sustainfarmfood/documents/hlsag-report080722.pdf>.

[53] See the Sheep Annual Premium Regulations 1992, SI 1992/2677; Beef Special Premium Regulations 1993, SI 1993/1734; Suckler Cow Premium Regulations 1993, SI 1993/1441; and the Hill Livestock Compensatory Allowances Regulations 1994, SI 1994/2740.

[54] It was envisaged that the main effect of the Mid-term Review would be upon the milk-quota system, on the basis that a decision would be taken to end milk quotas by 2006. Yet, in the event, the milk-quota system was one of the few areas of the Common Agricultural Policy that remained relatively undisturbed; milk quotas surviving until at least 31 March 2015: Council Regulation 1788/2003, OJ 2003 L270/123, and art.1. These rules are now contained in Council Regulation 73/2009, [2009] OJ L30/16.

[55] By Council Regulation 1782/2003 establishing common rules for direct support schemes under the Common Agricultural Policy and establishing certain support schemes for farmers [2003] OJ L270/1. See Council Regulation 73/2009, [2009] OJ L30/16, art. 1.

reform through further shifts from price support to direct payments'.[56] This was, in turn, intended to remove the incentive to greater intensification generated by production linked subsidies.[57]

The Agenda 2000 reforms and their Mid Term Review were driven in part by the need to reach agreement in the WTO for a new agreement to replace the Uruguay Round Agreement on Agriculture concluded in 1994.[58] The Mid-term Review marked the third, and arguably most important, phase in the reorientation of the CAP towards incorporating environmental concerns. It reconfigured the direct payments regime[59] by bringing most domestic support schemes within a new and simpler farm support regime based upon the single farm payment. The SFP is intended to be production neutral, in that a farmer does not receive payment differentiated according to the crop or other agricultural product produced. It is also claimed that the 'decoupled' support permits a more effective response to market signals. Although the 'decoupling' of support from production is the key attribute of the SFP, its definition remains elusive, and there are conceptual problems in arriving at a working definition.[60] A distinction can, for example, be drawn between 'fully decoupled' support and 'effectively decoupled' support. There remains a question whether the SFP implements 'effective' decoupling, as is arguably required by the WTO agreement on agriculture.[61]

The SFP rolled all of the principal agricultural support schemes into one decoupled payment regime. It applies to all agricultural products included in the arable crops regime, grain legumes, seeds, beef, and sheep.[62] The system is based on the allocation of payment entitlements to each farmer. These are allocated so that each farmer is entitled to a payment entitlement per hectare. The entitlement was calculated by dividing the reference amount by the three years average number of hectares that in the reference period (2000–2002) gave

[56] European Commission, *Agenda 2000: For a Stronger and Wider Union, Bulletin of the European Union, Supplement 5/97*, COM(97)2000, Part One, III.4.

[57] *The Development and Future of the CAP*, COM(91)100, 8.

[58] A consideration of the impact of the WTO negotiations on the Agenda 200 reforms, and the potential compatibility of the CAP measures with WTO disciplines, is beyond the scope of this work. For further discussion see inter alia: M. Cardwell and C. Rodgers, 'Reforming the WTO Legal Order for Agricultural Trade: Issues for European Rural Policy in the Doha Round' (2006) 55 *ICLQ* 805–38; J. Ride, 'Under the Green Box' (2001) 35 *Journal of World Trade* 1015; A. Swinbank and R. Tranter, 'Decoupling EU Farm Support: Does the New Single Payment Scheme Fit within the Green Box?' (2005) 6 *Estey Centre Journal of International Law and Trade Policy* 47.

[59] See, generally, eg J. Moody and W. Neville, *Mid Term Review: a Practical Guide* (Burges Salmon, 2004), pp. 32–165.

[60] OECD, *Decoupling: a Conceptual Overview* (Paris: OECD, 2001), 8. See also, eg M. R. Grossman, 'Multifunctionality and Non-trade Concerns', in M. Cardwell, M. R. Grossman, and C. P. Rodgers (eds), *Agriculture and International Trade: Law, Policy and the WTO* (CAB International, 2003), p. 85.

[61] Cardwell, Grossman, and Rodgers (eds) (2003), p. 9. And see definitions of decoupling developed in S. A. Cahill, 'Calculating the Rate of Decoupling for Crops under CAP/Oilseeds Reform' (1997) 48 *Journal of Agricultural Economics* 349.

[62] For the support schemes contained within the SFP, see now the 2009 Horizontal Regulation, Council Regulation 73/2009, [2009] OJ L30/16, Annex I.

rise to the direct payments that that farmer received.[63] The reference amount was the three-year average of the total amounts of payments which the farmer was granted under the relevant support schemes in each of calendar years 2000, 2001, and 2002.[64] This calculation generated a payment entitlement based upon that farmer's historic claim during the reference period. The member states could opt to apply the single payment at a regional level,[65] and this was done in England, but not Wales.[66]

Further reforms are posited post-2013 under the 'Europe 2020' reform process, and draft regulations have been published by the European Commission.[67] These would abolish the single farm payment, but replace it with a similar subsidy that can only be claimed by farmers who have activated at least one payment entitlement in 2011. It will apply 'greening' conditions to CAP support payments, including the set aside from production of 7 per cent of land in 'ecological focus areas', including forest areas, buffer strips around arable fields, and fallow land. Cross compliance will be maintained under the new support arrangements, although the number of conditions is likely to be reduced. The final shape of these reforms is awaited, but the broad thrust of the measures will maintain the current application of the CAP measures as they have relevance to issues of natural habitat management.[68]

(b) Cross compliance and environmental management

The concept of cross compliance was first introduced into European agricultural law under the 1992 reforms; for example, in relation to arable set aside and livestock production.[69] It was radically extended in scope by the Mid Term Review from 2003, and now applies to all payments under the SFP scheme. A farmer receiving a payment under the single payment scheme must observe the 'cross-compliance' conditions established in the European legislation[70] and the domestic

[63] Council Regulation 1782/2003 establishing common rules for direct support schemes under the Common Agricultural Policy and establishing certain support schemes for farmers [2003] OJ L270/1, art. 43.1 of Council Regulation 1782/2003.

[64] Art. 37.1 of Council Regulation 1782/2003.

[65] Arts. 58 and 59 of Council Regulation 1782/2003.

[66] In England, payments on a regional basis were phased in over the period 2005–2012: see the Common Agricultural Policy Single Payment and Support Schemes Regulations 2005, SI 2005/219, Schedule 1 (the regional element rising from 10 per cent in 2005 to 100 per cent in 2012, and the historic element falling correspondingly). For a detailed consideration see Cardwell, para. 52.16 et seq. in Scammell and Densham's *Law of Agricultural Holdings* 9th edn (Williams, Supplement 2011). This is now largely of historic interest.

[67] *Proposal for a Regulation of the European Parliament and the Council establishing rules for direct payments to farmers under support schemes within the framework of the common agricultural policy*, COM (2011) 625/2 Final.

[68] See further M. Cardwell, 'European Union Agricultural Policy and Practice: The New Challenge of Climate Change', (2011) 13 Env L Rev 271.

[69] See p. 123. For a review of the introduction and extension of the concept in European Agricultural Law see B. Jack, *Agriculture and EU Environmental Law*, (Ashgate, 2009) at pp. 66–79.

[70] Ie now Council Regulation 73/2009, [2009] OJ L30/16 following the 2008 CAP Health Check.

regulations implementing them.[71] Cross compliance consists of two separate elements:

- Adherence to a number of *statutory management requirements* relating to public, animal and plant health, the environment, and animal welfare.[72] The statutory standards relate to existing European Directives such as the Wild Birds Directive of 1979, the Nitrates Directive of 1991, and the Habitats and Species Directive of 1992 and require farmers to comply with the provisions of national legislation implementing them.
- Land that is no longer used for production purposes must be maintained in *good agricultural and environmental condition* (GAEC). Each member state is required to establish minimum requirements for good agricultural and environmental condition by reference to the criteria established in the Community legal order.[73]

Although the statutory management requirements reflect management standards that are already required under European environmental law, they provide an additional enforcement mechanism to secure appropriate land management; namely, the withdrawal of subsidy (the single payment) in cases of non-compliance. The statutory management requirements and standards of GAEC that must be met by farmers in receipt of the single farm payment are set out in separate regulations for England[74] and Wales.[75] In England, the Secretary of State was designated as the competent authority for the purpose of inspection of holdings, and the application of penalties and reduction in payments arising from non-compliance with the cross-compliance conditions.[76]

[71] The Common Agricultural Policy Single Payment and Support Schemes (Cross Compliance) (England) Regulations 2010 SI 2010/540 and the Agriculture (Cross Compliance) (No. 2) Regulations 2009, SI 2009/3365 (as amended); in Wales the Common Agricultural Policy Single Payment and Support Schemes (Cross Compliance) (Wales) Regulations 2004 SI 2004/3280 (W284), as amended; in Scotland the Common Agricultural Policy Schemes (Cross Compliance) (Scotland) Regulations 2004 SSI 2004/518 as amended; and in Northern Ireland the Common Agricultural Policy Single Payment and Support Schemes (Cross Compliance) Regulations (Northern Ireland) 2005 SR 2005/6 as amended.

[72] These were originally set out in Annex III of Council Regulation 1782/2003 establishing common rules for direct support schemes under the Common Agricultural Policy and establishing certain support schemes for farmers [2003] OJ L270/1. Following the 2008 CAP Health Check they are now set out in Council Regulation 73/2009, [2009] OJ L30/16, art. 4 and Annex II.

[73] Council Reg. (EC) 73/2009 art. 6 and Annex III. The criteria set out in Annex III relate to the prevention of soil erosion, maintenance of soil organic content and soil structure, and ensuring a minimum level of maintenance in order to avoid the deterioration of habitats. The 2008 CAP Health Check added a requirement that water management issues should also be addressed in standards of good agricultural and environmental condition.

[74] Agriculture (Cross Compliance) (No. 2) Regulations 2009, SI 2009/3365, reg. 3 and Schedule 1 (as amended by SI 2010/2941).

[75] Ie the Common Agricultural Policy Single Payment and Support Schemes (Cross Compliance) (Wales) Regulations 2004 SI 2004/3280 (W284), as amended, Schedule.

[76] Agriculture (Cross Compliance) (No. 2) Regulations 2009, SI 2009/3365, reg. 2.This function is carried out by the Rural Payments Agency. In Wales these functions can be administered by either the Environment Agency or the Countryside Council for Wales: the Common Agricultural Policy Single Payment and Support Schemes (Cross Compliance) (Wales) Regulations 2004 SI 2004/3280 (W284), as amended, reg. 6.

Several of the cross-compliance conditions that are applied to receipt of the single payment in England and Wales underpin environmental management for nature conservation. These include conditions relating to:

- *Overgrazing and unsuitable supplementary feeding.*[77] The Secretary of State can give a farmer written directions concerning the management of land which is in her opinion subject to overgrazing or the use of unsuitable supplementary feeding methods. 'Overgrazing' means grazing with so many livestock as to adversely affect the growth, quality, or diversity of any self-seeded or self-propagated vegetation characteristic of the area in which the land is situated.[78] 'Unsuitable supplementary feeding methods' include feeding livestock in a way that adversely affects the quality or diversity of any self-seeded or self-propagated vegetation characteristic of the area in which the land is situated.[79] In Wales, supplementary feeding must not be undertaken within 10 metres of a watercourse, and the feeding site must be regularly rotated.[80]
- *Protection of hedgerows and watercourses.* Several cross compliance conditions apply to protect hedgerows and watercourses. In England a farmer must not cultivate, or apply fertilizers or pesticides to land within 2 metres of the centre of a hedgerow and land which is covered by, forms the bank of, or is within 1 metre of the top of the bank of a watercourse or field ditch.[81] And a farmer must not remove a hedgerow in breach of the legislation protecting hedgerows.[82]
- *Environmental Impact Assessment.*[83] A farmer must not carry out a project to convert uncultivated land to intensive agricultural use, or to restructure the boundaries of a holding, without first obtaining a screening decision from

[77] Agriculture (Cross Compliance) (No. 2) Regulations 2009, SI 2009/3365, reg. 3 and Schedule 1 para. 3; Common Agricultural Policy Single Payment and Support Schemes (Cross Compliance) (Wales) Regulations 2004, SI 2004/3280, reg. 4 and Schedule para. 6.

[78] Agriculture (Cross Compliance) (No. 2) Regulations 2009, SI 2009/3365, reg. 3 and Schedule 1 para. 3(2). In Wales over-grazing is defined slightly differently, to mean grazing with so many livestock that the growth, quality, or diversity of natural or semi-natural vegetation is adversely affected. Semi-natural vegetation means any self-seeded or self-propagated vegetation characteristic of the area in which the land is situated: Common Agricultural Policy Single Payment and Support Schemes (Cross Compliance)(Wales) Regulations 2004, SI 2004/ 3280 reg. 4 and Schedule para. 6(3).

[79] Agriculture (Cross Compliance) (No. 2) Regulations 2009, SI 2009/3365, reg. 3 and Schedule 1 para. 3 (2); Common Agricultural Policy Single Payment and Support Schemes (Cross Compliance) (Wales) Regulations 2004, SI 2004/ 3280 reg. 4 and Schedule para. 6(3).

[80] Common Agricultural Policy Single Payment and Support Schemes (Cross Compliance)(Wales) Regulations 2004, SI 2004/ 3280 reg. 4 and Schedule para. 6(2)(d).

[81] Agriculture (Cross Compliance) (No. 2) Regulations 2009, SI 2009/3365, reg. 3 and Schedule 1 paras. 7 and 8.

[82] Ie the Hedgerow Regulations 1997 SI 1997/1160. See generally the Agriculture (Cross Compliance) (No. 2) Regulations 2009, SI 2009/3365, reg. 3 and Schedule 1 paras. 8 and 9; Common Agricultural Policy Single Payment and Support Schemes (Cross Compliance)(Wales) Regulations 2004, SI 2004/ 3280, reg. 4 and Schedule paras. 11, 12.

[83] Agriculture (Cross Compliance) (No. 2) Regulations 2009, SI 2009/3365, reg. 3 and Schedule 1 para. 1.

DEFRA[84] as to whether an environmental impact assessment will be required, or without a decision granting consent for the project.[85] Neither must he breach a stop notice or, without reasonable excuse, fail to comply with any requirement of a reinstatement notice served on him under the relevant regulations.[86]

- *Sites of Special Scientific Interest.*[87] Several cross-compliance conditions apply to protect SSSIs notified under the Wildlife and Countryside Act 1981.[88] A farmer must not carry out an OLDSI[89] in breach of the requirements of the 1981 Act. And he must not, without reasonable excuse, intentionally or recklessly destroy or damage any of the flora, fauna, or geological or physiographical features by reason of which that land is of special scientific interest, or intentionally or recklessly disturb any of that fauna.[90] This condition is wider than the controls imposed by the 1981 Act, and applies to prevent damage to an SSSI whether caused by potentially damaging operations notified in the site notification or otherwise.
- *Tree preservation orders.*[91] A farmer must not breach a tree preservation order,[92] and must comply with the provisions protecting trees in conservation areas.[93]

The Community legislation lays down penalties to be applied in cases of breach of the cross-compliance conditions. The penalties depend upon whether the breach was intentional or negligent. In the case of a first incident of intentional non-compliance, as a general rule 20 per cent of the payments made to the farmer should be deducted or withdrawn.[94] In cases of repeat infringements, the penalty can be increased to 100 per cent of all direct payments and can include exclusion from one or more aid schemes for one or more calendar years any one year. If the

[84] Or in Wales from the minister: see Common Agricultural Policy Single Payment and Support Schemes (Cross Compliance)(Wales) Regulations 2004, SI 2004/ 3280 reg. 4 and Schedule para. 14(1).

[85] Environmental Impact Assessment for projects involving the conversion of semi-natural areas to intensive agricultural use, and for the restructuring of holdings, is governed by the Environmental Impact Assessment (Agriculture)(England)(No. 2) Regulations 2006, SI 2006/2522.

[86] Agriculture (Cross Compliance) (No. 2) Regulations 2009, SI 2009/3365, reg. 3 and Schedule 1 para. 1; Common Agricultural Policy Single Payment and Support Schemes (Cross Compliance) (Wales) Regulations 2004, SI 2004/ 3280 reg. 4 and Schedule para. 14(4).

[87] Agriculture (Cross Compliance) (No. 2) Regulations 2009, SI 2009/3365, reg. 3, and Schedule1 para. 1; Common Agricultural Policy Single Payment and Support Schemes (Cross Compliance) (Wales) Regulations 2004, SI 2004/ 3280, Schedule para. 21.

[88] As to which, see Chapter 3, pp. 68 ff.

[89] Ie an operation likely to damage the conservation interest of the site: see Chapter 3, p. 84.

[90] Agriculture (Cross Compliance) (No. 2) Regulations 2009, SI 2009/3365, reg. 3, Schedule 1 para. 1; Common Agricultural Policy Single Payment and Support Schemes (Cross Compliance) (Wales) Regulations 2004, SI 2004/ 3280, Schedule para. 18(1).

[91] Agriculture (Cross Compliance) (No. 2) Regulations 2009, SI 2009/3365, reg. 3, Schedule 1 para. 1; Common Agricultural Policy Single Payment and Support Schemes (Cross Compliance) (Wales) Regulations 2004, SI 2004/ 3280, Schedule para. 22.

[92] Ie an order made under s. 198(1) Town and Country Planning Act 1990.

[93] See s. 211 Town and Country Planning Act 1990.

[94] See art. 24.3 Council Regulation 73/2009 OJ L30/16 18.2.2009.

breach was due to negligence, the penalty may be reduced to a minimum of 1 per cent or raised to a 5 per cent deduction from the single payment for that calendar year. In the case of repeated negligent infringements the penalty can be increased to 15 per cent.[95]

(c) Cross compliance, property rights, and the 'polluter pays' principle

Advocates of cross compliance stress its flexibility and potential, not only for linking financial support for farm production with environmental safeguards, but also for promoting the uptake of voluntary environmental schemes. In the US, where the concept originated in the 1970s,[96] three variants of the concept have been prominent in policy development. Under 'red ticket' or mandatory cross compliance, eligibility for certain agricultural support benefits is made contingent upon a farmers adherence to prefaced environmental land management standards. A 'green ticket' approach, on the other hand, offers enhanced direct support payments where the farmer voluntarily subscribes to a certified environmental management scheme. An 'orange ticket' approach combines both elements—mandatory obligation and voluntary incentives—by making eligibility for direct farm support conditional upon a farmer entering an otherwise voluntary incentive scheme. The existence of agri-environment schemes financed under the EC Rural Development Regulation,[97] together with direct support in the form of the single farm payment, meant that any of the three variants of cross compliance could (in theory) have been adopted by the Agenda 2000 and subsequent reforms to the CAP.[98] In the event, the cross-compliance rules applied through the single farm payment regulations are based squarely on a 'red ticket' approach, making the receipt of direct support mandatorily conditional upon the adherence of the producer to the basic statutory management requirements outlined earlier.

Cross compliance in this form has inherent limitations. As a tool of environmental management it is dependent upon the farmer applying for, and being granted, direct support; the single farm payment. It is therefore dependent upon the market for its efficacy and application; if market conditions dictate that farmers can produce food profitably without subsidy it will lose its relevance.[99] And opting

[95] Art. 24.2 Council Regulation 73/2009 OJ L30/16 18.2.2009. This is reached by multiplying the penalty by up to three; after a third infringement, future infringements are treated as intentional.

[96] For the development of cross compliance see B. Jack, *Agriculture and EU Environmental Law*, (Ashgate, 2009) at pp. 67–8; D. Baldock and K. Mitchell, *Cross Compliance within the Common Agricultural Policy: a review of options or landscape and nature conservation* (IEEP, 1995); M. R. Grossman, 'Good Agricultural Practice in the US: Conservation and Climate' (2011) 13 Env L Rev 296, 3026 ff.

[97] As to which, see pp. 131 ff.

[98] See J. Dwyer, D. Baldock, and S. Einschutz, *Cross Compliance under the Common Agricultural Policy—a report for the Department of the Environment Transport and the Regions* (IEEP, 2000).

[99] In practice, of course, this is an unlikely eventuality: see M. Cardwell, 'The Polluter Pays Principle in European Community Law and its Impact on UK Farmers' (2006) 59 *Oklahoma Law Review* 89–113 at 109; C. P. Rodgers, 'Agenda 2000, Land Use and the Environment: Towards a Theory of Environmental Property Rights' in Holder and Harrison (eds), *Law and Geography* (Oxford University Press, 2003) at p. 235.

for a 'red ticket' approach has meant that an opportunity to link the receipt of direct farm support to participation in agri-environmental schemes, which target more specific and extensive environmental benefits,[100] has been foregone. A more fundamental criticism, however, focuses on the nature of the conditions applied by the single payment scheme itself. The cross-compliance rules are an explicit attempt to apply the 'polluter pays' principle of EC environmental law to agriculture.[101] The statutory management requirements are all, however, matters that farmers should in principle already be observing under European and/or domestic law. It is therefore questionable whether the cross-compliance conditions deliver additional benefits in return for public expenditure.[102] Withdrawing the single farm payment, which is funded at public expense, for infringements of environmental law is arguably not an implementation of the 'polluter pays' principle; rather, it is a case of 'not paying the polluter'. Their inclusion in the cross-compliance conditions for the SFP does, however, provide an additional mechanism for enforcing compliance with pre-existing legal obligations viz. the withdrawal or reduction of farm support payments.[103] The withdrawal of subsidy is without prejudice to any additional penalties that may be applicable under the relevant Directives and domestic implementing regulations, and these unquestionably *do* apply the polluter pays principle, including in some cases potential obligations as to the restoration of damaged natural habitats.[104] It should also be noted that the requirement to keep land in good agricultural and environmental condition is more broadly based, and applies to land that is no longer in agricultural production—and the same sanctions are imposed for breach of the requirement to maintain land in GAEC.

A further aspect of the introduction of cross compliance (and one of particular relevance to the theme of this work) is its impact upon property rights. The original Agenda 2000 reform was explicitly based upon the assumption, given legal effect in the implementing regulations, that farmers should be obliged to perform basic environmental management obligations as an attribute of property rights:

> *The philosophy underpinning the environmental aspects of the CAP reform is that farmers should be expected to observe basic environmental standards without compensation. However, where society demands that farmers deliver an environmental service beyond the base line level, this service should be specifically purchased through the agri-environment measures.*[105]

This assumption sits uneasily with traditional common law notions of property, which do not recognize implicit limitations on the owner's rights of exploitation

[100] See pp. 131 ff.

[101] Art. 174 (2) TEU; 6th Community Environmental Action Programme, Decision 1600/2002 of the European Parliament and of the Council, 2002 OJ L 242/1. And see generally M. Cardwell, 'The Polluter Pays Principle in European Community Law and its Impact on UK Farmers' (2006) 59 *Oklahoma Law Review* 89–113.

[102] See, eg House of Commons Environment, Food and Rural Affairs Committee, *The Mid-term Review of the Common Agricultural Policy*, Third Report of Session 2002–03, HC 151, paras. 52, 76 ff.

[103] See Council Regulation 73/2009, arts. 6–7.

[104] As to which, see eg the Conservation of Habitat and Species Regulations 2010, SI 2010/690, Chapter 6, pp. 230–231, (implementing the requirements of the EC Habitats and Species Directive 1992).

[105] *Directions Towards Sustainable Agriculture*, COM (1999) 22 final, at para. 3.2.1.

and land use.[106] The difficulty, of course, is to define the 'base line' of environmental management that will be recognized as inherent in property rights, and the argument might be made that the Agenda 2000 reforms placed the obligations at too low a level in the cross-compliance conditions that were attached to the SFP. Future reforms to the CAP, under the *Europe 2020 Strategy*,[107] could lead to a more refined approach. The European Commission document *The CAP towards 2020*[108] posits the enhancement of environmental performance by the CAP, through a mandatory 'greening' component of direct payments by supporting environmental measures across the whole of the EU.[109] These could take the form of 'simple, generalised, non-contractual and annual environmental actions that go beyond cross compliance and are linked to agriculture; for example, permanent pasture, green cover, crop rotation, and "ecological" set aside'. The inclusion of the requirements of *Natura 2000* areas[110] in this 'green' element of the direct support regime is also proposed.[111]

Agri-Environment Schemes

Agri-Environment Schemes (hereafter 'AES') are funded by the Rural Development Programmes for England, Wales, and Scotland under Pillar 2 of the EU Common Agricultural Policy.[112] They offer farmers and landowners management agreements on a voluntary basis for environmental land management, and are an important land management instrument, both in complementing the land management targeted in SSSIs and other protected sites through management agreements under the nature conservation legislation,[113] and also in delivering sympathetic conservation management in the wider countryside. The earliest AES was the Environmentally Sensitive Areas ('ESA') programme, originally introduced in 1987 and substantially expanded after the 1992 reform to the CAP. This operated in geographically distinct areas, designated as Environmentally Sensitive Areas by the minister. ESA policy was an attempt to counteract the damaging

[106] See Chapter 1, pp. 25–6, and for an exploration of the impact of CAP reform on environmental property rights theory see C. P. Rodgers (2003) in Holder and Harrison (eds) *Law and Geography* (Oxford University Press, 2003).

[107] European Commission, *Europe 202: a Strategy for smart sustainable and inclusive growth*, COM (2010) 202 final (3.3.2010).

[108] EU Commission, *The CAP towards 2020: meeting the food, natural resources and territorial challenges of the future*, Communication for the Commission to the European Parliament, the Council, European Economic and Social Committee and the Committee of the Regions, COM (2010) 672 Final.

[109] See *Proposal for a Regulation of the European Parliament and the Council establishing rules for direct payments to farmers under support schemes within the framework of the common agricultural policy*, COM (2011) 625/2 Final.

[110] Ie sites designated under the Habitats Directive—see Chapter 6, pp. 209 ff.

[111] See COM (2010) 672 Final (see n. 103) at 8–9.

[112] See C. P. Rodgers, 'Rural Development Policy and Environmental Protection: Reorienting English Law for a Multifunctional Agriculture' (2009) 14 *Drake Jo. of Agricultural Law* 259–89; M. N. Cardwell, *The European Model of Agriculture* (Oxford University Press, 2004) 227–34.

[113] Pp. 112 ff.

impacts of intensive farming encouraged by the market subsidy policies pursued under what is now Pillar 1 (market management) of the CAP. ESA was complemented by the Countryside Stewardship scheme, which operated in England outside the ESA areas. The ESA and Countryside Stewardship programmes closed to new entrants in 2005, and have been superseded by a more widely based scheme in England (Environmental Stewardship) and by distinct schemes in Scotland and Wales. In 2009 there were over 58,000 AES agreements in England, of which 7639 were ESA agreements and 11,749 Countryside Stewardship agreements entered into prior to 2005; 33,367 were Environmental Stewardship agreements; and 3344 were Higher Level Stewardship agreements.[114] This means that 66 per cent of the utilized agricultural land area in England is being managed under AES agreements.[115] AES are administered in England by Natural England. In Scotland and Wales they are administered by the devolved administrations.

(a) Environmentally Sensitive Areas

The minister[116] has power, by statutory instrument, to designate an area of land an 'Environmentally Sensitive Area'[117] if he considers that the adoption of a particular agricultural method is likely to facilitate the conservation and enhancement of the natural beauty of an area, or the conservation of the flora, fauna, geological/physiographical features of an area, or the protection of buildings or other objects of archaeological, architectural or historical interest in that area. The ESA programme was therefore broadly based, taking in not only nature conservation interests, but also archaeology and historical features that could be preserved through the adoption of sympathetic farming techniques. The introduction of the scheme in 1986 was attributable to the UK using a facility in EC farm structures legislation to provide funding for environmental farming techniques.[118] The scheme was subsequently financed under the Rural Development Regulation with co-financing under Pillar 2 of the CAP.[119]

The designation of an area as an ESA did not alter the property rights of landowners. Its chief impact was to make available management agreements within the ESA under which farmers could adopt prescribed management practices in return for payment. This form of designation was very different to the notification of land as an SSSI or SAC, where the notification varies the property rights of landowners by imposing a consultation requirement for certain land use operations.[120] Where land had been designated an ESA the minister was able to enter

[114] See *Agri-Environment Schemes in England: a review of results and effectiveness* (Natural England 2009), at page 30: available at <http://www.naturalengland.org.uk/Images/AE-schemes09_tcm6-14969.pdf>, esp. Figure 10 at 28.

[115] *Agri-Environment Schemes in England: a review of results and effectiveness* (Natural England, 2009), Figure 13 at 30.

[116] Ie the Secretary of State for Environment Food and Rural affairs (DEFRA) or (in Wales) the Secretary of State for Wales.

[117] Ss. 18(1) and 18(2) Agriculture Act 1986.

[118] Council Regulation 797/85, art. 1 [1985] OJ L93 p. 1, 4.

[119] Now Council Regulation 1698/2005, [2005] OJ L277 p. 1.

[120] Chapter 3, pp. 84 ff. Chapter 6, pp. 220 ff.

into a management agreement wherever it appeared to him that any of the ESA's conservation purposes were likely to be facilitated by him doing so.[121] The ESA scheme was therefore firmly based on the voluntary principle and no provision was made for compelling appropriate land management to protect environmental features; this provides a clear contrast to, for example, the residual power of compulsion exercisable by Management Orders where a site has been designated an SSSI.[122]

The first generation of Environmentally Sensitive Area (ESA) agreements in England and Wales were based on a standard contractual model. Standardized and inflexible management prescriptions were applied to all participating farms in each ESA, with prescriptions appropriate for the type of farming predominant in each area. A more sophisticated approach was adopted in the second and third generation of ESA agreements from 1992, which combined participation in a basic tier of obligations with optional additional (or higher) 'tiers' of participation under which extra premiums could be paid for allowing public access to farmland or for additional environmental obligations targeted at particular habitat types. This was essentially a more sophisticated variant of the standardized or 'general' contractual model, in which prescriptions were targeted at particular ESA areas[123] rather than at individual farms and farm-based habitats.[124]

In the final phase of the programme, until its closure to new entrants in 2005, there were 22 ESAs in England:

Stage 1 ESAs: The Broads, Pennine dales, Somerset Levels and Moors, South Downs, and West Penwith.[125]
Stage 2 ESAs: Breckland, Clun, North Peak, Suffolk River valleys, and Test Valley.[126]
Stage 3 ESAs: Avon Valley, Exmoor, The Lake District, North Kent marshes, South Wessex Downs, and the South West Peak.[127]
Stage 4 ESAs: Blackdown Hills, Cotswold Hills, Dartmoor, Essex Coast, Shropshire Hills, and the Upper Thames Tributaries.[128]

Policy and payments within each ESA were subject to five-yearly review. The Secretary of State had wide power to enter into management agreements with farmers in the designated ESAs and terms of the management agreements in each ESA are specified in the relevant designation orders.[129] These provided both for capital payments and for annual payments for maintenance of the

[121] See s. 18(3) Agriculture Act 1986.
[122] See p. 96.
[123] Some of which were geographically very large, such as the Cambrian Mountains ESA in Wales: see the Environmentally Sensitive Areas (Cambrian Mountains—extension) Designation Order 1987, SI 1987/2026.
[124] See M. Whitby, (ed.), *Incentives for Countryside Management: the Case of Environmentally Sensitive Areas* (CABI 1994), esp. Chs. 10 (Colman) and 11 (Whitby).
[125] Environmentally Sensitive Areas (Stage I) Designation Order 2000 SI 2000/3049.
[126] Environmentally Sensitive Areas (Stage II) Designation Order 2000 SI 2000/3050.
[127] Environmentally Sensitive Areas (Stage III) Designation Order 2000 SI 2000/3051.
[128] Environmentally Sensitive Areas (Stage IV) Designation Order 2000 SI 2000/3052.
[129] S. 18(3) Agriculture Act 1986.

land using traditional farming methods. The capital activities to be carried out by the farmer would be specified in a capital works plan incorporated into the management agreement; for example, the recreation of herb-rich meadows, coppicing of hedges, or other works for the restoration or recreation of wildlife habitats.

The requirements for managing the land for environmental protection and for public access were also specified for each ESA in the Designation Order. These varied from one area to another, depending on the traditional nature of the husbandry practiced there and the nature of the terrain and locality. Payments were agreed up to a maximum rate per hectare laid down in each designating Order. The allowances for each management prescription reflected the importance and difficulty of modifying the participants' existing husbandry regime to accommodate the terms of the ESA agreement. Penalties were provided for the breach of a management agreement prescription.[130]

(b) Countryside Stewardship

The Countryside Stewardship scheme (CSS)[131] provided management agreements to farmers and other land managers, with land management obligations tailored to site-specific environmental issues. It also provided for the promotion of greater environmental stewardship on arable land, and included a number of arable land management options.[132]

Participation in the scheme required the preparation of a conservation plan for approval by the Secretary of State.

The scheme's objectives went beyond protecting existing environmental features, and included the recreation of new habitats or new landscape features. Each English county had target priorities set under the scheme. The scheme was aimed at protecting and enhancing priority habitats and landscape features identified in the England Rural Development Plan and in the various county programmes for the scheme. Management agreements were offered to those able to deliver environmental benefits matching the declared local priorities and those identified in the Rural Development Programme. Countryside Stewardship agreements were for 10 years, and payments were made annually on the basis of the benefits offered. Unlike other schemes in the England Rural Development Programme, Countryside Stewardship was not limited to farmers, and was open to local authorities, charities, wildlife groups, and other landowners. Grant aid could also be claimed for the preparation of whole-farm environmental audits of the land affected.[133]

[130] See reg. 6. of the England Rural Development Programme (Enforcement) Regulations 2000, SI 2000/3044, made under s. 2(2) European Communities Act 1972. The Secretary of State can withhold future payments under a management agreement where a farmer is in breach of its terms, and can also demand repayment of all monies paid under it and levy an additional penalty of up to 10 per cent of the payments made. Powers of entry to property are conferred on the Secretary of State and her officials to check and monitor performance of agreements, and to require the production of relevant documentation.

[131] See the Countryside Stewardship Regulations 2000, SI 2000/3048 as amended.

[132] See the Countryside Stewardship (Amendment) Regulations 2001, SI 2001/3991.

[133] Under the Countryside Stewardship (Amendment) Regulations 2004, SI 2004/114.

Box 4.2 Agri-environment measures and SSSI management: Scafell Pikes SSSI

Scafell Pikes is a large SSSI of 1102.2 ha lying largely within Eskdale common, a large upland area of dry sub-alpine heath in the western Lake District of England, and running up to the summit of Scafell Pike itself, the highest mountain in England. It is part of the High Fells SAC, and hosts several Annex 1 habitats under the Habitats Directive, including North Atlantic wet heath, European dry heath, alpine and boreal heath with bilberry. The Scafell Pikes SSSI was originally notified in 1965 and last re-notified in 1988. Its special conservation interest includes its extensive summit boulder field which hosts lichen-heaths, and a series of 'gills' running off the summit that host rare plant assemblages, inducing bilberry, several rare mosses, viviparous fescue, and alpine ladies mantle. Natural England's views about the management of the site stress the need to protect montane plant assemblages and encourage the regeneration of sub-alpine heather through sympathetic livestock management and grazing. Light summer grazing using sheep may be an acceptable form of management, with livestock being removed during the winter. Montane habitats, especially moss- and lichen-heaths, are vulnerable to heavy grazing, and where this has happened (as here) it may be necessary to temporarily remove grazing stock in order to allow the vegetation to recover. The SSSI was assessed as in unfavourable recovering condition in 2012.[134]

This requires a flexible approach to livestock management at different times and different locations. This cannot be delivered by the SSSI notification itself. The list of OLDSIs for Scafell Pikes SSSI[135] includes 30 operations requiring Natural England's consent—it includes ploughing or re-seeding land, introducing changes in the grazing regime for livestock (including the type of animals grazed and seasonal patterns of grazing), applying fertilizers, lime, or herbicides, introducing drainage, and using vehicles likely to disturb the flora and fauna. This can *prevent* obviously damaging land-use practices, but little more. The management sought by the SSSI notification is, in practice, delivered through the use of agri-environment agreements to target reductions in sheep grazing numbers at different times of the year, supplemented by SSSI agreements to 'cushion' the conservation interest in those areas where additional management is required. The whole of Eskdale common is in the Lake District Environmentally Sensitive Area, and was entered in a 10-year Tier 1 ESA management agreement in 1995. This required farmers to graze a maximum of 1.5 sheep per ha in summer and 1.125 per ha in winter. The ESA agreement was renewed in 2004. Farmers grazing sheep in the Scafell Pikes SSSI itself were then offered Sheep and Wildlife Enhancement Scheme Agreements to further reduce the grazing density on the SSSI to 0.8 sheep per ha. Some reduced their sheep-grazing numbers to accommodate the target, while two farmers removed their entire sheep flock from the common. It is too early to fully assess the impact of the management changes on heather and other montane vegetation, although its initial impact has been doubted.[136] When the ESA agreement expires in 2014 Natural England will seek to introduce a Higher Level Stewardship agreement on the SSSI, with mixed grazing by cows and sheep—cows have a more selective grazing pattern than sheep and will graze tall grasses and trample bracken infestations, enabling sheep to follow and graze down shorter grass and vegetation thus exposed. The property rights in the SSSI may make this difficult, as most of the land is common land with registered grazing rights for sheep only.[137]

134 See condition summary at <http://www.sssi.naturalengland.org.uk/Special/sssi/reportAction.cfm?report=sdrt13&category=S&reference=1001922>.

135 See <http://www.sssi.naturalengland.org.uk/Special/sssi/sssi_details.cfm?sssi_id=1001922> (Scafell Pikes SSSI—Operations likely to damage the conservation interest, and statement of views about management of the SSSI).

136 See J. Butler, *Interactions between ecological condition and the management of grazing rights on Eskdale Common in the Lake District National Park*, MSc Thesis, Newcastle University, September 2007.

137 See further Rodgers, Straughton, Winchester, and Pieraccini (Earthscan, 2010) at pp. 103–6.

(c) The Environmental Stewardship scheme

The Environmental Stewardship scheme replaced CSS and ESA in England in 2005, and marked a new approach to targeting and funding environmental land management. Environmental Stewardship seeks to adopt a whole farm and more 'holistic' approach to farmland biodiversity. Within the Environmental Stewardship scheme,[138] the Secretary of State can make grants for the management of land under one of four optional elements: Entry Level Stewardship (ELS), Organic Entry Level Stewardship (OELS), Higher Level Stewardship (HLS), and Upland ELS (UELS). The Secretary of State can also make a grant to any person who enters into, and complies with, the conditions of an environmental stewardship agreement.[139] The environmental stewardship agreement must require the beneficiary to carry out specified activities to further environmental protection on land in which he has an interest, and detailed prescriptions are set out in regulations governing the operation of the scheme.[140] The agreement can include elements from each of ELS, OELS, UELS, and HLS, and the conditions of each agreement can be varied by the Secretary of State either with the other party's agreement, or by notice (without agreement) where an alteration is necessary to comply with European legislation.[141]

Environmental Stewardship marked a new departure in that, while the scheme is open to all farmers, it adopts a 'bidding' model for the provision of environmental goods. Eligibility is determined by the applicant achieving the relevant points score for management undertakings under each of the four elements of the scheme.[142] Applicants must prepare a Farm Environment Record, and Natural England will set a points target for each farm dependant on its size. The scheme has 50 options (for example, hedgerow management, low input grassland, and various arable options) and entrants earn points for each option selected. If the scheme's requirements are met, and the points target satisfied, entry is guaranteed. Management agreements under ELS are for five years. Higher Level Stewardship is, on the other hand, more closely focused than entry level stewardship and targets environmental improvement in the most valuable farmland habitats and features. These include management options with annual payments for the preservation of environmentally valuable hedgerows; for the creation and maintenance of woodlands; the creation and maintenance of unfertilized conservation headlands in arable fields; and for the

[138] See the Environmental Stewardship (England) Regulations 2005, SI 2005/621, made under s. 2(2) European Communities Act 1972 and s. 98 Environment Act 1995. Amended by SI 2006/991, and see generally: <http://www.naturalengland.org.uk/ourwork/farming/funding/es/els/default.asp>.

[139] Reg. 3 SI 2005/621.

[140] Environmental Stewardship (England) Regulations 2005, SI 2005/621: basic prescriptions for ELS agreements are set out in Schedule 2 Part 2 and more advanced prescriptions for inclusion in HLS agreements in Part 3 of Schedule 2.

[141] Reg. 3(3) Environmental Stewardship (England) Regulations 2005, SI 2005/621.

[142] See reg. 5(2) (ELS), 5(3) (OELS), and also reg. 5(4) in relation to HLS obligations to be included in the agreement.

creation, restoration, and maintenance of species rich semi-natural grassland.[143] Many of these land management options offer valuable management tools for the creation and maintenance of valuable nature conservation features of the countryside.

(d) AES in Wales and Scotland

Several agri-environment schemes operate under the Wales Rural Development Plan 2007–13. *Tir Cynnal* is an entry-level scheme, while *Tir Gofal* offered a whole farm plan approach with a menu of positive obligations carrying appropriate rates of payment. Tir Gofal replaced the ESA scheme in Wales. It differed from the Wildlife Enhancement Scheme in England, in that it was not restricted to SSSIs and was available across the whole of Wales. Management agreements were for 10 years with a break clause after five years. The scheme requires participating farmers to subscribe to a mandatory schedule of farm management obligations to maintain existing habitats, and then choose from an optional range of additional land management obligations targeted at habitat restoration or creation. These were focused on the restoration of existing sites or the creation of new environmental features in four areas of concern: (i) the protection of landscape and historical features, such as traditional field boundaries, historic earthworks, or stone structures; (ii) the reduction of intense management on arable and improved land. Management options here include keeping unsprayed cereal crops, winter stubbles, and undersown spring cereals; (iii) grassland restoration such as the conversion of improved to semi-improved grassland, managing grassland for breeding lapwing or over-wintering wildfowl; and (iv) establishing new habitats and features such as new woodland, stream-side corridors, or new reed beds. The scheme also targets the creation of new permissive access to farmland.

Tir Gofal and Tir Cynnal were replaced from 2012 by a single new integrated scheme, *Glastir*.[144] *Glastir* has three elements: an all Wales entry-level element (AWE), based on a whole farm approach; a targeted element (TE) that will be available on part of a farm and targeted to delivering environmental improvements to key habitats, species, soils, and water; and a common land element aimed at delivering environmental benefits in the management of common land, of which there is a considerable amount in Wales. Management agreements will be for five years.

In Scotland, the Rural Development Contracts Land Managers Option (LMO) operates under the Scotland Rural Development Programme 2007–13.[145] The

[143] For the full list of HLS management options and payments, see s. 3.1 'Management Options and Supplements' in *Higher Level Stewardship: Environmental Stewardship Handbook* 3rd edn (Natural England, 2011 (NE227)), available at: <http://publications.naturalengland.org.uk/publication/31047?category=45001>.

[144] See <http://wales.gov.uk/topics/environmentcountryside/farmingandcountryside/farming/glastirhome/?lang=en>.

[145] See <http://www.scotland.gov.uk/Topics/farmingrural/SRDP/RuralPriorities/HowItWorks/SchemeRules>.

scheme offers participating famers 14 land management options under Axis 2, improving the environment and countryside; for example, summer cattle grazing, moorland management, biodiversity cropping on in-bye land, creation of conservation headlands, small-scale woodland creation, and woodland management. Acceptance into the scheme is based on proposals put forward by applicants, which are measured against the 'rural priorities' agreed with stakeholders for each of 11 regions within Scotland.

(e) Contractual models—impact and effectiveness

In the UK, AES have primarily been implemented using environmental contracts. It will be obvious from the outline of the various schemes given here that the design and implementation of environmental land management contracts has developed markedly since the first ESAs were introduced in 1987. The resources devoted to the instrument have also expanded dramatically since the 2003 reform of the CAP. The EC's Fifth Action Programme on the Environment originally set a target for 15 per cent of the utilized agricultural area of the Community to be under management contracts for the maintenance of natural habitats and minimizing natural risks, such as erosion, by 2000.[146] By 1997, approximately 1.35 million agreements had been concluded with farmers, covering 17 per cent of the Utilized Agricultural Area (UAA) of the EC at that time.[147] Expenditure on the agri-environment measures has now increased to a point where in the period 2007–2013 22 per cent of all expenditure on rural development measures in the European Union (just short of 20 billion Euros) will be spent on funding agri-environment measures.[148] The figures for the number of agreements in England have already been given; no less than 66 per cent of the utilized agricultural area of England was under agreements in 2009.[149]

An implementation strategy for European agri-environmental policy based upon the use of contractual instruments offers the member states considerable flexibility, and different contractual models have been used in differing member states to implement agri-environmental measures. Some, such as the *prime à l'herbe* scheme in France and the Rural Environmental Protection Scheme (REPS) in Ireland, have been based on the use of standard form agreements with prescribed terms that apply very basic requirements for environmental land management and stewardship, usually across either their whole territory, or in identified, but geographically large, zones. The effectiveness of this type of approach has been questioned, not least because it may be viewed as a socio-economic policy that effectively acts as a

[146] European Commission, *Towards Sustainability: A European Community programme of policy and action in relation to the environment and sustainable development* [1993] OJ C136/5, at 138/38.

[147] European Commission, Report from the Commission to the Council and the European Parliament on the application of Council Regulation (EEC) 2078/92 COM (97) 620 final, at 16/17.

[148] See <http://ec.europa.eu/agriculture/envir/measures/index_en.htm>.

[149] See *Agri-Environment Schemes in England: a review of results and effectiveness* (Natural England, 2009) at p. 30: available at: <http://www.naturalengland.org.uk/Images/AE-schemes09_tcm6-14969.pdf>, esp. Figure 10 at 28. See n. 115.

form of farm income support with little environmental focus.[150] The first generation of ESA agreements in England and Wales, as we have seen, was targeted at geographically designated ESA zones and was a variant of the standardized contractual model. Although a more sophisticated approach was adopted in the second and third generation of ESA agreements in the UK, this remained essentially a more sophisticated variant of the standardized or 'general' contractual model, in which prescriptions were targeted at particular ESA areas and not at individual farms and farm-based habitats.[151]

Comparisons of the effectiveness of the ESA programme with management agreements in SSSIs have concluded that the use of individually negotiated agreements in SSSIs delivers conservation management in a more cost effective manner per hectare than the use of ESA agreements.[152] A key determinant in this analysis is the fact that in the case of SSSIs, the notification mechanism delivers a base level of conservation management at nil cost through the consultation requirements for OLDSIs.[153] Viewed in another light, the property rights available to the farmer for trade in return for payment in a management agreement are restricted where the land is also an SSSI, as land use rights have been reallocated to the Conservation Body through the OLDSI mechanism.[154] It follows that any analysis of the efficacy of management agreements as an instrument for conservation management must take account of the reallocation of property rights, and the consequent reallocation of access to the land resource this represents,[155] brought about by notification of the land in question as an SSSI or SAC.[156] Where the land has *not* been notified for protection as either an SSSI or SAC, the landowner's property rights will be correspondingly amplified, whereas in the case of SSSI land they will be restricted, and the land use rights that can be included in an economic exchange will be correspondingly more limited.

The standardized approach to environmental contracts used in the ESA programme has now been superseded in the Environmental Stewardship scheme by a more sophisticated strategy based on the purchase by the state of 'environmental goods'. This facilitates the targeting of aid to projects offering the best environmental potential for the enhancement and restoration of farmland habitats and wildlife species, by requiring farmers to submit bids for contracts

150 See 'Protecting the European Environment from the Community: the case of agriculture', (Jack, 2001) 3 Env L Rev 44, esp. 55–60; and, more generally C. Potter, *Against the Grain: Agri Environmental Reform in the United States and the European Union* (CABI, 1998).

151 See M. Whitby (ed.), *Incentives for Countryside Management: the Case of Environmentally Sensitive Areas* (CABI, 1994), esp. Chs. 10 (Colman) and 11 (Whitby).

152 See M. Whitby and C. Saunders, 'Estimating the Supply of Conservation Goods in Britain; A Comparison of the Financial Efficiency of Two Policy Instruments' (1996) 72 *Land Economics* 313–25.

153 Ie s. 28E Wildlife and Countryside Act 1981. See Chapter 3, pp. 84 ff.

154 See further Box 8.1 at p. 290 below.

155 See Chapter 1, pp. 28–30.

156 See Chapter 8, at p. 290, and Box 8.1.

according to the environmental 'goods' to be purchased. The Countryside Stewardship scheme was the first agri-environment scheme in England to be implemented using this model of environmental contract, and the Environmental Stewardship scheme is also firmly based on this model. This type of approach enables the 'screening out' of cases where an agreement would offer no tangible environmental advantage,[157] limits participation to cases where a defined and measurable environmental 'good' is to be purchased by the taxpayer, and therefore represents a better use of public resources to fund agri-environment agreements.[158] The public goods model of environmental agreement also offers greater flexibility, in that management prescriptions can be tailored to the particular farm concerned, and facilitates the use of 'whole farm' plans in order to develop a holistic conservation strategy for the entire holding is increasingly common—a central feature of the Environmental Stewardship scheme in England. The reallocation of property rights in an SSSI or SAC notification remains centrally important in this context, however, as the state need not 'buy' property rights that have already been reallocated through the OLDSI mechanism to the Conservation Body; they are already, in effect, 'public' goods.

Development Control

The land use controls applied in SSSIs that were outlined in Chapter 3 apply principally where development consent is not required for damaging operations or land use. Where an operation that is likely to cause damage in an SSSI, or a change in land use, requires planning permission, then the law of town and country planning will also have a role to play. The bifurcated structure of the controls on land use applied for nature conservation is attributable to the definition of what is, and is not, considered 'development' in English planning law:

(a) If a development or land use operation is 'development' within the meaning of the Town and Country Planning legislation,[159] then planning permission will be required from the local planning authority—or National Park Authority if situated in a national park—before it can be lawfully carried out. In such cases the protection of the conservation interest will, if the development will impact upon an SSSI, be considered in the context of development control decision making.

(b) If an operation is *not* 'development' within the meaning of the planning legislation, then it will fall to be considered under the consultation procedures for OLDSIs established in the Wildlife and Countryside Act 1981.

[157] A major criticism of the first generation of ESA schemes in England, and of schemes such as *prime à l'herbe* in France: see the references in n. 150.

[158] See C. Potter, *Against the Grain: Agri Environmental Reform in the United States and the European Union* (CABI, 1998).

[159] As to which, see s. 55 (1) Town and Country Planning Act 1990.

These are considered in Chapter 3.[160] If they have not been notified as OLDSIs then no land use controls will apply. In this context, it is important to note that the use of land for agriculture and forestry is not 'development', and does not require planning permission,[161] and that agricultural and forestry operations will therefore commonly fall within the purview of the 1981 Act if carried out in SSSIs. Additionally, even where planning permission *is* required for development on agricultural land, automatic permission is granted for many minor types of agricultural development by the General Permitted Development Order.[162]

Where planning permission is required for development, a grant of permission will give a defence to any potential liability under the 1981 Act.[163] Where planning permission is required for a particular development, therefore, development control law and planning policy guidance has priority over the conservation legislation, and the planning application will provide the forum in which the conservation interest will be adjudicated upon. Planning policy now strongly supports the conservation of wildlife and landscapes.[164]

(a) Development plans

The implementation of the Habitats Directive[165] has had a major impact upon land use planning for the countryside. All local development plan documents must include policies in respect of the conservation of the natural beauty and amenity of the countryside and the landscape. The Habitats Directive requires EU member states to encourage, through their land use planning and development policies, the management of features of the landscape which are of major importance for the genetic exchange, dispersal, and migration of wild flora and fauna. Accordingly, local development plans and regional strategies must 'include policies encouraging the management of features of the landscape which are of major importance for wild flora and fauna'.[166] This is intended to ensure that consideration is given through the development control process to the protection of linear habitat features which are necessary for the migration, dispersal, and genetic exchange of wild

160 See Chapter 3, pp. 84 ff.

161 See s. 55(2) (e) and (f) Town and Country Planning Act 1990.

162 Town and Country Planning General Permitted Development Order 1995, SI 1995/418.

163 See 94 ff. and s. 28P(4) Wildlife and Countryside Act 1981, as amended by Countryside and Rights of Way Act 2000 Schedule 9.

164 For planning policy in England, see now the *National Planning Policy Framework* (Department for Communities and Local Government, 2012) paras. 109–125. This replaced Planning Policy Statement 9 *Biodiversity and Geological Conservation* (2005). Joint ODPM Circular 06/2005 and DEFRA Circular 01/2005 *Government Circular: Biodiversity and Geological Conservation—Statutory Obligations and their Impact within the Planning System* (16 August 2005) remain in force and contains detailed guidance to local planning authorities on statutory obligations. In Wales the relevant planning guidance is to be found in Technical Advice Note 5 *Nature Conservation and Planning* (2009); and in Scotland Scottish Planning Policy (2010) paras. 125 ff. and Planning Advice Note 60 *Planning for natural heritage* (2000, updated 2008).

165 Council Directive 92/EEC/43. See Chapter 6, pp. 225 ff.

166 Reg. 39 Conservation of Habitats and Species Regulations 2010, SI 2010/490.

species.[167] The features to be accommodated in plans are those which, 'by virtue of their linear or continuous structure' or their function as 'stepping stones' are essential to the migration, dispersal, and genetic exchange of wild species, features specified in the Directive within this category include rivers, field boundaries, ponds, or small woods.[168] Planning policy requires that local authorities should, when formulating their development plans, identify policies on the form and location of development that take a strategic approach to the conservation, enhancement, and restoration of biodiversity.[169] The *National Planning Policy Framework* recommends that, in order to minimize impacts on biodiversity, planning policies should plan for biodiversity at a landscape scale across local authority boundaries and also identity components of local ecological networks, including not only national and internationally designated sites but also wildlife corridors and stepping stones that connect them, and areas identified by local partnerships for habitat restoration or creation.[170]

Local authorities should, in their local development documents, indicate the location of designated sites, making clear distinctions between the hierarchy of international, national, regional and locally designated sites), and identify areas for the restoration and creation of new priority habitats which contribute to regional targets, and support the restoration and creation of habitats through appropriate policies.[171]

(b) Development control in SSSIs

The Wildlife and Countryside Act 1981 requires local authorities to take such reasonable steps as are consistent with the exercise of their functions, to further the conservation and enhancement of the special conservation features of an SSSI.[172] When granting planning permission, this would require them to consider whether it is necessary to impose planning conditions to secure the appropriate future management of the site, whether to include compliance monitoring of planning obligations, and to take such enforcement action as may be necessary.[173] If a planning authority intends to authorize or grant permission for the carrying out of operations likely to damage the special interest features of an SSSI, then it must notify Natural England before making its decision.[174] This will be so whether the development is to take place within, or

[167] This is a requirement of art. 10 HDB.

[168] Reg. 39(3) SI 2010/490.

[169] National Planning Policy Framework (DCLG 2012) para. 114.

[170] National Planning Policy Framework para. 117.

[171] National Planning Policy Framework para. 113. Further guidance is set out in Joint ODPM Circular 06/2005 and DEFRA Circular 01/2005 Government Circular: *Biodiversity and Geological Conservation—Statutory Obligations and their Impact within the Planning System* (16 August 2005).

[172] S. 28G(2) Wildlife and Countryside Act 1981, amended by Schedule 9 Countryside and Rights of Way Act 2000.

[173] See ODPM Circular 06/2005/DEFRA Circular 01/2005 at para. 60. An application for planning permission in an SSSI will also require an environmental impact assessment under the Town and Country Planning (Environmental Impact Assessment) Regulations 2011, SI 2011/1804.

[174] S. 28I Wildlife and Countryside Act 1981, amended by Schedule 9 Countryside and Rights of Way Act 2000. This would be the case, for example, where it intends to grant planning permission on

outside the boundaries of, an SSSI, in every case where the operation will impact upon the special interest of the site. Natural England then has 28 days in which to tender its advice, during which time the planning authority cannot grant planning permission or otherwise consent to the operation in question.[175] The authority must take account of Natural England's expert advice, including any suggestions as to the attaching of conditions to the permission. If they propose to give planning permission contrary to Natural England's advice they must notify the Conservation Body as to the terms of which it is proposed to grant it (including, for example, any planning conditions to be imposed) and how, if at all, it has taken the Conservation Body's advice into account. It must then allow a further period of 21 days before the operations can commence.[176] This will give Natural England time to consider its response including, if appropriate, taking legal action to challenge the validity of the planning permission.[177]

Special consultation arrangements apply before a local authority can grant planning permission for any development which is either:

- In or likely to affect an SSSI, or
- In a consultation area around an SSSI notified to the planning authority by Natural England or its predecessor English Nature, or
- In an area of particular natural sensitivity or interest which the local authority considers may be affected by development involving the siting of new establishments (or the modification of existing ones) which could have significant implications for major accident hazards, or which may increase the risk or consequences of major accidents.[178]

The Conservation Body can notify a consultation zone around an SSSI of up to 2 kilometres (km), within which it must be consulted on *any* planning application. Planning policy guidance in England also requires a consultation with Natural England where a development *is likely to affect* an SSSI, even if it is outside the notified consultation area around the site.[179] Consultation should take place as soon as possible and the local authority cannot determine a planning application that could affect an SSSI within 14 days of initiating a statutory consultation. If it proposes to give planning permission, and this will result in operations likely to damage the special interest of the site, then a longer consultation period of 28 days will apply.[180] The consultation requirements do not apply if Natural England has

application, or where it intends to authorize the exercise of permitted development rights without a full application.

175 S. 28I(4) Wildlife and Countryside Act 1981.

176 S. 28I(6) Wildlife and Countryside Act 1981.

177 For further explanation of the relevant procedures under the 1981 Act see ODPM Circular 06/2005/DEFRA Circular 01/2005 (see n. 164) paras. 62–66, and TAN 5 paras. 5.4.1 ff. (Wales).

178 Town and Country Planning (General Development Procedure) Order 1995, SI 1995/419 ('GDPO').

179 ODPM Circular06/2005/DEFRA Circular 01/2005, para. 71. This requirement applies both to consultations required by the GDPO 1995 and s. 28I Wildlife and Countryside Act 1981.

180 S. 28I Wildlife and Countryside Act 1981, as amended. For guidance, see ODPM Circular 06/2005/DEFRA Circular 01/2005 at para. 72.

advised the authority that it does not wish to be consulted or where it has provided 'standing advice' to the planning authority about specific types of planning application, of which the application is one.[181] Consultation with the Conservation Body will nevertheless be required if a planning authority proposes to give permission which will damage the special interest features of the site[182] or where it may give rise to major hazards.

The features comprising the special interest of an SSSI (and the potential impact of the development upon them) will be one of a number of 'material considerations' to be weighed when assessing an application for development consent, alongside the development plan.[183] Planning permission can be granted for an operation which has been notified as an OLDSI in the site notification.[184] If planning permission is given, this will constitute a 'reasonable excuse' for carrying it out without Natural England's consent.[185] Where an operation requires consent from both the planning authority and another public body, such as a statutory undertaker, then the permission of both must be obtained if this is to constitute a 'reasonable excuse'.[186]

If a proposed development on land within or outside an SSSI is likely to have an adverse effect on the site's special interest features, then planning guidance stresses that planning permission should *not* normally be granted.[187] This does not preclude the grant of planning permission where other material factors outweigh the conservation interest, but it signifies that special weight must be attached to the conservation interest in development control decisions. Where an adverse impact on an SSSI is likely, an exception should only be made, and permission given, where the benefits of development clearly outweigh both the impacts that it is likely to have on the features of the site that make it of special scientific interest and any broader impacts on the national network of SSSIs.[188] Where permission is granted then local authorities should use conditions and/or planning obligations to mitigate the harmful effects of the development and, where possible, to ensure the conservation and enhancement of the sites biodiversity or geological interest.

Development that may have a detrimental effect on an SSSI may in some circumstances be permitted without formal planning permission; for example,

[181] For the ability of Natural England to deliver standing advice, see ODPM Circular 06/2005/ DEFRA Circular 01/2005 at paras. 78 ff.

[182] See s. 28I Wildlife and Countryside Act 1981, as amended.

[183] See s. 70(2) Town and Country Planning Act 1990.

[184] For which see Chapter 3, pp. 84 ff.

[185] S. 28P(4) Wildlife and Countryside Act 1981 as amended. For an example, see *R v Poole B.C. ex parte BeeBee (1991) JEL 293.*

[186] S. 28P(5) Wildlife and Countryside Act 1981.

[187] *National Planning Policy Framework* (DCLG 2012) at para. 118.

[188] 'Where an adverse effect on the site's notified special interest features is likely, an exception should only be made where the benefits of the development, at this site, clearly outweigh both the impacts that it is likely to have on the features that make the site of special scientific interest and any other broader impacts on the national networks of SSSis': *National Planning Policy Framework* (DCLG 2012) para. 118.

where permission is granted by permitted development rights[189] or by a certificate of lawful development. Operations likely to damage the nature conservation interest of the site will be notified to the landowner with the SSSI site notification,[190] irrespective of whether they require planning permission. Where an OLDSI benefits from permitted development rights, the land owner has a choice: he can either apply to Natural England for operational consent,[191] or he can apply for full planning permission. If planning permission is granted it will constitute a reasonable excuse for carrying out the operation without Natural England's consent.[192] It is not necessary to request operational permission from Natural England before applying to the local planning authority for planning permission, but this may be advisable as it will be statutory consultee on the planning application and may be prepared either to give consent or negotiate a compromise that will protect the nature conservation interest of an SSSI.[193]

If development has taken place in breach of development control, the landowner can apply for a certificate of lawful development.[194] If granted by the local authority or Secretary of State this will legitimate the development for planning purposes and render it immune from enforcement action under the Town and Country Planning Act 1990. If the development is also an OLDSI, the grant of a lawful development certificate will not provide a reasonable excuse for the purposes of the Wildlife and Countryside Act 1981.[195] Even if a lawful development certificate is granted, therefore, the landowner will have committed an offence under the 1981 Act and will be vulnerable to prosecution by Natural England.

Development in European sites (SACs and SPAs notified under the European Habitats and Wild Birds Directives) is subject to more stringent restrictions than those in SSSIs. These are considered in Chapter 6.[196]

Environmental Liability

In addition to the habitat management measures already outlined, an additional element has now been added by the implementation of the Environmental Liability Directive.[197] This was to have been implemented in the member states by 30 April 2007. In the event, its requirements were only implemented in England, Wales,

[189] Ie under the Town and Country Planning (General Permitted Development) Order 1995, SI 1995/418.

[190] See Chapter 3, pp. 84 ff.

[191] See s. 28E Wildlife and Countryside Act 1981, amended by Schedule 9 Countryside and Rights of Way Act 2000.

[192] S. 28P(4) Wildlife and Countryside Act 1981.

[193] See ODPM Circular 06/2005/DEFRA Circular 01/2005, para. 75; TAN 5 para. 5.4.8 (Wales).

[194] Ss. 191–194 Town and Country Planning Act 1990.

[195] The 'reasonable excuse' exception to liability in s. 28P(4) Wildlife and Countryside Act 1981 is expressly limited to 'planning permission granted on an application under s. 28(1) Part III Town and Country Planning Act 1990' or permitted by a public authority (p. 94).

[196] See Chapter 6, pp. 225 ff.

[197] Directive 2004/35/CE of the European Parliament and of the Council on environmental liability with regard to the prevention and remedying of environmental liability, as amended by

and Scotland in 2009.[198] The Directive marks a new departure for the protection of natural resources, requiring that action is taken not only where environmental damage has already been caused to habitats and species, but also where damage is imminent. It seeks to apply the polluter pays principle to the application of liability for biodiversity damage by adopting an administrative liability approach, as explained further later, and is based on notions of public trust not dissimilar to these underpinning environmental legislation in the USA.[199]

Liability is applied by the Directive to two categories of damage: (i) 'Environmental damage' occurring as a result of occupational activities listed in Annex III to the Directive, to which a strict liability regime is applied, and (ii) 'Damage to protected species or natural habitats' to which strict liability applies if caused by occupational activities within Annex III, or to which liability based on negligence or fault applies if caused by occupational activities that are not listed in Annex III.[200]

(a) Strict liability

The Directive seeks to internalize external environmental costs by imposing strict liability for occupational activities causing environmental damage. Annex III of the Directive requires the member states to ensure that operators whose activities fall within the categories therein listed bear the cost of taking action to prevent or to clean up such environmental damage as they threaten or cause, irrespective of fault. The member states are required to establish strict liability regimes as regards administrative direction to prevent harm,[201] and to require operators to reimburse costs incurred by public bodies in undertaking remedial action.[202] The occupational activities listed in Annex III are mainly hazardous activities that are already regulated under European environmental directives, including, for example, damage arising from the operation of installations regulated under the Integrated Pollution Prevention and Control regime,[203] and environmental damage resulting from the deliberate release of Genetically Modified Organisms into the environment in accordance with the authorization procedures established under the Deliberate Releases Directive.[204]

Directive 2006/21/EC of the European Parliament and of the Council of 15 March 2006. For the consolidated text see [2006] OJ L102/15.

198 Environmental Damage (Prevention and Remediation) Regulations 2009, SI 2009/153 (England); Environmental Damage (Prevention and Remediation) (Wales) Regulations 2009, SI 2009/995 (Wales); Environmental Liability (Scotland) Regulations 2009, SSI 2009/266 (Scotland).

199 See generally E. H. P. Brans, 'Liability for Damage to Public Natural Resources under the 2004 Environmental Liability Directive' (2005) 7 Env L Rev 90–109.

200 See art. 3.1 of Directive 2004/35/EC.

201 Art. 5 Directive 2004/35/EC.

202 Art. 6 Directive 2004/35/EC.

203 Under Council Directive 96/61/EC concerning integrated pollution prevention and control [1996] OJ L257/26 and the Pollution Prevention and Control Act 1999.

204 Directive 2001/18/EC, OJ L106/1, 17.4.2001 on the Deliberate Release of GMOs into the Environment.

These activities will engage strict liability for any environmental damage they cause, even though they will have been preceded by an environmental risk assessment undertaken during the process of issuing the authorization for the activity concerned.[205] The Directive's approach to risk allocation is premised on the view that strict liability is a more efficient mechanism for internalizing costs than fault-based liability. Although widely accepted, this view has not gone without challenge.[206] Where the activity potentially attracting liability is preceded by a rigorous risk assessment (as for IPPC or authorizations for GMO releases) then it is clearly arguable that the imposition of strict liability will do little to change producer behaviour. It could also be argued that in this event the state should underwrite liability because the authorization procedures, and environmental risk assessment undertaken before the damaging activity took place, were flawed.

(b) Fault-based liability for biodiversity damage

Enhanced protection is given to protected species and natural habitats by the Environmental Liability Directive. The Directive extends the potential range of liability for biodiversity damage by providing for liability based on fault or negligence where an operator causes damage to a protected site as a result of *any* operational activity; that is, activities other than those hazardous activities in Annex 111 to which strict liability applies.[207] The widened ambit of potential liability would, for example, encompass damage to a wildlife site caused by negligent management, or by negligence in carrying out the requirements of the Habitats Directive or domestic legislation as to site management.

Fault-based liability has important limitations. It only applies to damage caused by 'operational activities'. This is defined to mean 'any activity carried out in the course of an economic activity, a business or an undertaking, irrespectively of its private or public, profit or non-profit character'.[208] Further, it must be carried out by an 'operator'; that is, someone who has control of an occupational activity or to whom 'decisive economic power over the technical functioning' of that activity has been delegated.[209] This would clearly cover activities by a farmer or contractor

[205] See Annex 111 paras. 11 and 12 of Directive 2004/35/EC on Environmental Liability. And in England reg. 5 and Schedule 2 Environmental Damage (Prevention and Remediation) Regulations 2009, SI 2009/153, listing the activities giving rise to strict liability. These include the operation of permitted installations under Directive 2008/1/EC (Integrated Pollution Prevention and Control); waste management operations (Directive 2006/12/EC); water discharges under licence (Directive 2006/11/EC); the manufacture, storage, processing, filling, or release into the environment of dangerous substances, plant protection products, or biocidal products (eg under Directive 91/414/EEC on plant protection products); and the contained use or release of GMOs to the environment (Council Directives 90/219/EEC and 2001/18/EC).

[206] See eg L. Bergkamp, 'The Commission's White Paper on Environmental Liability: A Weak Case for an EC Strict Liability Regime' (2000) EELR 105, at 108/9.

[207] Art. 3.1(b) of Directive 2004/35/EC on Environmental Liability. And see Commission of the European Communities, *White Paper on Environmental Liability*, COM (2000) 66 Final, at para. 4, p. 16.

[208] Art. 2.7 of Directive 2004/35/EC on Environmental Liability.

[209] Art. 2.6 of Directive 2004/35/EC on Environmental Liability.

working the land, but would exclude damage caused by a private trespasser or a fly-tipper, unless the latter was engaged in some kind of occupational activity at the relevant time.

The scope of the 'fault' or negligence required for liability is not defined. This is for each member state to define. The English liability regulations limit fault-based liability to cases where an operator intended to cause 'environmental damage', or was negligent as to whether environmental damage would be caused, to a protected habitat or species, or to an SSSI.[210] This will require proof of an intention to cause damage to a protected habitat or SSSI, or negligence that has this effect.[211] It is unclear whether the perpetrator must have knowledge that the habitat is an SSSI when committing the acts giving rise to the damage in question. Liability will extend to both the owner/occupier of the land, and also to third parties. The problems of establishing liability in similar circumstances under pre-existing criminal offences protecting SSSIs in English law led to the creation of a new strict liability offence by the Natural Environment and Rural Communities Act 2006; that is, one that does not require the perpetrator causing damage to its conservation features to have prior knowledge that a site is an SSSI.[212] This offence will continue to apply to protect SSSIs, and will overlap with the environmental liability regime in some contexts.

(c) 'Environmental' damage

'Environmental' damage has three possible components: it means, firstly, damage to protected species and natural habitats; secondly, water damage that significantly adversely affects the ecological, chemical, and/or quantitative status or ecological potential of the waters concerned; and thirdly, land damage, meaning any land contamination which creates a significant risk of human health being adversely affected as a result of the direct or indirect introduction in, on, or under the land of substances, preparations, or micro-organisms.[213] The Directive does not apply to damage to the person or goods, or to property damage, unless it falls within the narrow definition of 'land damage' used in the Directive, in that it creates a significant risk to human health.[214] With regard to protected species and habitats, liability only mandatorily extends[215] to damage to the conservation status of habitats and/or species that are either protected under the Wild Birds Directive

[210] See reg. 5(1) Environmental Damage (Prevention and Remediation) Regulations 2009, SI 2009/153; and reg. 4(1) ibid. (definition of environmental damage), discussed further on p. 150.

[211] This would follow from the definition of 'environmental damage' in reg. 4 of SI 2009/153, which is integral to the new offence in reg. 5 Environmental Damage (Prevention and Remediation) Regulations 2009.

[212] See s. 55(3) Natural Environment and Rural Communities Act 2006, inserting a new s. 28P(6A) in the Wildlife and Countryside Act 1981.

[213] Art. 2.1 Directive 2004/35/EC on Environmental Liability.

[214] See art. 2.1 (c) Directive 2004/35/EC on Environmental Liability.

[215] See art. 2.3 Directive 2004/35/EC on Environmental Liability.

of 1979[216] or listed for protection under the Habitats and Species Directive of 1992.[217] The Directive gives the member states the option, however, to extend the scope of liability to apply in cases of damage to conservation sites protected in domestic, but not EC, law.[218] The UK's initial stance was to resist an extension of the basis of liability beyond that mandatorily required, on the basis that this represented 'gold plating', and therefore as a matter of policy to be avoided in implementing the Directive.[219] The regulations implementing the Directive in both England and Wales have, however, used this facility to extend the scope of liability so that it will also apply to environmental damage to SSSIs notified under the Wildlife and Countryside Act 1981 (as amended).[220] The environmental liability regime has not been extended to SSSIs in Scotland, however, and only applies to European sites.[221]

'Damage' is defined in general terms to mean any measurable adverse change in a natural resource or measurable impairment of a natural resource service.[222] Although the Directive is innovative in applying liability to natural resources damage, it applies a restrictive definition to biodiversity 'damage' by closely aligning liability with breaches of existing Community environmental law.[223] Damage to protected species and habitats is defined as 'any damage that has significant adverse effects on reaching or maintaining the favorable conservation status' of the habitats or species in question, a concept that is closely tied to each site designation established under the relevant wildlife Directives.[224] The significance or

[216] See Council Directive 79/409/EEC, art. 4.2 and Annex 1; reg. 2(1) Environmental Damage (Prevention and Remediation) Regulations 2009, SI 2009/153.

[217] Council Directive 92/43/EC, Annexes 1, 2, and 4; reg. 2 (1) Environmental Damage (Prevention and Remediation) Regulations 2009 SI 2009/153. Note that it is sufficient for the potential application of the Environmental Liability Directive that there has been damage to a listed habitat or species: it is not necessary for the damage to occur in, or relate to, a designated Special Area of Conservation established under the terms of the 1992 Directive. This could give rise to difficulties if damage were to be caused to a site hosting a listed habitat type, but which had not been designated by the member state under the terms of the Directive.

[218] See arts. 2.1 (a) and 2.3 of Directive 2004/35/EC (definitions of, respectively, 'environmental damage', and 'protected species and natural habitats').

[219] See the DEFRA consultation paper on implementation of the Directive: *Consultation for Options for Implementing the Environmental Liability Directive* (HMSO, London, and Dept. of Environment, Food and Rural Affairs, 2006). The UK government's minimalist approach to implementation was criticized by the House of Commons Environment Food and Rural Affairs Committee in 2007: *Implementation of the Environmental Liability Directive, Sixth report of Session 2006–07* (HC 694, Stationery Office, and London 2007).

[220] See the Environmental Damage (Prevention and Remediation) Regulations 2009, SI 2009/153, esp. reg. 4(1)(a) (meaning of 'environmental damage') and reg. 2(1) (definition of 'natural resource'); Environmental Damage (Prevention and Remediation) (Wales) Regulations 2009, SI 2009/995 reg. 4.

[221] Environmental Liability(Scotland) Regulations 2009. SI 2009/266. It was considered that provisions protecting SSSIs in the Nature Conservation (Scotland) Act 2004 (which differ in some respects from those applicable to SSSIs in England) may prove sufficient; see *Environmental Liability Directive—A Consultation* (Scottish Government, 2006) at paras. 45 ff.

[222] See art. 2.2 of Directive 2004/35/EC on Environmental Liability.

[223] Ie the Wild Birds Directive 79/409/EEC, and the Habitats Directive 92/43/EEC.

[224] Art. 2.1(a) Directive 2004/35/EC on Environmental Liability. The criteria that will be relevant to assessing the significance of the likely effects are set out in Annex 1 of the Directive. And see Annex 1 to the Common Position (EC) 58/2003 [2003] OJ C277/E/10.

otherwise of any adverse effects on a site's conservation status are measured by reference to the baseline condition of the habitat or species in question; that is, the condition of the natural resources and services that would have existed had the environmental damage not occurred, estimated on the basis of the best information available[225] and taking account of criteria set out in Annex I.[226] The application of these concepts in the implementing regulations is explained in Box 4.3.

Recovery is excluded for damage that results from actions that were expressly authorized by the relevant authorities in accordance with provisions implementing the regime for the management of designated sites under the Habitats Directive, or in accordance with provisions of national law having an equivalent effect in relation to habitats or species.[227] There will, therefore, be no liability for damage that arises from notified operations likely to damage the conservation interest of either a European site,[228] or a site of special scientific interest (SSSI) if these have received operational consent from Natural England.[229] It is perhaps noteworthy that by linking recovery of natural resources damage exclusively to legally protected habitats, the Directive takes a narrower approach than the UN Convention on Biological Diversity, which defines biodiversity in much wider terms.[230] The European Commission rejected a wide approach, taking the view that the adoption of the concept of variability in living organisms as a qualification for defining biodiversity damage would raise difficult questions as to how such damage would be quantified and what would be the threshold of damage entailing liability.[231]

(d) The administrative liability model

The Directive is based squarely on an administrative liability model. It requires the member states to establish administrative mechanisms for preventing and remediating environmental damage where it occurs. They must also establish cost-recovery mechanisms to ensure that the financial cost of rectifying environmental damage is recovered from those responsible for causing it, and that remediation takes place at the polluter's expense. The Directive's framework for assessing damages focuses on developing plans to restore damaged natural resources and resource services, rather than assessing the monetary value of the

[225] Art. 2.14 Directive 2004/35/EC on Environmental Liability.

[226] Directive 2004/35/EC, Annex 1 sets out various criteria including the capacity of the habitat or species for natural regeneration, its capacity for propagation and for recovery without further legal protection measures.

[227] Art. 2.1(a) Directive 2004/35/EC.

[228] Ie a site notified under the Conservation of Habitats and Species Regulations 2010, SI 2010/490 or its predecessor the Conservation (Natural Habitats & Co.) Regulations 1994, SI 1994/2716.

[229] Ie under s. 28 Wildlife and Countryside Act 1981 as amended (SSSIs) or Conservation of Habitats and Species Regulations 2010 SI 2010/490 reg. 20(1) (European Sites). As to which, see Chapter 3, pp. 84 ff and Chapter 6, pp. 220 ff.

[230] See Art. 2 Convention on Biological Diversity 1992.

[231] *Proposal for a Directive on Environmental Liability*, COM (2002) 17 Final at p. 17.

Box 4.3 Environmental Damage under the Environmental Liability Directive[232]

The regulations implementing the Environmental Liability Directive in England define 'environmental damage' to natural habitats and species by reference to the objective of maintaining their favourable conservation status. Damage is defined in the following terms:

1. Protected Species or Natural Habitats (other than SSSIs)

The damage must have a significant adverse effect on reaching or maintaining the favourable conservation status of the protected species or natural habitat taking into account (a) the conservation status at the time of the damage; (b) the services provided by the amenities they produce; (c) their capacity for natural regeneration; (d) the number of individuals, their density or the area covered; (e) the role of the particular individuals or of the damaged area in relation to the species or to the habitat conservation and the rarity of the species or habitat assessed at the relevant level whether local, regional or Community-wide; (f) the capacity of the species for propagation, its viability, or the capacity of the habitat for natural regeneration; and (g) the capacity of the species or habitat to recover within a short time of the damage being caused to a condition that leads to its state at the time of the damage or better without any intervention other than increased protection measures.

2. The Conservation Status of Natural Habitats

Schedule 1 paragraph 2 defines this as 'the sum of the influences acting on that habitat and its typical species that may affect its long term natural distribution, structure and functions as well as the long term survival of its typical species'. It is favourable if (a) the natural range and areas covered within that natural range are stable or increasing; (b) the specific structure and functions which are necessary for the long-term maintenance of the natural habitat exist and are likely to continue to exist for the foreseeable future; and (c) the conservation status of its typical species is favourable.

3. The Conservation Status of Species

Schedule 1 paragraph 3 defines this as the sum of the influences acting on the species concerned that may affect the long-term distribution and abundance of its populations. It will be considered favourable if: (a) the population dynamics data on the species concerned indicate that it is maintaining itself on a long-term basis as a viable component of its natural habitat; (b) the natural range of the species is neither being reduced nor is likely to be reduced for the foreseeable future; and (c) there is, and will probably continue to be, a sufficiently large habitat to maintain its populations on a long-term basis.

4. Sites of Special Scientific Interest

To be remediable, damage to an SSSI must be to the notified species or habitats, or to protected species, or natural habitats. The damage must have an adverse effect on the integrity of the site, that is, on 'the coherence of its ecological structure and function, across its whole area, that enables it to sustain the habitat, complex of habitats or the levels of populations of the species affected'.

[232] See Schedule 1 Environmental Damage (Prevention and Remediation) Regulations 2009, SI 2009/153.

damage to the resource itself. In other words, the responsible party pays for the cost of implementing the compensatory restoration project, not the monetary value of the interim losses.[233]

Annex II of the Directive provides for 'primary restoration' damages to be assessed on the basis of measures taken to restore damaged natural resources—and natural resource services—to their baseline condition.[234] Compensatory measures include off-site measures, such as creating a replacement habitat elsewhere, where primary restoration is not possible. The person responsible for the damage can be held liable for the cost of restoring the injured natural habitat to baseline condition, compensation for interim loss of resource services during the restoration period, and, in addition, the costs of assessing damages and legal and enforcement costs.[235] Where it is impossible to reverse the damage to habitats or species, then compensatory remediation may require an alternative habitat to be established elsewhere[236] for the protected species whose habitat has been degraded or destroyed.[237]

Several rules will apply to limit the situations in which damage is recoverable:

(i) The Directive applies an absolute limitation period[238] for the application of liability and cost recovery. It does not apply to any damage if more than 30 years has elapsed since the 'emission, event, or incident' that resulted in the damage that has occurred.[239] The application of this rule will be problematic in cases where environmental damage arises over a long time frame. This could be the case, for example, with damage arising from the introduction of GMOs to the environment; where the replacement of wild non-GM weed species with volunteers or outcrosses from GM plant varieties may take considerably longer than 30 years to emerge, and the environmental impacts

[233] Art. 6 of Directive 2004/35/EC on Environmental Liability places the primary duty on the operator to take remedial action to contain control and remove contaminants so as to prevent further damage and rectify any damage that has occurred. Under art. 7 the competent national authorities have jurisdiction to determine the necessary measures to be taken to remedy environmental damage, in accordance with criteria set out in Annex II to the Directive.

[234] See Schedule 4 para. 4 Environmental Damage (Prevention and Remediation) Regulations 2009, SI 2009/153.

[235] Arts. 2 and 8 of Directive 2004/35/EC on Environmental Liability. This is implemented by Schedule 4 paras. 4(3) and 5(1) Environmental Damage (Prevention and Remediation) Regulations 2009, SI 2009/153 (England).

[236] Where possible, the alternative site should be geographically linked to the primary site that has been damaged, taking into account the interests of the affected population of affected species (Annex II, para. 1.1.2 Directive 2004/35/EC on Environmental Liability).

[237] It is perhaps worth noting that the recitals in the Preamble to the 2001 Deliberate Releases Directive refer to the fact that 'the effects of such releases [ie of GMOs] on the environment may be irreversible': see [2001] OJ L106/1 Preamble, Recital (4).

[238] As opposed to a qualified limitation period, ie one where the period fixed for barring legal claims starts to run when the damage concerned was discovered, or ought reasonably to have been discovered.

[239] Art. 17 Directive 2004/35/EC on Environmental Liability. This rule is applied in England by reg. 33 Environmental Damage (Prevention and Remediation) Regulations 2009, SI 2009/153, which provides that no enforcement action may be taken '30 years or more after the emission, event or incident concerned'.

may not be discernible for many years.[240] It will also be difficult in many cases to prove causation, linking damage with an 'emission, event, or incident'[241] as the causative factor leading to environmental damage.

(ii) The Directive does not confer legal standing on individuals or NGOs to bring claims for environmental damage.[242] Instead it gives NGOs and individuals who have been affected, or are likely to be affected, by environmental damage, a right to convey information to the competent authorities and request that they take action under the Directive.[243] The English implementing regulations provide, accordingly, that any person with a sufficient interest, or who is, or is likely to be, affected by environmental damage, may serve a notification to this effect on the enforcing authority.[244] The enforcing authority will notify the operator responsible for the alleged damage before taking a decision on enforcement action. The role of the enforcing authority as the arbiter on enforcement decisions and body with sole responsibility for cost recovery[245] underlines the 'public trust' nature of the administrative-liability model. The decision of the enforcing authority (for example, Natural England) will be open to judicial review in the courts, in the usual way.

(iii) The Directive allows the member states to apply a 'state-of-the-art' defence relieving an operator of the cost of rectifying damage caused by emissions or activities that were not considered harmful according to the state of scientific knowledge at the time when the damaging substance was released or the activity took place.[246] The implementing regulations in England provide that no liability applies where the operator was not at fault or negligent and the environmental damage was caused by an emission or activity, or any manner of using a product in the course of an activity, that the operator demonstrates was not considered to be likely to cause environmental damage according to the state of scientific and technical knowledge at the time when the emission was released or the activity took place.[247] Where an emission or activity has been authorized by a regulatory authorization, it

[240] For a discussion of the limitations of the environmental liability model in relation to damage from GMOs see Rodgers, 'Implementing the EC Environmental Liability Directive: GMOS and the Problem of Unknown Risk', Chapter 7 in L. Bodiguel and M. Cardwell (eds), *The Regulation of GMOs: Comparative Approaches* (Oxford University Press, 2009).

[241] See art. 17 of Directive 2004/35/EC on Environmental Liability and reg. 33 Environmental Damage (Prevention and Remediation) Regulations 2009, SI 2009/153.

[242] Art. 3.3 Directive 2004/35/EC on Environmental Liability.

[243] Art. 12 Directive 2004/35/EC on Environmental Liability.

[244] See reg. 29 Environmental Damage (Prevention and Remediation) Regulations 2009, SI 2009/153. For the enforcing authorities see reg. 11. This will be Natural England in most cases of damage to natural habitats or species, but will be the Environment Agency in the case of damage to water.

[245] See reg. 10 Environmental Damage (Prevention and Remediation) Regulations 2009, SI 2009/153.

[246] Art. 8.4(b) Directive 2004/35/EC on Environmental Liability.

[247] See reg. 19(3)(e) Environmental Damage (Prevention and Remediation) Regulations 2009, SI 2009/153.

will be very difficult to establish fault given the relevance of technical evidence on scientific issues to the environmental risk assessment undertaken prior to the grant of the relevant authorization.[248]

(iv) The Directive also permits the member states not to impose remediation costs on an operator where environmental damage is caused by 'an emission or event expressly authorized by . . . an authorization conferred by or given under applicable national laws and regulations' implementing Community environmental legislation.[249] This exclusion has potentially wide scope, and it could exclude damage flowing from activities permitted under a range of regulatory authorizations issued by the national regulatory bodies. In England, damage arising from a range of regulatory permits will not engage liability, unless the operator has been negligent or is at fault—including Integrated Pollution Prevention and Control and waste-management licences, water discharge consents, water abstraction licences, consents to the release of GMOs, and authorizations relating to the approval of genetically modified food and feed.[250]

(e) Conclusion

The Environmental Liability Directive makes no distinction between owned and 'un-owned' natural resources. Its transposition into English and Scots law therefore addresses a criticism often made of nature conservation law in the UK, that the law protects private property interests through nuisance and other tort remedies, while giving little or no protection to the 'un-owned' environment.[251] Most of the legal instruments relevant to habitat management operate by adjusting the property rights of landowners and others to restrict access to the land resource and prohibit certain types of damaging land use activity; this is the case, as explained earlier, with site notifications, such as SSSIs and SACs, with management agreements to promote conservation management, and with planning law instruments. The development of a public trust concept, with the state acting as a trustee for public natural resources, is a novel development and marks a significant break with property rights-based approaches to environmental remediation.

That is not to say, however, that the application of environmental liability can be entirely divorced from property concepts. The use of a public trust model is itself

[248] See eg M. Stallworthy, 'Environmental Liability and the Impact of Statutory Authority' (2003) 15 *Journal of Environmental Law* 3, 18. And in relation to damage from GMO releases see Rodgers (n. 240), and M. Lee, 'Regulatory Solutions for GMOs in Europe: the Problem of Liability' (2003) 12 *Journal of Environmental Law and Policy* 311.

[249] Art. 8.4(a) Directive 2004/35/EC on Environmental Liability. The relevant Community legislation is defined by reference to the list in Annex III (ie occupational activities engaging environmental liability under the Directive).

[250] See reg. 19(3)(d) and Schedule 3 Environmental Damage (Prevention and Remediation) Regulations 2009, SI 2009/153.

[251] See eg C. Reid, *Nature Conservation Law* 3rd edn (Thomson/W. Green, 2009) at 5.12.9.

redolent of property notions, with the public in the role of 'beneficiaries' for whom the enforcing authority acts as a trustee of natural resources. The application of environmental liability will also have implications for redistributing access to economic resources, and this is best understood applying a resource allocation model of property rights.[252] European environmental policy stresses the cost internalization and deterrence effects of environmental liability, and the Directive is explicitly based on the polluter pays principle of European environmental law.[253] It also performs economic functions, including the allocation and/or spreading of risk, and the internalization of environmental externalities.[254] If polluters have to pay for the remediation of damage they cause, they will restrict polluting activities to the point where the marginal cost of abatement exceeds the compensation thereby avoided.[255] Inasmuch as the cost of the polluting activity will increase, this will be reflected in output costs thereby increasing the price of, and reducing demand for, the products of the polluting process, a factor that will lead in turn to a reduction in pollution.

The role of environmental liability in resource allocation can usefully be understood using a law and economics analysis. The starting point is the theorem posited by Coase,[256] that the nature of the problem of allocating costs arising from environmental damage is always reciprocal.[257] If A's factory pollutes a natural habitat situated on his neighbour B's land, measures taken to avoid the harm to B will also inflict harm on A (a loss of production). In order to arrive at an optimum allocation of resources both parties (A and B) should take into account the harmful effect of the nuisance when deciding their course of action. It is not, however, simply a question of restraining those responsible for the harmful effects (A in our example); the key determinant is whether the gain from preventing the harm is greater than the loss that would be suffered elsewhere as a result of stopping the

[252] See Chapter 1, pp. 28 ff. and Box 1.3.

[253] Art 191(2) TFEU (ex Art. 174(2) European Treaty). See especially recitals 2 and 18 to Directive 2004/35/CE on environmental liability with regard to the prevention and remedying of environmental damage, OJ L143/56, 30.4.2004 (the Environmental Liability Directive), and see the white paper on Environmental Liability, COM (2000) 66 Final, para. 2.1 at p. 11.

[254] See eg L. Bergkamp, 'The Commission's White Paper on Environmental Liability: A Weak case for an EC Strict Liability Regime' (2000) EELR 105. Bergkamp is critical of the public liability model posited in the Environmental Liability Directive as a mechanism for delivering any of these objectives.

[255] See the White Paper on Environmental Liability, COM (2000) 66 Final, para. 2.1 at para. 3.1.

[256] See R. H. Coase, 'The Problem of Social Cost' (1960) 3 *Journal of Law and Economics* 1, at 13. And see R. H. Coase, *The Firm, the Market and the Law* (University of Chicago Press, 1986).

[257] The following analysis is essentially utilitarian. It should not be forgotten that the law may seek to protect living natural resources for deontological reasons, completely unconnected with considerations of resource allocation or the internalization of environmental externalities. The Coasean approach is fundamentally at odds with approaches based on deontological ethics, eg Aldo Leopold's 'land ethic' (see *A Sand County Almanac*, Oxford University Press, 1949). In other words, approaches that emphasize that we protect wildlife and natural resources because it is the right thing to do, irrespective of the economic consequences of so doing or of the impact of liability on questions of resource allocation. See eg C. Palmer, *Environmental Ethics and Process Thinking* (Clarendon Press, 1998) esp. Ch. 3.

action that produces it. This analysis requires us to view property rights as a factor of production, an approach that has much in common with the resource allocation role of property institutions, and with interpretations that stress the role of property rights in giving access to a resource or stream of benefits.[258] It follows that because the application of a liability mechanism to 'rectify' damage results in a rearrangement of property rights, with attendant economic costs, the courts are, in nuisance cases, making a decision on the economic problem of how to allocate and use resources.[259] The cost of exercising a right is always the loss that is suffered elsewhere in consequence of the exercise of that right; the inability to enjoy a fine view, or to breathe clean air, for example. When we choose which social arrangements to permit, a Coasean analysis would dictate that we should consider the total effect of the reallocation of property rights required to remedy the damage at issue.[260]

This approach has primarily been used to analyse the economic functions of the private law of nuisance, but it has considerable relevance to explain the wider economic and resource allocation implications of the application of environmental liability to protect natural resources and wildlife. Consider this notional example:

A owns Pinkacre, part of which is a wetland area notified as an SSSI for its rare flora and fauna. The SSSI includes a rare habitat for fen orchids and also hosts a breeding population of Bitterns (Botaurus stellaris) – both of which are protected under the Wildlife and Countryside Act 1981.[261] *B owns Blackacre, an adjacent farm. B established a farm waste disposal facility in 2008 which incinerates a miscellany of farm waste collected from neighbouring farms – including old tyres, oil and silage wrappers. Oil effluent stored in B's waste facility has escaped over a period of time and has seeped onto A's land, causing damage to the orchid habitat. A also alleges that toxic fumes and dust from B's incinerator are impairing the habitat, and that numbers of nesting bitterns have declined since the facility was established in 2008. Natural England have served a remediation notice on B alleging that his facility is causing environmental damage to the SSSI and its protected habitats and species. B has a waste management licence, but it is accepted on the facts that he is in breach of the duty of care imposed by the agricultural waste regulations.*[262]

The damage here is biodiversity damage, and as such is normally uncompensated by civil law mechanisms such as nuisance and negligence, which limit the range of

[258] See eg K. J. Gray, 'Property in Thin Air' (1991) 50 *Cambridge Law Journal* 252; K. Gray and S. F. Gray, 'The Idea of Property in Land', in S. Bright and K. Dewar (eds), *Land Law: Themes and Perspectives* (Oxford University Press, 1998); J. Waldron, 'What is Private Property?' (1985) 5 OJLS 313; C. P. Rodgers, 'Nature's Place? Property Rights, Property Rules and Environmental Stewardship' (2009) 68 Cambridge Law Journal 550. Cf. welfare economics approaches (criticized by Coase) eg A. C. Pigou, *The Economics of Welfare* 4th edn (Macmillan,1932), esp. part 2.

[259] Coase (see n. 256) (1960) 3 Journal of Law and Economics 1 at 27.

[260] Coase, (1960) 3 *Journal of Law and Economics* 1, at 44.

[261] Both the bittern and little bittern are protected by special penalties pursuant to Schedule 1 Wildlife and Countryside Act 1981, and the bittern is also an Annex 1 species requiring special conservation measures under article 4 of Directive 2009/147/EC on the conservation of wild birds. Fen orchids are listed for protection under Schedule 8 of the 1981 Act.

[262] See the Waste Management (England and Wales) Regulations 2006, SI 2006/937, amending the Waste Management Licensing Regulations 1994 SI 1994/1096. The duty of care is imposed by s. 34 Environmental Protection Act 1990 and SI 1991/2839.

available remedies to damage to the 'owned' environment.[263] If the application of environmental liability restricts B's right to operate his waste facility in a manner that damages the Pinkacre SSSI this will have the effect of reallocating B's property rights; it will increase his production costs. But this is arguably a unilateral effect, because it is not balanced by a reciprocal alteration in A's property rights. If, on the other hand, A is running an eco-tourism business on Pinkacre then the impact of the liability mechanism may be bilateral. Viewed as a resource allocation mechanism, the imposition of environmental liability will protect his access to a resource (the protected habitat) that will generate an economic stream of benefits. And in so doing it will prioritize this over B's right to run his waste facility in a manner which is damaging to neighbouring farmers. But if A's own land use is not contingent upon the habitat in this sense (he simply has an SSSI on his land and does not run an eco-tourism business) then the imposition of environmental liability will superficially have a unilateral effect on property rights in that it will restrict B's rights without necessarily amplifying those of A.[264]

If we also consider the property rights implications of the SSSI notification itself, however, this will enable us to take full account of the reallocation of property rights and resources brought about by the application of the environmental liability rule.[265] When the Pinkacre SSSI was notified A's property rights were partially reassigned to the state, in that decision making on operations likely to damage its scientific interest was reassigned to Natural England.[266] The land contained in the Pinkacre SSSI will arguably have taken on a 'quasi-public' character as a result.[267] If the damage to the protected habitat on Pinkacre SSSI results in a further reassignment of property rights resulting from the application of environmental liability, this will take place within a tripartite framework of reference, not a bilateral one. Depending on the facts, the environmental harm resulting from B's actions may impact upon A's property rights and/or those reassigned to the state by the SSSI notification, and the imposition of environmental liability will have bilateral effect in each case. It may also have tripartite effects; for example, if damage to the conservation interest of the SSSI is also coupled with damage to A's eco-tourism business. Any impact on A's property rights will, however, be incidental: the primary objective of the administrative liability mechanism is the protection of the property rights reassigned to the state by the site notification,[268] and any

263 See inter alia *Marquis of Granby v Bakewell* UDC (1923) 87 JP 105; *Pride of Derby and Derbyshire Angling Association Ltd v British Celanese* [1953] Ch 149; *Hunter v Canary Wharf* [1997] 2 WLR 684, and Chapter 1, pp. 3–4.

264 This is the criticism made by eg L. Bergkamp, 'Allocating Unknown Risk: Liability for Environmental damages Caused by Deliberately Released Genetically Modified Organisms' (2000) at 23–4 (Social Science Research Network).

265 This is essentially what Coase is arguing for: see R. H. Coase, 'The Problem of Social Cost' (1960) 3 *Journal of Law and Economics* 1, at 44 (see n. 260).

266 See s. 28E Wildlife and Countryside Act 1981 and Chapter 3, p. 84.

267 For a discussion of the wider characterization of 'quasi public' property concepts see 'Private Property and Public Propriety', Chapter 2 in J. McLean (ed.), *Property and the Constitution* (Hart Publishing, 1999) at 18–20; J. Waldron, 'What is private property?' (1985) 5 OJLS 313 at 327–33.

268 Or, to be more precise, the protection of the habitat that the modification of Jones' property rights by the SSSI notification seeks to protect.

Box 4.4 Environmental Liability: A Property Rights Analysis

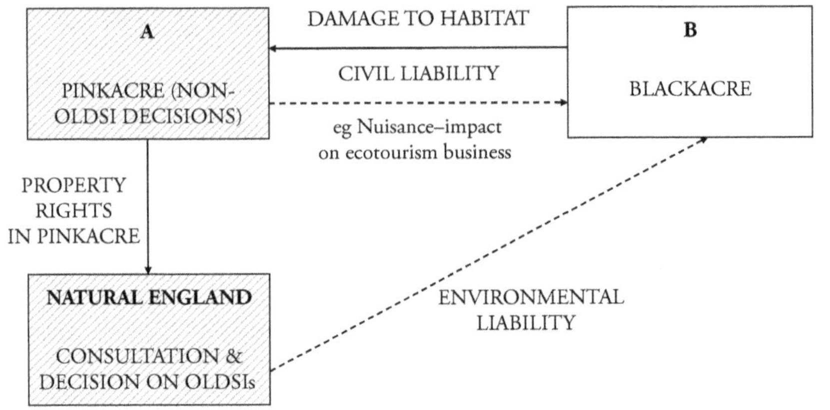

economic benefit accruing to A (for example, the protection of his eco-tourism venture) will be incidental. Viewed through the lens of a resource allocation model of property rights, therefore, environmental liability performs a similar function to the law of nuisance in situations where environmental harm has a purely bilateral effect; for example, where A's land has not been notified as an SSSI and the only question concerns damage to his business. The principal difference will lie in the different legal remedies available, and to whom, and by virtue of which the consequent reassignment of property rights is effected.[269] These interactions are explained in diagrammatic form in Box 4.4

Finally, a property rights analysis also assists in the interpretation of the rules in the Directive against double recovery for environmental damage.[270] The Directive omits to give guidance on how to deal with overlapping claims in private and public law. In our example, how should the double loss rule be applied if A sues for damages in nuisance for losses to his eco-tourism business, and Natural England also take remedial action to restore the SSSI habitat and claim recovery of their costs in doing so? Applying a property rights analysis, we can see that A is claiming damages in nuisance for B's interference with his reasonable use of the land—the measure of damages being the loss occasioned to his business by B's actions. Natural England, on the other hand, will be claiming for reimbursement of the cost of remediating damage to its conservation features (the 'un-owned' conservation

[269] Enforcement action to seek the imposition of environmental liability can only be taken by the public enforcement authorities, and not by A. And damages and injunctions are not available under the Environmental Liability Directive. So if A wishes to gain financial recompense for damage to his eco-tourism business venture in the example cited he will have to sue in nuisance or negligence and seek the imposition of civil liability.

[270] Art. 16(2) Environmental Liability Directive.

features of A's land) in which it now has a property right by virtue of the SSSI notification, in the sense that decision making on use of the resource has been reallocated to it in order to protect the site. The two claims are not overlapping, in that they relate to different aspects of the property rights in Pinkacre, which have been apportioned and reallocated by the SSSI notification. This is further illustrated in diagrammatical form in Box 4.4.

5

Protection of Wild Animals, Birds, and Plants

Legislation Protecting Animals, Birds, and Plants

Two distinctions run through the law as it applies to the protection of animals, birds, and plants in the UK. The first is between (i) protection of the habitats of rare and/or endangered species (considered in Chapters 3 and 4), and (ii) the protection of individual birds, animals, and plants themselves, which forms the subject of this chapter. The second is a distinction between the protection of *individual* animals, birds, and plants, on the one hand, and the protection of animals, birds, and plants at the *species* level on the other. While the law protects individual birds, animals, and plants, as we shall see in the remainder of this chapter, there is also legal provision for the protection of some types of bird, animal, and plant at a sustainable population level in order to maintain the viability of the species. This is the case, for example, in relation to European protected species of animal and bird under the terms of the European Habitats and Birds Directives.[1]

In the UK, legislation on nature conservation has historically adopted a twin approach to the protection of individual birds, animals, and plants: measures conferring protection on the habitats of such species are complemented by more direct legislation conferring legal protection on members of identified species, and prohibiting the taking, killing, or causing of damage to their eggs or young. The law adopts a twin policy approach: clearly, there is little point in conferring direct legal protection on individual members of protected species, if the habitats necessary to their survival, genetic exchange, and diversity are not also protected. The laws on habitat protection have a very important long-term importance, therefore, for the preservation and encouragement of growth in *species* populations. In this context, the law on habitat protection[2] is intimately connected with the law applied to protect animals, birds, and plants at sustainable levels of species population—'species protection'.[3] The more immediate protection conferred by criminalizing the destruction of individual plants, birds, and animals is nevertheless important, and this chapter will explore the ways in which the law confers protection on individual birds, animals, and plant, and how it seeks to prevent the interference with their nests, eggs, and young.

[1] See eg Council Directive 2009/147/EC (the Wild Birds Directive) arts. 2 and 5(d): Council Directive 92/43/EC (the Habitats Directive) art. 12.4. Both are discussed in Chapter 6.

[2] Discussed in Chapters 3 and 4.

[3] As to which, see Chapter 6, p. 216.

The Structure of Species Protection Law in England and Wales

Part I of the Wildlife and Countryside Act 1981 is the primary measure in the UK for the protection of individual members of protected species of animal, bird, and plants. The UK has international obligations to protect wild species of endangered bird, plants, and animals under:

- The *Wild Birds Directive of 2009*. Art 5 prohibits the deliberate killing or taking of birds, the deliberate destruction of nests and eggs, the deliberate disturbance of birds during the breeding season, and the keeping or taking of eggs. The taking of certain species by hunting is permissible, but the Directive expressly prohibits certain non selective methods of killing of birds.[4]
- The *Habitats and Species Directive of 1992* complements this by requiring the member states to establish a strict system of protection for European protected species of animal and plant. The protection must apply within their natural range and requires the prohibition of all forms of deliberate capture or killing of specimens in the wild, the deliberate destruction or taking of eggs and the destruction or deterioration of breeding or resting places.[5] Both the Habitats Directive and the Wild Birds Directive are considered further in Chapter 6.
- International treaties; for example, the *Bern Convention on the Conservation of European Wildlife and Natural Habitats 1979*. Appendices I and 2 require signatories to confer protection on the listed species of plants and animal, while Appendix 3 to the Convention prohibits certain methods of destruction for birds and animals otherwise not granted special protection.

Part 1 of the 1981 Act is the primary vehicle for the transposition of these obligations in to the domestic law of Scotland, England, and Wales. Rather than apply specific controls to protect different species directly, the approach adopted by the 1981 Act is to lay down a general standard of protection for all birds, plants, and animal species. This is then varied by reference to lists of species in the schedules to the Act, giving additional protection in the case of rare or endangered species, and reduced protection in the case of pests and animals/birds categorized as 'game' species subject to hunting at prescribed times of the year.

Following devolution, the 1981 Act has been varied in some respects by Scottish legislation as regards its application in Scotland, and by separate legislation implementing changes to the Act that apply in England and Wales. As a consequence, there are two different versions of Part 1 of the 1981 Act that are currently applicable in (i) Scotland, and (ii) in England and Wales. Although the principal thrust of the provisions is the same in both jurisdictions, there are some important differences of emphasis, and these will be highlighted in the following discussion. The overall effect of this is that the *form* in which the legislation is currently

[4] Council Directive 2009/147/EC, Annex IV (a) and (b). See Chapter 6, p. 207.

[5] Council Directive 92/43/EC (the Habitats Directive), esp. art. 12 and Annex IV(a) and (b) (defining protected species). See Chapter 6, p. 216.

presented is an unsatisfactory patchwork of legislative provisions. This is compounded by the addition of bespoke protection through the Conservation of Habitats and Species Regulations 2010 for species of animal and plants protected under the European Habitats Directive.[6] The Law Commission's Eleventh Programme of Law Reform[7] has initiated a review of wildlife legislation in order to rationalize what it referred to as 'succeeding geological strata of legislation with no coherent design'.[8] A principal objective of reform would be to rationalize the presentation of the law in Part 1 of the 1981 Act, which has been amended so many times that it is difficult to use unless one has specialist knowledge of this area of law. The project will also consider the extent to which the current legislation implements requirements of EU law efficiently, and in a manner that is open to easy amendment to reflect new requirements.[9]

The Conservation Bodies—acting through the Joint Nature Conservation Committee—have a duty to review the Schedules of Protected Animal and Plant[10] every five years. The Schedules can be amended by the Secretary of State by order (subject to negative resolution of either House of Parliament). The Secretary of State has a general power to vary Schedule 1, which confers protection on rare birds, at any time by order. Taken together, these provisions ensure that the Schedules can be amended from time to time to keep pace with changes not only in the conservation status of individual species of bird, animal, and plants, but also with the state of scientific and ecological knowledge of the status of the various species. The schedules have been revised in recent years, for example, to add water voles to the list of protected animal species, as a result of a large-scale decline due to predation by feral mink. Similarly the bluebell has been added to Schedule 8, having become rare in some areas as a consequence of the digging up of bulbs for private use or sale.

The 1981 Act is supplemented by additional measures for some specific species of animal requiring targeted protection; for example, the Protection of Badgers Act 1972 and the Conservation of Seals Act 1970.

[6] SI 2010/490, Chapter 6, pp. 216 ff.

[7] Law Commission, *Eleventh Programme of Law Reform* (Law Com No. 330, 2011) available at: <http://lawcommission.justice.gov.uk/docs/lc330_eleventh_programme.pdf>. The Law Commission intend to produce a Final Report and Draft Bill in 2014.

[8] Law Commission, *Eleventh Programme of Law Reform* (Law Com No. 330, 2011) at para. 2.84.

[9] See paras. 2.83–2.88. The Commission published a consultation paper in August 2012 reviewing the operation of both the domestic legislation and the regulations implementing the European Directives. This provisionally proposed a rationalization and simplification of the existing law into a single statute for wildlife management: see *Wildlife Law: A Consultation Paper*, Law Commission Consultation Paper No. 206 (2012), esp. paras. 5.19 et seq. and Provisional Proposal 5–1.

[10] Schedules 5 and 8 Wildlife and Countryside Act 1981. The duty to review does not, however, apply to the other Schedules in the 1981 Act, neither does the Secretary of State have to follow the advice given or give reasons for his failure to do so. The Law Commission have proposed that in order to improve transparency in the application of the law there should in future (i) be a duty to review all Schedules, and (ii) that the Secretary of State should be under a duty to give reasons for refusing to follow the advice of the Conservation Bodies on review: see *Wildlife Law: A Consultation Paper*, Law Commission Consultation Paper No. 206 (2012), esp. paras. 5.61–5.64 and Provisional Proposals 5–9 and 5–10.

Protection of Wild Birds

The general approach to the protection of birds, and set out in Part 1 of the Wildlife and Countryside Act 1981, is to enact a general offence applicable to the killing, taking, or injury of all wild birds, and then, by reference to the Schedules to the Act, to apply a stricter level of protection to members of certain species of protected or endangered birds, and a reduced level of protection to game birds and pests, which may be hunted at certain times of the year, or in the case of pests exterminated without sanction. The general offence is set out in section 1(1) of the 1981 Act, which makes it a criminal offence for any person to intentionally—or if the offence is committed in Scotland, recklessly[11]—kill, injure, or take any wild bird, to take, damage, or destroy the nest of a wild bird while it is in use or being built, or to take or destroy the egg of any wild bird.

A 'wild bird' is defined to include any bird ordinarily resident in or a visitor to Great Britain in a wild state, other than poultry or game birds.[12] The definition was expanded in 2004 so that it is now an offence to possess or sell any bird or egg that has been taken from the wild anywhere in the EU.[13] The law was changed to bring it into line with the requirements of the Wild Birds Directive of 1979.[14] This means that any person trading or keeping a bird taken elsewhere in the EU can be prosecuted in England, Scotland or Wales. The law was further widened in 2006[15] so that birds reintroduced into the wild as part of a repopulation or reintroduction programme are also given full protection as 'wild' birds under the 1981 Act. A good example would be the red kite, which has been successfully reintroduced to parts of Northern England and Scotland in recent years. A bird which has been bred in captivity is not, however, a 'wild' bird for these purposes unless it is lawfully released in to the wild as part of such a repopulation or reintroduction programme.[16] Where this question arises, the burden of proof will be on the defendant to show, on a balance of probabilities, that a bird in his possession was bred in captivity.[17]

[11] Ss. 50, 59, and Schedule 6 para. 2(2) (a) Nature Conservation (Scotland) Act 2003.

[12] S. 27 Wildlife and Countryside Act 1981.

[13] See the Wildlife and Countryside Act 1981 (England and Wales) (Amendment) Regulations 2004, SI 2004/1487, reg. 4 and (In Scotland) the Nature Conservation (Scotland) Act 2004, Schedule 6 para. 23.

[14] See Chapter 6, p. 205.

[15] By s. 48 of the Natural Environment and Rural Communities Act 2006, amending s. 1(6) of the 1981 Act.

[16] S. 1(6) and 1(6A) Wildlife and Countryside Act 1981. Its parents must have been lawfully in captivity at the time the egg was laid for the resulting progeny to have been born in captivity: s. 27(2) Wildlife and Countryside Act 1981.

[17] See *Hughes v DPP* [2003] EWHC 2470 (conviction for possession of live goldfinches). 'On a prosecution for an offence under s. 1 of the Act it is the defendant who must show, on a balance of probabilities, that a bird has been bred in captivity. This follows from the wording of s. 1(6) and is consistent with commons sense. Whether a bird has been bred in captivity may be known to the person in possession of it. He will know where he obtained the bird, if he did not breed it himself. The prosecution normally will only be able to refer to the condition and behaviour of the bird as indicative of its having been born in the wild' (Stanley Burnton J., judgment at para. 17).

The commission of the general offence in section 1 does not require the offender to have prior knowledge that the bird killed or destroyed was a 'wild' specimen. So, in *Kirkland v Robinson*[18] it was held that knowledge of the bird's 'wild' state was not necessary to ground a conviction under section 1(1) for deliberately killing a wild bird. The necessary 'intention'—in legal terms the *mens rea*—relates to the act of killing, taking, etc.; further knowledge of the wild status of the bird concerned is not necessary.

Despite this, it remains the case that proving the necessary intention on the part of the perpetrator in order to establish a conviction is not easy. For this reason, the 1981 Act supplements these offences with a range of others which criminalize the mere *possession* of live or dead wild birds and birds' eggs. Section 1(2) makes it a criminal offence for any person to have in his possession or control any live or dead wild bird (or part of one), or any wild bird's egg (or part of one). These are offences of strict liability: it is not necessary to prove intention on the part of a defendant found in possession of eggs or birds. All that is required to establish liability is that the defendant has in his possession a wild bird or wild birds' eggs. It follows that anyone who keeps dead or live wild birds or their eggs does so at his own risk. This is important, as it may be impossible to know, when a rare birds' nest is raided for eggs, or a bird is killed by poison, who the perpetrators were. That will only be known to those involved. The possession of wild birds' eggs or carcasses resulting from such illegal activity is, however, much easier to prove. The law therefore seeks to prevent anyone benefiting from the crime which has been committed, whether or not the initial offence of killing, etc. has been discovered.

Detecting this type of criminal activity can be difficult. The 1981 Act therefore supplements the basic criminal offences with special enforcement powers conferred on the police to detect and punish wildlife crime. Section 19 of the 1981 Act gives the police powers to stop and search any person, if they have reasonable cause to suspect that he is, or has, committed an offence. They can stop and search any person without a search warrant if they suspect that s/he is in possession of evidence of the commission of an offence; they can search any object in his/her possession (for example, a car or van) for evidence of the crime; and they can arrest a person for failing to give a satisfactory name and address. They also have powers to seize and detain anything which might be evidence of the commission of an offence under the 1981 Act, as well as wide powers of entry into private property, other than dwelling houses, for which a search warrant will be required.

(a) Protected bird species

Additional protection is given to species of rare and endangered bird listed in Schedule 1 to the 1981 Act, over and above the protection of the general offences (cited earlier) constituted by section 1(1) and 1(2). There is an additional offence making it illegal to intentionally or recklessly disturb any wild bird listed in

[18] [1987] Crim LR 643.

Schedule 1 while it is building a nest, or is at or near its nest containing young, or to disturb intentionally or recklessly the dependent young of such a bird.[19] The penalties for breach of the general offences in section 1(1) and (2) are also higher for protected Schedule 1 bird species. Some of the defences applicable to all wild birds also do not apply to protected species listed in Schedule 1 (these are considered later). Schedule 1 lists almost 100 species of rare bird which benefit from extra protection under these provisions; for example, red kites, ospreys, all breeds of harriers, barn owls, and corncrakes (see Box 5.1).

Box 5.1 Birds that are Protected by Special Penalties

Part 1: Birds Protected at all Times

- Avocet
- Bee-eater
- Bittern, and Little Bittern
- Bluethroat
- Brambling
- Bunting, Cirl; Bunting, Lapland; Bunting, Snow
- Buzzard, Honey
- Capercaillie
- Chough
- Corncrake
- Crake, Spotted
- Crossbills (all species)
- Curlew, Stone
- Divers (all species)
- Dotterel
- Duck, Long-tailed
- Eagle, Golden
- Eagle, White-tailed
- Falcon, Gyr
- Fieldfare
- Firecrest
- Garganey

(*Continued*)

[19] S. 1(5) Wildlife and Countryside Act 1981. The offence was extended to reckless conduct by s. 81(1), 103(2) and Schedule 12 para. 1 Countryside and Rights of Way Act 2000 (England and Wales); and in Scotland by ss. 50, 59, and Schedule 6 para. 2(5) the Nature Conservation (Scotland) Act 2003.

Box 5.1 Continued

- Godwit, Black-tailed
- Goshawk
- Grebe, Black-necked
- Grebe, Slavonian
- Greenshank
- Gull, Little
- Gull, Mediterranean
- Harriers (all species)
- Heron, Purple
- Hobby
- Hoopoe
- Kingfisher
- Kite, Red
- Merlin
- Oriole, Golden
- Osprey
- Owl, Barn
- Owl, Snowy
- Peregrine Falcon
- Petrel, Leach's
- Phalarope, Red-necked
- Plover, Kentish
- Plover, Little Ringed
- Quail, Common
- Redstart, Black
- Redwing
- Rosefinch, Scarlet
- Ruff
- Sandpiper, Green
- Sandpiper, Purple
- Sandpiper, Wood
- Scaup
- Scoter, Common
- Scoter, Velvet
- Serin
- Shorelark

- Shrike, Red-backed
- Spoonbill
- Stilt, Black-winged
- Stint, Temminck's
- Swan, Bewick's
- Swan, Whooper
- Tern, Black
- Tern, Little
- Tern, Roseate
- Tit, Bearded
- Tit, Crested
- Treecreeper, Short-toed
- Warbler, Cetti's
- Warbler, Dartford
- Warbler, Marsh
- Warbler, Savi's
- Whimbrel
- Woodlark
- Wryneck

Part 2 Birds Protected During the Close Season

Goldeneye; Greylag goose (in Outer Hebrides, Caithness, Sutherland, and Wester Ross only); and Pintail.

The Natural Environment and Rural Communities Act 2006 introduced a new offence to protect the nests of birds that return to the same nesting sites and reuse them. It is now an offence to take, damage, or destroy the nest of any wild bird listed in Schedule ZA1 to the 1981 Act.[20] The offence will be committed whether or not the birds are using the nest at the time damage takes place cf. the offence applied to all Schedule 1 birds (p. 165) which applies to prevent, damage, or disturbance only while the nest is being built or used.[21] Three species of rare bird are listed in Schedule ZA1 for protection against disturbance of their nests: golden eagles, white-tailed eagles, and ospreys. The white-tailed eagle is also protected in Scotland against harassment.[22]

20 Inserted by s. 47 Natural Environment and Rural Communities Act 2006.

21 S. 1(5) see n. 19.

22 See Schedule 1A inserted by ss. 50, 59, Schedule 6 para. 25 Nature Conservation (Scotland) Act 2004.

(b) Game birds and pests

While the level of protection is raised by Schedule 1 in the case of protected bird species, it is lowered in relation to birds categorized as Pests and Game Birds by reference to Schedule 2 to the 1981 Act. Game birds are not subject to the protection of the 1981 Act during the open season for that species to be hunted, and Schedule 2 Part 1 lists 19 species of game bird that can lawfully be killed or taken outside the close season.[23] For these purposes the 'close season' means in the majority of cases the period in any year commencing with 1 February and ending with 31 August.[24] A different close season is specified for certain species: for capercaillie and woodcock,[25] it is the period in any year commencing 1 February and ending 30 September; for snipe it is the period in any year commencing 1 February and ending 11 August; and in the case of wild duck and wild geese found in an area below the high-water mark of ordinary spring tides, it is the period in any year commencing 21 February and ending 31 August.[26] The Secretary of State has general power to vary the close season for any species of game bird by order[27] and can, furthermore, declare periods of up to 14 days as special protection periods for any wild birds, in which case the protection period takes effect in the same way as the close season for that species as a whole.[28]

Pests can be destroyed by an authorized person possessing a relevant licence issued by the public authorities. Originally, pests were excluded from the protection of the 1981 Act by Schedule 2 Part 2. This was considered to be a breach of the European Wild Birds Directive of 1979, which requires member states to confer protection on all wild species of bird. Accordingly, Schedule 2 Part 2 was replaced by a licensing system complying with the derogation permitted in the Directive. Licences made under the 1981 Act[29] are available from the Department of the Environment Food and Rural Affairs in England or the agriculture departments of the devolved administrations in Scotland and Wales, and from the statutory nature Conservation Bodies. The licences can be specific to individuals authorized to destroy pests, or they may be generic in that they apply to categories of person or pest, in which case individual applications are not necessary. Each devolved administration promulgates a general licence annually, for example, permitting the killing or taking by authorized persons of birds damaging crops and foodstuffs. The licensing system provides a widely applicable set of defences to liability and is considered in further detail from p. 170.

[23] S. 2(1) Wildlife and Countryside Act 1981.
[24] S. 2(4)(d) Wildlife and Countryside Act 1981 .
[25] Except in Scotland.
[26] S. 2(4) (a)-(c) Wildlife and Countryside Act 1981.
[27] S. 2(5) Wildlife and Countryside Act 1981.
[28] s. 2(6) Wildlife and Countryside Act 1981. This might apply to protect a geographically distinct sub-group of birds, for example, rather than the whole species (which will of course be protected during the close season declared under the Act for that species).
[29] S. 16 Wildlife and Countryside Act 1981.

(c) Exceptions to liability

(i) Defences

Section 4 provides a number of defences to liability. 'Humanitarian' actions such as taking a disabled bird in order to tend and release it will not attract liability,[30] nor the mercy killing of birds seriously injured with no chance of recovery, providing the original injury was not caused by the individual's own illegal act.[31] An 'authorized person' will also have a defence if s/he can show that their actions were necessary for the purpose of preserving public health or public (or air) safety, for preventing the spread of disease, or for preventing serious damage to crops, to livestock, to foodstuffs for livestock, to vegetables, fruit, growing timber, or to fisheries and inland waters.[32] It must also be shown that there was no other 'satisfactory' solution other than that adopted (the killing or taking of the birds in question)[33] and the defence will not be available in respect of actions the necessity for which became apparent at an earlier time, unless the landowner had taken steps to apply for a licence from the public authorities or, if he did in fact do so, where the licence has been refused.[34] Following the ruling of the European Court in *Commission of the European Communities v United Kingdom*[35] the range of potential application of the defence was narrowed, and it does not apply to acts that impact upon any bird that is a member of a protected species listed in Schedule 1. Protected species therefore enjoy the full protection of the offence in section 1 (preventing the killing, taking, or injury of such birds or their nests and eggs) even if the birds are causing damage to livestock or other crops, etc.

A further defence excludes liability where death or injury, etc. to wild birds is caused by an act that was the incidental result of a lawful operation and could not reasonably have been avoided.[36] Examples of the application of this defence might include incidental damage resulting from agricultural operations, such as destroying nests while ploughing arable crops or felling trees in woodland. This defence will apply to incidental killing, etc. of protected species of bird within Schedule 1. The defence is also more restrictedly applied in Scotland, where the relevant provisions in the 1981 Act have been amended to require that, if the defence is to be applicable, the defendant must have taken precautions to avoid causing damage in circumstances where the damage was unforeseeable, and have taken steps immediately upon the damage becoming apparent to minimize its impact.[37] It has been questioned whether, given its broad remit, this defence

[30] S. 4(2)(a) Wildlife and Countryside Act 1981.
[31] S. 4(2)(b) Wildlife and Countryside Act 1981.
[32] S. 4(3) Wildlife and Countryside Act 1981.
[33] S. 4(4) Wildlife and Countryside Act 1981.
[34] S. 4(5) Wildlife and Countryside Act 1981.
[35] (2005) Case C 06/04, [2005] E.C.R. 1–9017.
[36] S. 4(2)(c)Wildlife and Countryside Act 1981.
[37] S. 4(2A) Wildlife and Countryside Act 1981, amended by ss. 50, 59, and Schedule 6 para. 5(3) Nature Conservation Scotland Act 2004; SSI 2004/407 art. 2.

accords with the narrowly defined derogations from liability permitted by the Birds Directive.[38]

The way in which the defences are structured is central to the manner in which the law resolves the tension between the property rights of the landowner on whose land the birds are to be found, and the public interest in conserving individual birds and bird species. The general defence elevates the property interest of the landowner in preserving the economic resource to which his property right gives access, by permitting the destruction of birds causing damage to crops, livestock, or fruit, etc. The property interest of the landowner therefore has priority over the wider public interest in conserving the birds or bird species in question. Where damage is caused by a member of a Schedule 1 protected species, however, the position is reversed: the withdrawal of the defence has the effect of elevating the public interest in conserving the species above that of the landowner in protecting his property right and in maximizing the economic value of the land resource to which it gives access.

(ii) Licences

A more general exception to liability is granted by the licensing system established under the 1981 Act. Licences can be granted by the public authorities for a wide range of purposes, subject to the condition that there must be no other satisfactory solution, and in some cases on the basis that the licence is selective as to the birds to be killed or taken and is issued in respect of a small number of birds.[39] Licences can be issued under the 1981 Act for the killing or taking of wild birds for the following purposes:[40] for scientific, research, or educational purposes; for ringing or marking, or examining any ring or mark on, wild birds; for the purpose of conserving wild birds; for the purposes of the repopulation of an area with, or the reintroduction into an area of, wild birds, including any breeding necessary for those purposes; for the purpose of conserving flora or fauna; for the purpose of protecting any collection of wild birds; for the purposes of falconry or aviculture; for the purposes of any public exhibition or competition; for the purposes of taxidermy; for the purpose of photography; for the purposes of preserving public health or public or air safety; for the purpose of preventing the spread of disease; or for the purposes of preventing serious damage to livestock, foodstuffs for livestock, crops, vegetables, fruit, growing timber, fisheries, or inland waters. General licences are issued separately for Scotland, England, and Wales, and although they have, in general, the same effect, they are organized differently in each case.

Natural England uses these powers to issue three types of licence: general licences, class licences, and personal (individual) licences:

General Licences: Natural England uses a series of standard general licences that authorize acts (sale, killing, etc.) by those that qualify under the terms of each

[38] See C. T. Reid, *Nature Conservation Law*, 3rd edn (Thomson/W. Green, 2009) at 3.3.11.

[39] See s. 16(2) Wildlife and Countryside Act 1981.

[40] See s. 16(1) Wildlife and Countryside Act 1981 as amended by SI 1995/2825.

licence, and that would otherwise be illegal. The application of the dispensation from liability that these licences confer is automatic, and provided the terms of the licence in question are strictly adhered to it is not necessary to apply for permission to carry out the actions that each licence authorizes. General licences are issued for 12 months on 1 January annually and permit a wide range of activities including the sale, exhibition, and possession of protected species of bird. They allow the control of certain species of bird if they are in conflict with conservation or human interests.[41] Birds may be trapped, kept, and then released for rehabilitation or research under licence, and the police have power under licence to keep birds pending legal proceedings, and to take and retain tissue and blood samples for the purpose of prosecuting legal proceedings.[42] There is also a general licence permitting 'authorized persons'—in practice usually the landowner or occupier—to kill or take certain species of bird in order to prevent damage to flora or fauna; for example, to take ruddy ducks or their nests and eggs,[43] or Canada geese where they are threatening the viability of indigenous lapwing populations.[44] The general licence permitting the possession of wild birds for the purposes of rehabilitation allows authorized bodies such as the RSPCA and RSPB to possess birds that are intended for release back into the wild,[45] and veterinary surgeons and practitioners have permission under licence to possess wild birds for the purposes of providing veterinary treatment.[46] The licence will in most cases identify the birds that may be taken, sold, etc. by reference to the lists in the Schedules to the 1981 Act. An example is given in Box 5.2.

Class Licences: Class licences are similar to general licences in that they have a standard set of conditions and qualifications for their application in each case. They differ from general licences in that, in order to use the licence, a body or individual must apply to be registered to use the specific class licence that s/he wishes to use, and will remain eligible to use the licence only for so long as s/he remains registered with Natural England for its use. There is also a reporting requirement attached to many class licences, and annual reporting of the number of birds taken, possessed, etc. will be required as a term of continuing registration to use the class licence in question. The identity and eligibility of potential users varies, and the range of activities permitted also varies from licence to licence. So, for example, managers of airports licensed by the Civil Aviation Authority or the Ministry of Defence are

[41] General Licence WML-GL04 (Licence to kill or take certain birds to prevent serious damage or disease) which authorized killing or taking birds by authorized persons (ie landowners and occupiers). Available at: <http://www.naturalengland.org.uk/Images/wlc-gl04_tcm6-24149.pdf>.

[42] See General Licences WML-GL09 (Licence to keep certain birds pending legal proceedings (Schedule 4 birds)) and WML-GL10 (to retain blood and other tissue samples (wild birds and wild animals)). Available at: <http://www.naturalengland.org.uk/Images/wml-gl09_tcm6-24155.pdf>.

[43] General Licence WML-GL 21. Available at: <http://www.naturalengland.org.uk/Images/wml-gl21_tcm6-24169.pdf>.

[44] General Licence WML-GL06. Available at: <http://www.naturalengland.org.uk/Images/wml-gl06_tcm6-24151.pdf>.

[45] General Licence WML-GL07. Available at: <http://www.naturalengland.org.uk/Images/wml-gl07_tcm6-24153.pdf>.

[46] General Licence WML-GL08. Available at: <http://www.naturalengland.org.uk/Images/wml-gl08_tcm6-24154.pdf>.

Box 5.2 The Operation of General Licences–Preventing Damage

Natural England General Licence WML-GL04

One of the most important of the general licences issued by Natural England is Licence WML-GL04 which permits landowners, occupiers, and other 'authorized persons' to kill or take specified wild birds in circumstances that would otherwise constitute a criminal offence under the 1981 Act. It is a good example of the way in which the licence mechanisms works, the very detailed nature of the requirements attached to many licences, and some of the controversial aspects of the licence mechanism.

Purpose: the licence can only be used to prevent serious damage to livestock, foodstuffs for livestock, crops, vegetables, fruit, growing timber, fisheries and inland waters, and to prevent the spread of disease. It is not necessary to apply to use the licence, or to be registered with Natural England in order to do so.

Actions permitted by licence: authorized persons may kill or take any of the wild birds listed in the licence, and may take damage or destroy their nests or eggs. The birds covered by the licence are: (a) crow, collared doves, lesser black-backed gulls, jackdaw, jay, magpie, feral pigeons, rooks, and wood pigeons (all native species). In relation to these birds only, semi-automatic weapons may be used, hand-held, or propelled nets, and cage traps (for example with decoys); and (b) Canada goose, Monk parakeet, and ring-necked parakeet (non-native species).

Licence conditions: Perhaps the most important condition is that the licence can only be relied upon to kill or disturb native species ((a)) if the authorized person—for example, the landowner—'is satisfied that appropriate legal methods of resolving the problem such as scaring and proofing are either ineffective or impracticable'. This is a subjective and self-referential test. Proving that the landowner or occupier did not have this belief may be difficult on the facts, making it difficult to secure convictions in many cases. In the case of non-native species such as parakeets it is not necessary for landowners to satisfy themselves that non-lethal methods are ineffective, although they are encouraged to use non-lethal methods where possible.

The licence has limitations: it cannot be used for other purposes, such as to prevent noise or nuisance, or to prevent damage to vehicles or buildings. Neither does it confer a right of entry onto land. And if birds are to be found in an SSSI notified under Part 2 of the 1981 Act, it will not authorize any acts which are notified as operations likely to damage the conservation interest (OLDSIs) of the site or its flora and fauna.[47]

permitted under licence to manage wild birds for the purpose of preserving air safety.[48] Several class licences apply to authorize the possession and transport of live and dead specimens of wild bird and animals for scientific research purposes, including great crested newts and Annex IV species listed in the Habitats Directive.[49] An example is given in Box 5.3.

[47] As to which, see Chapter 3, pp. 84 ff.

[48] Licence WML-CL012. Available at: <http://www.naturalengland.org.uk/Images/wml-cl12_tcm6-24178.pdf>.

[49] See Class Licence WML-CL01, WML-CL07, 08 and 09. All available at: <http://www.naturalengland.org.uk/ourwork/regulation/wildlife/licences/classlicences.aspx>.

Box 5.3 The Operation of Class Licences—Scientific Research

Natural England Class Licence WML-CL01

This licence permits the possession and transport of dead specimens and derivatives of wild animals and plants listed in Annex IV of the Habitats Directive. This includes European species of protected animal, such as all bats, horseshoe bats, the wildcat, dormouse, Great crested newt, common otter, and smooth snake, and European protected species of plant including shore dock, lady's slipper, fen orchids, and early gentian. Possession of specimens or derivatives of any of these outside the terms of the licence is an offence.[50]

Possession is authorized by the licence for the purposes of science or education only, and only in circumstances where the specimen was taken from the wild without breaching the relevant laws of the member state where it was found. The Class Licence lists the organizations that can take advantage of the licence. These include museums with full accreditation under the Museums Accreditation Scheme, and educational establishments registered with the Department for Education and Skills, as well as DEFRA's food and environment research and veterinary agencies, DEFRA's Plant Health Division, English Heritage, and Natural England, NERC research centres, the Institute of Zoology London and the Royal Botanic Gardens (Kew). Although these bodies do not have to apply to be registered to use the class licence, they must notify Natural England's wildlife licensing unit within one month of the date of first possession of a dead specimen or derivative of an animal or plant covered by the licence. There are restrictions on the use of the licence by anybody convicted of a wildlife offence on or after 1 January 2010. Specimens kept under the terms of the licence must be catalogued and a register of specimens and derivates must be kept and updated annually in a form prescribed in the licence itself. This information must be made available to Natural England for inspection at any reasonable time. It is an offence to contravene the terms of the licence.[51]

Class licences were introduced in 2012, following a public consultation and review of Natural England's licensing functions carried out in 2011,[52] and several former general licences were reissued as class licences for future use. The practical import of this was to make it necessary for potential users to register for their future use, and to impose in some cases a reporting function on the manner in which the licences were being used.

Personal Licences: Natural England can also issue a personal licence to an individual or body authorizing specific acts that would otherwise be illegal under the 1981 Act. A personal licence must be applied for in each case, and each application will be

[50] Under the Conservation of Habitats and Species Regulations 2010, SI 2010/490, regs. 41(3) and 45(2). The protected species in question are listed in Schedules 2 (European protected species of animals) and 5 (European protected species of plant) to the 2010 Regulations. See further Chapter 6, p. 216.

[51] Under reg. 58 Conservation of Habitats and Species Regulations 2010, SI 2010/490. Contravention is on conviction subject to a level 5 fine of max £5000 and/or a six-month custodial sentence.

[52] For which, see <http://www.naturalengland.org.uk/ourwork/consultations/generallicense.aspx>.

assessed on its own merits before a licence specific to the situation and requirements is issued. An application for a personal licence will be necessary where the actions desired are not covered by an extant general or class licence.

The use of General and Class licences is intended to reduce the bureaucracy inherent in the administration of the licensing mechanism, and to reduced transaction costs for research establishments, landowners, and other potential user groups. Nevertheless, it remains the case that the licensing system currently operates in a way that makes it difficult to assess the current legal status, protected or otherwise, of many species of wild bird in different situations. Finding the applicable law can be difficult, and the law suffers a lack of transparency, with important changes in the status of members of protected bird species subject to variation by administrative action, through the issue or periodic variation of licences, without legislative scrutiny. The system still carries high transaction costs for farmers, landowners, and others who need to apply for licences in a wide range of situations. It is also arguable that a better licensing system would deliver administrative savings for the Conservation Bodies, such as Natural England, that have to administer it. The Law Commission review of wildlife law, to be undertaken in its *Eleventh Programme of Law Reform,*[53] will review the licensing system with a view to its simplification and improvement.

(iii) 'Authorized' persons

Most of the defences to the general offence of killing or taking wild birds, and also the ability to lawfully kill game birds in the open season, only apply to 'authorized persons'. This is widely defined to mean the owner or occupier of the land on which the authorized action takes place, or someone authorized by him.[54] It also includes any person authorized in writing by the local authority for the area where the authorized action takes place. In England and Wales it includes, in relation to wild birds, any person authorized by the Environment Agency, a water undertaker or sewage undertaker, or any of the statutory Conservation Bodies (for example, Natural England), and in Scotland also includes a salmon fishery board or district board for a fishery district.[55]

(d) Killing birds by unlawful means

Section 5 creates a separate offence prohibiting the use of certain means or devices for killing, trapping, or taking wild birds. These offences are founded in notions of

[53] Law Commission, *Eleventh Programme of Law Reform* (Law Com No. 330, 2011) at para. 2.86: available at <http://lawcommission.justice.gov.uk/docs/lc330_eleventh_programme.pdf>. *Wildlife Law: A Consultation Paper*, Law Commission Consultation Paper No 206 (2012), makes recommendations for standardizing the licensing system and introducing transparency into the administration of licences through the adoption of statutory factors to be taken into account by decision makers when issuing licences; see paras. 5.26–5.49 and 7.40–7.46.

[54] S. 27(1) Wildlife and Countryside Act 1981.

[55] Ie within the meaning of the Salmon Fisheries (Scotland) Act 1862; s. 27(1)(c)(ii) Wildlife and Countryside Act 1981.

fair play, and the avoidance of indiscriminate and large-scale methods of killing birds. As might be expected, the prohibited articles for taking or killing birds include the use of poisons, springes, traps, gins, snares, and lines and hooks, and the use of decoys. As to methods of killing or taking wild birds, the use of semi-automatic weapons, bows and crossbows, artificial lighting, and chemical wetting agents are all prohibited. This is a freestanding offence, and applies even where the bird killed could have been lawfully killed by other means; for example, because it is a game bird or pest within the meaning of the Act.

The use of poisoned baits is a criminal offence,[56] but in practice it is very difficult to prove in a criminal prosecution. The Natural Environment and Rural Communities Act 2006[57] therefore introduced a new offence of possessing pesticides harmful to wildlife that include ingredients proscribed by regulations made by the minister. Conviction will carry a possible term of imprisonment for up to 51 weeks and/or a fine not exceeding level 5 on the standard scale.[58] Wide powers of entry are conferred on wildlife inspectors appointed by the Secretary of State or Welsh Assembly Government to enter any premises if they have reasonable cause to suspect that they may find evidence of an offence being committed under this provision, to require the provision of information about any substance found on premises, and to seize any substance if they have reasonable grounds to believe it provides evidence of an offence being committed; that is, of illegal poisons being stored on the premises.[59]

(e) Prohibition on sale of wild birds or eggs

The law strictly prohibits the sale of any live or dead wild bird or its eggs. The offences here are widely drawn, and make it illegal[60] to (a) sell, offer, or expose for sale, or have in one's possession, or transport for the purpose of sale, any live or dead wild bird or an egg of a wild bird or any part of such an egg; or (b) to publish or cause to be published an advertisement likely to be understood as conveying that one will buy or sell, or intends to buy or sell, any of those things. The offence in (a) does not apply to wild birds listed in Schedule 3 Part 1 of the 1981 Act provided the specimens concerned have been bred in captivity, have been ringed or marked in accordance with the relevant regulations and have not been reintroduced into the wild as part of a reintroduction programme.[61] Schedule 3 lists 19 species of wild bird that may be sold if bred in captivity, including: blackbirds, bullfinches, chaffinches, greenfinches and goldfinches; jays, jackdaws and magpies; barn owls; starlings; song thrushes; and yellowhammers. The sale of dead wild birds, or any part of them, is also prohibited except for some species of game bird listed in

[56] Under s. 5 (1) Wildlife and Countryside Act 1981.

[57] S. 43 Natural Environment and Rural Communities Act 2006.

[58] S. 43(4) Natural Environment and Rural Communities Act 2006. At the time of writing the maximum fine is £5000.

[59] See s. 44(1) and (2) Natural Environment and Rural Communities Act 2006.

[60] See s. 6(1) and (2) Wildlife and Countryside Act 1981.

[61] See S. 6(5) Wildlife and Countryside Act 1981 and Schedule 3 Part 1; Wildlife and Countryside (Ringing of Certain Birds) Regulations 1982, SI 1982/1220.

Schedule 3 parts 2 and 3 of the 1981 Act. Wood pigeons can be sold dead at any time of the year,[62] while a number of game birds can be sold dead between 1 September and 28 February each year. The latter include capercaillie, coots, tufted ducks, mallards, pintails, common snipe, teal, and woodcock.[63] In Scotland a registration system operates for the purposes of registering those individuals authorized to sell dead birds.[64] It should be noted that the prohibition on the possession of dead wild birds is not limited to those recently captured and killed: the possession of stuffed and mounted wild birds can constitute an offence under the 1981 Act.[65]

(f) Keeping wild birds

Keeping wild birds will be an offence in most cases under the general prohibition on the possession of live and dead birds contained in section 1 of the 1981 Act.[66] There are, however, special provisions that apply to some types of bird (specified in Schedule 4 to the 1981 Act) that may be kept in captivity subject to certain conditions. The birds listed in Schedule 4 that may be kept in captivity include, in England and Wales, the honey buzzard, eagles (golden or white-tailed), harriers, goshawks, merlin, peregrine falcons, and ospreys.[67] The list for Scotland is somewhat longer. The bird(s) must be registered and ringed in accordance with regulations made by the minister.[68] If someone is convicted of an offence (for example, damaging nests, killing specimens, or taking eggs) in relation to golden or white-tailed eagles, or ospreys,[69] or any other protected species listed in Schedule 1, then a five-year ban on keeping birds is applied. As a consequence the offender will be guilty of a further offence if found in possession of wild birds within five years of the conviction, or if s/he knowingly disposes of a bird, etc.[70] irrespective of whether the birds are ringed and registered. The ban on keeping birds is three years following conviction if the conviction relates to birds *other than* protected species under Schedules 1 or ZA1. In Scotland a five-year ban on keeping Schedule 4 birds follows any conviction, and no distinction is made in this regard between offences against different categories of bird, their nests, or eggs.[71]

62 See Schedule 3 Part 2 Wildlife and Countryside Act 1981.

63 See Schedule 3 Part 3 Wildlife and Countryside Act 1981.

64 See the Wildlife and Countryside (Registration to sell etc. certain dead wild birds) Regulations 1982 SI 1982/1219 as amended by SI 1991/479. The registration scheme was repealed in England and Wales by the Countryside and Rights of Way Act 2000 Schedule 16.

65 *Robinson v Everett* [1988] Crim LR 699.

66 S. 1(2) Wildlife and Countryside Act 1981, p. 163.

67 Schedule 4 as amended by the Wildlife and Countryside Act 1981 (Variation of Schedule 4) Order 2008, SI 2008/2356, and in Wales by SI 2009/780.

68 S. 7(1) Wildlife and Countryside Act 1981. See the Wildlife and Countryside (Ringing of Certain Birds) Regulations 1982, SI 1982/1220 as amended by SI 1991/478, SI1994/1151, SI 2004/640 and SI 2008/2357 (England); Wildlife and Countryside (Registration, Ringing and Marking of certain Captive Birds)(Wales) Regulations 2003, SI 2003/3235 (Wales).

69 Ie species listed in Schedule ZA1 to the 1981 Act.

70 See s. 7(4).

71 S. 7(3) amended by the Criminal Justice (Scotland) Act 2003, ss. 77, 89(2)(b), Schedule 3 para. 2.

It is also an offence to keep a bird for the purposes of competitions or at premises where competitions are taking place.[72] This office applies to any bird *other than* a wild bird listed in Part 1 of Schedule 3, and/or any bird one of whose parents was a wild bird in this category. Schedule 3 birds, such as, for example, blackbirds, jays, barn owls, etc., bred in captivity, can be kept for competition showing, provided they have been ringed and registered under the relevant regulations.[73] In practice licences issued under section 16 of the 1981 Act cover the showing in competitions of most captive-bred wild birds.

General rules apply as to the conditions in which birds are to be kept in order to prevent unnecessary suffering. It is an offence to keep a bird in a cage or other receptacle which is not sufficient in height, length, or breadth to permit the bird to stretch its wings freely.[74] This offence applies to protect all bird species, and is not confined to the keeping of wild birds. There are several exceptions, however:[75] the offence does not apply to poultry, nor to the keeping or confining of any bird while it is in the course of conveyance, by whatever means, or is being shown for the purposes of a public exhibition or competition. If it is being shown in a competition or exhibition, the time during which the bird is kept or confined must not in the aggregate exceed 72 hours. Similarly, it is not an offence to keep a bird in confined conditions while it is undergoing examination or treatment by a veterinary surgeon or veterinary practitioner. It is also a criminal offence to organize, assist in or take part in an event at which wild birds are released by hand or otherwise for the purpose of being shot immediately after being liberated.[76] The owner or occupier of land used for these purposes will also be committing an offence.

Protection of Wild Animals

The law protecting individual wild animals, and species of animal, is based on a similar model to that applicable under Part 1 of the 1981 Act to wild birds. The modern law is, however, if anything even more fragmented than that applicable to wild birds. A general measure of protection is afforded to a wide range of wild animals by provisions in the 1981 Act, and described on pp. 178–84. These have been separately amended for Scotland, and for England and Wales. In addition to these, there are discrete legislative measures applicable to some types of wild animal; for example, badgers and seals. And the implementation of the Habitats Directive has resulted in additional (and separate) protection being afforded to European level species of animal and plant under the Conservation of Habitats and Species Regulations 2010 (England and Wales) and the Conservation etc. Regulations 1994[77] as amended (Scotland). The protection of European level species is

[72] S. 6(3) Wildlife and Countryside Act 1981.
[73] See s. 6(5) Wildlife and Countryside Act 1981.
[74] S. 8(1) Wildlife and Countryside Act 1981.
[75] See s. 8(2) Wildlife and Countryside Act 1981.
[76] S. 8(3) Wildlife and Countryside Act 1981.
[77] SI 1994/2716.

considered in Chapter 6. This chapter will confine itself to the protection of all other individuals and species of animals under the domestic law of England, Wales, and Scotland.

(a) Part 1 Wildlife and Countryside Act 1981

Protection similar in scope to that for wild birds is conferred on those species of animal listed in Schedule 5 to the 1981 Act.[78] Thus it is an offence to intentionally kill, injure, or take any animal listed in Schedule 5, and in Scotland it is also an offence to do so recklessly.[79] It is also an offence to have in one's possession any dead or live wild animal, any part thereof, or anything derived from such an animal.[80] It is also an offence to damage or destroy any structure or place which any wild animal specified in Schedule 5 uses for shelter or protection, to disturb a protected animal while it is occupying a structure or place which it uses for shelter or protection, or to obstruct access to any structure or place which any protected animal uses for shelter or protection.[81] For protected species see Box 5.4. Cetaceans and basking sharks are given special protection. It is an offence to intentionally or recklessly disturb a whale, dolphin, or basking shark—an offence that also extends to the disturbance of porpoises in Scotland, but not England and Wales.[82]

Similar defences and exceptions to liability apply to those discussed earlier in connection with wild birds. It is not an offence if one can show that the animal was not killed or taken in contravention of the 1981 Act or its predecessor.[83] Neither is it an offence to take an animal that has been disabled (other than by one's own unlawful act) for the purposes of tending it and releasing it when recovered, or to kill an animal that has been so severely disabled that there is no reasonable prospect of its recovery.[84] There is also a general defence that applies if the death or injury of a protected animal is the 'incidental result of a lawful operation and could not reasonably have been avoided'.[85] This will provide an exception to liability, for example, where the death of a protected animal is the result of lawful agricultural or forestry operations and could not have been foreseen. This defence is circumscribed in its application in Scotland by additional requirements for its application; the accused must have taken reasonable precautions to avoid the offence being committed, could not have foreseen that the injury or death to the animals in question would have resulted from the

text continues on p 182

78 See s. 9 Wildlife and Countryside Act 1981.

79 S. 9(1) Wildlife and Countryside Act 1981.

80 S. 9(2) Wildlife and Countryside Act 1981.

81 See s. 9(4) Wildlife and Countryside Act 1981.

82 See s. 9(4A) Wildlife and Countryside Act 1981. The offence was extended to porpoises in Scotland by ss. 50, 59, Schedule 6 para. 8(6) the Nature Conservation (Scotland) Act 2004 (asp 6); SSI 2004/407, art. 2.

83 Ie the Conservation of Wild Creatures and Wild Plants Act 1975. See s. 9(3) and (3A) Wildlife and Countryside Act 1981.

84 S. 10(3)(a)(b) Wildlife and Countryside Act 1981.

85 S. 10(3)(c) Wildlife and Countryside Act 1981.

Box 5.4 Protected Species of Animal[86]

Adder (in respect of section 9(5) only)
Allis Shad (in respect of section 9(1) and (4)(a) only)
Anemone, Ivell's Sea
Anemone, Startlet Sea
Bats, Horseshoe (all species but in respect of section 9(4)(b) and (c), and (5) only)
Bats, Typical (all species but in respect of section 9(4)(b) and (c), and (5) only)
Beetle Graphoderus zonatus
Beetle Hypebaeus flavipe
Beetle Parcymus aeneus
Beetle - Lesser Silver Water
Beetle - Mire Pill (in respect of section 9(4)(a) only)
Beetle - Rainbow Leaf
Beetle, Stag (in respect of section 9(5) only)
Beetle, Violet Click
Burbot
Butterfly, Northern Brown Argus
Butterfly, Adonis Blue
Butterfly, Chalkhill Blue
Butterfly, Silver-studded Blue
Butterfly, Small Blue
Butterfly, Large Copper
Butterfly, Purple Emperor
Butterfly, Duke of Burgandy Fritillary
Butterfly, Glanville Fritillary
Butterfly, Heath Fritillary
Butterfly, High Brown Fritillary
Butterfly, Marsh Fritillary Butterfly, Pearl-bordered Fritillary
Butterfly, Black Hairstreak
Butterfly, Brown Hairstreak
Butterfly, White Letter Hairstreak
Butterfly, Large Heath
Butterfly, Large Blue (in respect of section 9(4)(b) and (c), and (5) only)
Butterfly, Mountain Ringlet

(*Continued*)

[86] Source: Schedule 5 Wildlife and Countryside Act 1981, as amended.

Box 5.4 Continued

Butterfly, Chequered Skipper
Butterfly, Lulworth Skipper
Butterfly, Silver Spotted Skipper
Butterfly, Swallowtail
Butterfly, Large tortoiseshell
Butterfly, Wood White
Cat, Wild (in respect of section 9(4)(b) and (c), and (5) only)
Cicada, New Forest
Crayfish, Atlantic Stream
Cricket, Field
Cricket, Mole
Dameselfly
Southern Dolphins (all species but in respect of section 9(4A) and (5) only)
Dormouse (in respect of section 9(4)(b) and (c), and (5) only)
Dragonfly, Norfolk Aeshna
Frog, Common (in respect of section 9(5) only)
Goby, Couch's
Goby, Giant
Grasshopper, Wart-biter
Hatchet Shell, Northern
Hydroid, Marine
Lagoon Snail
Lagoon Snail, De Folin's
Lagoon Worm, Tentacled
Leech, Medicinal
Lizard, Sand (in respect of section 9(4)(b) and (c), and (5) only)
Lizard, Viviparous (in respect of section 9(5) only)
Marten, Pine
Mat, Trembling Sea
Moth, Barberry Carpet
Moth, Black-veined
Moth, Essex Emerald
Moth, Fiery Clearwing
Moth, Fisher's Estuarine (in respect of section 9(4)(b) and (c) and (5) only)
Moth, New Forest Burnet
Moth, Reddish Buff
Moth, Sussex Emerald

Mussel, Fan (in respect of section 9(1), (2), and (5) only)
Mussel, Freshwater Pearl
Newt, Great Crested or Warty (in respect of section 9(4)(b) and (c), and (5) only)
Newt, Palmate (in respect of section 9(5) only)
Newt, Smooth (in respect of section 9(5) only)
Otter, Common (in respect of section 9(4)(b) and (c), and (5) only)
Porpoises (all species but in respect of section 9(5) only)
Sandworm, Lagoon
Sea Fan, Pink (in respect of section 9(1), 9(2), and 9(5) only)
Seahorse, Short Snouted (with respect to England [and Wales] only)
Seahorse, Spiny (with respect to England [and Wales] only)
Sea Slug, Lagoon
Shad, Twaite (in respect of section 9(4)(a) only)
Shark, Angel (in respect of section 9(1) only and with respect to England [and Wales], other than the excluded waters, only)
Shark, Basking
Shrimp, Fairy
Shrimp, Lagoon
Sand Slow-worm (in respect of section 9(5) only)
Snail, Glutinous
Snail, Roman (in respect of section 9(1), (2), and (5) only and with respect to England [and Wales] only)
Snail, Sandbowl
Snake, Grass (in respect of section 9(5) only)
Snake, Smooth (in respect of section 9(4)(b) and (c), and (5) only)
Spider, Fen Raft
Spider, Ladybird
Squirrel, Red
Sturgeon (in respect of section 9(4)(b) and (c), and (5) only)
Toad, Common (in respect of section 9(5) only)
Toad, Natterjack (in respect of section 9(4)(b) and (c), and (5) only)
Turtle, Flatback Natator
Turtle, Green Sea (in respect of section 9(4)(b) and (c), and (5) only)
Turtle, Hawksbill (in respect of section 9(4)(b) and (c), and (5) only)
Turtle, Kemp's Ridley Sea (in respect of section 9(4)(b) and (c), and (5) only)
Turtle, Leatherback Sea (in respect of section 9(4)(b) and (c), and (5) only)
Turtle, Loggerhead Sea (in respect of section 9(4)(b) and (c), and (5) only)
Turtle, Olive Ridley Vendace
Vole, Water

(Continued)

Box 5.4 Continued

Walrus
Whale (all species) but in respect of section 9(4A) and (5) only
Whitefish

operation, and must have taken all reasonable steps in the circumstances to minimize damage and/or disturbance to the structure or place where the damage occurred.[87] No offence is committed[88] by actions that are undertaken pursuant to an order made by the ministers in relation to agricultural pest control,[89] or in relation to powers under the animal health legislation.[90]

Another defence applies to permit an 'authorized person' to kill or injure protected species of animal if s/he shows that his action 'was necessary for the purpose of preventing serious damage to livestock, foodstuffs for livestock, crops, vegetables, fruit, growing timber or any other form of property or to fisheries'.[91] This defence will apply of the benefit of the owner or occupier of the land on which the action causing death, etc. takes place, or someone authorized by him.[92] This provision prioritizes the property rights of the landowner above the public interest in nature conservation, in that it protects the landowner's right to protect the lands natural resources, and to take action against protected species of animal that threaten to impugn them. The defence will in practice, however, only be available in unforeseen emergencies: if it had become apparent that action would be necessary prior to it being undertaken, then the defence will not be available unless a licence to destroy the animals in question has been applied for as soon as reasonably practicable. The defence is also inapplicable if a licence has been applied for and refused.[93] In Scotland it is also necessary to inform the ministers as soon as reasonably practicable after the action has been undertaken.[94] This requirement does not apply in England and Wales.

It is not an offence to damage or disturb a shelter or place used by a protected species if it is within a dwelling house.[95] In relation to bats, which often roost in the lofts or attics of dwellings, this provision used to be limited to acts done in the living quarters of a dwelling. Bats are now a European protected species and therefore protected by the provisions in the Conservation of Habitats and Species

[87] S. 10(3A) Wildlife and Countryside Act 1981 (Scotland only) (inserted by Nature Conservation Scotland Act 2004, Schedule 6 para. 9(a)).
[88] See s. 10(1) Wildlife and Countryside Act 1981.
[89] Agriculture Act 1947 s. 98 (England and Wales); Agriculture (Scotland) Act 1948, s. 39 (Scotland).
[90] Ie Animal Health Act 1981.
[91] S. 10(4) Wildlife and Countryside Act 1981.
[92] See s. 27 (1) Wildlife and Countryside Act 1981 and p. 174.
[93] S. 10(6) Wildlife and Countryside Act 1981.
[94] See s. 10(6A) (Scotland only).
[95] S. 10(2) Wildlife and Countryside Act 1981.

Regulations 2010[96] (England and Wales) and the Conservation etc. Regulations 1994[97] (Scotland). These do not have an equivalent defence in relation to European protected species, and to avoid duplication all species of bat have been removed from the list of protected species under the 1981 Act. It is therefore illegal to disturb bats in any part of a dwelling, although the defence in the 1981 Act continues to apply to non-European level protected species of animal.

As with wild birds, it is an offence to offer for sale any dead or live wild animal or part thereof, or possess an animal for these purposes, and the advertisement of animals for sale is also an offence.[98] For the purposes of the offences against wild animals outlined earlier, including those of possession and offering for sale, it is presumed that an animal is a wild animal unless the contrary is shown.[99] The burden of proof is therefore on someone accused of killing, causing injury, possession, or sale, etc. to prove otherwise.

Schedule 6 lists a number of species for which the general standard of protection conferred by section 9 is lowered (see Box 5.4). The protection of Schedule 6 species is limited to the prohibition of certain methods of killing or taking them; for example the use of snares or nets, or poisonous or stupefying substances. Schedule 6 lists 14 species to which this applies, including badgers, horseshoe and common bats, bottle-nosed and common dolphins, hedgehogs, dormice, otters, polecats, shrew, and red squirrels. The proscribed methods of killing can chiefly be rationalized as proceeding from one of two concerns: (i) to prevent unnecessary suffering to animals trapped, etc., and (ii) to prohibit indiscriminate methods of killing.

In relation to the first policy concern, it is an offence to use a self-locking snare that is of a nature and so placed as to be calculated to cause bodily injury to an animal coming into contact with it, or to use a self-locking snare for the purpose of killing animals.[100] It is also an offence to fail, without reasonable excuse, to inspect any snare that has been set at least once a day.[101] This is intended to prevent suffering to animal trapped in a self-locking snare for any length of time. In Scotland, the minster has power by order to specify prohibited types of snare, and if he does so, the sale or offering for sale of such a device is also a criminal offence.[102] It is an offence to use a live mammal or bird as a decoy for the purpose of killing or taking a wild animal.[103] It is not only an offence to do this oneself, it is also an offence to knowingly cause or permit these activities to take place;[104] for example, in the case of a landowner knowingly permitting them to be carried out by hunters on his land. It is also an

[96] SI 2010/490, Chapter 6, p. 233.

[97] SI 1994/2716 (as amended).

[98] S. 9(5) Wildlife and Countryside Act 1981.

[99] S. 9(6) Wildlife and Countryside Act 1981.

[100] S. 11(1)(a)(b) Wildlife and Countryside Act 1981.

[101] See s. 11(3) ibid. In Scotland the snare or trap must be inspected a least once a day, at not more than 24-hour intervals, and any animal found trapped in the snare must be removed whether live or dead—s. 11(3) and (3A) Wildlife and Countryside Act 1981, inserted by Nature Conservation (Scotland) Act 2004, Schedule 6 para. 10(2).

[102] See s. 11(1)(a) and (3C) Wildlife and Countryside Act 1981, inserted by Nature Conservation (Scotland) Act 2004, Schedule 6 para. 10(2)(a) and 10(6)).

[103] S. 11(1)(c) Wildlife and Countryside Act 1981.

[104] S. 11(1)(d) Wildlife and Countryside Act 1981.

offence to use, or to place in such a way as to cause injury, any trap or snare, any electrical device for killing or stunning or any poisonous, poisoned, or stupefying substance, or to use nets to trap Schedule 6 animals.[105] In the case of snares or traps, it is a defence to show that the object was put in position for the purpose of killing or taking, in the interests of public health, agriculture, forestry, fisheries, or nature conservation, any wild animals which could be lawfully killed or taken by those means. The defendant must also show that s/he took all reasonable precautions to prevent injury thereby to any wild animals included in Schedule 6.[106]

In pursuit of the second policy concern (the prohibition of indiscriminate methods of killing) it is an offence to use any of the following for the purposes of killing or taking wild animals: bows, crossbows, or explosives;[107] any automatic or semi-automatic weapon; any device for illuminating a target or night sights; artificial lights ('lamping'), mirrors or dazzling devices; gas or smoke; or the use of sound recordings as a decoy.[108] It is an offence to use a mechanically propelled vehicle in immediate pursuit of an animal protected by Schedule 6 for the purpose of driving killing or taking the animal in question.[109] In all cases, it is an offence not only to commit the acts in question but also to knowingly cause or permit them to take place;[110] for example, on one's land if a landowner.

The Secretary of State has power, for the purpose of complying with an international obligation, to add to or omit from the list of prohibited methods of killing set out in the 1981 Act. This can be done by order, and in relation to animals generally or to those animal species specified in the order.[111] The Scottish ministers have further powers to specify by order the criteria that methods of killing must meet to come within or without the prohibition earlier, and also the circumstances in which snares, traps, or other methods of killing must be set in order to constitute an offence.[112]

(b) Species-specific protective legislation

Certain species of animal benefit from specific legal protection, in addition to that in Part 1 of the 1981 Act.

(i) Badgers

Badgers are protected against killing by unlawful means under Schedule 6 to the 1981 Act. They are also given more general protection by the Protection of Badgers Act

[105] See ss. 11(2)(a) and (b) Wildlife and Countryside Act 1981.
[106] See s. 11(6) and (7) Wildlife and Countryside Act 1981.
[107] S. 11(1)(b) Wildlife and Countryside Act 1981.
[108] S. 11(2)(c) and (d) Wildlife and Countryside Act 1981.
[109] S. 11(2)(e) Wildlife and Countryside Act 1981.
[110] S. 11(2)(f) Wildlife and Countryside Act 1981.
[111] See s. 11(4) Wildlife and Countryside Act 1981.
[112] See s. 11(4A) Wildlife and Countryside Act 1981 inserted by Nature Conservation (Scotland) Act 2004, Schedule 6 para. 10(7).

1992. This is structured in similar terms to the 1981 Act, with a general offence of deliberate killing or taking of badgers in similar terms to those applicable to other protected species of animal and bird, and set out in the 1981 Act (p. 178). The history and special characteristics of cruel practices applied to badgers, including badger-baiting and digging, and the problems of proof that can arise in cases of killing and cruelty, mean that some of the detailed provisions are different, and are specific to badgers as a species, however.

It is an offence to wilfully kill, injure, or take, or attempt to kill, injure, or take, a badger.[113] The burden of proof that applies is, however, reversed where someone is charged with killing, taking, or injuring a badger: when there is evidence from which it could reasonably be concluded that at the material time, the accused was attempting to kill, injure, or take a badger, s/he is presumed to have been attempting to kill, injure, or take the badger in question unless the contrary is shown.[114] It is also an offence to have in one's possession a dead badgers or any part or thing derived there one.[115] The possession of a live badger is also an offence, unless otherwise authorized under the Act (for example, by a licence), and it is also an offence to sell or offer for sale a live badger.[116] The marking of badgers, or attaching rings or tags to them, is also an offence, unless the badger is lawfully in one's possession under the terms of a licence issued by the public authorities.[117]

A number of offences of cruelty against badgers are also set out in the 1992 Act. It is an offence to cruelly ill-treat a badger, to use badger tongs in the course of killing or taking, or attempting to kill or take, a badger, or to dig for badgers. It is an offence to use firearms against them of other than specified size and power; it is illegal to use any firearm other than a smooth bore weapon of not less than 20 bore or a rifle using ammunition having a muzzle energy not less than 160 foot-pounds, and a bullet weighing not less than 38 grains.[118] In relation to digging for badgers, the onus of proof is again reversed, in that if there is evidence from which it can reasonably be concluded that a person has been digging for badgers, the onus is on him to prove otherwise.[119] Legal protection is also extended to badgers' setts. It is an offence to damage or destroy a sett, cause a dog to enter a sett, obstruct access to a sett, or to disturb a badger while it is occupying a sett.[120] This offence will be committed where accused acts are not only intentional, but where they are committed recklessly as to whether these consequences will follow. The Act only

113 S. 1(1) Protection of Badgers Act 1992.

114 See s. 1(2) Protection of Badgers Act 1992. The burden of proof is also reversed in relation to other offences involving badgers, such as digging setts.

115 S. 1(3) Protection of Badgers Act 1992.

116 S. 4 Protection of Badgers Act 1992. It is an offence not only to have a badger in one's possession but also 'under his control'.

117 S. 5 Protection of Badgers Act 1992.

118 S. 2(1) Protection of Badgers Act 1992. The intention in specifying a minimum size of weapon and projectile is to avoid unnecessary suffering caused by the injury, short of death, of badgers that are shot.

119 See s. 2(2) Protection of Badgers Act 1992.

120 S. 3(1) Protection of Badgers Act 1992.

protects the badger's 'sett' however: and this is defined in the 1992 Act to mean 'any structure or place which displays signs indicating current use by a badger'.[121] In *Green v DPP*[122] it was held that digging *above* a badger sett in such as way that the tunnels and chambers forming the occupied part of the structure were not damaged was not an offence under this provision. It is a defence that the actions were necessary to prevent serious damage to crops, poultry, or other property,[123] provided a licence has been applied for and is still under consideration.[124] And the 1992 Act provides a defence if the action damaging the sett was the incidental result of a lawful operation and could not reasonably have been avoided.[125] This defence does not apply to the destruction of setts or to the introduction of dogs to a sett.[126] The destruction of a badger sett will, therefore, require the prior grant of a ministry licence in all cases.[127]

Similar defences are available as apply under the 1981 Act. Killing a badger is not unlawful if necessary to prevent serious damage to crops poultry or livestock, but the circumstances must be such as to make it impossible to apply first for a licence to do so from the relevant authorities.[128] Similarly, taking a badger that has been injured, for the purposes of tending it, and killing a badger that has been seriously injured, such that it would be an 'act of mercy', will not constitute an offence.[129] It is also not an offence to unavoidably kill a badger as 'an incidental result of a lawful operation'.[130] This would apply, for example, to the unforeseen death of badgers during agricultural or forestry operations.

The Conservation Bodies and agriculture ministers have wide powers to grant licences that authorize actions that would otherwise be criminal offences prohibited by the 1992 Act. The Conservation Bodies can, for example, grant licences authorizing any person to kill, take, or possess badgers, or to interfere with badger setts, for educational or scientific purposes or for the conservation of badgers, for the purposes of zoological gardens, or for the marking of badgers.[131] A licence can also be granted that permits interference with a badger sett for the purposes of carrying out operations consented by permission under the Town Planning legislation, or to preserve ancient monuments that have been listed for protection under the Ancient Monuments and Archaeological Areas Act 1979.[132] The ministers may also grant licences to kill or take badgers, or interfere with their setts, for a wide range of purposes including: the prevention of the spread of disease; preventing

[121] See s. 14 Protection of Badgers Act 1992.

[122] [2001] Env LR 15.

[123] S. 8(1) Protection of Badgers Act 1992.

[124] See s. 8(2) applying s. 7(2) Protection of Badgers Act 1992.

[125] S. 8(3) Protection of Badgers Act 1992.

[126] Ie the offences in s. 3(b) and (d) of the 1992 Act.

[127] This will be the case even if it is an incidental result of a lawful operation, eg an agricultural operation that does not require planning consent, or an operation that has been granted planning permission under the Town and Country Planning Act 1990.

[128] See s. 7 Protection of Badgers Act 1992.

[129] S. 6 Protection of Badgers Act 1992.

[130] S. 6(c) Protection of Badgers Act 1992.

[131] S. 10(1) Protection of Badgers Act 1992.

[132] See s. 10(1)(d) and (e) Protection of Badgers Act 1992.

serious damage to land, crops, poultry, or any other form of property; and for the purpose of any agricultural or forestry operation.[133] The ministers must consult the statutory Conservation Bodies as to the exercise of these licensing functions, and cannot grant a licence of a particular description unless they have first been advised by the Conservation Body of the circumstances in which a licence of that description should be granted.[134] The grant of a licence will, in all cases (whether granted by the Conservation Body or minister) authorize actions only within a geographical area identified in the licence. Licences can contain conditions as to the manner of their exercise, and can be revoked at any time.[135] Failure to comply with the conditions stipulated in a licence will in itself constitute a criminal offence.[136] A licence must not, however, be unreasonably withheld or revoked.[137] Actions carried out pursuant to a licence granted under these provisions will not constitute an offence under the law restricting the placing of poisons, provided always that the conditions in the licence have been met[138]

The licensing powers are in practice of considerable importance. The use of licences granted by Natural England under the 1992 Act is, for example, the mechanism by which the trial programme of culling badgers in two areas of South West England was authorized in 2012 as part of DEFRA's Bovine TB Eradication Programme for England.[139] The latter has issued statutory guidance to Natural England[140] on the grant of licences in the two trial areas within the programme. The guidance envisages a four-year culling trial period, and sets out the conditions to be include in licences issued by the Conservation Body; these must include stipulations on the minimum area of land to be included in the licence (150 km^2), a requirement that participating farmers enter into a Badger Control Agreement with DEFRA,[141] and prohibit culling during a close season (1 December to 31 May for trapping and shooting badgers). The guidance also requires the inclusion of conditions as to the intensity and pace of the culling programme; for example, licences must require an intensive cull in the first year of the licence that removes a minimum of 70 per cent of adult badgers in the trial area.[142]

[133] S. 10(2) Protection of Badgers Act 1992.

[134] S. 10(6) Protection of Badgers Act 1992.

[135] S. 10(3) and (8) Protection of Badgers Act 1992.

[136] S. 10(8) Protection of Badgers Act 1992.

[137] S. 10(9) Protection of Badgers Act 1992.

[138] See s. 10(10) Protection of Badgers Act 1992.

[139] See <http://www.defra.gov.uk/news/2012/01/19/pilot-areas-confirmed/>. The trial culls were subsequently postponed to 2013: see <http://www.defra.gov.uk/news/2012/10/23/badger-cull/>.

[140] Under s. 15(2) Natural Environment and Rural Communities Act 2006.

[141] Ie an agreement under s. 13 Natural Environment and Rural Communities Act 2006. The terms of this agreement will be enforceable separately and in addition to those in the licence issued under the 1992 Act.

[142] Guidance to Natural England: Licences to Kill or Take Badgers for the purposes of preventing the spread of Bovine TB under s. 10(2)(a) of the Protection of Badgers Act 1992 (DEFRA 2012) available at: <http://www.defra.gov.uk/publications/files/pb13692-bovinetb-guidance-ne.pdf>. The conditions to be inserted in licences are set out paras. 9, 10, and 11 of the guidance at pp. 4–6.

(ii) Seals

Seals also benefit from special legal protection, in this case under the Conservation of Seals Act 1970. The protection is broadly similar to that described earlier for birds, animals, and plants, although the 1970 Act also imposes a close season during which it is illegal to wilfully kill, capture, or take either of the two seal species found in UK waters. For grey seals the close season is from 1 September to 31 December, and for common seals from 1 June to 31 August.[143] It is a criminal offence to kill, take, or injure a seal during the close season for that species.[144] The Secretary of State has wide power, furthermore, to prohibit the killing, injuring, or taking of seals of either species at any time if this is necessary for the proper conservation of seals in an area.[145] This power is exercisable by order, and was exercised in 1991 to prohibit the killing, taking, or injury of common seals in the Shetland Islands and adjacent territorial waters.[146] It is a criminal offence to use a poisonous substance to kill or injure seals, or to use for the purpose of killing, injuring, or taking any seal a firearm other than a rifle using ammunition having a muzzle energy of not less than 600 foot-pounds, and a bullet weighing not less than 45 grains.[147] The possession of poison or of a firearm that does not comply with this requirement, for the purposes of killing seals, is in itself a criminal offence.[148]

The defences available under the 1970 Act are similar to those applicable under both the Wildlife and Countryside Act and Protection of Badgers Act 1992. It is not an offence to take an injured seal for the purpose of tending it, neither is it an offence to kill a seal if it is seriously injured (mercy killing).[149] It is also not an offence to kill or injure a seal where this occurs as an incidental result of a lawful action; for example, where a seal is injured by nets during a lawful fishing operation. Neither is it an offence to kill seals in order to prevent damage to fishing equipment, tackle, or nets, or to protect fish in a net, provided that they are in the vicinity of the equipment/nets, etc. at the time they are killed.[150]

The Secretary of State has power to grant licences to any person to authorize the killing and taking of seals. This power can be exercised for a number of reasons, including the prevention of damage to fisheries, and, perhaps controversially, for the reduction of a population surplus of seals 'for management purposes' or the use of a 'population surplus' of seals as a 'resource'.[151] Licences can also be granted to further the conservation of flora and fauna in a nature reserve, SSSI, marine conservation area, or, in Scotland an area subject to a nature conservation

143 S. 2(1) Conservation of Seals Act 1970.
144 S. 2(2) Conservation of Seals Act 1970.
145 S. 3 Conservation of Seals Act 1970.
146 See the Conservation of Seals ((Common Seals) (Shetland Islands Area) Order 1991, SI 1991/2638.
147 S. 1(1) Conservation of Seals Act 1970.
148 See s. 8(2) Conservation of Seals Act 1970.
149 S. 9(1)(a) and (2) Conservation of Seals Act 1970.
150 See s. 9(1)(b) and (c) Conservation of Seals Act 1970.
151 See s. 10(1)(c) Conservation of Seals Act 1970. This begs two questions: what qualifies as a 'management purpose'? And how is a population surplus to be quantified?

order.[152] The Secretary of State must consult the Natural Environment Research Council before making a licence under these provisions, and cannot grant a licence to kill seals in a protected area, such as an SSSI, without the consent of the statutory Conservation Body; for example, Scottish Natural Heritage or Natural England.[153] The Secretary of State has power to grant written authorization to persons to enter land for the purpose of culling seals or obtaining information required for the performance of his duties under the Act.[154] Because many offences committed under the 1970 Act will take place at sea, it is provided that, for the purpose of conferring jurisdiction on any court to try alleged offences, they shall be deemed to have been committed at the place where the offender is found, or to which he is first brought after the commission of the offence.[155] The courts have power to order the forfeiture of seal skins, meat, and any firearms, poisons, or ammunition found in a convicted offenders possession at the time of the offence.[156] The Natural Environment Research Council has a duty to provide the Secretary of State with scientific advice on the management of seal populations.[157]

Seals are also listed for protection under Annex V of the Habitats and Species Directive. They are therefore also subject to the additional protection granted by the Conservation (Natural Habitats, etc.) Regulations 1994[158] and the Conservation of Habitats and Species Regulations 2010.[159] They are also protected against indiscriminate methods of killing and capture, and from methods of killing and capture that can seriously impact upon their population levels, by the Offshore Marine Conservation (Natural Habitats etc.) Regulations 2007.[160] These are focused on maintaining seal population levels at a favourable conservation status, and are discussed further in Chapter 6.[161]

Protection of Wild Plants

(a) The general law

Wild plants are treated differently to animals and birds in English law in that, unlike the latter, they are capable of ownership in their wild state and are subject to the rules of property law. Wild plants, trees, and flowers are part of the land and are therefore owned by the landowner of the property where they are to be found growing; they accrue, in other words, to the estate of the landowner.[162] The

[152] S. 10(1)(c)(iv) and (4) Conservation of Seals Act 1970.
[153] S. 10(3) Conservation of Seals Act 1970.
[154] S. 11 Conservation of Seals Act 1970.
[155] See s. 7 Conservation of Seals Act 1970.
[156] S. 6 Conservation of Seals Act 1970.
[157] S. 13 Conservation of Seals Act 1970.
[158] SI 1994/2716 (now limited in application to Scotland).
[159] SI 2010/490 (England and Wales).
[160] SI 2007/1842, as amended by SI 2009/7.
[161] See Chapter 6, pp. 232ff.
[162] See *Monsanto plc. v Tilly* [2001]Env LR 313; Blackstone's *Commentaries on the Law of England*, Vol. 2, p. 18.

protection accorded to wild plants at common law, is however, limited by the simple fact that they will normally have little or no commercial value. Causing damage to wild plants growing on someone else's land, either deliberately or negligently, will in principle give rise to liability in the law of torts; for example, for nuisance or negligence. Although causing damage to plants growing on a neighbour's land may constitute an actionable nuisance, however, it will be very difficult to quantify any 'damage' allegedly caused, as most wild plants lack a quantifiable financial value. The common law protects private interests, and does not recognize and protect 'public' (or shared) values such as the aesthetic or scientific value of wild plants, trees, or flowers—at least, it fails to do so in the absence of a quantified commercial loss that is capable of remedy by the award of damages or an injunction. In most nuisance cases, for example, the courts will award damages to compensate the claimant for the unreasonable interference with his land use that has resulted from the nuisance, such as lost production or the cost of replacing damaged goods, not for replacing damaged wild plants or repairing a habitat damaged by the nuisance.[163]

As plants are the property of the landowner, they are protected by the criminal law against theft and criminal damage. This is subject to exceptions in the law of England and Wales. It is not theft to pick flowers, fruit, or foliage from a wild plant, or to pick wild fungus, unless it is done for commercial reward, for sale, or for some other commercial purpose.[164] The uprooting and removal of an entire wild plant can, however, constitute theft. Similarly, it is not criminal damage to damage fungus or the flowers, fruit, or foliage of a wild plant, unless the entire plant is uprooted or destroyed.[165] These exceptions do not apply in Scotland, where the taking of any part of a growing wild plant can, therefore, constitute theft.[166]

(b) Protection under Wildlife and Countryside Act 1981

Because of the difficulties of establishing liability at common law, the protection of the 'public' interest in conserving wild plants has instead been prosecuted by legislative initiatives. Wild plants may be protected as an integral part of a habitat protected as an SSSI under the Wildlife and Countryside Act 1981[167] or a Special Area of Conservation under the Habitats Directive.[168] And where this is the case, the difficulties of quantification of damage referred to earlier are neatly sidestepped by the imposition of environmental liability for damage to protected habitats and species. The regulations implementing the Environmental Liability

[163] Damage to plants was for example an essential ingredient of several leading nuisance cases in the 19th century, when the parameters of the modern common law were laid down in the Industrial Revolution: see for example *St. Helens Smelting Co v Tipping* (1865) 11 HLC 642, *Salvin v Brancepeth Coal Co* (1874) 9 Ch App 705, 709.

[164] S. 4(3) Theft Act 1968.

[165] S. 10(1) Criminal Damage Act 1971.

[166] But for problems in establishing liability in Scots law see C. T. Reid (2009) at 6.1.6, 6.1.7.

[167] See Chapter 3, pp. 68 ff.

[168] Chapter 6, pp. 213ff.

Directive now require anyone convicted of damaging a protected habitat to restore it, failing which the nature Conservation Bodies can do so and reclaim their costs from the 'polluter'.[169] This avoids the necessity of placing a commercial 'value' on plants and other natural features of a habitat that have been impaired or damaged. Importantly, these measures also protect wild plants from damage by the landowner himself where they are in a protected habitat, something the common law failed to do, as it viewed them as part of the 'property' of the landowner and therefore available for exploitation by him.

The protection of wild plants that are integral to a protected habitat is supplemented by more general protection afforded to wild plants by the Wildlife and Countryside Act 1981, which applies to protect plants whether or not they are to be found in a protected area. The law treats the owner of the land on which the plant is growing differently to third parties; the owner is entitled to pick wild plants, provided they are not listed for protection in Schedule 8 to the 1981 Act. It is an offence for anyone other than an 'authorized person' to intentionally uproot any wild plant, unless the uprooting was an incidental result of a lawful act and could nor reasonably has been avoided.[170] 'Wild plants' are defined to mean any plant growing wild which is of a kind which ordinarily grows in Great Britain in a wild state.[171] Additional protection is conferred on those plants listed in Schedule 8. In this case it is an offence for anyone, including an authorized person, to pick, uproot, or destroy any of the plants listed. The lawful operations defence will, however, apply.[172] The sale or possession of any live or dead specimen listed in Schedule 8 is also prohibited.[173] The list of protected plants in Schedule 8 is varied from time to time in accordance with advice to DEFRA and to the devolved administrations from the statutory Conservation Bodies. The bluebell, one of the most iconic of British woodland flowers, was added to Schedule 8, and thereby granted legal protection, in 2007 in the light of extensive evidence of its decline. The latest amendments were made in 2011, with the addition of two species of plant to the list of protected plants in Schedule 8, the rock nail (Calicium corynellum) and tree lungwort (Lobaria pulmonaria), and the removal of four species from Schedule 8.[174]

Finally, in order to protect the habitat of wild plant species indigenous to the British Isles, the 1981 Act prohibits the introduction of certain invasive non-native species of plant, which it is a criminal offence to plant or to otherwise cause to grow in the wild.[175] The proscribed plants are listed in Part 11 of Schedule 9 to the 1981

[169] Environmental Damage (Prevention and Remediation) Regulations 2009, SI 2009153 (England). For the power to recoup costs from the operator causing damage, see reg. 24 ff.

[170] S. 13(1)(b) Wildlife and Countryside Act 1981. In Scotland this offence can also be committed by a reckless act: s. 13(1)(a) Wildlife and Countryside Act 1981 (Scotland).

[171] See s. 27(1) Wildlife and Countryside Act 1981.

[172] S. 13(3) Wildlife and Countryside Act 1981. The law in Scotland is stricter than in England and Wales, and requires evidence that reasonable precautions have been taken and that the damage was unforeseeable: s. 13(3)(b) Wildlife and Countryside Act 1981 (Scotland).

[173] S. 13(2) Wildlife and Countryside Act 1981.

[174] See the Wildlife and Countryside Act 1981 (Variation of Schedules 5 and 8) (England and Wales) Order 2011, SI 2011/2015, Schedules 3 and 4.

[175] See s. 14(2) Wildlife and Countryside Act 1981.

Act. They include the giant hogweed, Japanese knotweed, and Japanese seaweed. It is a defence if accused of this offence to show that all reasonable steps were taken and that all due diligence was exercised in order to avoid committing the offence.[176] The 1981 Act gives the minister power to authorize officials to enter land for the purposes of ascertaining whether an offence is being committed.[177]

(c) Tree Preservation Orders

Trees are a key element of many ecosystems, and also fulfil an important role in creating and enhancing different landscape types. They also perform important amenity functions. It is hardly surprising, therefore, that they enjoy extensive legal protection against destruction and felling. The strongest protection is afforded by the making of Tree Preservation Orders (TPOs) by the local authority, and additional controls apply both through the planning rules applicable to conservation areas and through the legislation governing the activities of the Forestry Commission in relation to the licensing of tree felling and tree planting. In addition, a number of publicly funded schemes encourage the planting and environmentally beneficial management of woodlands.

The local authority has power under the Town and Country Planning Act 1990 to make a TPO if 'it is expedient in the interests of amenity to make provision for the preservation of trees or woodlands in their area'.[178] In Scotland a TPO can also be made to protect trees or woodland of historic or cultural significance.[179] A TPO can apply to individual trees, to groups of trees, or to woodlands. A TPO can prohibit the cutting down, topping, lopping, uprooting, wilful damage, or wilful destruction of trees otherwise than with the consent of the local planning authority.[180] An order cannot apply, however, to prohibit the cutting down, uprooting, topping, or lopping of trees which are dying or dead, or which have become dangerous.[181] In England, the form and contents of a TPO and the procedure for making and confirming orders, are now governed by regulations made under powers introduced in the Planning Act 2008.[182]

When a local authority makes a TPO, it takes effect provisionally but must be confirmed within six months.[183] A copy of the order must be served on every person interested in the land affected by the order, with a statement specifying the reasons

[176] S. 14(3) Wildlife and Countryside Act 1981.

[177] S. 14(4) Wildlife and Countryside Act 1981 (Scotland: in England and Wales these powers are exercisable under the wider powers granted to wildlife inspectors by the Countryside and Rights of Way Act 2000, Schedule 12 (now s. 19ZA Wildlife and Countryside Act 1981).

[178] S. 198(1) Town and Country Planning Act 1990.

[179] See Planning (Scotland) Act 2006 s. 28(2), amending s. 160(1) ff. Town and Country Planning (Scotland) Act 1997.

[180] S. 198(3) Town and Country Planning Act 1990.

[181] S. 198(6) Town and Country Planning Act 1990.

[182] S. 202A–202G Town and Country Planning Act 1990, inserted by Planning Act 2008 s. 192. The Town and Country Planning (Tree Preservation)(England) Regulations 2012, SI 2012/605, came into force on 6 April 2012. The form in which orders must be made is specified in the Schedule to the 2012 Order.

[183] SI 2012/605.

for the making of the order and informing them that they can make written objections within 28 days of the making of the order.[184] When confirming a TPO the local authority must consider all objections that have been submitted within the time allowed, and can confirm the order with or without modifications. The confirmation of the order must be notified to all interested parties as soon as practicable after it is made,[185] and there are provisions for the subsequent variation and revocation of TPOs which must proceed subject to similar rules for notification and objections.[186] The local authority must keep a register of all TPOs that includes information on every application for consent under a TPO and its decision in respect thereof, a statement of the subject matter of every appeal under an order and details of any conditions with respect to replanting attached to consent to works taking effect under a TPO.[187] The register must be made available for public inspection at all reasonable hours.

The planning legislation offers no definition of what constitutes a 'tree' for these purposes. The protection afforded by TPOs is therefore potentially very wide, provided the plants involved can be properly described as 'trees', and its application is to some extent for the local planning authority to decide. The courts have taken a common-sense approach, upholding the validity of TPOs that are applied to any growth, such as a coppice,[188] that could properly be called a 'tree' in common parlance, as opposed to a shrub or bush.[189] In *Palm Developments Ltd v Secretary of State*[190] it was held that there is no minimum size exemption for a tree to come within the TPO powers, and that saplings could therefore be protected by a TPO.[191] It was there held, furthermore, that in the context of a 'woodland' TPO the order could extend to protect not only those trees existing at the time that the TPO was made, but also future growth by way of regeneration of the woodland. So saplings that grow naturally in the future would also be protected, as would small trees planted to enhance the wood. The purpose of a TPO in this context is to protect the 'undifferentiated mass of trees in the specified area' covered by the TPO, and not solely those trees existing at the date of the order—if it were otherwise, the order would cease to have effect once those trees had died out, a conclusion that was not intended by the legislature in enacting these powers.[192]

[184] Town and Country Planning (Tree Preservation)(England) Regulations 2012 reg. 5. The form in which objections can be made is set out in reg. 6.

[185] Town and Country Planning (Tree Preservation)(England) Regulations 2012 reg. 8.

[186] See Town and Country Planning (Tree Preservation)(England) Regulations 2012 reg. 10 (variation of a TPO) and 11 (Revocation).

[187] Town and Country Planning (Tree Preservation)(England) Regulations 2012 reg. 12.

[188] Ie a wood of small trees grown for periodical cutting.

[189] See eg *Bullock v Secretary of State for the Environment* (1980) 40 P&CR 246.

[190] [2009] EWHC 220 (Admin) (Cranston J.).

[191] It had been suggested obiter dicta by Lord Denning MR in an earlier case that a minimum size of 7 or 8 inches in diameter would be required for a sapling to qualify as a tree in a woodland setting; *Kent County Council v Batchelor* (1976) 33 P&CR 185, at 189. This suggestion has not been followed in subsequent cases and has been the subject of considerable criticism: see *Bullock v Secretary of State for the Environment* (1980) 40 P&CR 246 at 251.

[192] *Palm Developments Ltd v Secretary of State* [2009] EWHC 220 (Admin) judgment at para. 42. And see: *Evans v Waverley Borough Council* [1995] 3 PLR 80; *R (Plimsoll Shaw Brewer and others) v Three Rivers District Council* [2007] EWHC 1290 (Admin).

The scope and application of a TPO will depend upon the terms of the order itself.[193] The activities prohibited by a TPO are, however, standardized and are specified in regulations made under the Planning Acts.[194] It is forbidden to cut down, top, lop, uproot, wilfully damage, or wilfully destroy any tree to which an order applies, other than with the written consent of the planning authority. The authority's consent can be given with or without conditions,[195] and if conditions *are* imposed it is also forbidden to undertake any of the prescribed activities otherwise than in accordance with the conditions specified in the TPO. A number of exceptions are set out in the regulations made under the Planning Acts.[196] It is not a prohibited activity to cut down, lop, or uproot a tree which is dead, or to remove dead branches from a living tree. Neither is it prohibited to do such works if this is 'urgently necessary to remove an immediate risk of serious harm', or if it is necessary for the abatement of a nuisance.[197] Notwithstanding this exception, in practice, dead trees may provide an important habitat for some protected species of bird or animal—bats, for example, will often roost in holes in decaying trees. If this is the case, the removal of a dead tree may require permission from the statutory Conservation Body (for example, Natural England) even if within the exemption in the planning legislation for operations on trees covered by a TPO.[198] It is not prohibited to remove branches from a tree cultivated for fruit. Special exceptions apply to permit statutory undertakers, such as the water, sewage, and electricity or gas utilities, to lop or remove trees on operational land where this is necessary for the purposes of inspection or for the operation of the undertaking.[199]

Carrying out a proscribed activity without written permission, or in breach of the conditions attached to a consent granted by the local authority, is a criminal offence.[200] The offence is one of strict liability, and it is therefore unnecessary in order to ground a conviction to prove that the accused knew that the tree in question was subject to a TPO.[201] The penalties are potentially severe: an unlimited fine

[193] Guidance on the management of trees subject to TPOs is given in *Tree Preservation Orders: A Guide to the Law and Good Practice* (2000) Department of Communities and Local Government, (available at <http://www.communities.gov.uk/documents/planningandbuilding/pdf/tposguide.pdf>. This guide is often referred to as the 'Blue Book'.

[194] See The Town and Country Planning (Tree Preservation)(England) Regulations 2012, SI 2012/605, reg. 13 (England): Town and Country Planning (Tree Preservation Order and Trees in Conservation Areas)(Scotland) Regulations 1975, SI 1975/1204 as amended, Model Order paras. 3–7 (Scotland).

[195] For the form and manner of applying for consent see the Town and Country Planning (Tree Preservation)(England) Regulations 2012, SI 2012/605, regs. 16 and 17.

[196] See Town and Country Planning (Tree Preservation)(England) Regulations 2012 reg. 14(1).

[197] See Town and Country Planning (Tree Preservation)(England) Regulations 2012 reg. 14(1)(a)(ii) and 14(1)(c). The term 'nuisance' is here used in a legal sense: this exception will only apply where two properties are involved, eg where branches are overhanging the boundary of a neighbour's land and thereby constitute a nuisance. The exception will not apply to permit a householder to destroy or damage a tree on his own property (see *Tree Preservation Orders: A Guide to Good Practice* (2000) Department of Communities and Local Government at para. 6.10, available at: <http://www.communities.gov.uk/documents/planningandbuilding/pdf/tposguide.pdf>.

[198] See *Tree Preservation Orders: A Guide to Good Practice* at para. 6.3.

[199] Town and Country Planning (Tree Preservation)(England) Regulations 2012 reg. 14(1)(iii) and 14(3) (definition of statutory undertaker).

[200] S. 210 Town and Country Planning Act 1990.

[201] See *Maidstone BC v Mortimer* [1980] 3 All ER 552.

if convicted on indictment, or a fine not exceeding £20,000 on summary conviction.[202] The court must take into account any financial benefit that has accrued, or will accrue, to the offender as a consequence of the offence having being committed.[203] The planning legislation in both Scotland and England and Wales also imposes a duty on the landowner to replace any trees removed, uprooted, or destroyed in breach of a TPO or in contravention of the terms of a consent issued by the local authority under a TPO.[204] The replacements must be of an appropriate species and planted at the same place as those destroyed or at such another place as may be agreed with the local authority. The obligation to replace trees can be enforced by the local authority within two years of their becoming aware of a failure to comply with the obligation to do so (in Scotland)[205] or within four years of this occurring (in England).[206]

Compensation is not payable for the making of a TPO. It can, however, be claimed for losses flowing from a refusal of consent to carry out operations under a TPO, or for the effect of conditions attached to a consent.[207] In practice, significant losses may result from the imposition of the order itself, as this will restrict the land uses that the owner can put his land to and depress its market value.[208] The resale value of timber covered by the TPO will often be another significant loss. The rules in Scotland permit these losses to be claimed if the local authority refuses consent to fell trees covered by a TPO.[209] The rules in England are, however, more restrictive.[210] Compensation cannot be claimed for any loss if more than 12 months has elapsed since the authority's decision, and in respect of any loss of less than £500. Neither can compensation be claimed for any loss of development value or any other diminution in the value of the land, for any loss or damage that was not reasonably foreseeable when consent was refused or granted subject to conditions, or in any case where the claimant failed to take reasonable steps to avert the loss or to mitigate its extent. Where a loss arises as a result of a refusal of a licence to fell trees in the course of a forestry operation, compensation is payable to the owner of the land, but is limited to the depreciation in the value of the trees that is attributable to the deterioration in the quality of the timber attributable to the refusal, and not, in other words, a loss in their market value.[211]

[202] Town and Country Planning Act 1990 s. 210(2).

[203] S. 210(3) Town and Country Planning Act 1990.

[204] See s. 206 Town and Country Planning Act 1990 (England and Wales); s. 167 Town and Country Planning (Scotland) Act 1997 .

[205] See s. 168(2) Town and Country Planning (Scotland) Act 1997.

[206] S. 207 Town and Country Planning Act 1990s.

[207] The Town and Country Planning (Tree Preservation)(England) Regulations 2012, SI 2012/605, reg. 24(1).

[208] See *Bell v Canterbury City Council* (1988) 56 P&CR 211.

[209] See ss. 165–166 Town and Country Planning (Scotland) Act 1997. For a discussion of the position in Scotland, see Reid (2009) 293–94.

[210] See The Town and Country Planning (Tree Preservation)(England) Regulations 2012, SI 2012/605, reg. 24(2)–(4). These rules were introduced in 1999 and consolidated into the 2012 Order.

[211] See The Town and Country Planning (Tree Preservation)(England) Regulations 2012, reg. 24(3)(c).

Special rules also apply to protect trees in conservation areas. Local planning authorities have a duty to designate as conservation areas those 'areas of special architectural or historic interest the character or appearance of which it is desirable to preserve or enhance'.[212] This is a landscape designation and focused to the impact of trees in enhancing the appearance and amenity of an area. Nevertheless, the designation has important consequences for the protection of trees from damage or destruction, and also has an important indirect effect in protecting the habitats for wildlife that trees provide. It is a criminal offence to cut down, top, lop, uproot, or wilfully damage or destroy any tree in a conservation area without first serving a notice on the local planning authority.[213] The local authority then has six weeks in which to consider whether to make a TPO to protect the trees in question. If no TPO is made, the operations can be carried out once six weeks have elapsed, but if not carried out within two years a further notice of intent must be served before operations can lawfully be carried out. No notice is required to cut down, lop, or top, etc. a tree with a diameter not exceeding 75 millimetres, or not exceeding 100 millimetres if the operations are to thin out trees to improve their growth. This is in marked contrast to the position where a TPO has been made, as the latter can apply to small trees and saplings of any size.[214] In all other respects the same exceptions apply to permit operations as apply on trees covered by a TPO; for example, to permit the cutting or lopping of dead branches from a living tree or the uprooting of a dead tree.

Where a notice of intent is given for works on a tree in a conservation area, the appropriate response by the local authority in order to confer protection on the trees in question is the making of a TPO, in which case the tree will be subject to the rules outlined earlier—the local authority cannot respond by refusing consent or by granting consent with conditions.[215] There are therefore two possible responses: to make a TPO if this is justified in the interests of amenity; to decide not to make a TPO and allow the six weeks to expire, in which case the work can be carried out as long as it is done within two years; or to decide not to make a TPO and inform the applicant that the work can go ahead.[216] Carrying out any of the proscribed operations without notice, or within the six-week notice period, is a criminal offence and carries the same penalties as apply for breach of the terms of a TPO.[217] The offence is committed by the person carrying out the operations in question, and the landowner will come under an obligation to replace the tree with one of an appropriate species and size at the same place as that unlawfully destroyed

[212] S. 69(1) Planning (Listed Buildings and Conservation Areas) Act 1990; s. 61 Planning (Listed Buildings and Conservation Areas) (Scotland) Act 1997.

[213] S. 211(3) Town and Country Planning Act 1990; s. 172 Town and Country Planning (Scotland) Act 1997.

[214] See *Palm Developments Ltd v Secretary of State*, see n. 190.

[215] Guidance on these provisions and their application is given in Chapter 9 of *Tree Preservation Orders: A Guide to the Law and Good Practice* (2000) Department of Communities and Local Government, available at: <http://www.communities.gov.uk/documents/planningandbuilding/pdf/tposguide.pdf>.

[216] See *Tree Preservation Orders: A Guide to the Law and Good Practice* (2000) at para. 9.7.

[217] S. 211(4) Town and Country Planning Act 1990.

or uprooted.[218] If the local planning authority responds by making a TPO the protective regime applicable to TPOs will then apply as described earlier.

(d) The legal protection of hedgerows

Hedgerows are a traditional feature of the British countryside, and an important element in cultural conceptions of rural landscapes. They also provide an important linear network of habitats for a wide range of birds, invertebrates, and other wildlife, as well as containing many species of indigenous shrub, tree, and other flora that are deserving of legal protection in their own right. Although they are today seen as an element of the 'cultural' landscape, it is important to remember that their establishment and form in the English countryside, if not in Scotland, is intimately connected with the Enclosure Movement; hedgerows were often established in the eighteenth and nineteenth centuries as barriers to common land use, and instruments of the assertion of private property rights over the land enclosed.[219] The law itself played a part in the form that this took; in the early part of the enclosure movement most hedgerows were established to mark the boundaries established by inclosure agreements entered into by freehold owners consensually terminating common use of their land. This tended to be more piecemeal and haphazard than later enclosures that were achieved under private acts of Parliament, as the Inclosure Acts overrode the objections of landowners unwilling to give their consent to enclosure of their land, a process culminating in the General Inclosure Act of 1836 whereby enclosure was permitted without a local Act if two thirds of the landowners affected by it gave their consent to enclosure. This led to a more orderly process of enclosure, with the marking of field boundaries by hedgerows in a more orderly fashion into large rectangular fields, whereas the earlier process of piecemeal enclosure tended to produce smaller enclosures of less regular size and appearance. Although the law was intimately connected with the process of creating what is now viewed as the 'traditional' English countryside, therefore, it was more closely concerned with legitimizing private property rights than with issues of nature conservation or landscape protection.[220]

The role of the law in protecting hedgerows has only recently been recognized. In the first place, it has been recognized that the Inclosure Acts themselves, although of considerable antiquity, may still apply to protect hedgerows erected several hundred years ago following the enclosure of common land. In the second, bespoke legal protection for important hedgerows was introduced in 1997. The relevance of the Inclosure Acts came to prominence in the 1980s, and was judicially

[218] S. 213 Town and Country Planning Act 1990.

[219] See J. Holder, 'Law and Landscape: The Legal Construction and Protection of Hedgerows' (1999) 62 MLR 100, esp. 104–105; C. Mynors, 'Hedgerows, Biodiversity and Rupert Bear' in N. Herbert Young (ed.), *Law, Policy and Development in the Rural Environment* (University of Wales Press, 1999).

[220] For a review of the implications of enclosure patterns for conceptions of cultural landscape see J. Holder, 'Hedgerows, Laws and Cultural Landscape', Ch. 5 in J. Holder and D. McGillivray (eds), *Locality and Identity: Environmental Issues in Law and Society* (Ashgate, 1999).

tested in *Seymour and Yorkshire Wildlife Trust v Flamborough Parish Council.*[221] In this case, it was found that an inclosure award made under the Flamborough Inclosure Act 1765 required the owner 'to build and forever maintain a quick wood hedge' along the boundary of enclosed land between the land and a public road. As this provision of the award endured for the benefit of the public as well as the landowner, the hedge adjoined a pubic road, it was held that aggrieved local residents and the Wildlife Trust had locus standi to enforce it before the courts. The local authority was therefore prohibited from removing the hedgerow. Each case will turn on the specific terms of any local Inclosure Award and Inclosure Act;[222] but as 4804 private Inclosure Acts were passed by Parliament between 1700 and 1845[223] this decision has substantial implications for the potential use of inclosure awards to secure the protection of ancient hedgerows.

Traditional hedgerows are now also given legal protection against grubbing up and damage by the Hedgerow Regulations 1997.[224] The 1997 Regulations apply to 'important' hedgerows. Much of the detail in the regulations is devoted to amplifying, not necessarily with great success, what this concept means, and hence delimiting the scope of the regulations themselves. The basic position is that a hedgerow is 'important' if it (or the hedgerow of which it is a stretch) meets two criteria: it must have existed for 30 years or more, and it must also satisfy at least one of the qualifying criteria that are set out in Part II of Schedule 1 to the 1997 Regulations.[225] Schedule 1 set out very detailed prescriptions for qualifying hedgerows that include criteria relevant to their role both in relation to historical and archaeological sites and in relation to nature conservation. A hedgerow is 'important', and therefore protected, if, for example, it contains any protected bird species listed in Schedule 1 to the 1981 Act, and/or any protected animals or plants listed under the latter.[226] It will also be classified as important if it contains any breed of bird identified as a declining breeder, or any species of animal and/or plant identified as endangered, extinct, rare, or vulnerable in the relevant British Red

[221] (1997) (Unreported). See *The Times*, 3 January 1997, 253 (Hull County Court). The relevant facts and decision are set out in evidence supplied to the House of Commons Select Committee on Environment Transport and Rural Affairs: Supplementary memorandum by the Department of Environment Transport and Rural Affairs (FB 7(a)) *The Protection of Field Boundaries—Statutory Controls* (July 1998) available at: <http://www.publications.parliament.uk/pa/cm199798/cmselect/cmenvtra/969/8072921.htm>. See also: House of Commons Select Committee on Environment Transport and Rural Affairs, *Protection of Field Boundaries*, 13th Report of 1997–8 (HC Paper 869); C. Mynors, 'Hedgerows, Biodiversity and Rupert Bear', in N. Herbert Young (ed.), *Law, Policy and Development in the Rural Environment* (University of Wales Press, 1999), 153–7.

[222] Establishing locus standi to enforce an inclosure award may, for example, be problematic if there is no clear public benefit: see *Marlton v Turner* [1998] 2 EGLR 185.

[223] Supplementary memorandum by the Department of Environment Transport and Rural Affairs (FB 7(a)) *The Protection of Field Boundaries—Statutory Controls* (July 1998), at para. 7: and see the Report of the Royal Commission on Common Land (Cmnd 462, 1958).

[224] SI 1997/1160, made under s. 97 Environment Act 1995.

[225] The Hedgerow Regulations 1997, SI 1997/1160, reg. 4(1).

[226] Ie listed in Schedule 1 Part 1, Schedule 5 (animals) or Schedule 8 (plants) Wildlife and Countryside Act 1981, SI 1997/1160, Schedule 1 para. 6(1)(3).

Data Books.[227] A hedgerow will also be classified as important if it is recorded in a record held by a biological record centre maintained by or on behalf of the local authority, and is recorded as containing any of these animal or bird species in the last five years, or any of the plant species in the last 10 years.

The 1997 Regulations also go into considerable detail as to the mix of woody tree species[228] that must be a constituent part of the hedge for it to be classified as 'important'.[229] The number of woody species required will also depend upon whether additional hedgerow features (such as hedge banks or walls, ditches, and small gaps) are present. The regulations require there to be at least seven woody species present in the hedgerow, or a lesser number if additional features are also in evidence, six woody species if at least three of the additional features are present, and five woody species if there are four additional features. A hedgerow will also be 'important' if it contains at least six woody species including at least one of the following species of tree characteristic of traditional hedgerows—the black-poplar tree (Populus nigra ssp. betulifolia), large-leaved lime (Tilia platyphyllos), small-leaved lime (Tilia cordata), and the wild service-tree (Sorbus torminalis).[230] The number of woody species required is also differentiated by geographic location; for the northern counties of England the number required in each case is reduced by one.[231] To add to the complexity of the regulations, one of the additional features that will lead to the classification of a hedgerow as important, and protected, is the presence of at least three woodland plant species within 1 metre, in any direction, of the outermost edges of the hedgerow, and the identity of the plants concerned are set out in considerable detail.[232]

The legal protection given to important hedgerows is based upon a similar model to that for trees under the town and country planning system (pp. 192–7). If an owner of land or a utility operator[233] wishes to remove or destroy all or part of a hedge they must first give notice to the local planning authority.[234] The local authority then has 42 days in which to consult the local parish or community

227 Wildlife and Countryside Act 1981, Schedule 1 para. 6(3)(c)(4). The Red Data Books include eg 'Red Data Birds in Britain', L. A. Batten, C. J. Bibby, P. Clement, et al. (eds), (Nature Conservancy Council and the Royal Society for the Protection of Birds, 1990); 'Vascular Plants', F. H. Perring and L. Farrell, 2nd edn (Royal Society for Nature Conservation, 1983); 'Insects', D. B. Shirt (ed.), (Nature Conservancy Council,1987); and 'Invertebrates other than insects', J. H, Bratton (ed.), (Joint Nature Conservation Committee, 1991).

228 These are defined and listed in The Hedgerow Regulations 1997, SI 1997/1160, and in particular in Schedule 3. The latter lists 56 woody species relevant to this question. A further 57 woodland species are listed in Schedule 2—a hedgerow will be classified as important (and protected) if it contains at least three woodland species within 1 metre, in any direction, of the outermost edges of the hedgerow.

229 See The Hedgerow Regulations 1997, Schedule 1 para. 7.

230 See The Hedgerow Regulations 1997, Schedule 1 para. 7(1)(c).

231 The Hedgerow Regulations 1997 Schedule 1 para. 7(2).

232 The Hedgerow Regulations 1997 Schedule 1 7(4)(f). No less than 57 woodland plant species are listed in Schedule 2 for this purpose.

233 This includes a gas, or electricity utility company, a telecommunications operator or a sewage or water undertaker; see The Hedgerow Regulations 1997 reg. 2.

234 See The Hedgerow Regulations 1997 reg 5(1). The form of notice is set out in Schedule 4 to the 1997 Regulations.

council. They can issue a hedgerow retention notice.[235] If they do so it will then be a criminal offence to remove or damage the hedgerow in contravention of the notice.[236] There are a number of exceptions, however, where works that damage a hedgerow may be permitted without engaging criminal liability.[237] Some of the exceptions are broadly conceived. It is permissible, for example, to remove a section of hedgerow in order to make a new opening for access to land, in substitution for an existing access point, provided that the existing access is filled by the planting of a new hedge within eight months.[238] It is also permissible to create a new access point to land by removing a section of hedgerow if no access is otherwise available, and to lop or trim trees and hedgerow growth if necessary to prevent obstruction of utility supplies, such as electricity wires, using powers in the relevant legislation to do so,[239] or for public bodies, such as the Environment Agency, to do so in connection with the exercise of their land, drainage, or flood-defence powers.

The widest exception permits damage 'for the proper management of the hedgerow'.[240] This was considered in *R (Conwy County Borough Council) v Lloyd,*[241] where it was held that the regulations must be construed as permitting the total removal of a hedge if that is required for its proper management. In that case, therefore, no offence was committed where 100 metres of ancient hedgerow was removed without permission, in circumstances where expert evidence was given for the defence to the effect that it was dangerous and liable to collapse.[242] This decision also exposed other flaws in the practical protection afforded by the 1997 Regulations; principally, that failure to serve a hedgerow removal notice before carrying out work to remove all or part of a hedge is not in itself a criminal offence. As a result, if a hedgerow has been removed unilaterally by a landowner without prior notification to the local authority, the latter will have difficulty in assessing the status of the (former) hedgerow for the purposes of ascertaining whether it was 'important' and therefore protected. This will make it difficult to ground a prosecution for unlawful removal after the event, in cases where unilateral action to destroy a hedgerow has been taken without prior notice to the local authority.

The Hedgerow Regulations present a very complex and detailed regime for the protection of traditional hedgerows as a feature of the countryside. They have been heavily criticized for the inflexibility of the regulation that this delivers, and the inability to exercise administrative discretion in the manner of their enforcement. The degree of scientific detail that is deployed to identify woody and woodland species of hedgerow plants, and the protected species of bird, animal, and plant

[235] See The Hedgerow Regulations 1997 regs. 5(2) and (6).

[236] The Hedgerow Regulations 1997 reg. 7. It is an offence punishable on summary conviction by a fine not exceeding level 3 on the standard scale, or on indictment by a fine not exceeding the statutory maximum (The Hedgerow Regulations 1997 reg. 7(4)(5)).

[237] The Hedgerow Regulations 1997, reg. 6.

[238] See The Hedgerow Regulations 1997 regs. 6(1) (a) and 6(2).

[239] Electricity Act 1989, Schedule 4 para. 9.

[240] Hedgerow Regulations 1997, SI 1997/1160, reg. 6(1)(j).

[241] [2003] EWHC 264 (Admin).

[242] [2003] EWHC 264 (Admin), judgment para. 12 (Maurice Kay J.).

that may be present in protected hedgerows, also means that it will be difficult to ascertain where a hedgerow is protected or not without specialist scientific analysis. One especially pertinent criticism of the regulations is that they act primarily to prevent damage or destruction of hedgerows; for example, by grubbing out of component shrubs. They do nothing to prevent deterioration that occurs naturally as a result of neglect. Hedgerows are a classic example of a habitat type that requires positive management to retain its conservation features; in this case, periodic, usually annual, cropping to prevent components of the hedgerow maturing very quickly into trees. Some of the protective measures introduced in the Countryside and Rights of Way Act 2000, including the use of management schemes and management notices,[243] could be used to require the positive management of hedgerows in this context, although there is little evidence that has been the case in the period since the 2000 Act came into force. In practice the use of funding under agri-environment schemes funded by under the Rural Development Plans for England and Wales are of greater significance in ensuring the vibrancy and health of the hedgerow network as 'green corridors' in the countryside. Both the Higher Level Stewardship scheme (in England) and Glastir (in Wales) provide funding to farmers for the maintenance of traditional hedgerows in good condition, with appropriate conditions for periodic cutting and infilling of gaps to maintain hedgerows in good condition as a habitat for birds, invertebrates, and other wildlife.[244]

[243] Ss. 28J, 28K Wildlife and Countryside Act 1981, as inserted by Countryside and Rights of Way Act 2000, Schedule 9. See Chapter 3, pp. 94–6 for further discussion of these powers.

[244] See eg HLS management options HB11 and 12 (Higher Level Stewardship Handbook, 4th edn, Natural England, 2013) available at: <http://publications.naturalengland.org.uk/publication/2827091?category=45001>.

6

The Impact of European Environmental Law

The domestic law as to the protection of both wildlife and natural habitats in England Scotland and Wales has been strongly influenced by European Union environmental policy. More specifically, the modern law of nature conservation has been shaped by the need to implement the requirements of European Directives on the protection of both wild birds and of wildlife habitats. The Directive on the Conservation of Wild Birds was adopted in 1979.[1] The Wild Birds Directive was one of the earliest of the Community's environmental policy initiatives, and was introduced before there was express power in the EC treaty for the Community to take action on environmental matters. The Single European Act of 1987 subsequently added a new environmental title to the Treaty,[2] in order to give environmental protection a legal basis as an objective of the Community. The integration of environmental protection into existing policy and law was also made a Community priority. Since 1987 a number of measures have been adopted that reflect the new importance attached to environmental protection within EU policy making. Several of these have an important bearing on the law of nature conservation, including the Directive on the Conservation of Habitats and Species of 1992[3] and the Environmental Liability Directive of 2004.[4] The implementation of these Directives in domestic English law is the principal subject of this chapter and is considered further later. An outline of the principal conservation objectives of the Wild Birds and Habitats Directives, and of the legal obligations they impose on the member states, will be offered, however, before we turn to consider their implementation in the UK.

[1] Council Directive 79/409/EC, OJ L103, 25.4.79, p. 1. The Directive (and the various amendments made to it since 1979) has now been consolidated into Directive 2009/147/EC of the European Parliament and the Council of 30 November 2009 on the conservation of wild birds [2010] OJ L 20/7, 26.1.2010. The codified 2010 version will be cited hereafter in this chapter (hereafter 'Wild Birds Directive').

[2] Article 130 EC Treaty (subsequently art. 174 Treaty of the European Community): now Title XX, articles 191–193 of the Treaty on the Functioning of the European Union (TFEU) [2010] OJ C83/132, 30.3.2010.

[3] Directive 92/43/EEC on the Conservation of Habitats and Species, [1992] OJ L206/7 (hereafter 'Habitats Directive').

[4] Directive 2004/35/EC of the European Parliament and of the Council on environmental liability with regard to the prevention and remedying of environmental liability, as amended by Directive 2006/21/EC of the European Parliament and of the Council of 15 March 2006. For the consolidated text see [2006] OJ L102/15.

The Wild Birds Directive

The Wild Birds Directive is concerned with the conservation of all 'species of naturally occurring birds in the wild state' in the European territory of the member states.[5] It places a general duty upon the member states to take the requisite measures to maintain the population of all species of naturally occurring wild birds at a level which corresponds in particular to ecological scientific and cultural requirements, while taking account of economic or recreational requirements.[6] This rather vague obligation[7] is to be achieved by each member state taking the requisite measures to preserve, maintain, or re-establish a sufficient diversity and areas of habitats for all the species of birds covered by the Directive, including the creation of protected areas, biotopes, and the upkeep and management in accordance with their ecological needs of habitats both inside and outside protected zones.[8]

(a) Habitat protection

The protection of the natural habitats of wild birds lies at the heart of the Directive, and has proved to be one of its more controversial aspects. The endangered species identified in Annex 1 to the Directive are to be the subject of special conservation measures in order to ensure their survival and reproduction in their area of distribution. The Directive therefore requires the member states to classify as Special Protection Areas ('SPAs') 'the most suitable territories' in number and size for the conservation of Annex 1 bird species.[9] The Directive went on to provide that,[10] within these areas the member states 'shall take appropriate steps to avoid pollution or deterioration of habitats or any disturbances affecting the birds' insofar as these would be significant having regard to the Directive's objectives. For good measure, the member states are also obliged to 'strive' to avoid pollution or deterioration of habitats outside the SPAs designated under the Directive.

The Directive's provisions for the designation and management of SPAs have proved controversial. They raise two separate issues, to which the courts have given different answers. The first is the extent to which economic and recreational factors can be taken into account when selecting sites for designation as SPAs. The second is the extent to which these factors can be allowed for when considering the authorization of plans and projects within an SPA, in the context of the Directive's rules for the management of protected sites. In *Leybucht Dykes*[11] the European

[5] Directive 2009/147/EC art. 1.

[6] Directive 2009/147/EC art. 2.

[7] Article 2 has been held to be insufficiently precise to create directly enforceable obligations that can be the subject of direct effect in EU Law; see *Kincardine and Deeside District Council v Forestry Commission* 1992 SLT 1180.

[8] Directive 2009/147/EC art. 3.

[9] Directive 2009/147/EC art. 4.1.

[10] See Directive 2009/147/EC art. 4.4.

[11] *Commission of the European Communities v Germany* [1991] ECR I–883 ECJ.

Court had held that the economic and recreational requirements mentioned in article 2 of the Birds Directive[12] are subservient to the Directive's ecological objectives when member states are classifying SPAs. This has been upheld in subsequent cases, which have confirmed that economic considerations cannot be taken into account when selecting geographical areas for designation as SPAs and determining their boundaries; this must be done according to ornithological criteria alone.[13] The member state has a limited discretion when applying the ornithological criteria to determine the boundaries of the site to be included in the SPA, and can use the existing boundaries of protected sites, such as SSSIs, that are to be included in the SPA.[14] But that is the limit of the discretion that is permitted.

The relevance of economic and social factors in determining whether development should be permitted within an SPA, following designation, has on the other hand to be considered separately. Article 4 of the Directive, as originally drafted, made no allowance for economic considerations to be taken into account; the member states had a duty to take appropriate steps to avoid pollution or any disturbance of birds whether or not there were economic or social considerations dictating that a project or development should otherwise be permitted within an SPA. In *Leybucht Dykes*[15] it was held, on this basis, that activities that would damage the conservation features of the site could only be permitted in very limited and exceptional circumstances. This was felt by some member states to be too restrictive. Consequently the 1992 Habitats Directive[16] amended the provisions for the management of SPAs to bring them into line with the management regime for Special Areas of Conservation ('SACs') designated under the Habitats Directive. The Habitats Directive applies a unified management regime to both SPAs and SACs, and this allows for considerations of an economic or social nature to be considered when consenting operations and activities in SACs and SPAs, provided they are reasons of overriding public interest, the damaging activity is preceded by an environmental assessment of its implications, and, if necessary compensatory measures are taken to ensure the coherence of the *Nature 2000* network. The only situation where the original, and much stricter, Birds Directive formulation applies is where the site hosts a priority habitat or species.

There is no prescribed procedure for designating SPAs under the Birds Directive, and this is left largely to the member states, who must notify the Commission when a site has been classified and must add it to the statutory register of European sites.[17] There is no separate category of 'candidate' SPAs with provisional legal protection, as there is for prospective SACs under the Habitats Directive pp. 213 ff. The member state has an obligation to review whether it has designated all the sites

[12] Above n. 6.

[13] See *R v Secretary of State for the Environment ex parte RSPB* [1996] ECR I–33804 (Lappel Bank); *Commission v Spain* [1993] ECR I–4221 (Santona Marshes).

[14] See *WWF-UK Ltd v Secretary of State for Scotland* [1999] Env LR 632.

[15] *Commission of the European Communities v Germany* [1991] ECR I–883.

[16] See arts. 6.2–6.4 of Council Directive 92/43/EC.

[17] Reg. 13(2)(d) Conservation of Habitats and Species Regulations 2010, SI 2010/490. This must be done 'as soon as they are classified'.

that are the most suitable territories in number and size for the conservation of Annex 1 bird species within its territory.[18] It was held by the European Court of Justice in the *Basses Corbieres* case,[19] moreover, that sites that should have been classified as SPAs but have not, are entitled to the higher level of protection afforded by the original text of article 4 of the Directive; that is, that applied in the *Leybucht Dykes* case, and not the formulation for classified SPAs under the Habitats Directive. As a consequence, damaging activities and the disturbance of species cannot be permitted on social or economic grounds pending an area's formal classification as an SPA. While this may appear idiosyncratic, it is in fact an interpretation which creates a strong incentive for the member states to uphold the terms of the Directive and adhere to their obligations to classify all areas that meet the criteria for SPA classification. Once classified, the less rigorous management regime for SPAs substituted by the Habitats Directive will apply.[20] The *Basses Corbieres* approach will only apply, however, where it is established that the non-classification of the area as an SPA is a breach of the terms of the Directive; it will not apply to every area that is being considered for classification.[21]

(b) Species protection

The Wild Birds Directive establishes a general standard for the protection of wild bird species, and then provides for a lower level of protection to apply to certain species designated as pests or game species, and subject to hunting in some members states. It also enables the member states to apply for derogations from these standards in certain limited circumstances. This approach—setting a general standard of protection and then relaxing or varying it by reference to Annexes containing lists of pet and game species—is replicated in the Wildlife and Countryside Act 1981, which implemented the 1979 Directive in UK law.[22]

The general obligation imposed on the member states as to species protection is set out in article 5 of the Birds Directive. This requires that the member states take the requisite measures to establish a general system of protection for all species of birds that occur naturally in the wild state in the territory of the member states to which the Treaty applies. This general obligation applies to both migratory and non-migratory species, and will apply to migratory birds even if they are normally found for short periods in the territory of one or more of the member states annually. The member states must, in particular, take measures to prohibit the following:

(i) The deliberate killing or capture of wild birds by any method,

(ii) The deliberate destruction of, or damage to, their nests or eggs or the removal of their nests,

[18] See *Commission of the European Communities v Greece* [2007] ECR I–9215.

[19] *Commission of the European Communities v France* [2001] ECR I–10, 799.

[20] See further the excellent analysis by G. Machin, 'Protecting Bird Habitat of European Importance—the view from Basses Corbieres' (2004) 6 Env L Rev 174.

[21] See *Humber Sea Terminals Ltd v Secretary of State for Transport* [2006] Env L Rev 4.

[22] See Chapter 5, pp. 163 ff.

(iii) Taking their eggs in the wild and keeping eggs even if empty,

(iv) The deliberate disturbance of wild birds, particularly during the period of breeding and rearing, *in so far as disturbance would be significant having regard to the objectives of the Directive.*[23] This obligation therefore requires the member states to avoid disturbance that would impair the maintenance of the species at a population level which corresponds to ecological, scientific, and cultural requirements.[24]

(v) The keeping of birds of species the hunting and capture of which is prohibited.

The member states are also required to prohibit the sale, transport for sale, keeping for sale, and offering for sale of all live or dead wild birds, and of 'any readily recognizable parts or derivatives of such birds'.[25] The prohibition on the sale or transport etc. of wild birds does not apply to species listed in Annex III/A of the Directive, and in the case of a number of further species listed in Annex III/B the member states have a discretion to allow these activities subject to restrictions, provided in both cases that the birds in question have been legally captured or killed, or otherwise legally acquired.[26] Where a member state wishes to relax the prohibition on the sale or transport/keeping of wild birds listed in Annex III/B, it must first consult with the European Commission to establish jointly whether the marketing of specimens of the species could reasonably be expected to result in the population levels, geographical distribution, or reproductive rate of the species, becoming endangered throughout the European Union. If the Commission concludes that a species will become endangered as a result of the member state authorizing sale and transport, etc., then it must issue a reasoned recommendation to the member state concerned stating its opposition to the relaxation of the prohibition on the marketing and sale, etc., of the species. This will be communicated to the member state in question and published in the Official Journal of the European Union.[27]

The hunting of wild birds is permitted for those species listed in Annex II, provided that hunting does not jeopardize conservation efforts in their distribution area.[28] Some species (those listed in Annex II/A) may be hunted throughout the geographical sea and land area of the European Union,[29] while those specified in Annex II/B can only be hunted in the territory of the member state indicated in the Table appended to Annex II/B.[30] Where hunting is permitted, the member states must ensure that it is carried out in accordance with what the Directive calls the 'wide use and ecologically balanced control' of the species of birds concerned, and that the hunting does not endanger the maintenance of the bird population at a

[23] Directive 2009/147/EC, art. 5(d) (emphasis added).
[24] Wild Birds Directive art. 2.
[25] Wild Birds Directive art. 6.1.
[26] Wild Birds Directive arts. 6.2 and 6.3.
[27] See Wild Birds Directive art. 6.3.
[28] Wild Birds Directive art. 7.1.
[29] Wild Birds Directive art. 7.2.
[30] Wild Birds Directive art. 7.3.

level compatible with the Directive objectives.[31] The member states must not permit the hunting of species under their national hunting laws during the rearing season or during the various stages of reproduction. Whether hunting is permitted or not, the Directive requires the member states to prohibit all means, arrangements, or methods for the large-scale or non-selective capture or killing of birds, and all means capable of causing the local disappearance of a species.[32] A number of such methods are specified in Annex IV, and must be prohibited in all cases; these include the use of snares, hooks, live birds (if blinded or mutilated for use as decoys), tape recorders, electrocuting devices, artificial light sources, explosives, nets, traps, poisoned or anaesthetic bait, and semi-automatic or automatic weapons. The use of aircraft or motor vehicles, or of boats driven at speeds greater than 5 km/hour, is also prohibited.[33] The list in Annex IV, which is extensive, is not, however, exhaustive—*any* indiscriminate means of killing or capturing wild birds should be proscribed by the member states if capable of causing the large-scale or non-selective capture or killing of wild birds.

The member states are able to derogate from the specific obligations laid down in the Directive, but only 'where there is no other satisfactory solution',[34] and for one or more of a limited number of closely defined reasons.[35] Derogation is permitted in the interests of public health and safety; for reasons of air safety; in order to prevent serious damage to crops livestock, forests, fisheries, or water;[36] and for the protection of flora and fauna. Derogations are also permitted for the purposes of research and teaching, of repopulation, of reintroduction, and for breeding necessary in connection with repopulation or reintroduction schemes. It is also permitted, under closely supervised conditions, for member states to permit the capture, keeping, or 'other judicious use' of certain birds in small numbers.[37] Hunting can be a judicious use of birds, and thus permissible, but not if it is allowed in the close season or during periods when the species concerned is breeding or raising young.[38] The grounds justifying action against the birds in question must be specified and the methods of killing permitted under the derogation must be justifiable by reference to them. They must also contain controls to ensure that a small number of birds (and no more) are killed or taken. What constitutes a 'small number' for

[31] See Wild Birds Directive art. 7.4, and art. 2 for the overall objectives of the Directive's protection regime.

[32] Wild Birds Directive art. 8.1.

[33] Wild Birds Directive art. 8.2 and Annex IV(b).

[34] It is not sufficient if there is another solution but it is merely less convenient—there must be no other available solution in order for the derogation power to become exercisable: *Ligue Royale Belge pour la Protection des Oiseaux v Region Wallonne* [1996] ECR I–6775.

[35] See Wild Birds Directive art. 9.1.

[36] It is, perhaps, noteworthy that this derogation enables the member states to give primacy to property and commercial interests over the conservation interest in species protection. This underlines the anthropocentric focus of the legal provisions, and works against an argument that nature conservation law is ecocentric in its focus and implementation.

[37] Wild Birds Directive art. 9.1(c).

[38] See *Ligue Royale Belge pour la Protection des Oiseaux v Premier ministre* [2003] ECR I–12, 105; *Commission v Finland* [2005] ECR I–11,033. Hunting during periods when the birds are not breeding, which is permitted under the Directive, will be a 'satisfactory' alternative solution in these cases.

these purposes will be guided by the work of the scientific committee established under the Directive; the ORNIS committee.[39] In the UK the control of pests is now undertaken through the grant of annual generic licenses issued by the Welsh Assembly Government, DEFRA, and the Scottish Executive.[40] These include a general licence to permit the killing or taking of birds to prevent damage to crops, livestock, vegetables, and fruit, and additional licences for the protection of public health and safety, air safety, and for the conservation of wild birds. Species categorized as pests, and covered by the general licences issued by all three devolved administrations, include crows, collared doves, herring and greater black-backed gulls, magpies, pigeons, jackdaws, rooks, and wood pigeons. There are some variations in the coverage of the regional licences and the species to which they apply, in addition to the species specified here.[41]

The list of grounds for derogating from the species protection provisions in the Directive is exhaustive,[42] and the member states must not only notify each derogation to the Commission, but also confirm the identity of the public authority that will have responsibility for declaring whether its terms have been met in individual cases.[43] One consequence of exercising the derogations permitted by the Directive in the UK through the issuance of annual generic licences to control pest species is a lack of transparency in the legislative process. The detailed law in England, Scotland, and Wales is contained in the terms of the licences issued under the Wildlife and Countryside Act 1981. These can be amended without parliamentary scrutiny, and ascertaining whether actions undertaken by landowners and others are lawful will depend upon scrutiny of the relevant licence issued by the devolved administrations.

The Habitats Directive[44]

The European Habitats and Species Directive is a more ambitious and far-reaching instrument than the Birds Directive. Its principal aim is ambitious; to contribute to ensuring biodiversity through the conservation of natural habitats, and of wild fauna and flora, in the member states.[45] The Directive is more broadly based than the Birds Directive, however, and its objectives are to be pursued while also taking

39 The 'Committee for Adaptation to Technical and Scientific Progress' established by Wild Birds Directive art. 16.1. In practice, this means that small numbers will equate to less than 1 per cent of the total annual mortality of the bird species in question. See also *Commission v Finland* [2005] ECR 1–11,033. See generally *Review of the Implementation of Species Action Plans of Threatened Birds in the European Union (2004-2010) Final Report* (BirdLife International 2011) available at: <http://ec.europa.eu/environment/nature/conservation/wildbirds/action_plans/docs/Final%20report%20BirdLife%20review%20SAPs.pdf>.

40 S. 16 Under Wildlife and Countryside Act 1981. These have replaced a more generic system whereby a general licence was granted by the 1981 Act to all 'authorized persons' to destroy pests, of indefinite duration. This was incompatible with the more restrict terms of the Directive. See further Chapter 5, pp. 170 ff.

41 Eg in England and Wales the licence also permits the destruction of jays and lesser black-backed gulls.

42 *Commission v Spain* [2004] ECR I–11,619; *Commission v Austria* [2007] ECR II–5939.

43 Wild Birds Directive art. 9.2(d).

44 Council Directive 92/43/EC of 21 May 1992 on the Conservation of Natural Habitats and of Wild Flora and Fauna, [1992] OJ L206, 22/07/1992, p. 7 (hereafter 'Habitats Directive').

45 Art. 2 Habitats Directive.

into account economic, social, cultural, and regional requirements, in a manner that also contributes to sustainable development.[46] The measures deployed in the Directive are based upon identifying natural habitats, and species of flora and fauna, that are of 'Community Interest'.[47] The conservation measures taken by the member states under the Directive must be intended to maintain or restore at 'favourable conservation status' the natural habitats, and populations of wild species of flora and fauna, that have been designated as of Community interest.[48] 'Favourable' conservation status is further defined in the case of natural habitats to mean: that the natural range of the habitat and the areas it covers within that range are stable or increasing; its specific structure and the functions necessary for its long-term maintenance exist and are likely to continue to exist for the foreseeable future; and the conservation status of its typical species is also favourable.[49] The conservation status of any wild species of flora and fauna of Community interest will be favourable when population dynamics data indicates that it is maintaining itself on a long-term basis as a viable component of its natural habitats, its natural range is not being reduced, and it has a sufficiently large habitat to maintain its populations on a long term basis.[50]

The Directive seeks to attain these goals by providing for the creation of an ecological network of 'special areas of conservation' (hereafter SACs), to be known collectively as *Natura 2000*. Member States are required to contribute to the *Natura 2000* network by designating sites hosting the natural habitat types listed in Annex 1 to the Directive, and the habitats of those species listed in Annex 11.[51] When complete, *Natura 2000* will consist of three types of site:

- SACs which host the natural habitat types listed in Annex 1 to the Directive,
- SACs which comprise the habitats of the rare species listed in Annex 2 to the Directive, and
- Special Protection Areas designated under the Wild Birds Directive.[52]

Each member state is required to contribute to the creation of the *Natura 2000* network in proportion to the representation within its territory of the natural habitats and habitats of species specified in the Directive.[53] Natural habitats of Community importance are identified by reference to three criteria: they are either habitat types that are in danger of disappearance in their natural range, or are habitats that have a small range following their regression or because of their restricted area, or which present outstanding examples of typical characteristics of one of five bio-geographic areas within the Community viz. the Alpine, Atlantic, Continental, Macronesian (that is, the Seychelles) and Mediterranean bio-geographic regions. The UK is wholly within the Atlantic bio-geographical region.

[46] See Habitats Directive Preamble, recital 3.
[47] Art. 2.2 Habitats Directive.
[48] Habitats Directive art. 1 (a) (definition of 'conservation').
[49] Art. 1(g) Habitats Directive.
[50] Art. 1(i) Habitats Directive.
[51] Art. 3.1 Habitats Directive.
[52] Ie SPAs designated by the member states under arts 4(1) or (2) of Council Directive 2009/147/EC on the Conservation of Wild Birds or its predecessor, Council Directive 79/409/EEC (pp. 203 ff.).
[53] Art. 3.2 Habitats Directive.

The timetable for selecting and designating SACs is complex, and is further explained in Box 6.1. After public consultation on the draft proposals, a list of candidate sites in the UK was sent to the European Commission in 1995. The next stage in the implementation process required the Commission to draw up two

Box 6.1 Procedure for Classifying Special Areas of Conservation under the Habitats Directive

Stage 1	Member state identifies candidate sites using criteria in Annex III Habitats Directive. Priority habitat types and habitats for priority species must be indentified in the site proposal. These sites will automatically be considered as Sites of Community Importance (SCI). The identification of candidate sites can proceed on the scientific criteria in Annex III only—economic considerations are irrelevant to this exercise.[54]
Stage 2	European Commission moderates member state's list of candidate SCIs by reference to the criteria in Annex III, in the context of the bio-geographical area in which it is situated, and in the context of the EU as a whole. It produces draft list of sites of Community importance (SCI). Annex III requires that all sites that host priority natural habit and/or species be considered as SCIs. In other cases the evaluation must take account of the site's contribution to the maintenance or restoration of Annex I habitat/s and/or Annex II species to favourable conservation status and its contribution to the coherence of the *Natura 2000* network of protected sites.[55]
Stage 3	The final list of SCIs is agreed by the member state and European Commission. Some flexibility is built into the process at this stage. If the member state has sites that host one or more priority habitat or species and total more than 5% of its national territory, it may request that the Annex III criteria be applied more flexibly in selecting the final SCIs in its territory.[56] The full list of SCIs was originally to be adopted by the Council of Ministers within 6 years of the Directive's notification (May 1998).[57] A considerable number of sites have now been designated, but slippage in the timetable and the accession of new member states mean this is an ongoing process.
Stage 4	Following adoption as an SCI, the member state must designate a site as a Special Area of Conservation 'as soon as possible and within 6 years at most'.[58]

[54] *R v Secretary of State for the Environment ex parte First Corporate Shipping Ltd* [2001] ECR I–9235 (Case C-371/98). See as well *R (Newsum) v Welsh Assembly Government* (No 2) [2005] EWHC 538 Admin.

[55] Annex III Stage 2.2 Habitats Directive. This must take account of the site's relative value at national level, its geographical location (eg on migration routes or as hosting an ecosystem crossing national boundaries), its size, the global ecological value of the site for the bio-geographical area in which it is located, and for the European territory.

[56] Art. 4.2 Habitats Directive. This may enable social or economic criteria to be considered at this (third) stage in appropriate cases where the qualifying criteria in art. 4.2 for flexibility are met, whereas they cannot be considered at stage 1 (as established in *R v Secretary of State for the Environment ex parte First Corporate Shipping Ltd* [2001] ECR I–9235).

[57] Art 4.3 Habitats Directive. The Council is advised in doing so by a committee chaired by the European Commission with representatives from each member state (art. 21).

[58] Art. 4.4 Habitats Directive.

separate site lists. Firstly, the Directive required the Commission to draw up, by 5 June 1998, a list of 'Sites of Community Importance'. This involved a selection process from among the candidate sites notified to the Commission by member states, using criteria set out in Annex III to the Directive. Secondly, from the draft lists presented by member states, the Commission must also produce a separate list of *priority sites;* that is, those sites hosting a priority habitat or priority species identified in Annexes I or II of the Directive. All priority sites must be designated Sites of Community Interest under Annex III. There are special consultation procedures applicable where the Commission considers that a member state has left a site hosting a priority habitat, or a site comprising the habitat of a priority species, out of its list of national candidate sites. In this case the Commission can, of its own volition, initiate a bilateral consultation between itself and the member state for the purpose of comparing the scientific data used by the latter and by the Commission. If this fails to produce agreement, the Commission can put a proposal to the Council for the designation of the site as a Site of Community Importance—and the Council can, by unanimous vote, accept the recommendation and designate the site.[59] There is no comparable procedure under the Birds Directive for the designation of sites by the European Commission, rather than by the member state in whose territory it falls.

Once the list of Sites of Community Importance has finally been agreed, the Directive requires member states to designate the sites as SACs as soon as possible and by the end of six years at most.[60] In principle, therefore, the full list of SACs should have been designated, and *Natura 2000* completed, by 5 June 2004. The process remains well behind schedule, and the European Commission has undertaken infringement proceedings against several member states for including insufficient sites in their national lists of candidate sites.[61]

The criteria for selecting UK sites for possible inclusion in *Natura 2000* were developed by the Joint Nature Conservation Committee and closely follow and apply the scientific criteria in the Directive.[62] They include the presence of an identified priority habitat type or species, rarity of habitat type in the European context, whether a high proportion of the extant habitat type or species is present, and representivity; that is, the need under the Directive to select sites which represent the best examples in extent and quality of the main types, as well as the main variants of habitat and species across the geographical range for the Atlantic bio-geographic region. The Directive also places emphasis on the structure and function of selected sites, leading to the selection for designation as SACs of sites that provide good quality examples for habitat types and species, often in larger sites that host complex ecosystem mosaics. The criteria in the Directive also place the

[59] Art. 5 Habitats Directive.

[60] Art. 4.4 Habitats Directive.

[61] See, for example, *Commission v France* [2001] ECR I–5831; *Commission v Ireland* [2001] ECR I–5757; *Commission v Germany* [2001] ECR I–5811.*Commission v United Kingdom* [2005] ECR I–9017.

[62] *The Habitats Directive: selection of Special Areas of Conservation in the UK* (Joint Nature Conservation Committee 2006).

UK under a special responsibility for certain habitat types in Annex 1 because of the large proportion of the European natural resource in the UK territory; for example, Caledonian pine forest and old oak woods with Ilex and Blechnum. In these cases the number of sites selected in the UK was higher than for other habitat types and species, and was intended to make a significant contribution to maintenance of their favourable conservation status in the Atlantic bio-geographical region as a whole. There are currently 611 designated SACs, of which the overwhelming majority (538 sites) are terrestrial SACs, with 73 Marine SACs.

The omission of important wildlife sites from national lists of SACs put forward for designation under the directive may generate significant legal challenges to the member states implementation programmes. Cases brought before the national courts and the European Court of Justice under the Wild Birds Directive have challenged both the non-designation of important sites and the drawing of the site boundaries in cases where sites have been designated. The *Basses Corbieres* case,[63] discussed on p. 205, is an example of a successful challenge based on non-designation; the *Lappel Bank* litigation[64] and *WWF-UK Ltd v Secretary of State for Scotland*[65] are two examples of (unsuccessful) challenges to the manner in which the boundaries of protected sites are drawn on designation. It should perhaps be noted, however, that the procedures for designating sites under the two Directives are materially different. Under the Wild Birds Directive, the choice of sites and their designation is left to each member state. The legal challenges here have therefore focused on whether individual member states have correctly applied the criteria laid down in the Directive. Site selection under the Habitats Directive is a far more complex process, and dialogue between the European Commission and the member states, is an integral element in identifying and designating SACs. This will make it more difficult to challenge the non-designation of sites by the member states and may make legal challenges more difficult. Although the Commission has powers to itself put forward sites omitted from the national lists, it is very unlikely to challenge details of those designations to which it has been—through consultation and the identification of sites of Community Importance—a party. Having said that, the UK's original implementation strategy has been successfully challenged on the basis that it excluded the seabed up to the limit of the continental shelf and territorial waters (200 miles).[66] This resulted in the extension of protected areas policy to include all those marine areas over which the UK claims jurisdiction.[67] Challenging the non-designation of territorial SACs would, however, be more difficult for the reasons outlined earlier.

[63] *Commission of the European Communities v France* [2001] ECR I–10.

[64] *R v Secretary of State for the Environment ex parte RSPB* [1996] ECR I–3805.

[65] [1999] Env L Rev 632 (concerning the drawing of the boundaries of an SPA in the Cairngorm Mountains in a manner that excluded land to be developed as a funicular railway for ski development).

[66] See *R v Secretary of State for Trade and Industry ex parte Greenpeace Ltd (No. 2)* (2000) Env L Rev 221 (the Directive was there held to apply to all areas over which the member states exercise sovereign rights, and should therefore have been applied to applications for exploration licences for gas and oil in the North West Atlantic).

[67] See the Offshore Marine Conservation (Natural Habitats etc.) Regulations 2007, SI 2007/1842.

(a) Habitat protection

The Habitats Directive requires member states to deliver a high level of legal protection for designated European sites. They must establish the 'necessary conservation measures' including appropriate management plans designed for the sites and integrated into other development plans, together with appropriate statutory, administrative, or contractual measures that correspond to the ecological requirements of the natural habitat types in Annex 1 of the Directive, and the Annex II species present on each SAC.[68] The Directive requires the member states to 'take appropriate steps to avoid, in the special areas of conservation, the deterioration of natural habitats and the habitats of species as well as disturbance of the species for which the areas have been designated, in so far as such disturbance could be significant in relation to the objectives of the Directive'.[69] Further, any plan or project not necessary to the management of the site must be subjected to an environmental assessment of its implications for the conservation objectives of the site designation. A project can only be allowed to proceed if the competent national authorities have ascertained that it will not adversely affect the integrity of the site concerned, or if there are 'imperative reasons of overriding public interest'. The latter can include public interest considerations of an economic or social nature provided, of course, that they are of overriding importance.

If the site hosts a *priority* species or habitat type identified by the Directive, then development can only be permitted if there are overriding considerations connected with human health or public safety, or what the Directive terms 'beneficial consequences of primary importance for the environment'.[70] Under article 6.4 of the Habitats Directive those 'imperative reasons of overriding public interest' which can justify the member state permitting a damaging development expressly include reasons of a social and economic nature. Social or economic reasons are only excluded where the site hosts a priority species or habitat identified in accordance with the procedures in Annex III to the Directive. Where the site host a *priority habitat type* or *priority species,* the only considerations that can be raised are:

- Those relating to human health or safety,
- To beneficial consequences of primary importance for the environment, and
- Other imperative reasons of overriding public interest—subject in this case to approval from the European Commission.

The express inclusion of social and economic criteria, as a justification for development in sites not hosting priority habitats or species, effectively reverses the decision in *Commission v Germany*[71] (the *Leybucht Dykes* case) on the parallel provisions in the Wild Birds Directive. In effect, the *Leybucht Dykes* test is retained solely for priority sites. As we have seen, however, in *Basses Corbieres* the court ruled that it did not apply to sites that should have been designated as SPAs, but have not yet

[68] Art. 6.1. Habitats Directive. [69] Art. 6.2 Habitats Directive.
[70] See arts. 6.3 and 6.4 of the Habitats Directive. [71] [1991] ECR I–883.

been so designated. It should be added that the European Court of Justice ruled in the *Santona marshes* litigation that article 4(4) of the Wild Birds Directive had direct effect under European law. As the key articles of the Habitats Directive are in this respect drafted in virtually identical terms, it is likely that its requirements would also be regarded as having direct effect.

The European Commission has published guidance to the member states on the interpretation and implementation of the habitat management provisions in article 6 of the Habitats Directive.[72] This makes it clear that the Directive imposes obligations to adopt positive measures to promote conservation through the maintenance and restoration of sites adopted as SACs, as well as preventative measures to prevent damage and deterioration of European sites.

(i) The Directive requires the member states to adopt conservation measures for all SACs, applicable to all the natural habitat types in Annex 1 and the species of Annex II present on these sites. 'Conservation' in this sense imposes positive obligations—the Directive requires the member states to take measures designed to maintain or restore at a *favourable conservation status*, all natural habitats and wild flora and fauna of Community interest.[73] Article 6 requires, furthermore, that positive conservation measures to promote this overarching objective should respect the ecological requirements of the natural habitat and/or species for which the site is designated viz. the ecological needs of 'abiotic and biotic factors necessary to ensure the favourable conservation status of the habitat types and species, including their relation with the environment (air, water, soil, vegetation, etc.)'.[74] The necessary conservation measures can take the form of management plans for protected sites addressed to all foreseeable activities—unforeseeable activities that may damage the conservation status of habitats or species can be dealt with through preventative measures, including the subsequent environmental assessment of plans and projects. Whether or not a management plan is adopted, however, the member state *must* chose to implement either statutory, contractual, or administrative measures to prosecute the Directive's objectives for maintaining or restoring the conservation status of protected sites. The use of agri-environmental schemes would, for example, be an appropriate measure to protect and restore some man-made habitats, such as hay meadows.[75]

(ii) The obligation to avoid the deterioration of natural habitats in SACs[76] is based on the prevention principle and requires the member state to take all actions that are reasonable to ensure that no significant deterioration or

[72] *Managing Natura 2000 Sites—the provisions of Article 6 of the Habitats Directive 92/43/EEC* (Luxembourg: Office for Official Publications of the European Communities 2000) (hereafter '*Managing Natura 2000 Sites*').

[73] Art. 2.2 Habitats Directive.

[74] *Managing Natura 2000 Sites*, n. 72 at p. 18.

[75] See *Managing Natura 2000 Sites* at 21.

[76] Art. 6.2 Habitats Directive, see n. 69.

disturbance occur. It is not limited to intentional acts, but could cover accidents, such as fire or flood, if they are predictable, and it may also require measures to be implemented outside an SAC if external events have an impact on the site's conservation status.[77] Deterioration or disturbance is measured against the conservation status of the species and habitats concerned. Therefore, habitat deterioration will occur when the area covered by the habitat on a site is reduced, or the specific structure and functions necessary for the long-term maintenance of the good conservation status of the typical species that are associated with the habitat in question are reduced in comparison with their initial status. The assessment is made by reference to the contribution that the site makes to the coherence of the overall *Natura 2000* network.[78]

(iii) Finally, the Commission guidance gives a wide interpretation to the scope of the 'plans or projects' that must be subject to an appropriate assessment before being consented by the member state.[79] Whether a plan or project will have 'significant' effects must be assessed objectively, against the conservation objectives of the site: something that may have significant effects on one site may not, for example, do so on another.[80] Furthermore, the safeguards in article 6.3 and 6.4 apply where there is a 'likelihood' of significant effects—there is no requirement for certainty of effects for the provisions to apply—and this can arise from plans and projects located *outside* the boundaries of a protected site. Clearly, damage to a SAC hosting a rare wetland habitat will be likely to arise, for example, from a proposal to drain land adjacent to but outside the site's boundaries. The 'appropriate' assessment that must be carried out before the member state can authorize the plan or project is confined to its implications for the site's conservation objectives, and these will be established and set out in the SAC standard data form submitted to the Commission when the site was adopted. This is therefore the point of reference for the assessment, which will be somewhat narrower in scope than a full environmental impact assessment carried out under the Environmental Impact Assessment Directive.[81]

[77] *Managing Natura 2000 sites* at p. 25.

[78] *Managing Natura 2000 Sites* at 27.

[79] Art. 6.3 and 6.4 Habitats Directive, see n. 70.

[80] The example given in the Commission guidance is a loss of 100 m^2 of habitat in a small SAC hosting a rare orchid site: this would be 'significant', whereas such a loss of habitat may not be on a large steppe site of many hundreds or thousands of hectares. See *Managing Natura 2000 Sites, Managing Natura 2000 Sites* at 33.

[81] Ie under Council Directive 85/337/EEC, now consolidated in Directive 2011/92/EU of the European Parliament and of the Council of 13 December 2011 on the assessment of the effects of certain public and private projects on the environment [2012] OJ L26/1. For further guidance on the methodology to be employed for assessments under the Habitats Directive see: European Commission, *Assessment of plans and projects significantly affecting Natura 2000 sites: methodological guidance on the provisions of Article 6(3) and (4) of the Habitats Directive 92/43/EEC* (Luxembourg: Office for Official Publications of the European Communities 2002).

(b) Species protection

The Habitats Directive complements the Birds Directive in making provision for the protection of individual species of animal and plant. The general approach is similar, however, in that this is done by reference to lists of protected species set out in the Annexes to the Directive, defined in scientific terms.

- *Animals.* Annex IV (a) lists those animal species protected under the Directive. Article 12 requires the member states to establish a system of strict protection for these species in their natural range prohibiting all forms of deliberate capture or killing of specimens in the wild, the deliberate disturbance of the species (especially during breeding rearing hibernation and migration), the deliberate destruction or taking of eggs, and the destruction or deterioration of breeding sites or resting places. Member states must establish a monitoring system to monitor the incidental capture and killing of the animal species listed in Annex IV, and must ensure that any killing or capture detected does not have a 'significant negative impact' on the species concerned.[82] Member states can derogate from the strict requirements of the Directive, but only in limited and stated circumstances; for example, to prevent serious damage to livestock and crops, or in the interests of public health. Where derogation is applied, each state must report to the Commission every two years on the operation of the derogation, and the latter will give an Opinion on its operation.
- *Plants.* For the species listed in Annex IV (b) member states must prohibit the deliberate picking, collecting, cutting, uprooting, or destruction of such plants in their natural range in the wild. They must also prevent their sale, transport, or exchange.[83]
- *Lawful Taking and Killing.* The taking and/or killing of certain species of plant and animal is permissible. The species to which this applies are listed in Annex V. In the case of animals, however, the Directive requires member states to outlaw 'the use of all indiscriminate means capable of causing local disappearance of or serious disturbance to, populations of such species'. This ban must include the methods specifically listed in Annex VI; for example, the use of blind animals as decoys, artificial lights, explosives, poisons, and semi-automatic weapons.

Habitat Protection—Implementing European Standards

The requirements of the Habitats Directive as to the management and protection of natural habitats and of wildlife species are implemented in England and Wales by the Conservation of Habitats and Species Regulations 2010 (hereafter referred to as

[82] Art. 12.4 Habitats Directive.

[83] See art.13 Habitats Directive.

'the Conservation Regulations 2010').[84] They are implemented in Scotland by the Conservation (Natural Habitats etc.) Regulations 1994, as amended.[85] Their impact is broadly similar, although the 1994 Regulations have been amended several times since 1994 to introduce provisions specific only to Scotland.[86]

The Conservation Regulations 2010 provide for the relevant national authorities[87] to maintain a register of 'European sites' in England and Wales. These will comprise the following:[88]

- Special Areas of Conservation (SACs) formally designated by the Secretary of State under the Habitats Directive.
- Any site adopted by the European Commission as a 'site of Community Importance'. This is the second stage of the designation process, following the submission of national lists of candidate Special Areas of Conservation to the Commission. In such cases all that remains is for the national authorities to formally designate them as SACs to complete the process.
- Candidate SACs identified by the European Commission as satisfying the criteria for selection in Annex 1 or 11 of the Directive. These sites will not have been submitted by the member state, and are only given the status of 'European sites' during the consultation between the Commission and the national authorities that will take place under article 5 of the Directive, pending their full adoption, or otherwise, as candidate SACs.
- 'Special protection areas' (SPAs) designated under the European Wild Birds Directive of 2009 or its predecessor.

The number and extent of the European sites designated in the UK is explained in Box 6.2. Taken together, these sites will form part of the Europe-wide *Natura 2000* conservation programme of protected wildlife sites instituted by the Habitats Directive.

In the United Kingdom, all European sites will already have been notified as SSSIs under the Wildlife and Countryside Act 1981. The relevant authorities are under a duty to identify sites in England and Wales that are eligible for identification as Sites of Community Importance.[89] Once a Site of Community Importance has, following consultation with the European Commission, been adopted under article 4 of the Habitat Directive as a candidate SAC, the Secretary of State is placed under an obligation to designate the site as a SAC as soon as possible, and within six years at most.[90] The chosen approach to implementation of the Directive has been

[84] SI 2010/490. The regulations came into force on 1st April 2010, with some minor exceptions relating to marine protected areas (reg. 1, SI 2010/490).

[85] SI 1994/2716. The 1994 Regulations also applied in England and Wales prior to the coming into force of SI 2010/490.

[86] By Scottish SI 2004/475; Scottish SI 2007/80; and Scottish SI 2007/349.

[87] Ie in England the Secretary of State and in Wales the Welsh Ministers: SI 2010/490, reg. 13(1).

[88] SI 2010/490, reg. 13(2).

[89] SI 2010/490, reg. 10.

[90] SI 2010/490, reg. 11(1).

Box 6.2 European sites in the UK

Country	SPAs		Potential SPAs	SACs		Candidate SACs	
	No.	Area (ha)	No. of sites	No.	Area (ha)	No.	Area (ha)
England	79	1,050,704	2	230	845,856	7	181,870
England (offshore)				0		2	231,273
England/ Scotland	1	43,637	0	0		0	
England/Wales	3	208,041	0	0		0	
Northern Ireland	16	113,998	0	52	65,913	2	1259
Scotland	146	850,364	7	236	921,225	0	
Wales	17	123,015	0	85	590,871	0	
United Kingdom	262	2,389,758	9	613	2,631,415	15	1,391,973

Notes

1. *Source*: Joint Nature Conservation Committee, UK SAC/SCI Sites Summary and UK SPA sites summary. Available at <http://www.jncc.gov.uk/page-1399 and http://www.jncc.gov.uk/page-1456>. The figures give the status of sites as at 20 August 2010.
2. In addition to these, there are 5 Sites of Community Importance in UK Offshore Waters covering 268,409 hectares.
3. Candidate SACs are sites submitted to the European Commission but not yet formally adopted as either SCIs or full SACs.

to designate existing SSSIs, and to apply additional controls on land use and development by

(i) amending the procedures for agricultural and other operations in the 1981 Act, and

(ii) imposing tighter planning controls on development within European sites.

It was noted earlier that the Habitats Directive requires member states to 'take appropriate steps to avoid, in the special areas of conservation, the deterioration of natural habitats and the habitats of species, as well as disturbance of the species for which the areas have been designated, insofar as such disturbance could be significant in relation to the objectives of the Directive'.[91] Further, any plan or project not necessary to the management of the site must be subjected to an environmental assessment of its implications for the conservation objectives enumerated in the site designation. A project can only be allowed to proceed if the competent national authorities have ascertained that it will not adversely affect the integrity of the site concerned, or if there are 'imperative reasons of overriding

[91] Art. 6.2 Habitats Directive, pp. 214 ff.

public interest'. These can include public interest considerations of an economic or social nature (provided, of course, that they are of overriding importance) but if the site hosts a *priority* species or habitat type identified by the Directive, the development can only be permitted if there are overriding considerations connected with human health or public safety, or what the Directive terms 'beneficial consequences of primary importance for the environment'.[92]

The relevant provisions implementing these requirements in England and Wales are now contained in Part 2 (conservation of natural habitats and habitats of species) and Part 6 Chapter 2 (planning) of the Conservation Regulations 2010, and, in relation to England, in the *National Planning Policy Framework* (2012) as amplified in ODPM Circular 06/2005.[93]

The original transposing regulations[94] were subjected to extensive amendment following their introduction in 1994. Substantial amendments were, in particular, required to close loopholes in the UK's transposition of the Directive highlighted by the European Court of Justice ruling in *Commission v United Kingdom,*[95] which concluded that in material respects they failed to fully implement the requirements of the Directive. The overall implementation strategy, encapsulated in the provisions discussed from pp. 220ff, was to confer specific powers on the statutory Conservation Bodies and then to impose upon them a general duty to exercise those functions so as to secure compliance with the Directive. This approach was criticized because the creation of general duties can render transposition of a Directive by specific regulatory measures superfluous only if those rules *actually ensure* the full application of the Directive by the national authorities. The general duty imposed upon the statutory Conservation Bodies (to exercise their powers to secure compliance with the Directive)[96] was held by the European Court to be inadequate to give effect to the Directive with sufficient precision and clarity to satisfy the demands of legal certainty. Neither, in the ECJ's view, did it impose a sufficiently clear legal framework to ensure the full compliance with the Directive's requirements. It was not capable of filling any gaps left by the specific provisions in the 1994 transposing regulations targeted at securing compliance.[97] The UK's transposition of the Directive was also found to be deficient in relation to a number of specific Directive obligations including the following:

[92] See arts. 6.3 and 6.4 of the Habitats Directive, p. 214.

[93] See in particular paras. 118 and 119 of the *National Planning Policy Framework* (DCLG 2012); Joint ODPM Circular 06/2005 and DEFRA Circular 01/2005 *Government Circular: Biodiversity and Geological Conservation—Statutory Obligations and their impact within the Planning System* (16 August 2005). In Wales, planning guidance is to be found in Technical Advice Note 5 *Nature Conservation and Planning* (2009); and in Scotland in *Scottish Planning Policy* (2010) paras. 125 ff, and in Planning Advice Note 60 *Planning for natural heritage* (2000, updated 2008).

[94] The Conservation (Natural Habitats & Co.) Regulations 1994, SI 1994/2716.

[95] *Commission v United Kingdom* Case C-06/04, [2005] ECR I–9017. For earlier criticism of the implementing provisions see S. Ball, 'Reforming the Law of Habitat Protection' in Rodgers (ed.), *Nature Conservation and Countryside Law* (University of Wales Press, 1996), Ch. 4.

[96] At that time reg. 3(2) of SI 1994/2716. This provision is now to be found in reg. 9(1) Conservation of Habitats and Species Regulations 2010 (SI 2010/490) in its application in England and Wales; the 1994 Regulations still apply in Scotland.

[97] Case C-6/04, Judgment paras. 24, 26, and 27.

- they did not require an environmental assessment of development plans prior to their adoption in order to assess their implications for SACs.
- No statutory duty was imposed on the relevant national authorities to monitor the conservation status of European sites. This was held to be a breach of articles 11 and 14 of the Directive, although in practice, monitoring of sites by the Conservation Bodies is carried out on a regular basis.
- The transposing regulations did not contain a general prohibition on the use of indiscriminate means of killing protected species of fauna. The UK legislation does ban killing by a range of specified methods, and the list is reviewed periodically, but this was held to be insufficient as new means of killing might be developed and escape proscription until the statutory list was periodically reviewed. As there was no statutory duty on the Conservation Bodies to review the list of prohibited methods of killing this was a clear lacuna in the legislation.[98]
- Both the Wildlife and Countryside Act 1981 (in relation to SSSIs) and the 1994 regulations (in relation to European sites) initially provided landowners with a defence if they could show that the destruction or disturbance of a protected species was the incidental consequence of an otherwise lawful activity. The landowner accidentally ploughing up the nests of a protected species of ground-nesting bird would, for example, be potentially within the ambit of this defence. This did not accord with the provisions in the Habitats Directive protecting endangered species identified in its Annexes.

This decision led to a number of amendments to the transposing regulations between 2007 and 2009.[99] The law applicable in England and Wales has now been consolidated and clarified in the Conservation Regulations 2010. The fundamental implementation strategy has not, however, changed. The 2010 regulations are closely modelled on the approach in SSSIs protected under the Wildlife and Countryside Act 1981, with additional restrictions on land use imposed on the owners and occupiers of land in European sites, and additional powers conferred on the Conservation Bodies to secure compliance with the requirements of the Directive.

(a) Restrictions on potentially damaging operations

All sites adopted as SACs will also be notified as SSSIs under the Wildlife and Countryside Act 1981. The Conservation Regulations 2010 impose restrictions on

[98] Judgment Case C-6/04, paras. 91 ff.

[99] The most important were made by the Conservation (Natural Habitats etc) (Amendment) Regulations 2007, SI 2007/1843. Following a reasoned opinion delivered by the European Commission in 2008, the 2007 Regulations were themselves further amended by SI 2008/2172 and SI 2009/6 in order to specify in greater detail the arrangements to be made by the Secretary of State for the surveillance of European protected species and of their conservation status, and to specify in clearer detail what duties apply in the light of that surveillance. This secured the withdrawal of the reasoned opinion and the threat of further proceedings in the ECJ. A separate amending regulation—the Offshore Marine Conservation (Natural Habitats etc.) Regulations 2007—extended the scope of the 1994 Regulations to apply to areas where the UK has jurisdiction beyond its territorial seas.

land use which supplement those in the Wildlife and Countryside Act 1981[100] in order to guarantee the higher level of protection afforded to European sites under the Directive. As with SSSIs, the administration of conservation in these sites is overseen by the Conservation Bodies, who enjoy a range of statutory powers and duties in relation to European sites that mirror those in SSSIs. The 2010 regulations impose an overarching duty on the Secretary of State and the Conservation Bodies to exercise their functions under the law of nature conservation so as to secure compliance with the Habitats Directive.[101]

The close relationship between the identification of sites as SSSIs and as European sites is recognized in the 2010 regulations, which principally confer additional protection on European sites by adding additional restrictions to the land use proscriptions imposed by the SSSI notification in each case. Thus, any notification already in force under the 1981 Act has effect for the purpose of the 2010 regulations.[102] The SSSI notification can, however, be amended by the Conservation Body where a site is also a European site, in order to secure compliance with the Habitats Directive. They may, for example, wish to specify additional operations that may be likely to damage the conservation interest of the SAC or vary the area of the notification. Any changes to the site notification must be given to the owner or occupier of the SSSI, and only take effect when notice has been given.[103] If the SSSI notification has been registered as a local land charge, it must be varied in accordance with the amendment to the site notification.[104]

While an SSSI notification is in force in relation to a site that is also a European site, an amended and somewhat more stringent set of land use restrictions will apply to deliver the management required by the Directive. Thus, the owner or occupier[105] of the site must not carry out any notified potentially damaging operation unless he has given written notice of his intention to do so.[106] It will only be lawful to proceed in certain circumstances;[107] if four months have elapsed following the giving of written notice of intent, if the operation is carried out with the written consent of the Conservation Body, or if it is carried out under the terms of a management agreement with the Conservation Body. If the Conservation Body has not given consent to the proposed operation, but consider there to be a risk, nevertheless, that it will be carried out before the expiry of the four-month 'waiting' period, it must take appropriate steps to notify the Secretary of State. This must be done at least one month before the end of the four months for which the operations are legally proscribed under the regulations.[108] This will enable the Secretary of

[100] See s. 28E Wildlife and Countryside Act 1981, pp. 89ff.
[101] SI 2010/490 reg. 9(1).
[102] SI 2010/490 reg 20.
[103] SI 2010/490 reg. 19(2) and (3).
[104] SI 2010/490 reg. 19 (4).
[105] Note the interpretation of the parallel wording in s.28 Wildlife and Countryside Act 1981 by the House of Lords in *Southern Water v Nature Conservancy Conservation Council* [1992] 3 All ER 481.
[106] SI 2010/490 reg. 20(1). Note that if the site is solely an SSSI, s. 28E of the 1981 Act does not require the owner's notice of intent to be made in writing—it can be made verbally. See Chapter 3, p. 85.
[107] These are specified in reg. 20(2) SI 2010/490.
[108] SI 2010/490 reg. 22.

State to make a special nature conservation order protecting the site if necessary (as to which see later).

(b) 'Appropriate' assessment of operational proposals

Where the Conservation Body receives an application for consent to a potentially damaging operation, they must carry out an environmental assessment of its implications for the conservation status of the site, an exercise in which the conservation objectives identified in the site notification will be the primary point of reference. They can only consent to the operation after having ascertained that the operation will not adversely affect the integrity of the site.[109]

The owner or occupier of land within a European Site can require a reference to the Secretary of State in two situations. He can do so within two months of receiving the Conservation Body's notice of refusal of operational consent for a potentially damaging operation if he wishes to challenge the decision. Alternatively he can refer the matter to the Secretary of State within three months of an application for operational consent being made, if no notice of decision has been received within that time. The Secretary of State can direct the Conservation Body to consent if (i) he is satisfied that there is no alternative solution, and (ii) the plan or project must be carried out for 'imperative reasons of overriding public interest'. Where the site does not host a priority habitat or species type, identified in the Directive and site designation, the public interest consideration dictating consent *can* include reasons of an economic or social nature. Where, however, the site hosts a priority habitat or species type, the overriding reasons of public interest justifying consent are restricted to reasons relating to public health, public safety, and 'beneficial consequences of primary importance to the environment'.[110]

If a damaging operation is allowed on appeal to the Secretary of State, he is under a duty to ensure that compensatory measures are taken to ensure the overall coherence of the *Natura 2000* programme.[111] The scope of this duty is not specified, but it could, clearly, encompass designating an alternative site with similar habitat characteristics to replace that whose conservation status has been compromised as a consequence of the consent.

(c) Special nature conservation orders

The appropriate authority[112] has power to make a special nature conservation order in respect of land in a European Site under the Conservation Regulations 2010.[113] An order can only be made following consultation with the relevant nature Conservation

[109] Reg. 21 SI 2010/490.
[110] Reg. 62 SI 2010/490.
[111] Art. 6.4 Habitats Directive; reg. 27(7) SI 2010/490 (permission on appeal against stop notice where special nature conservation order in force).
[112] Ie the Secretary of State in England, the Welsh Ministers in relation to land in Wales: SI 2010/490 reg. 3.
[113] Reg. 25 SI 2010/490.

Body (for example, Natural England). An application by the Conservation Body for an order may be triggered for example, where they consider it likely that a potentially damaging operation in a protected site may be carried by the landowner without operational consent. The order, if made, can specify 'operations . . . which appear to the appropriate authority to be of a kind which, if carried out in certain circumstances or in a particular manner, would be likely to destroy or damage the flora, fauna, or geological or physiographical features by reason of which the land is a European site'.[114] Although the primary legal mechanism for conferring protection is similar to that used in SSSIs (proscribing potentially damaging operations that require the consent of the Conservation Body prior to being carried out), the impact of the land use restrictions that can be applied by a special nature conservation order is somewhat broader. The order can prohibit operations both within and outside a European site, and on land that is not specified in the order itself. The legal proscription on carrying out notified operations is indefinite and not time-limited to four months, as is the case in a European Site where no order has been made. And it potentially applies to third parties, and not only the owner or occupier of the site.

The Conservation Body also has power to issue a 'stop' notice to prevent the carrying out of operations specified in the order as potentially damaging.[115] Where a stop notice has been served, the operations can only be carried out lawfully with the written consent of, or under a land management agreement with, the Conservation Body.[116] If the owner or occupier of the land applies for operational consent to carry out a plan or project prohibited by the stop notice, the Conservation Body must carry out an appropriate assessment[117] of its implications in view of the site's conservation objectives, and can only give consent if satisfied that it will not adversely affect the integrity of the site.[118] It is a criminal offence to contravene the terms of a stop notice unless the operation is carried out with a 'reasonable excuse'.[119] The Regulations in effect give a defence—that is, a 'reasonable excuse'—where the operation is carried out with planning consent, or is an 'emergency' operation that was notified to the Conservation Body as soon as practicable after its commencement.[120] Compensation must be paid by the Conservation Body if the value of property interests in the land affected by a stop notice is diminished as a result of it being served.[121]

Where a person carries out damaging operations in contravention of a special nature conservation order, the courts have power to impose restoration orders in addition to the other sanctions available under the Conservation Regulations. Restoration orders can require an offender to carry out 'such operations for the purpose of restoring the land to its former condition as may be specified'.[122] The

[114] Reg. 25(1) SI 2010/490. [115] Reg. 26(1) SI 2010/490.

[116] Reg. 26(6) SI 2010/490. [117] As to which, see p. 222.

[118] Reg. 27(1) and (2) SI 2010/490. [119] Reg. 26(4) and (8) SI 2010/490.

[120] Reg. 26(9) SI 2010/490. For discussion of the identical provisions in the 1981 Act, see Chapter 3, p. 94.

[121] See Reg. 28 SI 2010/490. The interest of the owner (and that of any other person with a property interest in the site) is valued at the date that the stop notice is served; reg. 28(4) SI 2010/490.

[122] Reg. 29(1) SI 2010/490.

court can specify a fixed period within which the remedial work must be carried out. Failure to comply with a restoration notice is a separate offence from that initially prosecuted—and which gave rise to the order in the first place—and is punishable on summary conviction by a fine not exceeding level 5 on the standard scale.[123] If he fails to comply, the offender can be proceeded against again until the order is met.[124]

(d) Restrictions on farm capital grants

Special rules apply to the making of farm capital grants in European sites. These would, for example, apply to capital grants for farm diversification under the CAP or for other projects within the rural development policy of the EU.[125] When making a capital grant, the authorities have a general duty to exercise their grant-making functions so as to further the conservation of the flora, fauna, geological, or physiographical features by reason of which the land has been designated as a European site.[126] The authority will consult the relevant Conservation Body[127] before awarding a grant, and must consider any objections that they make. They can reject the grant application in consequence of an objection from the Conservation Body that the activities have damaged, or are likely to damage, the conservation features of the site. If this is the case, however, the Conservation Body must offer the applicant a management agreement imposing restrictions on the activities in question and making provision for payments to be made to the unsuccessful applicant. This provision is controversial, as it is premised on the principle that the landowner can carry out operations on his land without restriction, and with public subsidy, however damaging to the environment and wildlife they may be. This is arguably an inversion of the polluter pays principle. This provision no longer applies in SSSIs and is one of the provisions applicable to European sites in England and Wales, but not Scotland, that is out of step with the changes made to the Wildlife and Countryside Act 1981 in 2000.

(e) Power to make by-laws

The 2010 regulations extend the powers of the Conservation Bodies to make by-laws for nature reserves so as to enable them to make by-laws for the protection of European sites.[128] By-laws may prohibit or restrict a wide range of activities in or near a European site: they can prohibit the entry onto the site by persons, vehicles, boats, or animals (for example, pets), and may prohibit or restrict the killing or

[123] Reg. 29(5) SI 2010/490.

[124] Reg. 29(6) SI 2010/490.

[125] The restrictions apply to grants made under s. 29 Agriculture Act 1970, and under the European Communities Act 1972. The latter are the only likely to be encountered in practice—no grant schemes under the 1970 Act have been made for some years.

[126] Reg. 24(1) SI 2010/490.

[127] Ie Natural England if the land is in England, CCW if in Wales.

[128] Reg. 30 SI 2010/490. The principal powers are contained in S. 20 of the National Parks and Access to the Countryside Act 1949 (and are extended by reg. 30 to European sites).

disturbance of any creature or its eggs, or interference with the vegetation, soil, or any other objects within the site. The dumping of rubbish and lighting of fires can also be prohibited. The by-law can apply these restrictions outside the confines of the site itself to an area adjoining or surrounding it, if this appears to the Conservation Body to be necessary for the protection of the site.[129] By-laws cannot, however, restrict the exercise of public rights of way, or the rights of the owner, tenant or occupier of the land. Neither can they restrict exercise of their functions by statutory undertakers (for example, the utility companies) and certain public bodies such as internal drainage boards.[130] Compensation is payable by the Conservation Body if the introduction of by-laws results in a diminution in the value of interests subsisting in the land covered by them.[131]

(f) Compulsory purchase powers

The final instrument in the 'conservation law toolkit' available to the Conservation Bodies to secure appropriate management of European sites is the power of compulsory purchase. The 2010 regulations confer compulsory purchase powers on the Conservation Body, but these can only be exercised to acquire an interest in land in two situations: (i) where they are unable to secure a management agreement 'on terms appearing to them to be reasonable', or (ii) where there is a management agreement, but breaches of it mean the site's satisfactory management cannot be secured.[132] In cases where there are breaches of an existing management agreement, the power is further restricted if the breaches are remediable. The Conservation Body must serve notice on the party in default requiring the acts or omissions in question to be remedied, and can only proceed to exercise the right of compulsory purchase if the recipient fails to comply within a reasonable time after the giving of the notice.[133] Disputes as to whether there has been a breach of agreement leading to possible compulsory purchase are referable to arbitration by an arbitrator appointed by the Lord Chancellor.[134] The exercise of the power to compulsorily acquire land (or an interest in land) must be authorized by the appropriate authority; in England, for example, by the Secretary of State.

Habitat Protection and the Control of Development

The rules for the control of operations that could have damaging impacts on European level protected habitats, and outlined earlier, apply where operations do *not* require planning permission from the local planning authority or other public bodies. These are activities that would not, therefore, require administrative

[129] Reg. 30(4) SI 2010/490. [130] See reg. 31 SI 2010/490.

[131] Reg. 32 SI 2010/490. [132] See reg. 34 SI 2010/490.

[133] Reg. 34(2). What constitutes a 'reasonable' period for compliance is not specified. This will be a question of fact and will depend upon the nature of the actions necessary to rectify the breach of the agreement.

[134] Reg. 34(3) SI 2010/490.

consent prior to being carried out unless brought within the special consenting regime set out in the 2010 regulations. This is important, as many of the activities that in practice have the potential to impact adversely on wildlife habitats do not require planning consent; most agricultural and forestry operations are, for example, not considered 'development' for the purposes of planning control.[135] Where, however, an operation in a European site involves 'development' that requires planning permission prior to being carried out,[136] then the 2010 regulations apply more stringent planning rules that restrict the public bodies' ability to grant planning permission more extensively than is the case in other protected areas, such as, for example, in an SSSI. The terms and conditions upon which the decision maker must proceed are the same as those applicable to non-planning matters (p. 222) and replicate the same protective provisions in the Directive. They are integrated into the more complex decision-making apparatus of the Town and Country Planning legislation in the manner set out on pp. 227–30. The combined effect of Part IV of the Conservation Regulations 2010, and governmental guidance to local authorities and other decision makers,[137] is to raise a stronger presumption against development of land in European sites than applies in other protected areas. Permitted development rights are also subject to extensive restrictions in European sites. The special planning provisions apply to development in SACs and SPAs, and to development in potential SPAs (pSPA) and candidate SACs (cSAC) as if they had already been classified or designated.

The discussion that follows will concentrate on the implementation of the Directive through planning law and development control. It should be appreciated, however, that the controls apply to all 'plans and projects' requiring consent, and that their potential scope is somewhat wider than planning decisions—the controls discussed later can apply to a range of administrative consents required for various operations, other than the grant of planning permission,[138] if they have significant impacts on protected habitats; for example, the grant of licences by public bodies to kill wildlife species that are considered pests.[139]

(a) Environmental assessment

If the planning authority considers that a plan or project is likely to have a 'significant' effect on a European site, they must consult Natural England and

[135] See s. 55(2)(e) and (f) Town and Country Planning Act 1990.

[136] Eg the erection of a building that does not benefit from permitted development rights under the Town and Country Permitted Development Order 1995.

[137] In para. 119 of the *National Planning Policy Framework* (DCLG 2012) as amplified in Joint ODPM Circular 06/2005 and DEFRA Circular 01/2005 *Government Circular: Biodiversity and Geological Conservation—Statutory Obligations and their impact within the Planning System* (16 August 2005).

[138] The phrase is to be interpreted purposively and given a broad meaning to accord with the objectives of the Directive: *R (Friends of the Earth) v Environment Agency* [2004] Env LR 31 at [60].

[139] But the notification by English Nature of an area as an SSSI is not itself a 'plan or project': *Boggis v English Nature* [2009] EWCA Civ 1061 esp. at [29] (Sullivan LJ.) (reversing the decision of Blair J. at first instance on this point: [2008] EWHC 2954 (Admin)).

carry out 'appropriate assessment' of the project's implications for the site in view of the site's conservation objectives. They can only agree to the development after having ascertained that it will not adversely affect the integrity of the European site.[140] The assessment required by the Conservation Regulations 2010 should not be confused with the project-based environmental impact assessment (EIA) required under the Town and Country Planning (Environmental Impact Assessment) Regulations 2011.[141] The 'appropriate assessment' under the 2010 regulations is more narrowly focused to an assessment of the impacts of development on the conservation status of the habitat and species for the protection of which the site has been designated. A full EIA will look at a wider range of potential environmental impacts flowing from the development.[142] Where a full EIA is also required, information gathered for the purposes of the latter can also be used for the purposes of the appropriate assessment required by the Habitats Directive.

The local planning authority's power to grant planning permission is further restricted in that the regulations put a positive onus on the planning authority to satisfy itself that the proposal *will not* adversely affect the site's conservation features. If there is any uncertainty as to its effects, the application must be notified to the Secretary of State. This will give him the opportunity to consider whether to call in the application. If the Secretary of State calls in the application and subsequently grants permission, he must secure the necessary compensatory measures required by the Conservation Regulations 2010. Planning guidance indicates that he will expect to see, and be satisfied by, evidence that necessary compensatory measures will be secured when applications are referred to him by planning authorities proposing to grant planning permission in European sites.[143]

The requirements outlined earlier for the scrutiny of planning applications in European protected sites are also applied to require the review of existing permissions and consents granted before a site was designated a European site.[144] The decision maker (for example, the local planning authority) must review existing permissions and consents on the same terms as apply to applications for planning permission for new development in the site, and carry out an appropriate assessment of their impact on the site's integrity. If their exercise is likely to cause significant disturbance to protected species or the conservation status of the site, then the permission must be revoked—unless the imposition of planning conditions or planning obligations can avoid adverse impacts that have been identified.[145] Revocation of consents or permissions will have implications for the

140 Conservation of Habitat and Species Regulations 2010, reg. 61.

141 SI 2011/1824 as amended.

142 See reg. 2 and Schedules 1 and 2 of SI 2011/1824 for development requiring a full environmental impact assessment.

143 See para. 10 of Joint ODPM Circular 06/2005 and DEFRA Circular 01/2005 *Government Circular: Biodiversity and Geological Conservation—Statutory Obligations and their impact within the Planning System* (16 August 2005).

144 See reg. 69 Conservation of Habitat and Species Regulations 2010, reg. 61.

145 See reg. 70(1) Conservation of Habitat and Species Regulations 2010, reg. 61.

payment of compensation; for example, in the case of the revocation of a planning permission.[146]

(b) Criteria for environmental assessment

The assessment under the Conservation Regulations 2010 must be carried out in accordance with criteria and guidance set out in the National Planning Policy Framework and supplementary planning guidance. If the development is not directly connected with or necessary to the site's management, then the authority[147] must first determine whether the proposal will have a 'significant' effect on the European site. This decision must be made on a precautionary basis, and an environmental assessment is required where there is a probability or a risk that the project will have significant effects on the site.[148]

The plan or project's implications must be assessed in view of the site's conservation objectives, so as to ascertain whether it will prejudice the *integrity* of the site, either individually or in combination with other plans or projects.[149] The maintenance of *site integrity* is the central objective of the assessment provisions, and this is defined to mean 'the coherence of [the site's] ecological structure and function, across its whole area, that enables it to sustain the habitat and/or the levels of populations of the species for which it was classified'.[150] Natural England will advise on the technical aspects of the assessment; for example, on the impact of land-take issues or hydrology. An assessment must be made for each interest feature for which a site is classified and for each designation where a site is classified under more than one international obligation; for example, both as an SPA and as a Ramsar site. Moreover, all aspects of the plan or project which can, either by themselves or in combination with other projects, affect the sites conservation objectives must be identified the light of the best scientific knowledge currently available.[151]

The planning authority cannot grant planning permission unless, having carried out an appropriate assessment, it determines that the proposal will not adversely affect the integrity of the site, taking into account all likely and foreseeable effects.[152] If the project would adversely affect site integrity, or the effects are uncertain but could be significant, then planning permission should not be granted. The decision maker can only grant permission if it has made certain that the plan or project will not adversely

[146] Under s. 107 Town and Country Planning Act 1990. See reg. 72 Conservation of Habitat and Species Regulations 2010, for special provision as to calculation of the compensation payable in such cases.

[147] Or Secretary of State if the application has been called in.

[148] See para. 13, Joint ODPM Circular 06/2005 and DEFRA Circular 01/2005 *Government Circular: Biodiversity and Geological Conservation—Statutory Obligations and their impact within the Planning System* (16 August 2005).

[149] See *Landelijke Vereneging tot Behoud van der Waddenzee v Staatssecretaris van Landbouw, Natuurbeheer en Visserij* [2004] ECR I–7405, Case C 127–02 (the *Waddenzee* case).

[150] Para. 20, Joint ODPM Circular 06/2005 and DEFRA Circular 01/2005 *Government Circular: Biodiversity and Geological Conservation—Statutory Obligations and their impact within the Planning System* (16 August 2005).

[151] See the *Waddenzee case* (n. 149) and ODPM Circular 06/2005 paras 17 and 18.

[152] Regs. 61(5) and 68 Conservation Regulations 2010.

affect the integrity of the site, in the sense that no reasonable scientific doubt remains as to the absence of adverse effects.[153] This test requires the authority to have regard to the scientific evidence in order to ascertain the presence or absence of scientific doubt as to the likely impacts of the development, and in this endeavour the advice of the statutory Conservation Bodies (who will be statutory consultees on all planning applications of this nature) will be very important. In giving advice, it is important that the Conservation Body has the primary test in view; that is, whether there is *no reasonable scientific doubt* as to the presence or absence of adverse impacts on site integrity flowing from the proposed development.[154] This involves the prediction of future consequences, based on the available scientific evidence, and the court is unlikely to set aside a decision reached on the advice of the statutory consultees, including the nature Conservation Bodies, which necessarily involves an evaluation of the scientific evidence to make predictions of likely impacts on the site in the future.[155] The planning authority must also consider the way in which the developer intends to carry out the proposal, and can impose planning conditions or planning obligations if they consider that this would avoid the adverse effects that have been identified.[156] In this case, the decision maker should identify the potential risks as far as may be reasonably foreseeable in the light of such information as can reasonably be obtained and put in place a legally enforceable framework with the aim of preventing the risks from materializing.[157]

If the decision maker is unable to ascertain that the development will not have adversely affects the site's integrity, then planning permission cannot be granted unless one of a number of closely defined circumstances applies.[158] The planning authority must be satisfied that there are no alternative solutions that would have a lesser effect than the proposed development on the site's integrity. If an alternative solution is identified, then planning permission must be refused. If, on the other hand, no alternative solution is identified then permission can be granted only if the proposed development has to be carried out for *imperative reasons of overriding public interest.* These can include considerations of a social or economic nature, and the government will obtain the opinion of the European Commission as to whether particular reasons can be considered imperative and overriding for these proposals.[159] In every case, the overriding importance of the public interest in development must be such as to override the ecological importance of the

[153] See the *Waddenzee case* (n. 149) and ODPM Circular 06/2005 para. 21 for explanatory guidance.

[154] The *Waddenzee* test (n. 149). See *Skye Windfarm Action Group Ltd v Highland Council* [2008] CSOH 19 at [135].

[155] See *R (Lewis) v Redcar and Cleveland District Council* [2008] EWCA Civ 746; *R (Hart District Council) v Secretary of State for Communities and Local Government* [2008] 2 P&CR 16.

[156] Reg. 68(2) Conservation of Habitat and Species Regulations 2010.

[157] See para. 22 of Joint ODPM Circular 06/2005 and DEFRA Circular 01/2005 *Government Circular: Biodiversity and Geological Conservation—Statutory Obligations and their Impact within the Planning System* (16 August 2005).

[158] See Conservation of Habitat and Species Regulations 2010, regs. 61 and 62.

[159] Conservation of Habitat and Species Regulations 2010, reg. 61 and reg. 62(4). And see generally Joint ODPM Circular 06/2005 and DEFRA Circular 01/2005 *Government Circular: Biodiversity and Geological Conservation—Statutory Obligations and their Impact within the Planning System* (16 August 2005) at paras. 25 et seq.

designation, and the Conservation Regulations require the planning authority to consult with and consider the views of other competent authorities before agreeing to the development.[160] Planning guidance makes it clear that permission will be given in these circumstances in very few cases.

If the site hosts a 'priority' habitat or species type identified in the Habitats Directive, then the grounds on which consent can be granted are narrower.[161] The only considerations of overriding public interest which can justify a grant of planning permission are those relating to public health or safety, 'beneficial consequences of primary importance for the environment', or other reasons which the authority consider, having regard to the opinion of the European Commission, to be imperative reasons of overriding public importance.[162] If there are other grounds, their status as imperative reasons must be confirmed by the European Commission. The Court of Appeal considered the meaning of this provision in *Duke of Westminster's Settlement v Welsh Assembly Government*[163] where it was held that the words 'other imperative reasons of overriding public interest' in the regulations[164] could not allow the preservation of a protected species to itself constitute the 'public interest' legitimizing the grant of a licence; their preservation was instead the *objective* of the regulations and the controls they impose on planning and licensing decisions.[165]

(c) Compensatory measures

Where a plan or project is agreed to on grounds of overriding public interest—notwithstanding a negative assessment of its implications for a European site—the appropriate authority must secure that any necessary compensatory measures are taken to ensure that the overall coherence of the *Natura 2000* network is protected.[166] This might include, for instance, the designation of an alternative site hosting the same habitat type as that lost to the development. In the second reporting period for member state implementation of the Directive (2001–2006), the UK implemented compensatory measures for nine projects affecting SACs, and

[160] Conservation of Habitat and Species Regulations 2010. reg. 55.

[161] See reg. 62(2) Conservation of Habitat and Species Regulations 2010.

[162] Conservation of Habitat and Species Regulations 2010 reg. 62(2)(b). For a review of the cases in which the European Commission has given guidance see L. Kramer, 'A Review of the European Commission's Opinions under Article 6(4) of the Habitats Directive' (2009) 21 JEL 59.

[163] [2004] EWCA Civ 1565.

[164] The decision turned on the interpretation of the phrase in reg. 44(2) of the Conservation (Natural Habitats etc.) Regulations 1994, which provided for the grant of licences for the disturbance of a protected species (in this case, great crested newts) in cases of overriding public interest.

[165] The reasoning in this case is somewhat Byzantine and unsatisfactory, if the result otherwise eminently sensible and sound. See further the commentary by J. Holder at [2004] 16 JEL 377. And see further at p. 233 in the context of the species protection provisions applicable to European protected species by the 2010 Regulations.

[166] Conservation of Habitats and Species Regulations 2010, reg. 66. See further Joint ODPM Circular 06/2005 and DEFRA Circular 01/2005 *Government Circular: Biodiversity and Geological Conservation—Statutory Obligations and their impact within the Planning System* (16 August 2005) at paras. 29–32.

seven affecting SPAs under the Birds Directive.[167] In 2004, for example, a project to improve and extend the Immingham Outer Harbour resulted in the loss of 22 ha of intertidal habitat within the Humber Estuary SPA and the Humber Estuary cSAC. This was compensated by the creation of two managed realignment sites adjacent to the Humber estuary at Welwick and Chowder Ness—and a further loss of 4 ha of intertidal habitat in the SPA was compensated by the creation of 6 ha of managed habitat at Chowder Ness the following year.

(d) Permitted development rights

In many cases where minor development is in prospect, automatic permission is granted by permitted development rights under the General Development Order 1995 (GDO),[168] without the need for the developer to apply to the local planning authority for a grant of planning permission. Because no administrative consent is required for the development, this causes problems where it is to take place in a European site—especially as an environmental assessment must be conducted prior to the development being authorized in order to evaluate its likely impact on the site's integrity. The Conservation Regulations 2010[169] therefore limit the exercise of permitted development rights to ensure that their exercise will not breach the site management requirements of the Habitats Directive. It is a condition of any planning permission granted by the GDO that any development that is likely to have a significant effect on a European site, and is not directly connected with or necessary for the management of the site, must not be begun until the developer has received prior written approval from the local planning authority.[170] The developer can make an application to the nature Conservation Body, for example Natural England, for an opinion as to whether the development will have a relevant effect on the conservation status of the site.[171] The Conservation Body's written opinion is conclusive on the significance or otherwise of the likely impacts of the development. The developer can then subsequently make an application to the local planning authority for permission to exercise the permitted rights in question, appending the consultation body's opinion to his application.[172] The planning authority must consult the Conservation Body on the application, and must take account of any representations they make.[173] If the planning authority cannot be certain that the development will not significantly affect the integrity of the site, then they must refuse to give their written approval. In this event, the developer

[167] See Joint Nature Conservation Committee, 2007, *Second Report by the United Kingdom under article 17 on the Implementation of the Habitats Directive from January 2001to December 2006*, Peterborough JNCC, Annex A Para. 6.1 and Appendix 4 (available at: <http://www.jncc.gov.uk/article17>).

[168] See s. 59 Town and Country Planning Act 1990 and art. 3 and Schedule 2 of the Town and Country Planning (General Permitted Development) Order 1995, SI 1995 No. 418.

[169] Conservation of Habitat and Species Regulations 2010, regs. 73–76.

[170] Reg. 73 Conservation of Habitats and Species Regulations 2010.

[171] See reg. 74 Conservation of Habitats and Species Regulations 2010.

[172] See reg. 75 Conservation of Habitats and Species Regulations 2010.

[173] Reg. 75(3) Conservation of Habitats and Species Regulations 2010.

must apply for full planning permission, and the requirements outlined earlier will then apply to the determination of the application. The criteria for assessing the significance of impacts on the site's integrity discussed earlier will be applied, as will the rules concerning overriding public interest in development.

Species Protection—Implementing European Standards

The species protection measures in the Habitats Directive and the Wild Birds Directive are similar in scope and structure to those applicable in domestic law under Part 1 of the Wildlife and Countryside Act 1981. Unfortunately, their implementation has not been integrated with the species protection provisions in domestic English and Scottish law very effectively, and the result is a patchwork of protective legislative that applies parallel—and sometimes overlapping—rules depending upon whether an animal or plant is or is not a member of a European protected species. The Conservation (Natural habitat etc.) Regulations 1994 sought to implement the Habitats Directive by applying more stringent protective provisions to those European Protected species of animal and plants given protected status by the Directive, meaning that two sets of rules—those in the 1994 Regulations and those in Part 1 of the 1981 Act—had to be considered in order to ascertain the relevant law protecting European species. This overlap was removed by amending regulations in 2007,[174] which removed European Protected Species of *animals and plants* from the scope of the 1981 Act. These are now protected by one set of rules, contained in Part 3 of the Conservation of Habitats and Species Regulations 2010.[175] The rules set out in Part 3 of the 2010 Regulations are modelled on those in the 1981 Act, nevertheless, although they apply more stringent penalties for the protection of European level species. There are also minor, but potentially problematic, differences in the terminology used in the 2010 Regulations as opposed to the 1981 Act; for example, it is an offence to 'deliberately' capture, kill, or injure a wild animal of European protected status, whereas the 1981 Act requires an 'intention' to kill, capture, etc., under the parallel offence for non-European protected species. The 2010 Regulations also create a strict liability offence of damaging or destroying a breeding site or 'resting place' of a European protected species of animal; the parallel offence under the 1981 Act requires proof of intention as the requisite mens rea for establishing commission of the offence. A more satisfactory, and less complex, statement of the law could have been achieved by consolidating and integrating the relevant species protection rules into one piece of legislation.

The rules for the protection of European level *bird species* are less complex. The Wildlife and Countryside Act 1981 was enacted to implement the requirements of the 1979 Wild Birds Directive. The species protection provisions of the Directive are implemented primarily by the 1981 Act itself. These have been considered in

[174] Regs. 7(7) and 7(8) Conservation (Natural Habitat etc.) (Amendment) Regulations 2007, SI 2007/1843.

[175] SI 2010/490, regs. 40–47 discussed further at pp. 230 ff.

Chapter 5 and will be considered in outline to highlight differences in the protection afforded to European protected species of bird as opposed to animals and plants, and to European protected species of bird as opposed to members of non-European species.

(a) Protected animals

European protected species of animals requiring protection under Annex IV of the Habitats Directive, and which have a natural range that includes Great Britain, are set out in Schedule 2 of the Conservation Regulations 2010. Individual members of these species enjoy the full protection of the provisions of the 2010 Regulations.[176] Schedule 2 lists for protection several species of bat indigenous to the UK and several other endangered species totalling 16 in all, including the dormouse, otters, great crested newt, and all species of dolphins porpoises and whales. It is a criminal offence for a person to deliberately capture, injure, or kill any animal of a European protected species; to deliberately disturb wild animals of these species; or to deliberately take or destroy the eggs of any such protected animal. It is also an offence to damage or destroy the breeding site or resting place of such an animal.[177] 'Disturbance' is widely defined to include[178] any disturbance which is likely to impair an animal's ability to survive, to breed or reproduce or rear their young, or to hibernate or migrate, or to 'affect significantly the local population or abundance of the species to which they belong'.[179] This protection is, in several respects, more extensive than that conferred by the 1981 Act on other species of animal; the disturbance of European species is an offence, for example, irrespective of whether they are disturbed while nesting or using a place of rest of shelter. The defences available were also restricted after the European Court of Justice's ruling in *Commission v United Kingdom.*[180] In particular, as noted earlier,[181] the regulations were amended to remove the defence for incidental damage arising from lawful actions, and to remove the defence for actions taken by authorized persons to prevent serious damage to livestock, crops, fisheries, fruit, or timber. One practical consequence has been that, where the development of land encounters populations of European protected species, such as greater crested newts or otters, it will now be necessary to obtain a licence to proceed, and this will require an environmental assessment prior to its grant.[182]

176 Reg. 40 Conservation of Habitats and Species Regulations 2010. See Box 6.4.

177 Reg. 41(1) Conservation of Habitats and Species Regulations 2010.

178 Note that this is an inclusive, not an exhaustive, definition—'disturbance' could legitimately be interpreted to include any action interfering with the natural rhythm of a protected animals lifecycle or natural behaviour patterns.

179 See reg. 41(2) Conservation of Habitats and Species Regulations 2010.

180 *Commission v United Kingdom* Case C 06/04, [2005] ECR I–9017. For earlier criticism of the implementing provisions see S. Ball, 'Reforming the Law of Habitat Protection', in Rodgers (ed.), *Nature Conservation and Countryside Law* (University of Wales Press, 1996), Ch. 4.

181 See p. 220.

182 See *R (Newsum) v Welsh Assembly Government* [2004] EWCA Civ 1565; *R v Cornwall County Council ex parte Hardy* [2001] Env LR 25 (on the need for the assessment to be made before grant of planning permission or a licence, and not subsequently pursuant to planning conditions imposed by the planning authority or other decision maker).

The general offence of killing, capturing, injuring, or disturbing a member of a European protected species is supplemented by several additional offences aimed at preventing trade in protected animals and removing any incentive for their capture. It is, therefore, an offence to have a live or dead protected animal that has been taken from the wild, or any part of a protected animal,[183] in one's possession or control. It is also an offence to transport, sell, or exchange (or offer for sale or exchange) a live or dead protected animal or any part of such an animal.[184] An animal is presumed to be a wild animal, or to have been taken from the wild, for the purposes of the prosecution of offences unless the contrary is shown.[185]

It is not an offence to have in one's possession an animal that has been disabled, if its capture was undertaken for the purposes of tending it and then releasing it when recovered.[186] Similarly there is a defence for 'mercy' killings and the disposal of dead animals where a specimen has been seriously disabled, other than by the defendant's own unlawful act, and there was no reasonable chance of it recovering.[187] The possession and sale offences are not committed if it can be shown that the animal or part of an animal in question was lawfully taken from the wild,[188] unless it is a member of a European protected species and is being kept or transported for the purposes of sale or exchange.[189] Where specimens are claimed to have been lawfully taken from the wild within the EU, this defence only applies if the animal was originally taken from the wild before the implementation date of the Habitats Directive, that is, before 10 June 1994. Where it is claimed it was taken lawfully within the territory of a member state that has subsequently joined the Union, then it must have been lawfully taken before the date on which the state in question became a member.[190] In all cases, the defences only apply if two overriding conditions are met: there must have been no satisfactory alternative, and the defendant's action must not have been detrimental to the maintenance of the population of the species concerned at a favourable conservation status in their natural range.[191]

The 2010 Regulations also prohibit certain indiscriminate methods of capture or killing of wild animals. This additional offence applies to two categories of case. Firstly, using any of the proscribed methods to capture or kill a member of a European protected species will be illegal, even if it would have otherwise been lawful under the regulations; for example, in the case of a 'mercy' killing. Secondly, a limited degree of protection is also extended to certain species that do not enjoy

183 Or anything derived from such an animal or part of an animal—reg. 41(4)(b). This would render it a criminal offence to have in one's possession, for example, parts of a protected animal that have been treated or powdered or otherwise altered in composition, eg as a traditional medicine.

184 Reg. 41(3) and 41(4) Conservation of Habitats and Species Regulations 2010.

185 Regs. 41(6) and (7) Conservation of Habitats and Species Regulations 2010.

186 Reg. 42(1) Conservation of Habitats and Species Regulations 2010.

187 Reg. 42(2) Conservation of Habitats and Species Regulations 2010.

188 Reg. 42(5) Conservation of Habitats and Species Regulations 2010, ie in a manner that is not contrary to the law of the place where it was captured.

189 Reg. 42(6) Conservation of Habitats and Species Regulations 2010.

190 Reg. 42(7) Conservation of Habitats and Species Regulations 2010.

191 Reg. 42(10) Conservation of Habitats and Species Regulations 2010.

full protection as European protected species, in that their capture, and/or killing is also prohibited if effected by any of the proscribed means.[192] The species granted partial protection in this manner are listed in Schedule 4 to the 2010 Regulations and include all species of naturally occurring seal in British waters, polecats, pine martens, mountain hares, and several species of freshwater fish; for example, barbel, grayling, and lampreys. The prohibited means of killing or capturing mammals include the use of blind or mutilated animals as live decoys, tape recorders and artificial light sources, the use of electrical devices capable of killing or stunning, mirrors and devices for dazzling, sighting devices for night shooting, explosives, non-selective nets and traps, crossbows, poisons and poisoned, or anaesthetic bait, gassing or smoking out, and the use of automatic or semi-automatic weapons.[193] In the case of fish it is illegal to capture or kill them using poison or explosives.[194] For good measure, it is illegal to employ any method of capture or killing—not limited to those cited earlier—if it is done using aircraft or moving motor vehicles.[195] European protected species of animal and plant are set out in Box 6.3.

(b) Protected plants

The species of plants given additional protection under the terms of the Habitats Directive are set out in Schedule 5 to the 2010 Regulations (see Box 6.3). This protection is extended to only nine species of extremely rare and endangered plant species, including fen orchids and yellow marsh saxifrage. The protection mirrors that granted to all plant species by the 1981 Act,[196] but with more wide-ranging offences and greater penalties for breach of the law. It is an offence to deliberately[197] pick, collect, cut, uproot, or destroy a wild plant of a European protected species, and it is also an offence to be in possession or control of any such plant, or to transport, sell, or exchange or offer for sale or exchange a European protected plant.[198] The protection applies to plants at all stages of their biological cycle,[199] thus rendering it an offence to possess or damage seeds and bulbs as well as fully grown plants. The possession and transport/sale offence also applies to both live and dead plants of these species, provided they have been taken in the wild.[200] There is a defence to the possession, sale, and exchange offences if it can be shown

192 Reg. 43(1) Conservation of Habitats and Species Regulations 2010.

193 See Reg. 43(3) Conservation of Habitats and Species Regulations 2010.

194 Reg. 43(4) Conservation of Habitats and Species Regulations 2010.

195 Reg. 43(5) Conservation of Habitats and Species Regulations 2010.

196 See Chapter 5, pp. 189 ff.

197 In Scotland the offence is wider and applies to both deliberate and reckless acts: see reg. 43(1) Conservation (Natural Habitats etc.) Regulations 1994.

198 See Reg. 45(2) Conservation of Habitats and Species Regulations 2010.

199 Reg. 45(4) Conservation of Habitats and Species Regulations 2010.

200 Reg. 45(3). A plant is presumed to be taken in the wild for this purpose unless the contrary is shown—Reg. 45(5) Conservation of Habitats and Species Regulations 2010.

Box 6.3 European Protected Species of Animal and Plant[201]

Horseshoe bats (all species)
Typical bats (all species)
Large Blue butterfly
Wild cat
Dolphins, porpoises, and whales (all species)
Dormouse
Pool frog
Sand lizard
Fisher's estuarine moth
Great crested newt
Common otter
Lesser Whirlpool Ram's Horn snail
Smooth snake
Sturgeon
Natterjack toad
Marine turtles

European Protected Species of Plants:
Shore dock, Killarney fern, early gentian, Lady's slipper, creeping marshwort, slender naiad, fen orchid, floating-leaved water plantain, yellow marsh saxifrage.

the specimen was lawfully taken in the wild,[202] but the defence does not apply if the plant was in the defendant's possession for the purposes of sale or exchange.[203]

(c) Surveillance and monitoring

In response to the European Court of Justice's ruling in *Commission v United Kingdom*[204] provision was introduced in 2007 for the monitoring of the incidental capture and killing of protected European species of animal and plant, and for the surveillance of the conservation status of habitats and species. This function is

[201] Schedule 2 and 5 Conservation of Habitats and Species Regulations 2010.

[202] See reg. 45(3) Conservation of Habitats and Species Regulations 2010. As with animals (see earlier) the plant must have been taken in the wild before the Habitats Directive came into force, or before the member state in whose territory it was taken joined the Union, or was taken from a territory outside the Union without a breach of the local law applicable—reg. 45(5) Conservation of Habitats and Species Regulations 2010.

[203] Reg. 45(4) Conservation of Habitats and Species Regulations 2010.

[204] *Commission v United Kingdom* Case C 06/04, [2005] ECR I–9017.

carried out by the statutory Conservation Bodies; for example, Natural England or Scottish Natural Heritage.[205] These rules are now contained in Part 4 of the Conservation Regulations 2010. This includes an obligation to ensure that any taking or exploitation of protected species is compatible with the maintenance of the species at a favourable conservation status.

The provisions on monitoring the incidental capture and killing of animals require that the Conservation Body identify the risks to which European protected species found in England and Wales are subject, and maintain a record of those instances of incidental capture and killing of animals in those species of which they are aware.[206] The risk analysis undertaken will inform advice that the Conservation Body must give the Secretary of State as to whether a programme of monitoring is required.[207] If necessary the authority must ensure that any incidental killing or capture of members of a protected species does not have a negative impact on the species.[208] This requirement implements the protective guarantees required by the Directive and applies protection, ultimately, at the population level of the species to ensure it remains in a favourable conservation status.

(d) Licensing function of Conservation Bodies

Actions that are otherwise prohibited can be sanctioned by the grant of a licence by the Conservation Bodies. Licences will normally be granted for a specific purpose and the grant of licences (for example, to disturb kill or capture members of a protected species) will be granted subject to strict conditions, and only in carefully circumscribed circumstances. The only purposes for which a licence can be granted are those of a scientific or educational nature; ringing or marking, or examining rings or marks on wild animals; conserving wild animals or plants or introducing them to particular areas; protecting a zoological or botanical collection; preserving public health or public safety; preventing the spread of disease; preventing serious damage to livestock, feedstuff for livestock crops or vegetables; and 'other reasons of imperative public interest, including those of a social or economic nature and of beneficial consequence to the environment'.[209] If granted, a licence must specify not only the species of animal or plant to which it relates, but also the number of specimens that may be taken or be in the possession or control of the licence holder and the means by which the taking or capture of specimens is authorized.[210] Any act undertaken pursuant to the terms of a licence will not be an offence under the terms of the 2010 Regulations.[211]

205 Reg. 48(6) Conservation of Habitats and Species Regulations 2010.
206 Reg. 50(4) Conservation of Habitats and Species Regulations 2010.
207 Reg. 50(4)(c) and (5) Conservation of Habitats and Species Regulations 2010.
208 See Reg. 51(2) Conservation of Habitats and Species Regulations 2010.
209 See reg. 53(2) Conservation of Habitats and Species Regulations 2010.
210 Reg. 53(8) Conservation of Habitats and Species Regulations 2010.
211 Reg. 53(5) Conservation of Habitats and Species Regulations 2010. This provision disapplies regs. 41, 43, and 45 (offences of killing or capture, etc. of animals, indiscriminate methods of killing, etc., wild animals, and the offences of deliberately picking, uprooting, or destroying protected plants).

Coordinating Conservation Management

The Joint Nature Conservation Committee plays a central role, not only in establishing the scientific criteria for the identification of European sites, but in co-coordinating the monitoring of their conservation status and publishing periodic assessments and reports. The obligation imposed on each member state by the Habitats Directive to undertake surveillance of the conservation status of natural habitats and species[212] is implemented in the UK through the system of Common Standards Monitoring (CSM). This has been developed by JNCC and is applied by the country conservation agencies to monitor features of SSSIs, SACs, and SPAs. This is especially important in measuring compliance with the target set by the Habitats Directive for the conservation of habitats and species in SACs and SPAs—namely, to maintain or restore at 'favourable' conservation status the natural habitats and species of wild flora and fauna that are of Community interest.[213] The objective of CSM is to assess the *trend* in the conservation status of the protected feature or species, by reference to the presence or absence of relevant attributes—such as the extent of the feature, its quality or the presence or absence of supporting processes in the relevant ecosystem. Where a feature is reported as 'unfavourable–no change', or 'unfavourable–declining', then a change in site management may be necessary to address the problem and target a return to favourable conservation status. If it is assessed as 'favourable' or 'favourable–recovering', then no change in management is necessary. The categorization applied by CSM to protected sites and the relevant criteria and attributes are explained more fully in Box 6.4.

It will be apparent from the discussion earlier that the legal mechanisms adopted for the implementation of the Directive in UK law are largely based on pre-existing models of land use control (for terrestrial sites) and the creation of management plans for coordinating the management of marine sites. In addition to the controls outlined in this chapter, the implementation of the Directives has also necessitated the extensive review of existing regulatory and planning consents affecting SACs and SPAs. The Conservation of Habitats and Species Regulations 2010[214] require the nature Conservation Bodies to review existing operational consents that they have granted under the 1981 Act[215] in relation to any land which, on or after 1 April 2010, becomes land with a European site, and they can modify or withdraw the consent if it is incompatible with the site's conservation objectives. Similarly, each planning authority must review existing planning permissions applicable to any land that becomes (or is included in) a European site on or after this date, unless the development to which it relates has been completed.[216] The Environment Agency

[212] Art. 11 Habitats Directive.

[213] Art. 22 Habitats Directive.

[214] Reg. 23 Conservation of Habitats and Species Regulations 2010.

[215] Ie under s. 28E Wildlife and Countryside Act 1981, in respect of operations likely to damage the conservation interest of the site (as to which, see Chapter 3, pp. 84 ff).

[216] Reg. 69 Conservation of Habitats and Species Regulations 2010. And see p. 227.

Box 6.4 Defining Conservation Status: Common Standards Monitoring (CSM)

The methodology employed for monitoring the conservation status of protected sites is set out in a JNCC Report: *Statement on Common Standards Monitoring (1998)*. The 'interest features' of each site are monitored—in the case of *Natura 20000* sites these will be the features for which the site was designated—and which are recorded in the SAC site data form submitted to the European Commission. Conservation objectives are assigned for each interest feature present in the site. The objectives define what is 'favourable' conservation condition for each site feature by describing targets that must be met if the feature is to be recorded as 'favourable'. Each feature will have one or more 'attributes' that can be used to help define favourable condition. In the case of protected species of flora or fauna, for example, the attributes may be the population size present in the site or the habitat requirements that the site presents for the species in question. In the case of a protected natural habitat, it might include the geographical area covered by the habitat, the key species present and sustained by it, and the composition, processes and supporting structure of the habitat. Broad targets are then set for those attributes that most effectively define the conservation interest of the feature. The condition of the site features are then recorded using the following classification:

Favourable–maintained. An interest feature will be recorded as *maintained* when its conservation objectives were being met at the most recent assessment, and are still being met.

Favourable–recovered. An interest feature will be recorded as having *recovered* if it has regained favourable condition, having been recorded as unfavourable on the previous assessment.

Unfavourable–recovering. An interest feature can be recorded as *recovering* after damage if it has begun to show, or is continuing to show, a trend towards favourable condition.

Unfavourable–no change. An interest feature may be retained in a more-or-less steady state by repeated or continuing damage; it is unfavourable but neither declining nor recovering.

Unfavourable–declining. Decline is another possible consequence of a damaging activity. In this case, recovery is possible and may occur either spontaneously or if suitable management input is made.

Features can also be recorded as partially or wholly destroyed if the interest features have been destroyed with no possibility of recovery. All statutory sites must be monitored once in a six-year period, to comply with the reporting cycle for the Habitats and Wild Birds Directives. Within that period, the JNCC guidance stresses that interest features for each site should be monitored once every three years, to enable an interim report to be made assessing the overall proportion of the national site network (SSSIs, SACs, SPAs, etc.); that is, in favourable and unfavourable condition in these categories.

Source: *Statement on Common Standards Monitoring* (1998, JNCC Peterborough) available at: <http://jncc.defra.gov.uk/page-2198>.

And see J. M. Williams (ed.) 2006. Common Standards Monitoring for Designated Sites: First Six Year Report. Peterborough, JNCC.

must, likewise, review existing regulatory authorizations, granted under, for example, its pollution control powers, if they affect land in a European site.[217]

The administrative task required by these provisions is considerable. In a process that concluded in 2010, all existing licences affecting *Natura 2000* sites in England and Wales were reviewed by the Environment Agency. The process was undertaken in four stages, corresponding to the requirements in articles 6.3 and 6.4 of the Directive[218] for the approval of plans and projects; stages 1 and 2 involved identifying relevant plans/projects, with stage 3 applying an appropriate assessment to those licences likely to have 'significant' effect on a site's conservation objectives. Stage 4 involved an appraisal of options and decisions where there was significant effect, and the licence was found to be incompatible with the European site's conservation objectives. By far the largest number of licences subject to an appropriate assessment of their effects (stage 3) was licences relating to water quality (47,000); for example, discharge consents granted under the Water Resources Act 1991.[219] Coordinating and overseeing the conservation work of the various public bodies with relevant roles in the protection and management of European sites is a large undertaking for the JNCC.

[217] Reg. 63 Conservation of Habitats and Species Regulations 2010 (see reg.7 for the definition of 'competent authorities' subject to his requirement to review decisions).

[218] Pp. 214–15.

[219] See Joint Nature Conservation Committee, 2007, *Second Report by the United Kingdom under article 17 on the Implementation of the Habitats Directive from January 2001to December 2006*, Peterborough JNCC, Annex A Para 5.1 (available at: <http://www.jncc.gov.uk/article17>).

7

Marine Conservation

Introduction

The conservation of marine habitats and living resources presents difficult challenges that require a response somewhat different to that adopted for terrestrial habitats and species, and examined in the earlier chapters in this work. The international law on marine conservation has, until comparatively recently, been piecemeal and poorly developed. One of the key problems in this regard has been, until comparatively recently, the historic treatment of the marine resources of the high seas as a common pool resource, open to free exploitation by all without control. The marine environment is therefore uniquely prone to the alleged 'tragedy of the commons', the phenomenon whereby appropriators will take unlimited quantities of its living resources (fish, shell fish, cetaceans, etc.) leading to degradation of the common pool resource available to others and to future generations.[1] The depletion of the fish stocks in the high seas is testament to this. This is arguably attributable not only to the common pool nature of fisheries and other marine living resources, but also to the absence of any pre-capture private property rights in marine resources.[2]

The unique character of the marine environment presents difficulties for the development of an effective legal framework for promoting marine conservation.[3] The dynamic nature of the marine environment and its natural variability mean that natural processes can cause fundamental change in marine ecosystems and habitats quite independent of human activity. The same is true to a certain extent with land-based habitats, where climate change and other natural processes are constantly in play; but the inherent variability of marine ecosystems is much more marked, and the marine environment is, as a result, inherently dynamic and subject to change. This makes it difficult to establish clear conservation objectives for specific habitats or species, and for protected areas. The marine environment also demonstrates a number of attributes, absent in terrestrial habitats and ecosystems, that make the establishment of effective common pool resource governance problematic. These

[1] G. Hardin, 'The Tragedy of the Commons', (1968) 162 *Science* 1243–48.

[2] R. Barnes, *Property Rights and Natural Resources* (Hart, 2009) at 8–10; R. Churchill and V. Lowe, *The Law of the Sea* (Manchester University Press, 1999) at 281.

[3] See generally L. M. Warren, 'Law and Policy for Marine Protected Areas' in C. Rodgers (ed.), *Nature Conservation and Countryside Law* (University of Wales Press, 1996), Ch. 3, especially at pp. 65–71.

include[4] problems of connectivity and scale, as living marine resources (for example, fish species) frequently range over very large distances, meaning that protected areas that are geographically discrete and separate may have a functional connection for marine ecosystems, whereas this is less commonly the case for terrestrial ecosystems. And where human activities impact upon marine ecosystems and habitats, this is invariably perceived as damaging. There is little scope for the creation, and legal recognition and protection, of 'semi-natural' marine habitats created by human intervention, whereas this is not only possible but often a key objective for management regimes protecting terrestrial habitats, especially in a UK context.[5] Where human activities (fishing, dredging, recreation use, etc.) are a major factor impacting adversely on the marine environment, the challenge is nevertheless essentially the same as with terrestrial nature conservation measures: how to limit, adapt, or prohibit access to the marine resource in a manner that is effective and enforceable, while also promoting sustainable development?

We saw in Chapters 3 and 4 that in the case of land-based habitats, the principal legal response has been to deploy a range of legal and economic instruments that modify and adapt the way in which property rights give access to the land resource. Indeed, addressing the resource allocation function of property rights is fundamentally important to an understanding of the way in which the law of nature conservation operates to protect the terrestrial environment. When we turn to consider marine conservation, however, we are faced with a dilemma: the allocation of marine resources is not itself (with a few exceptions) mediated by property rights. And the number of stakeholders with an interest in using marine resources in a given area may also be far greater; this may typically include commercial fishing interests, dredging and mineral extraction, oil and gas exploration activities and extraction, recreational use for fishing, sailing, etc., and rights of passage through protected areas by vessels. Whereas the primary focus of nature conservation law in a terrestrial context is on preventing damage by a landowner of natural habitats to be found on his own land, or by others with property rights giving access to the land resource, the focus in a marine context is on preventing damage by, and managing a wide range of activities by, a much wider range of stakeholders, none of whom will commonly have a property right on which legal enforcement measures can impact.

It follows that the development of an effective strategy for marine conservation law cannot be based on the same private property rights model as, for example, that obtaining in English law for the regulation and allocation of land-based resources. This is not to say, however, that a property rights analysis is irrelevant in the context of marine conservation. The thrust of recent developments in nature conservation law with regard to the protection of the marine environment has been to give coastal states sovereign jurisdiction over living natural resources in large areas of contiguous seas, and this has enabled them to develop rights-based models for

[4] See eg P. J. S. Jones and J. Burgess, 'Building Partnership Capacity for the Collaborative Management of Marine Protected Areas in the UK: A Preliminary Analysis' (2005) 77 *Journal of Environmental Management* 227, esp. at 233 ff.

[5] For example through the Agri-Environment schemes available under the Rural Development Plans for England, Wales, Scotland, and N. Ireland; see Chapter 4, pp. 132 ff.

managing living natural resources; quotas on fish catches, and licensing regimes for oil and gas exploration and other marine activities are but two examples of this. It is therefore possible to argue that the law is gradually moving towards a property rights-based model for the allocation and management of living marine resources, but one in which the public interest attributes of property as a social construct have greater prominence than private interests.[6] The use of private rights-based approaches must, however, be seen as but one element in the wider context of the development of what may be termed a 'management planning' model, in which the use of living marine resources is managed through the development of spatial plans, and then implemented through a composite system of rights-based measures such as licences and quotas, alongside more generally applicable (non-rights-based) measures such as conservation orders and by-laws. In the UK context this composite approach can be seen most clearly in the development of protective regimes in Marine Protected Areas, including Marine Conservation Zones designated under the Marine and Coastal Access Act 2009. This will be examined in detail on pp. 251 ff.

Marine Areas—Legal Classification

The contemporary legal response to these problems has been heavily influenced and shaped by the 1982 United Nations Convention on the Law of the Sea (UNCLOS), which adopted an approach based on giving powers to exercise regulatory control over marine resources to coastal states; in other words, withdrawing a large proportion of fish stocks and other marine living resources from the category of common pool resource by sanctioning the creation of Exclusive Economic Zones (EEZ) up to 200 miles from the coast of signatory states, and within which the coastal state would have exclusive jurisdiction to control fishing and other resource exploitation. The development of the domestic law applied in the UK has, in recent years, been heavily influenced by developments in the international law on marine conservation, and by UNCLOS 1982 in particular. This chapter will consider the implementation of the concepts developed in international conservation law[7] in order to provide for effective marine conservation in the coastal waters of the United Kingdom.

The classification of areas that are wholly, permanently, or periodically covered by sea water is important in terms of defining the jurisdiction of relevant public bodies over the activities carried out on the seabed or in the aquatic environment above it, and in terms of delimiting the powers to notify different categories of protected area over it. The following areas are treated differently for these purposes:

[6] See R. Barnes, *Property Rights and Natural Resources* (Hart, 2009), esp. Chs. 1, 7, 8, and 9. Barnes presents a clear and persuasive case for public property concepts, or 'stewardship', as dominant elements of the emerging regimes for protecting marine resources, using fisheries management systems in five jurisdictions to illustrate these themes (see Ch. 8).

[7] For an excellent account of which, see P. Birnie, A. Boyle, and C. Redgewell, *International Law and the Environment* 3rd edn (Oxford University Press, 2009), Ch. 13.

(i) The intertidal zone, that is, the shore between the mean low- and high-watermarks. This is land that is periodically covered by the sea. It is owned by the Crown, in most cases, unless ownership has been transferred into private hands at some prior time.

(ii) The territorial sea, an area of 12 nautical miles from the coast.[8] In estuaries and many other bays or inlets, the extent of the territorial sea is measured from straight baselines across the estuary or bay, etc. These are established by Order in Council.[9] Sea which is landward of a baseline adopted for the purpose of defining the territorial sea is referred to in the relevant legislation as 'internal waters'.[10] The United Kingdom has full jurisdiction in these areas, and powers are exercised by the devolved governments in Scotland and, to a lesser extent, Wales.

(iii) Sea beyond the territorial sea, up to 200 nautical miles from the coast (offshore waters). Within this expanded area the United Kingdom has limited jurisdiction over certain activities for certain purposes, most importantly fisheries and mineral exploitation. The most important are categorized within the Exclusive Economic Zone (EEZ) which extends up to 200 nautical miles from the low water baseline of the territorial sea.[11]

The Marine Strategy Framework Directive

The development of marine protected areas policy, and especially the designation of Marine Conservation Zones under the Marine and Coastal Access Act 2009, has also been strongly influenced by the need to implement the requirements of the European Marine Strategy Framework Directive, which was adopted in 2008.[12] The Directive has given an added impetus to the development of a cohesive and integrated network of marine protected areas, as well as shaping the monitoring, reporting, and regulatory functions that will underpin the conservation objectives of zones that are designated for protection under the Marine and Coastal Access Act 2009.

The Directive applies to 'marine waters', defined to include waters, the seabed, and subsoil on the seaward side of the baseline from which the extent of territorial waters is measured out to the outmost reach of the area over which the state has and/or exercises jurisdictional rights under UNCLOS, in addition to coastal waters.[13] The Directive requires the member states to take the necessary measures

[8] Article 3 United Nations Convention on the Law of the Sea 1982 (UNCLOS).

[9] See Territorial Waters Order in Council 1964, as amended by the Territorial Sea (Amendment) Order 1998, SI 1998/2564.

[10] This includes for example the whole of the Minch, the area of sea lying landward of the Outer Hebrides off the coast of north-west Scotland.

[11] See Arts. 55–57 of UNCLOS 1982.

[12] Directive 2008/56/EC of the European Parliament and of the Council of 17 June 2008 establishing a framework for community action in the field of marine environmental policy, OJ L164/19.

[13] Art. 3.1 Directive 2008/56/EC of the European Parliament and of the Council of 17 June 2008.

to achieve or maintain good environmental status in the marine environment by 2020 at the latest.[14] The introduction of a marine protected areas network by each member state with coastal waters is a key element the strategy at the core of the Directive. The Directive directs the member states to establish programmes of measures that include 'spatial protection measures'. These must contribute to the creation of coherent and representative networks of marine protected areas, adequately covering the diversity of the constituent ecosystems, such as special areas of conservation designated under the Habitats Directive, special protection areas under the Wild Birds Directive, and other marine protected areas established or agreed by the Community or Member States within other international or regional agreements to which they are parties, such as the OSPAR Convention.[15] The programme of measures must be designed to achieve or maintain 'Good Environmental Status' in marine waters, and must be implemented by the member states by 2016 at the latest.[16]

The Directive requires that programmes of measures adopted by the member states should be based on an ecosystem-based approach to the management of human activities, and that they should implement the precautionary principle.[17] Reference is also made to the fact that measures to establish good environmental status of the marine environment in the member states should be based not only on the precautionary principle, but also on the polluter pays principle, adopting a preventive approach, and seeking rectification of environmental damage at source.[18]

The concept of 'good environmental status' is at the heart of the Directive, and it is the creation and maintenance of this in the marine environment which the measures to be implemented must target. The Directive adopts a definition that reflects the dynamic nature of marine ecosystems, the multiple human and non-human impacts upon the marine environment and its constantly shifting nature.[19] 'Good environmental status' means the environmental status of marine waters where these provide ecologically diverse and dynamic oceans and seas which are clean, healthy, and productive within their intrinsic conditions, and where the use of the marine environment is at a level that is sustainable, thus safeguarding

[14] Art. 1.1 Directive 2008/56/EC of the European Parliament and of the Council of 17 June 2008.

[15] Art. 13.4 Directive 2008/56/EC of the European Parliament and of the Council of 17 June 2008. The reference is to the regional Convention for the Protection of the Marine Environment of the North East Atlantic 1992('OSPAR'). See n. 40.

[16] Art. 5.2(b) Directive 2008/56/EC of the European Parliament and of the Council of 17 June 2008.

[17] Recital 44 Directive 2008/56/EC of the European Parliament and of the Council of 17 June 2008.

[18] Recital 27 Directive 2008/56/EC of the European Parliament and of the Council of 17 June 2008.

[19] See Recital 34 Directive 2008/56/EC of the European Parliament and of the Council of 17 June 2008: 'In view of the dynamic nature of marine ecosystems and their natural variability, and given that the pressures and impacts on them may vary with the evolvement of different patterns of human activity and the impact of climate change, it is essential to recognize that the determination of good environmental status may have to be adapted over time. Accordingly, it is appropriate that programmes of measures for the protection and management of the marine environment be flexible and adaptive and take account of scientific and technological developments.'

the potential for uses and activities by both current and future generations.[20] The criteria are more fully explained in Box 7.1. The definition also seeks to capture the relationship between human interactions and impacts, on the one hand, and the conservation status of the marine environment on the other. Thus, waters are in good ecological status if 'the structure, functions and processes of the constituent marine ecosystems, together with the associated physiographic, geographic, geological and climatic factors, allow those ecosystems to function fully and to maintain their resilience to human-induced environmental change'.[21]

For the purposes of preparing and implementing the marine strategy, good environmental status is to be determined at the level of the marine region or sub-region. The waters around the territories of the EU member states are designated into four regions for these purposes by the Directive, and UK waters are part of the North East Atlantic region.[22] Within each region and sub-region the member states are required to apply 'adaptive' management using an ecosystem-based approach with the aim of achieving good environmental status of the marine environment. The member states must adopt a marine strategy for each region and sub-region within its jurisdiction.[23] The two sub-regions within the North East Atlantic Ocean region of relevance to the UK strategy are the Greater North Sea, including the English Channel, and the Celtic Seas. The development of a marine strategy will require a baseline assessment to be undertaken of the current ecological status of the marine environment and of the human activities impacting upon it by 15 July 2012; the determination of the essential characteristics of good environmental status by the same date; and the establishment of environmental targets and appropriate indicators to measure the status of the marine environment. The member states are also required to establish monitoring programmes by 15 July 2014.[24]

The Directive was transposed into national law by the Marine Strategy Regulations 2010,[25] which apply to England, Wales, Scotland, and Northern Ireland. The 2010 regulations are of a framework nature, and impose the general duties upon the public authorities to take the necessary steps to ensure that marine strategies with appropriate environmental targets and monitoring arrangements are in place within the time scales required by the Directive. The regulations apply the requirements of the Directive within the UK 'marine strategy area', which is defined for these purposes as: (i) the area of sea within the seaward limits of the territorial sea adjacent to the United Kingdom, and the seabed and its subsoil in that area of sea; (ii) any area of sea within the limits of the renewable energy zone and the seabed and its

[20] Art. 3.5 Directive 2008/56/EC of the European Parliament and of the Council of 17 June 2008.

[21] Art. 3.5(a) Directive 2008/56/EC of the European Parliament and of the Council of 17 June 2008.

[22] See art. 4.1 Directive 2008/56/EC of the European Parliament and of the Council of 17 June 2008.

[23] Art. 5 Directive 2008/56/EC of the European Parliament and of the Council of 17 June 2008.

[24] See art. 5.2(a) and (b) Directive 2008/56/EC of the European Parliament and of the Council of 17 June 2008.

[25] SI 2010/1627. Transposition was required by 15 July 2010.

Box 7.1 The Marine Strategy Framework Directive—'Good Environmental Status'

The European Marine Strategy Framework Directive[26] sets out 11 'qualitative descriptors' which the member states are required under article 9 of the Directive to use for the purpose of determining the good environmental status of each of its marine regions or sub-regions classified under the Directive. The 11 indicators are the following.[27]

(1) Biological diversity is maintained. The quality and occurrence of habitats and the distribution and abundance of species are in line with prevailing physiographic, geographic, and climatic conditions.

(2) Non-indigenous species introduced by human activities are at levels that do not adversely alter the ecosystems.

(3) Populations of all commercially exploited fish and shellfish are within safe biological limits, exhibiting a population age and size distribution that is indicative of a healthy stock.

(4) All elements of the marine food webs, to the extent that they are known, occur at normal abundance and diversity, and levels capable of ensuring the long-term abundance of the species and the retention of their full reproductive capacity.

(5) Human-induced eutrophication is minimized, especially adverse effects thereof, such as losses in biodiversity, ecosystem degradation, harmful algae blooms, and oxygen deficiency in bottom waters.

(6) Sea-floor integrity is at a level that ensures that the structure and functions of the ecosystems are safeguarded, and benthic ecosystems, in particular, are not adversely affected.

(7) Permanent alteration of hydrographical conditions does not adversely affect marine ecosystems.

(8) Concentrations of contaminants are at levels not giving rise to pollution effects.

(9) Contaminants in fish and other seafood for human consumption do not exceed levels established by Community legislation or other relevant standards.

(10) Properties and quantities of marine litter do not cause harm to the coastal and marine environment.

(11) Introduction of energy, including underwater noise, is at levels that do not adversely affect the marine environment.

The application of the indicators is more fully explored in the Annex to the Commission Decision of 1 September 2010 on criteria and methodological standards, on good environmental status of marine waters.[28]

[26] Directive 2008/56/EC of the European Parliament and of the Council of 17 June 2008 establishing a framework for community action in the field of marine environmental policy, OJ L164, 25.6.2008, 19–40.

[27] See Annex 1 to the 2008 Directive.

[28] Commission Decision 2010/477/EU: OJ L 232/14, 2.9.2010.

subsoil in that area of sea; and (iii) the seabed and its subsoil within the limits of any areas designated as part of the continental shelf.[29]

The ecosystem-based approach required by the Directive is defined in greater detail in the 2010 regulations, which refer to it comprising two elements: it is an approach that ensures that the collective pressure of human activities in the marine strategy area is kept within levels that are compatible with the achievement of good environmental status, and do not compromise the capacity of marine ecosystems to respond to human-induced changes.[30] By 15 July 2012, the Secretary of State must have carried out an assessment of the environmental status of waters within the marine strategy area,[31] and by the same date determine the characteristics of good environmental status for those waters in accordance with the Directive.[32] The regulations also place a duty on the Secretary of State, with the assistance of the devolved administrations, to establish indicators and targets to help secure good environmental status. The Directive contains an indicative list of pressures and impacts to assist with setting targets, and the Secretary of State is required to have regard to this when fulfilling his statutory duty.[33]

The Secretary of State and devolved administrations must also, by 31 December 2015, each publish a programme of measures necessary to achieve or maintain good environmental status in marine waters in the marine strategy area,[34] This 'must include spatial protection measures, to contribute to coherent and representative networks of marine protected areas' as required by the Directive.[35] The implementation of this requirement will be based principally on the designation of spatial marine protection zones through the marine conservation zone project, described more fully on pp. 257ff. The dynamic nature of the marine environment means that guaranteeing the achievement of targets for environmental status cannot be guaranteed, and the regulations therefore empower the Secretary of State and devolved administrations to identify situations in which the environmental targets for good environmental status cannot be achieved in all its aspects. These include situations[36] where the target cannot be achieved without action or inaction for which the United Kingdom is not responsible, where it is prevented by natural causes or force majeure ('act of God'), where modifications or alterations to the physical characteristics of marine waters are brought about by actions taken for reasons of 'overriding public interest' which outweigh the negative impact on the environment,[37] and, finally, where natural conditions do not allow timely improvement in the status of the marine waters concerned.

[29] Ie under s. 1(7) of the Continental Shelf Act 1964.
[30] Reg. 5(4) Marine Strategy Regulations 2010, SI 2010/1627.
[31] Reg. 10 Marine Strategy Regulations 2010.
[32] Reg. 11 Marine Strategy Regulations 2010.
[33] See Annex 3 Table 2 and Annex 4 of Directive 2008/56/EC.
[34] Reg. 14(1) Marine Strategy Regulations 2010.
[35] Reg. 14(3) Marine Strategy Regulations 2010. The reference is to art. 13(4) of Directive 2008/56/EC.
[36] See reg. 15(2) Marine Strategy Regulations 2010.
[37] Including any trans-boundary impact.

The Directive's core requirement to develop a marine protected areas network will be delivered by the network of European Marine sites, Ramsar sites, SSSIs, and by Marine Conservation Zones designated under the Marine and Coastal Access Act 2009.[38] This is discussed in greater detail later.

Marine Protected Areas Policy in the UK

The protection of the marine environment in the waters around the UK is founded upon the establishment of a comprehensive and integrated Marine Protected Areas (MPA) Network.[39] When fully concluded, this will not only implement the requirements of the EC Water Strategy Framework Directive (pp. 244 ff) but also those of the regional OSPAR Convention,[40] under which signatories have undertaken to establish an ecologically coherent network of marine protected areas. When complete, the MPA network will comprise sites under six marine designations: SSSIs, Ramsar sites, *Natura 2000* sites (SACs and SPAs), Marine Conservation Zones designated under the Marine and Coastal Access Act 2009, Scottish Marine Protected Areas under the Marine (Scotland) Act 2010, and sites under the Northern Ireland Marine Act 2011. Progress towards the completion of the MPA network took a major step forward with the passing of the Marine and Coastal Access Act 2009, and will be largely complete when Marine Conservation Zones (MCZs) designated under the 2009 Act come into being in 2013, together with those designated in Scotland and Northern Ireland. The remainder of this chapter will consider each category of protected area, including the provisions in the 2009 Act for the designation and protection of MCZs.

Protected Areas—Extension to Marine Sites

(a) Sites of Special Scientific Interest

The legislation on SSSIs is shaped by its origins as primarily a tool of land use planning. Under the original provisions in the National Parks and Access to the Countryside Act 1949, notification by the Nature Conservancy Council was an adjunct of planning control, and as the jurisdiction of local planning authorities only extends to the low-water median mark, SSSIs are notified to the low water-mark and not beyond into coastal waters. Many SSSIs are notified in practice over the intertidal zone, but even here the regulatory tools conveyed by the designation offer only a limited measure protection that is inappropriate for the unique

[38] See s. 123 Marine and Coastal Access Act 2009.

[39] For the development of legislative policy, see L. M. Warren, 'Law and Policy for Marine Protected Areas', in Rodgers (ed.), *Nature Conservation and Countryside Law* (University of Wales Press, 1996), Ch. 3, esp. at pp. 71–88.

[40] The Convention for the Protection of the Marine Environment of the North East Atlantic 1992. This came into force in March 1998. The UK ratified the OSPAR Convention in 1998.

character of coastal and marine habitats. In the first place, the primary focus of the legislation is on protecting habitats from damage by their owners and occupiers. Accordingly, the service of a list of operations likely to damage the conservation interest (OLDSIs) in an SSSI will only restrict operations by an owner or occupier of the land in the intertidal zone. In practice, open access to beaches and water in the intertidal zone means that the range of conservation risks and threats is often more prosaic and varied than is the case with terrestrial SSSIs. This might include fishing by the public, bait digging,[41] and other recreational uses such as sail-boarding and recreational boating, quite apart from commercial extraction of sand and gravel. In some parts of the country where coastal marshes are registered as common land, there are also common rights for inhabitants to remove sand, gravel, and vegetation, and to shoot wildfowl.[42] The statutory consultation mechanism provided by the notification of OLDSIs[43] therefore gives little purchase over the kind of conservation risks that coastal sites face.

An SSSI can be notified over any land lying above the mean low watermark and land covered by estuarine waters.[44] Following amendments introduced in the Marine and Coastal Access Act 2009,[45] an area of the seabed can also be included in an SSSI if it is adjacent to land notified above the mean low watermark (referred to as 'area A'), and this may include land below the low watermark ('area B'). The conditions for the inclusion of such adjacent areas of the seabed are: (i) that the flora, fauna, or features leading to the notification of area A must also be present in area B; (ii) that the notification of area A is by reason of any flora or fauna which are dependent, wholly or in part, on anything which takes place in, or is present in, area B; and finally (iii) that, without the inclusion of area B, the identification of the boundary of the land notified as an SSSI would be impossible or impracticable; for example, with regard to exercising functions in relation to it. The statutory conservation agencies also have power to notify additional land that is sub-tidal, or to enlarge an SSSI to include land that is sub-tidal, provided these conditions are met.[46] In all cases of the notification, enlargement to include, or the addition of, sub-tidal land, the minister has power to call in the notification and to give directions to Natural England as to whether the land is to be included, to be excluded, or to be included in part in an SSSI notification.[47] The 2009 Act also gives the statutory Conservation Body power to de-notify an SSSI if the land

[41] See *Anderson v Alnwick District Council* [1993] 3 All ER 613.

[42] Eg in North Norfolk, as to which see C. P. Rodgers, E. A. Straughton, A. Winchester, and M. Pieraccini, *Contested Common Land: Environmental Governance Past and Present* (Earthscan, 2010), Ch. 9, esp. 175 ff.

[43] See Chapter 3, p. 84.

[44] S. 28(1)(1A) Wildlife and Countryside Act 1981, inserted by Marine and Coastal Access Act 2009, s. 148 and Schedule 13 para. 2(3).

[45] S. 28(1)(1C) Wildlife and Countryside Act 1981 inserted by s. 148 and Schedule 13 para. 2(3) Marine and Coastal Access Act 2009.

[46] See s. 28 B(2A–2C) and s. 28 C(2A–2C) inserted by Marine and Coastal Access Act 2009, s. 148 and Schedule 13 paras. 5 and 6.

[47] S. 28CB Wildlife and Countryside Act 1981, as inserted by s. 148 and Schedule 13 para. 8 Marine and Coastal Access Act 2009.

contained within it is subsequently included in a Marine Conservation Zone designated under the 2009 Act.[48]

(b) National Nature Reserves

Similar amendments were made by the Marine and Coastal Access Act 2009 to the possible geographical extent of National Nature Reserves; areas managed by the Conservation Bodies themselves or by other organizations approved for this purpose by the Conservation Bodies.[49] A National Nature Reserve can include land lying above the mean low watermark and land covered by estuarine waters.[50] The reserve can now also include land lying *below* the mean low watermark[51] if it is adjacent to the land designated above the low watermark, provided always that the flora and fauna that have led to the management of the land as a nature reserve are also present in the sub-tidal area, that those flora and fauna are dependant, wholly or in part, upon anything that takes place, or occurs, in the sub-tidal area, and that without the inclusion of the sub-tidal area in the reserve its management and the delineation of its boundaries would be impracticable or impossible.[52] Where the statutory Conservation Body proposes to designate a national nature reserve that includes sub-tidal land, the minster has the power to call in the designation and make directions as to the land to be included within the reserve, or to be omitted from it.[53] There is no power to de-notify a National Nature Reserve if it is subsequently included within an MCZ; cf. the position for SSSIs, discussed earlier. This is because the principal consequence of designation as a national nature reserve is that the land, and adjacent sub-tidal area, is to be managed by the Conservation Body itself or a body approved by it for this purpose. This will not change whether the land is within an MCZ or not.

(c) European marine sites

Both the European Habitats and Species Directive and the Wild Birds Directive[54] include marine habitats and species and require the designation of SASCs and SPAs for their protection. European sites can, accordingly, extend to those offshore, and not simply to terrestrial habitats to be found on land. Transposition of the two

[48] S. 148 and Schedule 13 para. 9 Marine and Coastal Access Act 2009, amending s. 28D of the 1981 Act.

[49] For National Nature Reserves see Chapter 3, pp. 99ff.

[50] S. 35(1A) Wildlife and Countryside Act 1981, inserted by Schedule 13 para. 10 Marine and Coastal Access Act 2009 ('Area A').

[51] 'Area B', s. 35(1B) Marine and Coastal Access Act 2009.

[52] S. 35(1B)(1C) Wildlife and Countryside Act 1981.

[53] See s. 35A inserted by Schedule 13 para. 11 Marine and Coastal Access Act 2009.

[54] Council Directive 92/43/EC of 21 May 1992 on the Conservation of Natural Habitats and of Wild Flora and Fauna, [1992] OJ L206, 22/07/1992, p. 7; and Directive 2009/147/EC of the European Parliament and the Council of 30 November 2009 on the conservation of wild birds [2010] OJ L20/7, 26.1.2010. For a more detailed consideration of both Directives and their implementation see Chapter 6, pp. 203ff.

Directives has resulted in the designation of 96 SACs with marine components, of which 84 are wholly inshore waters and 10 wholly offshore. In addition, there are 4 Annex 1 habitats present in UK waters for which the European Commission has indicated that additional SACs must be identified and designated: reefs, sandbanks slightly covered by the sea at all times, submarine structures made by leaking gases, and sea caves which are wholly or partially submerged.[55] Four marine species listed for protection in Annex II of the Habitats Directive also occur away from the coast in large numbers in UK waters; grey seals, common seals, bottle-nose dolphins, and harbour porpoises. All four species range across wide areas of the offshore marine environment, however, and the JNCC do not consider it likely that a discrete geographical area for designation as an SAC can be identified in any of these cases.[56]

The Habitats Directive was transposed into English Law in 1994, and the transposing regulations recognized the possibility of protected sites extending offshore by providing for the designation of SACs in territorial waters up to 12 miles from the coast.[57] This was successfully challenged before the English Courts, in a case concerning the grant of oil and gas exploration licenses off North West Scotland, on the basis that the Habitats Directive required the designation of marine habitats and the seabed up to the limit of the continental shelf and territorial waters (200 miles).[58] A partial response resulted in the application of controls on oil and gas exploration licensing in the offshore marine area.[59] This resulted in infraction proceedings before the European Court of Justice, which ruled in *Commission v UK*[60] in 2005 that the UK was in breach of its obligations under the Directive in failing to fully implement the Directive in offshore areas within its jurisdiction beyond the territorial sea, including the exclusive economic zone. This resulted in the introduction of further transposing regulations in 2007 that now extend protected areas policy for SACs and SPAs to include all those marine areas over which the UK claims jurisdiction.[61]

The 2007 regulations remain in force, and the result of this piecemeal extension of protection under the Directives to UK marine waters is that protection for European marine sites is governed by two different regulations:

(i) European marine sites in the territorial sea

The Conservation of Habitats and Species Regulations 2010[62] integrate the protection of European marine sites with that applied to terrestrial SACs and SPAs. A European marine site is simply a European site insofar as it consists of a marine

[55] See further <http://jncc.defra.gov.uk/p.-1447>.

[56] <http://jncc.defra.gov.uk/p.-1446>.

[57] Conservation (Natural Habitats etc.) Regulations 1994, SI 1994/2716.

[58] See *R v Secretary of State for Trade and Industry ex parte Greenpeace Ltd (No.2)* (2000) Env LR 221.

[59] The Offshore Petroleum Activities (Conservation of Habitats) Regulations 2002, SI 2002/1754.

[60] Case C-6/04, [2005] ECR I–9017.

[61] See the Offshore Marine Conservation (Natural Habitats etc.) Regulations 2007, SI 2007/1842.

[62] SI 2010/490. The Conservation (Natural Habitats etc.) Regulations 1994, SI 1994/2716, as amended, continue to apply in Scotland.

area,[63] which in this context means the English inshore region and the Welsh inshore region.[64] It could therefore comprise any of the following, if found in the inshore region: an SAC, a site of Community importance, a site hosting a priority habitat or species in respect of which consultation has been instituted with the European Commission under article 5 of the Habitats Directive, an area classified as an SPA under the Wild Birds Directive, and a site proposed by the European Commission as a site of Community importance.[65] The same protective regulations apply as in terrestrial sites, and as described in Chapter 6.[66] Natural England[67] has responsibility for the control of potentially damaging operations in a marine site, and both it and the Secretary of State are subject to the general duty to exercise their powers so as to secure compliance with the Habitats Directive, and this duty extends in marine sites also to any 'competent authority'[68]—this extends the duty in marine sites to a wider range of public and quasi-public bodies than is the case in terrestrial sites. These include not only ministers of the Crown but also government departments, statutory undertakers, public bodies of any description, and any person holding public office.[69] The 2010 regulations apply the controls on plans and projects in a European site to marine sites, as to terrestrial ones, so that an appropriate assessment must be made of any proposal to carry out a potentially damaging operation or plan, and the ability of the Conservation Body to grant consent is limited to cases where there is an overriding public interest that the operation be carried out.[70] Some additional powers extend solely to European marine sites. The statutory Conservation Body can install markers to indicate the existence of the marine site, and must, as soon as possible after the site becomes a European marine site, inform other relevant authorities of the site's conservation objectives and of any operations that may cause deterioration of the natural habitats or habitats of species, or disturbance of species for which the site has been designated.[71]

A wide range of 'relevant' authorities, acting together or alone, have power to make a management scheme for a European marine site.[72] These include not only the Conservation Body, but also the Marine Management Organisation, local authorities, the environment agency, a water or sewerage undertaker, a navigation authority, harbour or lighthouse authority, inshore fisheries and conservation committee, local fisheries committee, or a National Park authority.[73] Only one management plan can be made for each marine site, and the Secretary of State and

[63] Reg. 8(4) Conservation of Habitats and Species Regulations 2010.

[64] Reg. 3(1) Conservation of Habitats and Species Regulations 2010.

[65] Ie under the mechanism in article 10 of the Habitats Directive for designation following identification of a site by the Commission (rather than the member state)—see Chapter 6, p. 210.

[66] See Chapter 6, pp. 216 ff.

[67] And in Wales, the Countryside Council for Wales; in Scotland, Scottish Natural Heritage.

[68] Reg. 9(3) Conservation of Habitats and Species Regulations 2010.

[69] Reg. 7(1) Conservation of Habitats and Species Regulations 2010.

[70] See Chapter 6, pp. 213 ff.

[71] Reg. 35 Conservation of Habitats and Species Regulations 2010.

[72] For a review of 15 case studies of management plans in inshore SACs see Jones and Burgess, 'Building Partnership Capacity for the Collaborative Management of Marine Protected Areas in the UK: A Preliminary Analysis' (2005) 77 *Journal of Environmental Management* 227.

[73] See reg. 6 Conservation of Habitats and Species Regulations 2010.

statutory Conservation Body both have power to give directions as to the conservation measures to be included in the scheme, to time limits within which any steps under it are to be taken, and requiring the approval of the authority before the scheme is established.[74] The Marine Management Organisation can make by-laws for the protection of a European marine site in England, on the same basis as applies in Marine Conservation Zones.[75] This power is exercisable by the Welsh ministers in relation to any European marine site in Wales. The provisions relating to by-laws in Marine Conservation Zones apply in all cases; for example, to determine the possible content and subject of by-laws and their enforceability.[76]

(ii) Offshore European marine sites

The Offshore Marine Conservation etc. Regulations 2007 apply a similar regime to marine areas outside territorial waters, and up to the limit of UK jurisdiction. Thus, a 'European offshore marine site' is defined as including any of the European site designations that are made in the offshore marine area.[77] The offshore marine area is defined[78] to mean, in this context, any part of the seabed and subsoil situated in the continental shelf,[79] and any part of the waters within British fishery limits except the internal waters of, and the territorial sea adjacent to, the United Kingdom, the Channel Islands, and the Isle of Man. As with inshore European sites, a wide range of competent authorities must exercise their functions so as to secure compliance with the Directive—including the Secretary of State, devolved administrations, statutory undertakers, and government departments.[80] The provisions for the designation of SACs and SPAs mirror those in the 2010 regulations and applicable to terrestrial European sites.[81] The most important variation applied to marine sites concerns habitats for species that have a wide natural range—a very common feature of marine mammal and fish species, of course. The 2007 regulations provide that in respect of

[74] See reg. 37 Conservation of Habitats and Species Regulations 2010.

[75] Reg. 38 Conservation of Habitats and Species Regulations 2010, ie under s. 129 Marine and Coastal Access Act 2009.

[76] As to which see further pp. 279ff.

[77] See reg. 15 Offshore Marine Conservation etc. Regulations 2007 SI 2007/1842.

[78] See reg. 2(2) Offshore Marine Conservation etc. Regulations 2007.

[79] As designated under s. 1(7) of the Continental Shelf Act 1964.

[80] Regs. 5(1) and 6(1) Offshore Marine Conservation etc. Regulations 2007. This duty is applied by reg. 6(2) to functions under a wide range of statutory provisions including: the Whaling Industry (Regulation) Act 1934; the Coast Protection Act 1949 (restriction of works detrimental to navigation); the Sea Fish (Conservation) Act 1967; the Prevention of Oil Pollution Act 1971; the Fishery Limits Act 1976; the Fisheries Act 1981; Part 2 of the Food and Environment Protection Act 1985 (deposits in the sea); the Radioactive Substances Act 1993; the Merchant Shipping Act 1995 (preventing pollution from ships); the Pollution Prevention and Control Act 1999; the Merchant Shipping (Prevention of Oil Pollution) Regulations 1996; the Merchant Shipping (Oil Pollution Preparedness, Response and Co-operation Convention) Regulations 1998; the Offshore Installations (Emergency Pollution Control) Regulations 2002; and The Offshore Marine Conservation Regulations themselves.

[81] See Offshore Marine Conservation etc. Regulations 2007 regs. 11 and 12. For the multi-stage designation process for SACs see Chapter 6, p. 210, and for the designation of SPAs, see Chapter 6, pp. 203–5.

an aquatic species which ranges over wide areas, a site is only eligible to be selected for designation as an SAC or SPA if it constitutes a clearly identifiable area which is distinct in providing the physical and biological features essential to that species for life and reproduction. As noted earlier, this requirement is one reason why the JNCC consider it to be unlikely that discrete marine sites will in future be designated for the protection of four Annex 2 marine species to be found in UK waters; grey seals, common seals, bottle-nose dolphins, and harbour porpoises.

Once an offshore site has been designated, the JNCC is the Conservation Body responsible for overseeing the management and protection of its conservation features. As soon as practicable after a site has been designated, it must establish conservation objectives for the site and notify these to all relevant competent authorities, together with notice of the operations it considers will be likely to adversely affect the integrity of the site.[82] Any of the competent authorities that have functions in relation to an offshore marine site can put forward proposals for a management scheme for the site. This must take account of the conservation objectives fixed for the site, and must be consulted upon with the JNCC prior to promulgation.[83] And once a management scheme has been established, every competent authority that has functions that impinge upon the site must take steps to exercise them in accordance with the scheme.[84] They also have general duties to exercise their functions in order to secure that the management objectives set out in the Habitats Directive are secured,[85] in particular, that there is no disturbance of protected species and that the management of habitats accords with the standards set out in article 6 of the Directive.[86] The 2007 regulations also apply restrictions to the power of competent authorities to grant permission for plans or projects in marine offshore sites, such that they can only do so if there is an overriding public interest in accordance with the Habitats Directive's protective provisions.[87] The same measures are applied as to compensatory habitat provision, where consent is granted that will damage a protected habitat, and for the review of existing consents, as apply in terrestrial European sites.[88] Finally, a number of criminal offences underpin the management regime established for offshore sites.[89] It is an offence to intentionally disturb Annex 11 species of animal while they are in a marine offshore SAC, or intentionally to disturb a protected species of bird in an SPA if this likely to impair the bird's ability to survive, breed, or rear or nurture its young. It is also an offence to intentionally or recklessly damage or destroy an Annex 1 natural habitat type listed in the Habitats Directive if it is situated in an offshore SAC.[90]

[82] Offshore Marine Conservation etc. Regulations 2007 reg. 18.

[83] Offshore Marine Conservation etc. Regulations 2007 reg. 19.

[84] Offshore Marine Conservation etc. Regulations 2007 reg. 20.

[85] As to which, see Chapter 6, pp. 213ff.

[86] See regs. 22 and 23 Offshore Marine Conservation etc. Regulations 2007.

[87] Reg. 25 Offshore Marine Conservation etc. Regulations 2007.

[88] See regs. 26–31 Offshore Marine Conservation etc. Regulations 2007.

[89] These are set out in reg. 32 Offshore Marine Conservation etc. Regulations 2007.

[90] The offences set out in regulation 32 are complex and detailed, and mirror those in the 2010 Regulations applied to terrestrial sites. This is a summary; for full detail on those in the 2010 Regulations see Chapter 6, pp. 220ff.

Marine Nature Reserves

The difficulties of developing a regime appropriate for managing marine areas, and their distinctive habitats and species, meant that the first specific measure addressed to this had to wait until 1981, when the Wildlife and Countryside Act introduced powers for the Conservation Bodies to propose the designation of Marine Nature Reserves. The 1981 Act provided for the designation as a Marine Nature Reserve of 'any land covered, continuously or intermittently, by tidal waters or parts of the sea which are landward of the baselines from which the breadth of the territorial sea adjacent to Great Britain is measured or are seaward of those baselines up to a distance of three nautical miles'.[91] Designation was by the Secretary of State, following an application made to him by the statutory Conservation Body. The chief importance of designation was the ability to introduce by-laws governing the movement of persons, vehicles, and vessels, prohibiting the killing, taking, destruction, and disturbance of animals or plants of any description, of any actions that may disturb the seabed, and the dumping of rubbish.[92] A copy of the proposed MNR by-laws had to be submitted to the Secretary of State with the application. In the absence of by-laws the only other power available to the Conservation Body was the putting down of markers to indicate the existence and extent of the reserve.[93]

Only three Marine Nature Reserves were designated under the 1981 Act: Lundy Island (England), Skomer Island (Wales), and Strangford Lough (Northern Ireland).[94] A number of voluntary Marine Conservation Reserves have also been established, but these lack statutory force and are entirely reliant on the voluntary participation of stakeholders and user groups for the achievement of their conservation objectives. The limited nature of the regulatory powers available to the Conservation Bodies in MNRs—focused principally on by-laws—and the difficulty of engaging all the stakeholders and public authorities whose activities can impact upon the marine environment in conservation planning and management, has meant that MNRs had limited impact as a tool for developing an integrated strategy for coastal and marine conservation. Statutory Marine Nature Reserves are therefore to be replaced by Marine Conservation Zones designated under the Marine and Coastal Access Act 2009. Lundy Island has already moved to MCZ status.[95] The legislative provisions for designating MNRs have been repealed by the 2009 Act, except as regards areas not within MCZs in Wales.[96] The legislative

[91] S. 36(1) Wildlife and Countryside Act 1981 amended by ss. 1, 3, and Schedule 1 para. 6(a) Territorial Sea Act 1987.

[92] Under s. 37(1), (2) Wildlife and Countryside Act 1981.

[93] S. 36(5) of the 1981 Act.

[94] Designated under the Nature Conservation and Amenity Lands (Northern Ireland) Order 1985.

[95] See the Lundy Field Society website for further information: <http://www.lundy.org.uk/inf/mnr.html>; and <http://www.lundymcz.org.uk/>.

[96] S. 36 and 37 Wildlife and Countryside Act 1981 were repealed with regard to England and Wales by ss. 146, 321, and 324 (2)(b) and Schedule 11 para. 2(2) the Marine and Coastal Access Act 2009.

provisions for the establishment of by-laws have also been repealed in Scotland.[97] The Marine Conservation Zone project offers the possibility for the development of an integrated and comprehensive programme of marine protected areas around the UK coastline, and the remainder of this chapter will consider the implementation of the MCZ project under the 2009 Act.

Marine Conservation Zones

Proposals to comprehensively reform the law relating to marine conservation in coastal waters around the UK have now culminated in the Marine and Coastal Access Act 2009, part 5 of which provides for the designation of 'Marine Conservation Zones'(MCZs). Designation is by the Secretary of State, or the Welsh ministers or Scottish ministers in relation to an area in (respectively) Wales or the Scottish offshore region.[98] In Scotland any zone designated under these provisions will be known as a 'marine protected area',[99] and the Marine (Scotland) Act 2010 makes additional and specific provision for the management of marine habitats in Scotland.

The 2009 Act represents a new approach not only to the protection of marine ecosystems and resources within MCZs, but also to the process of designation itself; a 'bottom-up'rather than wholly state-mediated approach was taken to the identification of possible areas for designation, with regional MCZ projects and stakeholder groups undertaking extensive research and consultation between 2009 and 2012 to identify candidate MCZs. At the same time, an element of 'top-down' direction has been retained, in that the regional MCZ proposals had to adhere to ecological network guidance produced by the JNCC in order to ensure that the protected areas network can deliver the conservation objectives dictated by, for example, European environmental law. This top-down element is also represented in the formal review of the MCZ proposals by the statutory Conservation Bodies and DEFRA against the JNCC guidance, and in the fact that statutory power to designate an area an MCZ rests ultimately with the Secretary of State. There is an inherent tension between bottom-up approaches to common pool resource governance, which focus on stakeholder preferences (potentially at the expense of conservation objectives) and top-down approaches in which state mediated direction risks alienating stakeholders and leading to problems of free-riding, non-enforcement, and non-participation. Conservation interests tend to favour top-down approaches, so as to avoid the vested interests of fishing and other appropriator groups from undermining conservation objectives for marine biodiversity, while fisheries conservation interests tend to favour a bottom-up approach.

[97] S. 37 Wildlife and Countryside Act 1981 was repealed with regard to Scotland by the Marine (Scotland) Act 2010 s. 167, 168, and Schedule 4 para. 5(b).

[98] S. 116(5) Marine and Coastal Access Act 2009.

[99] S. 116(6) Marine and Coastal Access Act 2009.

The process for identifying and then designating MCZs is an example of a balanced approach that combines bottom-up and top-down approaches, with public bodies and stakeholder groups working together in partnership. As such it is an example of a collaborative management model, although difficult questions will remain as to the balance of power within the partnership that it establishes.[100] This issue comes into sharp focus in relation to 'no take zones'[101] in particular, where conservation and fisheries interests are often in direct conflict—and we shall see examples of this in the discussion of the MCZ project later. In this context it can be argued that the formulation of MCZ proposals in the initial consultation/project phase represented a balanced approach, with stakeholder 'bottom-up' participation shaped by guidance from public bodies such as the JNCC. Whereas the subsequent designation process itself under the 2009 Act is primarily a top-down, government-led exercise and less participative.[102]

The consultation and designation process is discussed in greater detail later. At the time of writing candidate MCZs have been identified by the regional projects, but no designations have yet been made.

(a) Designating Marine Conservation Zones

The criteria to be satisfied for areas to be considered for designation as MCZs are set out in some detail in the 2009 Act.

(i) Geographical location

An area can be included within an MCZ if it is an area of the sea within the seaward limits of the territorial sea adjacent to the UK, or if it is an area of sea within the EEZ, or, finally, if it is an area of the seabed or subsoil within the limits of the UK sector of the continental shelf outside the limits of the EEZ.[103] It will be recalled that the EEZ extends to 200 nautical miles from the coast, or to be more precise, 200 nautical miles from the low-water baseline of the territorial sea.[104] Scottish and Northern Irish inshore regions are excluded.

[100] See P. J. S. Jones 'Collective Action Problems Posed by No-Take Zones' (2006) 30 *Marine Policy* 143–56; P. J. S. Jones 'Marine Protected Areas in the UK: challenges in combining top-down and bottom-up approaches to governance' (2012) 39 *Environmental Conservation* 248–58. The process for designating marine Special Areas of Conservation, by contrast, is primarily 'top-down' (as to which, see pp. 252ff.).

[101] These are referred to as 'reference areas' in the 2009 Act and associated guidance—see further p. 264. For a discussion of management problems and approaches to no take zones in particular see P. J. S. Jones, 'Equity Justice and Power Issues raised by No-Take Marine Protected Area Proposals' (2009) 33 *Marine Policy* 759–65; P. J. S. Jones, 'Collective Action Problems Posed by No-Take Zones' (2006) 30 *Marine Policy* 143–56.

[102] For a fuller discussion of these aspects see P. J. S. Jones, 'Marine Protected Areas in the UK: challenges in combining top-down and bottom-up approaches to governance' (2012) 39 *Environmental Conservation* 248–58.

[103] See s. 116(2) and s. 118 Marine and Coastal Access Act 2009.

[104] Above, p. 244.

(ii) Identifying the boundaries of an MCZ

An order designating an MCZ must identify the boundaries of the site. These can be determined by reference to mean high-water spring tide.[105] If an MCZ includes an area of the territorial sea adjacent to the coast, it may also include an area of the seashore lying above the mean high-water spring tide if the inward area has common protected features with the seaward area of the MCZ, and the zone is designated for the conservation of marine flora and/or fauna which are dependent on anything that takes place or is present in the inland area of the proposed protected zone.[106] It must be necessary to designate the landward area in order for the protection of, or carrying out of functions necessary for the protection of, the MCZ and its protected features. The protection afforded by the MCZ designation is intended to apply both to habitats on, and integral to, the seabed as well as the flora and fauna—fish, mammals, and plants—subsisting in the waters above it. To this end, it is provided that an MCZ designation order *must* designate an area of land, whether or not covered by water; this would include, for example, small islands, and the seabed or subsoil. It *may* also designate some or all of the water covering that land.[107]

(iii) Grounds for designation

The grounds on which an MCZ can be designated are broad.[108] The appropriate authority can make a designation order if it thinks it is desirable to do so for the purpose of conserving marine flora or fauna, marine habitats or types of marine habitat, or for conserving features of geological or geomorphological interest. The designating order must state the protected features of, and the conservation objectives for, the MCZ. Natural England and the Joint Nature Conservation Committee have published guidance on the ecological criteria to be applied when identifying candidate MCZs for possible designation.[109]

(iv) Designation—procedure and consultation

Before it can make an order designating an MCZ, the designating authority[110] must publish a notice of its proposals to make the order. This must contain a statement of the terms of the order and be published in such a manner as the authority considers is most likely to bring the proposal to the attention of any

105 Spring tides represent the largest inward and outward ingress of the sea due to tidal movements.

106 S. 118(4) and (5) Marine and Coastal Access Act 2009. The inland area is referred to as 'area B' and the seaward area as 'Area A'.

107 S. 118(6) Marine and Coastal Access Act 2009.

108 See s. 117 Marine and Coastal Access Act 2009.

109 Natural England and the Joint Nature Conservation Committee (2010), *The Marine Conservation Zone Project: Ecological Network Guidance.* Sheffield and Peterborough, UK. This is referred to for brevity in the following discussion as the 'Ecological Network Guidance'.

110 Ie the Secretary of State (England), or Scottish or Welsh ministers in relation to an area of Scottish Offshore waters or an area in Wales—s. 116(5) Marine and Coastal Access Act 2009.

persons who are likely to be affected by the making of the order.[111] The designating authority then has 12 months in which to make a designation order.[112] The designating authority has a duty to consult any persons whom it thinks are likely to be affected by, or interested in, the making of the order.[113] It can make regulations for the consultation procedure that is to be followed, and this can either give an opportunity to appear and be heard in person before someone appointed for that purpose (for example, a planning inspector) or provide for written representations to be made to such a person.[114] Where the proposed MCZ is to be designated by the Welsh or Scottish ministers, they must consult the Secretary of State before proceeding to formal designation,[115] and there are provisions requiring consultation with the Welsh or Scottish ministers in cases where an MCZ designation will affect activities in the Scottish or Welsh offshore waters.[116] If the designation order is not made within the 12 months allowed by the 2009 Act, any consultation undertaken will be deemed not to have been undertaken and the process will have to be restarted afresh.[117] Where a designation order is made, notice of designation must be published in a manner that the authority considers most likely to bring it to the attention of any persons likely to be affected by it.[118] The notice must give the address at which a copy of the order can be inspected, and the authority must make a copy of the order available for inspection at all reasonable hours without payment.[119] It must also provide a copy of the order to anyone requesting one, and although it can charge a fee for doing this, the fee cannot exceed its costs in providing the copy.[120]

In limited circumstances, where the authority considers that there is 'an urgent need to protect' the area proposed for designation as an MCZ, it can proceed to designation without carrying out the public consultation otherwise required by the provisions discussed earlier. In this case, however, the designation takes effect for a period not exceeding two years, and must be confirmed by a further designation order that takes effect following full consultation in accordance with the terms of the 2009 Act.[121]

(b) Network approach and focus

The legal basis for the designation of MCZs differs from that which applies to the selection and notification of terrestrial protected areas, such as SSSIs, in that it has

111 S. 119(2) and (3) Marine and Coastal Access Act 2009.
112 S. 119(10) Marine and Coastal Access Act 2009.
113 S. 119(4) Marine and Coastal Access Act 2009.
114 See s. 121 Marine and Coastal Access Act 2009. At the time of writing, regulations have not yet been laid.
115 S. 119(5) Marine and Coastal Access Act 2009.
116 S. 119(6)—(9) Marine and Coastal Access Act 2009.
117 This is the import of s. 119(10) Marine and Coastal Access Act 2009 which deems 'anything done... by the appropriate authority... to be treated as not having been done'.
118 S. 120(3) Marine and Coastal Access Act 2009.
119 S. 120(4) Marine and Coastal Access Act 2009.
120 S. 120(5) Marine and Coastal Access Act 2009.
121 See ss. 119(11) and (12) Marine and Coastal Access Act 2009.

an explicit focus on the wider contribution of each candidate MCZ to the creation of a *network* of protected sites. When considering whether to designate an area as an MCZ, the authority must have regard to the objective that the site, taken together with any other MCZs designated by the authority and to any others designated within the UK marine area,[122] and with any other relevant marine conservation sites, form a *network* that satisfies three conditions.[123] These are:[124]

- That the network contributes to the conservation or improvement of the marine environment in UK marine waters (Condition 1),
- That the features which are protected by the sites contained in the network represent the range of features present in UK marine waters (Condition 2), and that
- The designation of sites contained in the network reflects the fact that the conservation of the feature may require the designation of more than one site (Condition 3).

This is a very different approach to that found in the legislation on terrestrial habitats protected under the Wildlife and Countryside Act 1981, where the focus in relation to identifying and then designating SSSIs and nature reserves is single-site-specific.[125] The focus there is on whether *the area of land* to be notified as a protected area is of special interest by reason of its flora, fauna, or geological and/or physiographical features.[126] The contribution of the SSSI to the wider network of protected sites is, in that context, captured by the non-statutory Biological Guidelines on SSSI selection published by the Joint Nature Conservation Committee.[127] These emphasize, for example, that the 'special' scientific interest of a terrestrial habitat should require the selection of 'exemplar' habitats that are representative of indigenous habitats. In relation to terrestrial habitats, the representative network function of protected areas is more directly addressed by the European Habitats and Species Directive,[128] which requires each member state to contribute to the creation of the *Natura 2000* protected areas network in proportion to the representation within its territory of the natural habitats and habitats of species specified in the Directive.[129] In contrast, the Marine and Coastal Access Act 2009 elevates the network function of protected areas to be a central objective of the

[122] So eg the Secretary of State would, when considering whether to designate an MCZ in England, have to have regard to MCZs designated by the Scottish and Welsh ministers in the context of the overall contribution of the MCZ under consideration to the 'network' of UK marine sites.

[123] S. 123(1) and (2) Marine and Coastal Access Act 2009.

[124] See s. 123(3) Marine and Coastal Access Act 2009.

[125] See Chapter 3, pp. 68ff.

[126] See s. 28(1) Wildlife and Countryside Act 1981, Chapter 3, p. 69.

[127] See *Guidelines for the Selection of Biological SSSIs* (JNCC, Peterborough) at para. 3; Natural England, 2008, *Sites of Special Scientific Interest (SSSI): a notification strategy for England* at Appendix 1 and Table 1. Available at: <http://www.naturalengland.org.uk/Images/Notification%20strategy%20for%20web_tcm6-15235.pdf>. Both are discussed Chapter 3, pp. 70–3.

[128] Council Directive 92/43/EC of 21 May 1992 on the Conservation of Natural Habitats and of Wild Flora and Fauna, [1992] OJ L 206, 22/07/1992, p. 7 (hereafter 'Habitats Directive').

[129] Art. 3.2 Habitats Directive. See further Chapter 6, p. 209.

designation process, and this enhanced legal status is reflected in the fact that the Act places a statutory duty on the authority in every case when considering designation of an MCZ to have regard to the objectives set out on p. 261.[130]

The network of protected sites, to the creation of which regard must be had when designating MCZs, includes not only other MCZs already designated in the UK marine area, but also European marine sites, SSSIs, and the whole or any part of a Ramsar wetland site.[131] Condition 2, for example, will require the Secretary of State (or Scottish or Welsh ministers) to consider whether the features protected by MCZs and other sites contained in the network (SSSIs, etc.) together represent the range of features present in the UK marine area. Condition 3 also emphasizes the more broadly based designation criteria applicable to marine sites under the 2009 Act: the Secretary of State must consider not whether the conservation feature under consideration in a candidate MCZ itself makes that area 'special', but rather where the designation of more than one site, including that under consideration, is required to contribute to the ecological objectives of the network.

The duties to adopt a strategic 'network' focus when designating MCZs is underpinned by reporting duties imposed by the 2009 Act. The appropriate authority[132] must prepare a statement setting out the principles it intends to follow in order to achieve the objective of creating a protected areas network that satisfies the statutory conditions set out earlier. This must be laid before the relevant legislature viz. Parliament in the case of the Secretary of State, the National Assembly of Wales (Welsh ministers) or the Scottish Parliament (Scottish ministers).[133] The statement must be kept under review and can be amended as appropriate, in which case a revised statement must be laid before the relevant legislature.[134]

(c) Identifying candidate MCZs—the consultation process

The range of stakeholders with an interest in using the marine environment and exploiting its resources is larger and more diverse than that associated with most terrestrial protected areas. The MCZ project ran from 2009 to 2012 and adopted a new 'bottom-up' approach to identifying recommended sites for public consultation and designation. The MCZ project required the balancing of (i) local stakeholder engagement in a bottom-up process of site identification and the negotiation of relevant controls, with (ii) the application of carefully structured

[130] When complying with this statutory duty the authority must also have regard to any obligations under EU or international law that relate to the conservation or improvement of the marine environment: s. 123(5) Marine and Coastal Access Act 2009.

[131] See s. 123(4) Marine and Coastal Access Act 2009.

[132] Ie the Secretary of State, the Welsh ministers, or the Scottish ministers as the case may be: see s. 116(5) Marine and Coastal Access Act 2009.

[133] S. 123(6) and (9) Marine and Coastal Access Act 2009. The statement must be laid within two months of s. 123(6) coming into force. S. 123 came into force, except as regards MCZs in Wales, two months after the passing of the 2009 Act on 12 November 2009: s. 324(2)(b)(i) Marine and Coastal Access Act 2009. The duty in s. 123(6) had, therefore, to be complied with by 12 March 2010.

[134] S. 123(8) Marine and Coastal Access Act 2009.

ecological criteria aimed at ensuring that the ecological objectives which the network is intended to deliver could be appropriately identified and captured.

The application of structured ecological criteria as an essential ingredient in the designation process is important, given the MCZ project's contribution to meeting the UKs obligations under the European Marine Strategy Framework Directive, and in delivering protection for marine protected areas under, for example, the Habitats Directive. This was achieved by requiring each regional stakeholder working group to take into account the Ecological Network Guidance provided by Natural England and the JNCC. The process therefore involved not only wide stakeholder engagement to reach a consensus on the sites to be protected within the MCZ network, and the restrictions to be applied within them on resource use and exploitation, but also the consideration of the JNCC guidance in formulating the final list of recommended MCZs for presentation to the Secretary of State for public consultation prior to possible designation under the 2009 Act. Four regional projects were established, with working groups representing a diverse range of stakeholders to identify and map potential sites for subsequent consultation and designation. The recommended MCZs (rMCZs) identified by each project were then put to public consultation before being finalized for consideration by the Secretary of State for formal designation under the 2009 Act.

(i) Establishing conservation objectives

The stakeholder groups also had an important role in selecting whether a conservation objective should be framed so as to *maintain* or to *recover* the feature to be protected. Each of the four stakeholder working groups was required to produce draft conservation objectives for each protected feature in an rMCZ, and guidance on the criteria and methodology for doing this was provided by the statutory nature Conservation Bodies.[135] The guidance required the fixing of conservation objectives for each feature at either 'maintain' or 'recover' status, depending on the sensitivity of the protected features to the pressures to which it is exposed. In order to do this, the guidance required the stakeholder groups to undertake a vulnerability assessment of each feature, assessing both its sensitivity to a pressure and its exposure to that activity—if a feature had a high to moderate vulnerability to significant impacts, then the conservation objective would be set as 'recover', identifying the impacts to be managed in the process of achieving recovery. In all other cases, the conservation objective should be set as 'maintain', and new management measures will not be required to reduce the perceived pressures on the conservation feature.[136] The use of conservation objectives for features in each zone, specifying whether the sites features are to be maintained in that condition or

[135] Available at: <http://jncc.defra.gov.uk/pdf/mcz%20project%20conservation%20objective%20guidance%20summary.pdf>.

[136] See <http://jncc.defra.gov.uk/pdf/mcz%20project%20conservation%20objective%20guidance%20summary.pdf> at 3.

recovered to it,[137] is important as it will facilitate the application of the JNCC common standards monitoring methodology applied in other protected areas—SSSIs, SACs, and SPAs, for example—to assess the conservation status of MCZ protected features post-designation.[138] The regional stakeholder groups played a central role in this process; as marine users with current knowledge of human activities in each area, they were regarded as being best placed to identify those activities that present a threat of damage to protected features, and which may put them at risk of not achieving favourable conservation status.

(ii) Reference areas

Each regional project was also required to identify a small number of 'reference areas' in which all human depositional, extractive, damaging, or disturbance activities would be prohibited or removed, the object being to enable each protected conservation feature in the reference area to retain, or return to, its unimpaired or unimpacted conservation condition. This will also then provide a reference point for assessing the relative condition of protected features in the larger MCZ to which it refers, and in which managed exploitation of resources will be continuing. The reference areas must either be within an rMCZ, or may be the entire rMCZ if appropriate. In practice, most of the regional projects identified small reference areas within larger proposed MCZ areas. Guidance on the identification and ecological criteria for reference areas was provided by Natural England and the JNCC.[139]

(iii) The regional MCZ projects

The four regional projects in England and Wales were:

Balanced Seas Regional Stakeholder Group (South East England)[140]
The Balanced Sea project identified 30 rMCZs with conservation objectives for each and management objectives that were developed with local regional and public authority stakeholders. The project recommend 25 reference areas within which all extraction, human-based deposit, and disturbance would be prohibited, 24 within the rMCZs and one in an existing SAC designated under the Habitats Directive. The reference areas were identified for 42 out of the 45 conservation futures identified in the Ecological Network Guidance that occurred in the region. The inherent tension between encouraging strict adherence to the Ecological Network Guidance and promoting a stakeholder-led consultation process is evident

[137] See for an example of this methodology deployed the Balanced Seas MCZ report (below, n. 140) at 59–60: <http://www.balancedseas.org/p./national_mcz.html>.

[138] As to which, see Chapter 6 and Box 6.4, at p. 239.

[139] <http://www.naturalengland.org.uk/Images/MCZ-regional-guidance_tcm6-23451.pdf>.

[140] See *Balanced Seas Marine Conservation Zone Project, Final Recommendations*, 7th September 2011 available at: <http://www.balancedseas.org/p./national_mcz.html>.

in this group's recommendations: one recommended reference area[141] had virtually no support from the regional stakeholder group, but was included in the report's recommendations because it was recognized that this would be necessary if the ecological network guidance objectives were to be observed.

Finding Sanctuary project (South West England and Scilly Isles)

This project engaged widespread stakeholder involvement, with a steering group of 41 members representing a wide range of stakeholder groups with an interest in the use and exploitation of the marine environment, representing commercial fishing interests, recreational use (for example, kayaking, scuba-diving, recreational angling), tourism, the aggregates industry, ports, environmental NGOs, scientific advisers, government agencies (Natural England and the Environment Agency), and the Ministry of Defence. This produced a final report in mid-2011[142] which identified 58 recommended MCZs (rMCZs), 13 in the offshore area beyond 12 miles, 32 rMCZs within 12 nautical miles of the south-west coastline, and a further 13 reference areas within which all extraction, human-based deposit, and disturbance would be prohibited.[143] These formed the basis for public consultation on the proposals under the terms of the 2009 Act prior to formal designation.

Irish Sea Conservation Zones project[144]

The Irish Sea project covered the Irish Sea region from the Scottish border at the Solway Firth to South West Wales. It had a stakeholder group of 40, representing a wide range of users and industries including: commercial fishing interests; leisure and recreational groups; heritage interests; landowners; research bodies; and local government and other public bodies. Focus groups were held with user groups at a number of locations in Scotland, the Isle of Man, Wales, and Northern Ireland, and its proposals were developed in a series of eight workshops. The project recommended 14 rMCZs in the Irish Sea offshore between the coast of the UK and Ireland, and two estuarine rMCZs, the Solway Firth and the Lune and Wyre estuaries (Lancaster).

Net Gain (North Sea Marine Conservation Zone Project)[145]

This project covered the whole of the east coast of England north of London, with a stakeholder advisory panel and four regional 'hubs'—sub-groups of stakeholders covering the North East, Yorkshire and Humber, Lincolnshire, and the East of England. The regional hubs recommended the establishment of the following: six

141 St Catherine's Point West, off the Isle of Wight, included because of its sub-tidal broad-scale habitats. See *Balanced Seas Marine Conservation Zone Project, Final Recommendations,* 7 September 2011, at para. 2.3 and Table 12.

142 Available at: <http://www.finding-sanctuary.org/p./news/442>.

143 See *Finding Sanctuary: Final Recommendations* (Summer 2011) at 14–19 for maps showing the rMCZs proposed.

144 Available at: <http://www.irishseaconservation.org.uk/MCZ-recommendations>.

145 Available at: <http://www.netgainmcz.org/docs/Net_Gain_Final_Rec_v1_1.pdf>.

rMCZs and three reference areas in the North East region; five rMCZs and two reference areas in the Yorkshire region; four rMCZs and seven reference areas in the Lincolnshire region; and three rMCZs and one reference area in the East of England regional hub. The Lincolnshire hub within the Net Gain project covers the Wash and North Norfolk coasts, which are an ecologically rich area with a large number of existing protected areas, including the North Norfolk SAC,[146] North Norfolk Coast SPA,[147] North Norfolk Cost Ramsar Wetlands,[148] and a number of SSSIs and National Nature Reserves. The rMCZs in this area were designed to complement the existing protected area network, and include the largest number of reference areas in the entire Net Gain project area, and in which no human extraction or resource use will be permitted post-designation. The reference areas are targeted to protecting important populations of starlet sea anemone, coastal salt marshes, saline reed beds, and sea grass.

(d) The ecological network guidance

The MCZ project sought to balance the need for wide stakeholder consultation and consensus with the application of scientific data to identify (i) the conservation features in each rMCZ, (ii) conservation objectives for each site, and (iii) the management required to maintain its features to maintain them or to bring them into a recovering condition post-designation. Although the designation process is explicitly less technocratic than that applied to the identification and notification of terrestrial protected areas, such as SSSIs, the application of scientific criteria and evidence is nevertheless essential if the MCZ network is to deliver the meaningful conservation of key marine habitats, and of species of marine plants, invertebrates, and fish. Ecological cohesion was injected into the designation process by requiring each stakeholder group to follow the Ecological Network Guidance (hereafter ENG) provided by the JNCC and Natural England, and by provision for the review of the rMCZs against the ecological criteria by DEFRA's scientific advisory panel. Although there is, therefore, a substantial technocratic element within the designation process, this is quite different to that applied in relation to terrestrial protected areas, where the JNCC guidance for the selection of biological and geological SSSIs and SACs[149] plays the central role in identifying sites for notification and protection, without formal prior stakeholder consultation on site identification, on identifying and devising conservation objectives or appropriate habitat management.

[146] For which see the *Natura 2000 Standard Data* form available at: <http://www.jncc.gov.uk/ProtectedSites/SACselection/n2kforms/UK0019838.pdf>.

[147] <http://www.jncc.gov.uk/default.asp. x?page=2008>.

[148] On which see the *Information Sheet on Ramsar Wetland (RIS)* available at: <http://www.jncc.gov.uk/pdf/RIS/UK11048.pdf>.

[149] Guidelines for the Selection of Biological SSSIs (JNCC Peterborough) available at: <http://www.jncc.gov.uk/page-1457>. Discussed in Chapter 3, at pp. 70ff.

(i) Network design principles

The ENG sets out seven network design principles. The steps in the designation process, and the different stages at which each design principle is relevant, are set out in Box 7.2.

Representivity. The marine protected area network, including MCZs, needs to protect the range of biodiversity found in the seas around the UK. The ENG seek to ensure this by classifying habitats and species into 'broad-scale habitat types' and ensuring the protection of examples of these across the network as a whole. The Guidance also identifies those features that are of conservation importance because they are known to be rare, threatened, or declining (FOCI), and stipulates that examples of each of the 22 FOCI should be protected within MPAs *in each regional MCZ area* where they occur.[150] The guidance also identifies low or limited mobility FOCI that should be protected in each regional MCZ project area where the occur.[151] The range of marine habitats and species is immense and defies full categorization. To ensure a representative protection of the full range of habitats the ENG groups habitat types with shared ecological requirements and sets out 'broad-scale' habitats that should be protected within MPAs; for example, high-, moderate-, and low-energy intertidal rock, coastal salt marshes, and saline reed beds, sub-tidal coarse sediment, sub-tidal sand, sub-tidal mud, and the deep seabed, which encompasses different habitat sub types.[152]

Replication. The guidance recommends that at least two examples of each broad-scale habitat type should be protected in each MCZ project area where their distribution allows, and that at least three to five separate examples of each FOCI where they are present and their distribution so allows.[153] This is important to reduce the risk of damaging events impacting the habitat type and to reduce the impact of long-term change negatively affecting the features of protected areas.

Adequacy. Adequacy dictates that an MPA *network* must be sufficiently large and include a large enough proportion of features in order to deliver its ecological objectives and enable the features long-term protection and recovery. The guidelines therefore specify that for each broad-scale habitat the MPAs within each MCZ project area should collectively protect a proportion of the habitat known to occur in that area. For most broad-scale habitat types, the proportions are fixed at

[150] Natural England and the Joint Nature Conservation Committee (2010), *The Marine Conservation Zone Project: Ecological Network Guidance*. Sheffield and Peterborough, UK, at para. 4.2.2, and Table 2 on p. 31 of the 22 FOCI. The FOCI include for example blue mussel beds, deep sea sponge aggregations, file shell beds, maerl beds, horse mussel beds, honeycomb worms, sea grass beds, and estuarine rocky habitats.

[151] Natural England and the Joint Nature Conservation Committee (2010), *The Marine Conservation Zone Project: Ecological Network Guidance*, Table 3 atp. 32.

[152] See Natural England and the Joint Nature Conservation Committee (2010), *The Marine Conservation Zone Project: Ecological Network Guidance*, Table 1 at p. 31 for broad-scale habitats. The guidance uses the EUNIS pan-European habitat types classification system, for which see <http://eunis.eea.europa.eu/habitats.jsp>.

[153] Natural England and the Joint Nature Conservation Committee (2010), *The Marine Conservation Zone Project: Ecological Network Guidance* at para. 4.3.3.

Box 7.2 Marine Conservation Zones—Identification, Design, and Designation

The Marine and Coastal Access Act 2009 and JNCC/Natural England Ecological Network Guidance (ENG) provide for each regional MCZ project to adhere to the following process prior to formal designation of an area as an MCZ under the 2009 Act.[154]

Step 1: Assess existing MPAs for their contribution to the ENG under the criteria of representivity, adequacy, replication, and connectivity (regional MCZ project).

Step 2: The priority is to ensure that the MCZ network protects habitats representing the range of biodiversity present in UK waters, and habitats and species that are rare, threatened, or declining in UK waters ('Features of Conservation Importance' or FOCI) (regional MCZ project).

Step 3: Each conservation feature needs to be replicated in two or more protected areas, and an adequate amount for each feature protected in order to ensure its long-term protection or recovery (replication and adequacy). Selection of possible MCZs applying criteria in steps 1–3 (regional MCZ project)

Step 4: Selection of rMCZs. Choice between areas that are comparable in meeting the principles of replication, representivity, and adequacy. The ENG principles of viability, connectivity, protection, and best available evidence are key to completing the process of selection. Each MCZ must be large enough to ensure that viable populations of species and areas of habitat are protected (viability); it should contributes to maximizing connectivity between relevant habitats, and to include areas of particular ecological importance (connectivity); and knowledge of the vulnerability of its features to impacts, knowledge of its condition, and its value to science, and for monitoring purposes should also be used to select between comparable sites for possible designation (regional MCZ project).

Step 5: Draft conservation objectives and fix boundaries for rMCZ (regional MCZ project).

Step 6: Review of rMCZ by Scientific Advisory Panel of DEFRA (SAP).

Step 7: Public Consultation.

Step 8: Review of rMCZ, conservation objectives and management plan, taking into account recommendations of SAP, responses to public consultation (regional MCZ project).

Step 9: Designation (Secretary of State).

The procedure seeks to provide a balanced approach that meets the needs for both wide stakeholder consultation on the identification and designation of MCZs, while at the same time ensuring that the conservation objectives for each site meet relevant scientific criteria and that appropriate management techniques are deployed in the designation in order to achieve the MCZ's stated conservation objectives.

[154] A detailed flow-chart showing the iterations between the different stages of the designation process is to be found in the Ecological Network Guidance: Natural England and the Joint Nature Conservation Committee (2010), *The Marine Conservation Zone Project: Ecological Network Guidance*. Sheffield and Peterborough, UK. Figure 3 at 25.

between 21 per cent and 38 per cent, and in some cases a lower figure; for example, between 15 and 31 per cent for high-energy infralittoral rock.[155] This equates to the protection of between 10 per cent and 40 per cent of the total area of broad-scale habitats within MPAs in each MCZ regional project area.[156] For features of conservation interest (FOCI), insufficient reliable data exist to calculate the percentages needed to settle proportions necessary for adequacy of protection, and the guidance therefore suggests that adequacy of protection can best be achieved by following the guidelines on replication viability and connectivity.[157]

Viability. If the focus of the principle of adequacy is the MPA network, viability is determined by the size and shape of each individual marine conservation zone, and its effective management. Each individual rMCZ must be able to maintain the integrity of its features—in other words, it must be able to maintain the population of the species it harbours, or the condition and extent of the marine habitat to be found within it. The ENG therefore recommend that MCZs for broad-scale habitats should have a minimum diameter of 5 m with the average size being 10–20 km in diameter.[158] The guidance also specifies the size of minimum patches of FOCI within each MCZ.[159]

Connectivity. The connectivity principle is intended to ensure that populations of a different parts of a species range are linked by the movement of eggs, larvae, juveniles, and adults. If there is scientific evidence of the dispersal areas for life cycles of FOCI the guidelines recommend that these by sued to determine the separation distances between individual MCZs. But in the absence of such scientific data the guidance recommends that MCZs of similar habitat should be no more than 40–80 km apart.[160]

Protection. The level of protection deemed appropriate for each MCZ will be linked directly to its conservation objectives and the aspirations that these set out of the conservation of its features. These will be set out in the site designation order, which will provide the central reference point for identifying and managing activities that may impact upon MCZ features if left uncontrolled. The guidelines therefore recommend that conservation objectives should ensure that MCZs

[155] See Natural England and the Joint Nature Conservation Committee (2010), *The Marine Conservation Zone Project: Ecological Network Guidance* Table 5 at p. 38. Table 6 gives broad-scale habitat types for which principles of connectivity are important to determine adequacy, eg in the case of coastal salt marshes or habitats on the deep seabed.

[156] Natural England and the Joint Nature Conservation Committee (2010), *The Marine Conservation Zone Project: Ecological Network Guidance* at para. 4.4.4 at p. 39.

[157] Natural England and the Joint Nature Conservation Committee (2010), *The Marine Conservation Zone Project: Ecological Network Guidance* para. 4.4.4 at p. 40.

[158] These minimum size criteria were determined following research commissioned by natural England that examined the distances moved by mature adults of 72 species of invertebrate, fish, and seaweed groups: this showed that 43 per cent did not move at all after settlement and a further 38 per cent typically moved less than 10 km after reaching maturity: see Natural England and the Joint Nature Conservation Committee (2010), *The Marine Conservation Zone Project: Ecological Network Guidance* at 4.5.4.

[159] Natural England and the Joint Nature Conservation Committee (2010), *The Marine Conservation Zone Project: Ecological Network Guidance* 4.5.3 and Tables 7 and 8.

[160] Natural England and the Joint Nature Conservation Committee (2010), *The Marine Conservation Zone Project: Ecological Network Guidance* at 4.6.3.

collectively contribute to the protection and recovery of the marine environment by determining the protection levels that are necessary to support the features in favourable conservation condition.[161] Conservation objectives will depend upon the specific features for which each MCZ is designated, and the sensitivity and condition of those features. This means that different levels of restriction on human activities within an MCZ may be necessary and appropriate to satisfactorily achieve different site objectives. In this context the identification of 'reference areas'[162] in which all human activity is prohibited will provide an important opportunity to demonstrate the unimpacted state of a broad range of marine habitats. The guidance therefore recommends that reference areas should ideally cover the range of broad-scale habitats and FOCI found throughout each MCZ Project areas. These can be MCZs in their own right or can be nested within proposed zones in order to reduce so-called 'edge effects' that are often experienced along the boundaries of highly protected areas.[163]

(ii) Application of precautionary principle

It is self-evident that the best available scientific information and evidence should be used to ensure that an ecologically coherent network of MCZs is built. The ENG recommend using a precautionary approach, suggesting that where there is scientific uncertainty, a precautionary approach should be used in designating MPA networks, and this will involve using the best available evidence and information to make decisions rather than waiting for new information.[164] Identifying MCZs should also take account of local and lay knowledge, and not be based solely upon scientific data, however.[165]

(iii) Relevance of additional ecological considerations

Areas of additional ecological importance are issues that make a disproportionately greater contribution than other areas to ecosystem function, biodiversity, or resilience in the marine environment. There may, for example, be areas that support specific ecological processes, or support particular life stages of a protected species

[161] Natural England and the Joint Nature Conservation Committee (2010), *The Marine Conservation Zone Project: Ecological Network Guidance* at 4.7.2. For favourable conservation status, see Chapter 6, p. 238 and the statutory nature Conservation Body's common standards monitoring standards, discussed further at p. 239.

[162] Ie areas within each MCZ within which all human extraction or depositional activity is prohibited: see p. 264.

[163] Natural England and the Joint Nature Conservation Committee (2010), *The Marine Conservation Zone Project: Ecological Network Guidance* 4.7.4 at 51.

[164] 'Lack of certainty should not be a reason for postponing proportionate decisions on site selection'. DEFRA, ministerial statement on the creating of a network of marine protected areas (2010); The Government's strategy for contributing to the delivery of a UK Network of Marine Protected Areas (London, DEFRA, 2010).

[165] See Natural England and the Joint Nature Conservation Committee (2010), *the Marine Conservation Zone Project: Ecological Network Guidance.* Sheffield and Peterborough, UK, at para. 4.8.3.

(for example, breeding grounds) or are especially important because they support a high level of biodiversity. The ENG therefore suggests that where they are present, such additional ecological criteria should be taken into account in MCZ identification and design. A good example is provided by areas that are important for key life cycle stages and behaviours in marine species; breeding, foraging, resting, and wintering, for example. A marine species may be dispersed for a large part of the year, but congregate in a specific location for breeding and other purposes, and this factor should be taken into account in ensuring this key life cycle feature is protected. The ENG therefore suggest that when selecting MCZs for broad-scale habitats and FOCI, special attention should be given to including important areas for key life cycle stages of species, such as spawning, nursery or juvenile areas, and to include areas important for foraging, breeding, moulting, wintering, or resting.[166]

(iv) Review of rMCZs against the ecological guidance

The recommendations of the four regional projects were assessed by DEFRA's science advisory panel (SAP) for their coherence, and for the degree to which they demonstrated compliance with the Ecological Network Guidance.[167] The SAP report drew attention to some underlying methodological flaws in the operation of the Guidance itself, and also made criticisms of some of the regional project recommendations for MCZ designation.

The principal methodological flaws identified by the SAP concerned, firstly, the use of conservation objectives that aimed at enabling a feature to 'recover' and, secondly, the identification and designation of reference areas in which all human extraction and disturbance would be prohibited. 'Recovery' does not, in the context of the marine environment, necessarily involve returning a habitat or feature to a condition in which it has formerly existed. The SAP therefore criticized the assumption in the guidelines that the removal of anthropogenic pressures will return a feature to a pre-existing 'good' status. This is unsafe, because habitats and species are exposed to many non-human threats, including predation and climate change, and many of these cannot be mediated locally.[168] It also means that post-designation assessment of whether conservation objectives are being met would be impossible. Given that ecological changes within an rMCZ are inevitable, they recommended that the primary focus should instead simply be on the removal of damaging activities within MCZs, as this will bring long-term beneficial consequences, even if the time scales are uncertain.[169] The SAP also criticized the formulation of conservation objectives in several of the regional MCZ recommendations; for example, the preponderance of

[166] See Natural England and the Joint Nature Conservation Committee (2010), *The Marine Conservation Zone Project: Ecological Network Guidance* at 5.2.3.

[167] Science Advisory Panel, Assessment of the Marine Conservation Zone Regional Projects Final Recommendations (15 November 2011) available at: <http://www.defra.gsi.gov.uk/publications/>.

[168] Science Advisory Panel, Assessment of the Marine Conservation Zone Regional Projects Final Recommendations (n.163 at para. 7.1.2.2.

[169] Science Advisory Panel, Assessment of the Marine Conservation Zone Regional Projects Final Recommendations at paras. 7.1.4, 8.5.2.3.

conservation objectives set to 'maintain', rather than improve, conservation features in rMCZs in the Net Gain project report,[170] and inconsistencies between the conservation objectives set for similar broad-scale habitats, such as offshore sediment habitats, by different MCZ projects.[171]

The other overarching criticism was that the regional MCZ projects had failed to meet the requirements set out in the guidance to identify a complete set of viable reference areas.[172] This highlights the inherent tension in a stakeholder-led designation process between, on the one hand, achieving consensus to the designation of protected areas—and the accompanying resource use limitations that will follow—and on the other of establishing and maintaining the ecological coherence and objectives of the MCZ network. In the case of inshore habitats, for example, the SAP concluded that the regional projects had ignored the guidance 'in response to socio-economic pressures, and the fraction of near and inshore habitats that are afforded strong protection is [as a result] disappointingly small'.[173] This is a major failing, as it potentially compromises the ability of reference areas to provide the minimum feasible protection to threatened and/or rare flora and fauna, and also compromises the establishment of sound scientific benchmarks for the future evidence-based management of the protected areas network itself.[174] The report recommended that DEFRA reconsider the design criteria for reference areas with a view to expanding them in accordance with the Ecological Network Guidance.

The statutory nature Conservation Bodies also published advice to the Secretary of State on the regional MCZ project outcomes. This concluded, as had the SAP, that the recommendations failed to meet the ENG criteria for the designation of reference areas. They also recommended the alteration of the conservation objectives of a number of rMCZs; some 20 features across the network should move from 'recovery' to 'maintain' and 29 from 'maintain' to 'recovery'.[175] A three-month public consultation on the four regional projects' recommendations is to take place from December 2012. Following public consultation, the rMCZs, their boundaries and conservation objectives will be refined taking into account the public consultation responses, the views of the stakeholder groups, the SAP advice, and that of the statutory Conservation Bodies, before each MCZ is planned to proceed to formal designation in 2013.

170 See Science Advisory Panel, Assessment of the Marine Conservation Zone Regional Projects Final Recommendations at 5.1.6, 5.2.6.

171 See Science Advisory Panel, Assessment of the Marine Conservation Zone Regional Projects Final Recommendations 7.1.8; contrasting the conservation objectives in the rMCZs in the Finding Sanctuary project set as 'recovery' with those in the net gain project for the same habitat feature which were largely set as 'maintain'.

172 Science Advisory Panel, Assessment of the Marine Conservation Zone Regional Projects Final Recommendations para. 7.4.1.

173 Science Advisory Panel, Assessment of the Marine Conservation Zone Regional Projects Final Recommendations para. 7.4. The number of reference areas proposed by the Balanced Seas project was eg criticized as falling far short of the ENG recommendations to an extent that compromised the scientific basis of the network of protected areas: para. 4.2.7.

174 See Science Advisory Panel, Assessment of the Marine Conservation Zone Regional Projects Final Recommendations para. 7.4.1.

175 See Marine Conservation Zone Project Newsletter 10 July 2012. Available at: <http://jncc.defra.gov.uk/p.-6240#regionaladvice>.

Marine Conservation Zones: Management and Protection

(a) Marine planning and licensing

The management and protection of MCZs and their conservation features must be set in the context of the new regime for marine planning and marine licensing established under the Marine and Coastal Access Act 2009. The problems inherent in implementing effective conservation strategies for the marine environment are essentially of the same character as those faced in relation to terrestrial habitats: adjusting rights to resource exploitation in order to pursue a public interest objective in conservation. The difficulty in the marine context is, however, that there are many more stakeholders with resource entitlements and interests whose activities may impact upon the environment; and the allocation of access to marine resources is not mediated through property rights in most cases. As we saw in Chapter 4, the management and protection of terrestrial protected areas is primarily mediated by varying property rights in land, or in some cases, removing them, and this provides the principal means by which access to land-based resources and the means to exploit them is adjusted in the interests of nature conservation. The marine environment has, in contrast, the character of a common pool resource in which user rights are open, and to which property rights have little relevance. This has changed in recent years, with many marine resources withdrawn from the common pool model by the introduction of requirements for appropriators to obtain licenses permitting exploitation of certain resources (oil, gas, commercial fishing, for example) and in the case of commercial fishing by the introduction of quantitative limitations through quotas on the numbers of fish of different species that can be caught; for example, under the European Common Fisheries Policy.

The 2009 Act adopts an approach to the conservation of marine habitats and species that is based on a strategy comprising two complementary legislative pillars:

- The Act provides for integrated marine planning throughout UK inshore and offshore waters, and extends the licensing regime by applying a more broadly based requirement for 'marine licences' before a wide range of activities can lawfully be carried out. This extends to the whole of the UK marine waters.
- Within the geographically more defined parameters of each MCZ the 2009 Act then subjects the carrying out by public bodies of a wide range of licensing and other functions to a general duty to further the conservation objectives of the zone, and to a statutory consultation requirement if it wishes to carrying out operations or activities that may damage the conservation interest of the area. This requires consultation with the statutory Conservation Body prior to action being taken.

The planning framework for the marine environment is based upon, firstly, the establishment of a Marine Policy Statement by the Secretary of State and Scottish and Welsh ministers in which they set out their general policies for achieving sustainable development in the UK marine area.[176] The waters around the UK are divided by the 2009 Act into eight planning regions: the English, Scottish, Welsh, and Northern Ireland inshore and offshore regions. Marine planning authorities are then established for each of these regions, with the exception of the Scottish and Northern Ireland offshore regions.[177] The planning authority will be the Secretary of State in relation to the English inshore and offshore regions, the Scottish and Welsh ministers, and the Department of Environment in Northern Ireland. The marine planning authority can produce a marine plan for all or any part of the area within its planning remit.[178] Any public authority with responsibility for granting authorizations or permits within the area covered by a Marine Policy Statement and, where one has been adopted, a marine plan 'must take any authorization or enforcement decision in accordance with the appropriate marine policy documents, unless relevant considerations indicate otherwise'.[179] This gives the marine plan a status akin to that of a development plan under the Town and Country Planning legislation,[180] and means that the issuance of permits and authorizations for extraction activities, fishing, leisure, and other activities within a protected marine area will be plan-led.

A licence is required before any 'licensable marine activity' can be carried out,[181] and it is a criminal offence to carry out a licensable activity without one, or to break the conditions attached to a licence if granted.[182] The licensing authority can confer on the enforcement authority the power to issue fixed and variable monetary penalties in appropriate cases as an alternative to prosecution.[183] The activities requiring the grant of a licence are widely drawn in the 2009 Act.[184] They include depositing in the sea, or on or under the seabed, in any part of the UK marine licensing area any substance or object from any vessel, vehicle, aircraft, or marine structure, or from any structure adapted to make deposits at sea or from any container floating in the sea.[185] A licence is also required to scuttle any vessel or structure in the licensing area; to construct or adapt any structure in the sea or on or under the seabed; to use a vessel or aircraft to remove any substance from the sea or seabed; to carry out any form of dredging; to use or deploy explosive substances in the sea or on the seabed; to incinerate a substance on any vehicle, vessel, marine, or floating container in the UK marine licensing area, and to load any vessel, vehicle, or floating structure at any British port with the intention of incinerating it

[176] S. 44 Marine and Coastal Access Act 2009.

[177] Ss. 49, 50 Marine and Coastal Access Act 2009.

[178] See s. 51 Marine and Coastal Access Act 2009. There are detailed provisions in Schedule 6 for the preparation and publication of draft plans and for their adoption.

[179] S. 58(1) Marine and Coastal Access Act 2009.

[180] See s. 70 Town and Country Planning Act 1996.

[181] S. 65 Marine and Coastal Access Act 2009.

[182] S. 85(1) Marine and Coastal Access Act 2009.

[183] See s. 93–97 and Schedule 7 Marine and Coastal Access Act 2009.

[184] See s. 66 Marine and Coastal Access Act 2009.

[185] If the deposit, etc. is made from a British ship, aircraft, or marine structure, or is controlled from such a vessel, etc., then the licence requirement applied wherever the deposit is made, even if outside the UK marine licensing area: S. 66(1) 1 and 2 Marine and Coastal Access Act 2009.

anywhere in the world. Licences can be granted either unconditionally or subject to conditions, or they may be refused.[186] The licensing requirement is subject to exceptions, principally in cases where the activity concerned is already subject to an authorization procedure under pre-existing legislation; for example, in the case of dredging undertaken on behalf of a harbour authority under the Harbours Act 1964 or under a local Act of Parliament,[187] or for oil and gas exploration activities and the building of oil extraction facilities that require a licence under the Petroleum production legislation.[188]

(b) Duties imposed on public bodies

The 2009 Act imposes a number of general duties on public bodies that must be adhered to in the carrying out of any management or other functions in relation to marine areas that are within or comprise MCZs. These duties apply to any 'public' authority, and this includes ministers of the Crown, public bodies, and public office holders. A public body for these purposes includes a local authority, local planning authority, government department, Northern Ireland Department, and a statutory undertaker.[189] The reference to public authorities is also widely drawn: in England it includes any county council, district council, parish council, London Borough Council, the council of the City of London, and that of the Scilly Isles; in relation to Scotland it includes a council for any local government area: and in relation to Wales it means a county council, county borough council, or community council; and in Northern Ireland any district council.[190] Statutory undertakers subject to the duty are widely defined by reference to the planning legislation,[191] and this will include electricity undertakers, water management companies, and other utility companies.

The duty has three facets:

- Every public authority must exercise its functions in a manner which the authority considers best furthers the conservation objectives stated for the MCZ, and where it is not possible to further those objectives it must exercise them in a manner which the authority 'considers least hinders the achievement of those objectives'.[192] If it considers the exercise of its functions will hinder the conservation objectives of an MCZ, it must inform the statutory nature Conservation Body of that fact.[193]

[186] S. 71 Marine and Coastal Access Act 2009.

[187] See s. 75.

[188] See s. 77 Marine and Coastal Access Act 2009. The relevant legislation in this case is the Petroleum Act 1998, Petroleum (Production) Act 1934, and the Energy Act 2008 (storage of carbon dioxide).

[189] S. 322(1) Marine and Coastal Access Act 2009.

[190] S. 322(2) Marine and Coastal Access Act 2009.

[191] Ie Town and Country Planning Act 1990 Part 11, Town and Country Planning (Scotland) Act 1997 Part 10 and the Planning (Northern Ireland) Order 1991, SI 1991/1220.

[192] See s. 125(2) Marine and Coastal Access Act 2009 to be adjudged by the authority itself or (for example) the statutory Conservation Body is unstated.

[193] S. 125(3) Marine and Coastal Access Act 2009.

- If a public authority intends to carry out an act which is capable of affecting the protected features of a MCZ or 'any ecological or geomorphological process on which the conservation of any protected feature of an MCZ is . . . dependant', and it considers that there is a significant risk of this hindering the conservation objectives of the MCZ, then it must inform the statutory Conservation Body of that fact.[194]
- If the public authority has given notice to the statutory Conservation Body that its actions are likely to hinder the conservation objectives of an MCZ, then it must wait 28 days from the giving of the notification before deciding whether to carry out the act in question.[195] This creates, in effect, a statutory consultation period within which the authority and the statutory Conservation Body can investigate whether an alternative is available that protects the conservation features at risk. The consultation period does not apply if the Conservation Body notifies the authority that it need not wait before carrying out the operation or if 'the authority thinks that there is an urgent need to do the act'.[196]

It will be immediately apparent that the statutory duty created by these provisions is of a very limited and weak nature. In the first place the overall duty is of a balancing nature—the duty is imposed only 'in so far as consistent with the [function's] proper exercise'.[197] Secondly, a de minimis rule is applied—the duty only applies where the exercise of the functions will 'significantly' impact upon the conservation objectives of the MCZ.[198] Whether the evaluation of the significance or otherwise of the function's exercise is to be in the sole competence of the public authority itself, or, for example, the statutory Conservation Body, is left unresolved in the Act. Thirdly, the duty to notify the Conservation Body only arises if the public authority or public body concerned—not the Conservation Body—considers that the action will lead to a significant risk of hindering the conservation objectives of the MCZ. And (finally) even if the duty applies, the statutory consultation period does not apply if the authority considers that there is an urgent need to do the act. The basis on which this decision is to be made is left at large and entirely for the public authority. In view of these limitations, it is extremely unlikely that an alleged failure to act in accordance with the duty in the 2009 Act would be justiciable.

A public authority that, in the course of exercising its functions, becomes aware of the commission of an offence that may significantly hinder the conservation objectives of an MCZ must bring this to the attention of the statutory Conservation Body and 'the relevant authority'.[199] In England this will be the Marine Management Organisation, and in Scotland and Wales, respectively the Scottish

[194] S. 125(4) and (5) Marine and Coastal Access Act 2009.
[195] S. 125(7) Marine and Coastal Access Act 2009.
[196] See s. 125(8) Marine and Coastal Access Act 2009.
[197] See s. 125(2) Marine and Coastal Access Act 2009.
[198] See s. 125(1) Marine and Coastal Access Act 2009: 'any function the exercise of which is capable of affecting (other than insignificantly)' the protected features of a MCZ.
[199] S. 125(9), (10) Marine and Coastal Access Act 2009.

and Welsh ministers.[200] The statutory Conservation Bodies can produce advice or guidance on the matters capable of damaging protected features, or ecological, and/or geomorphological processes, and how MCZ conservation objectives can be promoted.[201] The guidance can either be of general application or limited to specific MCZs. Where guidance has been issued, all public authorities and public bodies must have regard to it when exercising their functions in relation to any MCZ to which the guidance applies.[202]

(c) Duties with regard to decision making

Similar duties apply where a public authority has responsibility for determining an application for an authorization to carry out any activity or action. These will apply to the grant of any licence, consent, permission, or any approval or confirmation required for the carrying out of any action affecting an MCZ.[203] The duty is widely drawn, and will apply not only to marine licensing decisions, but to, for example, development control decisions made by local planning authorities, oil and gas exploration and extraction licenses, and licenses for fishing and dumping material in an MCZ.

A statutory consultation period is imposed when a public authority has to consider the grant of an authorization that is capable of affecting the protected features of an MCZ or any of the ecological or geomorphological processes on which their conservation is dependant. The authority must inform the statutory Conservation Body, and it must then wait 28 days until deciding whether to grant or refuse an authorization for carrying out the act in question. As well as imposing a requirement for a statutory consultation with the Conservation Body, the 2009 Act also places limitations on the circumstances in which an authorization can be given. A public authority cannot grant an authorization for the doing of an act that is capable of affecting the protected features or processes in an MCZ[204] unless:

- The applicant for the authorization satisfies the authority that there is no significant risk of the act hindering the achievement of the conservation objectives of the MCZ.
- If the applicant is unable to do so, then s/he must instead satisfy the authority that there is no other means of proceeding with the act that would create a substantially lower risk to the conservation objectives of the MCZ. It must also be established that the public benefit of proceeding with the act outweighs the risk of damage to the environment, and the person seeking the authorization must undertake measures of equivalent environmental benefit to the damage that the act will or is likely to have in or on the MCZ.[205]

[200] S. 125(11) Marine and Coastal Access Act 2009.
[201] See s. 127 Marine and Coastal Access Act 2009.
[202] S. 125(12) Marine and Coastal Access Act 2009.
[203] S. 126(10) Marine and Coastal Access Act 2009.
[204] S. 126(5) Marine and Coastal Access Act 2009.
[205] See s. 126(7) Marine and Coastal Access Act 2009.

Where the authority considers there to be a risk to the conservation objectives of the conservation zone, satisfying the second of the conditions discussed earlier imposes a number of requirements on the applicant. In the first place, it will be necessary to demonstrate that alternative options for the action or development have been considered, either in terms of its location or the processes to be used in its execution.[206] Secondly, the applicant will have to undertake a cost–benefit analysis to demonstrate that the public benefit outweighs the risk of damage to the environment. The 2009 Act gives no guidance on how this is to be done. And, finally, the Act applies a measure of conservation offsetting; that is, if the project or action goes ahead the applicant will have to make arrangements to ensure that 'measures of equivalent environmental benefit' replace the damage to the MCZ that will ensue. The public authority can impose conditions on the grant of a license or permission, etc. to ensure that offsetting measures are undertaken after the authorization has been granted.[207] Guidance can be issued by the statutory Conservation Bodies, and must be taken into account by the authority when exercising its decision making powers.[208] The Act itself gives little guidance on the nature of the cost–benefit analysis required by the limitations on the power to grant permission, or on the evaluation of conservation measures offered by an applicant in order to comply with the offsetting requirement, and in both cases the statutory guidance will prove especially helpful.

(d) Breach of duty

Sanctions of a very limited kind are applied by the 2009 Act in cases where a public authority has allegedly acted in contravention of its statutory duties in sections 125 and 126 of the 2009 Act outlined earlier, as to decision making or the exercise of its functions in relation to an MCZ. If the statutory Conservation Body is of the opinion that it has failed to comply with either of the statutory duties (p. 275), or that it has failed to follow the advice or guidance provided to it by the Conservation Body, then it may request an explanation from the authority of its failure to do so. The only sanction is a requirement that, in this case, the public authority provide an explanation in writing to the statutory Conservation Body. The sufficiency or adequacy of the explanation is beyond review and there is no further sanction available to the Conservation Body if it is dissatisfied with the explanation given.

Furthermore, the nature of the duties imposed on public authorities by sections 125 and 126 is such that they will be impossible to enforce by judicial review. The duty in section 125 is expressed in statutory language that presents a classic example of the formulation of a 'balancing' duty—the duty to exercise public functions to assist the conservation objectives of an MCZ only applies 'so far as consistent with

[206] See s. 126(8) Marine and Coastal Access Act 2009, which refers to carrying out the act 'in another manner' or 'at another location'.

[207] S. 126(9) Marine and Coastal Access Act 2009.

[208] S. 126(10) Marine and Coastal Access Act 2009. The guidance will be issued under s. 127.

[the functions] proper exercise'. And the duty that arises in both sections 125 and section 126 is, in each case, subject to the pre requisite that the authority itself forms a subjective view of what the conservation objectives of the MCZ require for their fulfilment. The duty in section 125 is one that requires the authority to exercise its functions *in the manner which the authority considers* best furthers the conservation objectives stated for the MCZ.[209] And the duty as to decision making applies *if the authority believes that there is or may be a significant risk* of the action requiring consent, etc. hindering the conservation objectives of the MCZ in question.[210] There is no provision in the 2009 Act for the evaluation of the merits of the authority's decision against ecological or other criteria, or for its review by the statutory Conservation Body. This means that, in common with many statutory duties of this type, their exercise will be almost impossible to challenge in the courts on judicial review, other than on grounds of *Wednesbury* irrationality; that is, on the basis that a decision—for example, to grant a marine license—is so unreasonable that no reasonable authority could ever have arrived at it on the evidence presented.[211] This has already been discussed in Chapter 2.[212]

(e) By-laws and orders for protecting MCZs

Where potentially damaging activities in an MCZ require the grant of a license or authorization before the can be lawfully carried out, then protection is primarily delivered through the controls on the administrative permitting procedures already discussed. In those cases where no administrative authorization is required for a particular type of activity in a MCZ, on the other hand, protection is principally delivered by the imposition of by-laws (in England) and orders (in Wales) controlling the circumstances in which certain types of activity can be carried out, and prohibiting the disturbance, taking, or killing of wild species of bird, plant, fish, or animal. By-laws will be especially relevant to the control of leisure activities, and the control of the free passage of vessels and vehicles through or within an MCZ.

(i) By-laws (England)

The Marine Management Organization (MMO) has power to make by-laws for the furtherance of the conservation of MCZs in England.[213] The power is wide-ranging and flexible,[214] and can be used to create by-laws that:[215]

209 S. 125(2)(a) Marine and Coastal Access Act 2009 (emphasis added).

210 S. 126(2) Marine and Coastal Access Act 2009 (emphasis added).

211 *Associated Provincial Picture Houses Ltd v Wednesbury Corporation* [1948] 1 KB 223 at 229–230 (Lord Greene MR).

212 See Chapter 2, pp. 56ff, and generally De Smith's *Judicial Review* 6th edn (2007) at pp. 551ff.

213 S. 129(1) Marine and Coastal Access Act 2009.

214 It can be exercised so as to make provision for different parts of an MCZ, for different times of the year, and to restrict or regulate different means or methods of carrying out any activity; see s. 129(8) Marine and Coastal Access Act 2009.

215 See s. 129(3) Marine and Coastal Access Act 2009.

- Prohibit or restrict entry into the MCZ by any persons or animals, or their movement or activity with the zone,
- Prohibit or restrict entry into the MCZ by vessels or vehicles, and their movement within and activities in the zone,
- Restrict the speed at which any vessel may move in an MCZ, or in an area outside the boundaries of the MCZ if that movement might hinder the conservation objectives of the zone, prohibit or restrict the anchoring of any vessel in an MCZ,
- Prohibit or restrict the anchoring of any vessel within an MCZ,
- Prohibit or restrict the killing, taking, destruction, molestation, or disturbance of animals or plants of any description in an MCZ, or
- Prohibiting or restricting the doing of anything in a MCZ which could interfere with the seabed or damage or disturb any object in the MVCZ.

The use of by-laws can also be used to facilitate a licensing function vested in the MMO, allowing it to require the grant of permits authorizing actions that would otherwise be unlawful under the terms of the by-laws in place for an MCZ. The licence requirement must be included in the by-law itself, and its exercise will be subject to the general duty outlined earlier to exercise decision-making powers to further the conservation objectives of the zone.[216] The power to make by-laws can also be exercised so as to prohibit or restrict entry into or any movement or activity on any part of the seashore that adjoins an MCZ by persons, animals, or vehicles.[217]

The MMO must publish notice of its intention to make a by-law for an MCZ, and must do so in such a manner as is most likely to bring it to the attention of any persons who are likely to be affected by it.[218] It must make copies of the draft by-law available for inspection and state the time within which representations about it must be made to the MMO. A by-law must be confirmed by the Secretary of State before it comes into force, and will enter into force either on such date as is specified by the Secretary of State or, if none is specified, one month after the date on which it is confirmed.[219] The confirmation of the Secretary of State is dispensed with in two cases: the making of emergency by-laws, and of interim by-laws. The MMO can make an emergency by-law[220] if it considers that there is an urgent need to protect an MCZ, and in this case it will take effect without confirmation by the Secretary of State. It will, however, only remain in force for a maximum period of 12 months and can only be extended by a further emergency by-law if the MMO

[216] S. 129(5) Marine and Coastal Access Act 2009, and see s. 126(2) Marine and Coastal Access Act 2009 (pp. 277ff).

[217] S. 129(4) Marine and Coastal Access Act 2009.

[218] See ss. 130(6)(7) Marine and Coastal Access Act 2009.

[219] S. 130(8) Marine and Coastal Access Act 2009. The making of a by-law must be published by notice likely to bring it to the attention of those affected by it, and a copy must be made available for inspection at the MMO offices: s. 130(9)(10) Marine and Coastal Access Act 2009.

[220] See generally s. 131 Marine and Coastal Access Act 2009.

intends to make a permanent by-law to replace it and has given notice of this fact.[221] Interim by-laws, on the other hand, are intended to protect areas that the MMO considers should be designated as an MCZ, in situations where they consider there is an urgent need to protect its conservation features pending formal designation. The order will endure for a maximum of 12 months and does not require the Secretary of State's confirmation.[222]

(ii) Orders for protecting MCZs (Wales)

In relation to an MCZ in Wales, the Welsh ministers have power to make an order for the purpose of furthering the conservation objectives of an MCZ.[223] The scope of activities that can be controlled by an order are the same as those applicable to by-laws in England and described earlier, and like a by-law, an order can apply to the whole or any part of an MCZ in Wales.[224] An order creating a protection order can provide for the Welsh ministers to issue permits authorizing anything that would otherwise be unlawful if carried out in breach of the order, thus granting flexibility in the manner in which regulation can be applied to address the conservation objectives and needs of each MCZ. The consultation provisions require the publication of draft orders in a manner that will bring them to the attention of those likely to be affected by the order, unless the Welsh ministers consider that there is an urgent need to make an order in order to protect an MCZ.[225] The Welsh ministers must consult the Secretary of State before confirming on order.[226] Interim orders can be made in order to protect areas that the Welsh ministers think should be considered for designation as an MCZ, and this can be done on similar terms as those described earlier for interim by-laws in England.[227]

(iii) Offences

It is a criminal offence to contravene a by-law that is in force in relation to an MCZ in England, or an order protecting an MCZ in Wales. The offence is punishable on summary conviction with a fine not exceeding level 5 on the standard scale.[228] The offence can be committed by omission where the accused fails to comply with a requirement in a by-law or order; for example, by failing to remove a vessel in contravention of the terms of a permit or where its presence is prohibited by a

[221] See s. 131(7)(8) Marine and Coastal Access Act 2009.

[222] S. 132 Marine and Coastal Access Act 2009.

[223] S. 134(1) Marine and Coastal Access Act 2009.

[224] See s. 134(3) Marine and Coastal Access Act 2009, applying the by-law provisions in s. 129(3)(4) and (7)–(9).

[225] See s. 135 Marine and Coastal Access Act 2009.

[226] S. 135(1) Marine and Coastal Access Act 2009.

[227] S. 136 Marine and Coastal Access Act 2009.

[228] S. 139(1)(2) Marine and Coastal Access Act 2009.

by-law.[229] Although there are separate provisions for the making of orders in Wales and by-laws in England, proceedings for an offence under the 2009 Act can be brought in any part of England and Wales for an offence committed in either.[230] The 2009 Act also makes provision for the Secretary of State or, in Wales, the Welsh ministers to confer on the enforcement authority the power to impose fixed monetary penalties (civil sanctions) for offence committed by breach of by-laws or orders protecting MCZs.[231]

(f) Criminal liability for damage to MCZ features

The 2009 Act also creates a more widely based offence applicable where a person does one or more of a number of prohibited acts which significantly hinders, or may significantly hinder, the achievement of the conservation objectives for the MCZ.[232] The offence may be committed where one or more of four prohibited acts are undertaken by an accused:[233]

- S/he intentionally or recklessly kills or injures an animal in an MCZ which is a protected feature of the zone,
- S/he intentionally picks or collects, or intentionally or recklessly cuts, uproots or destroys, any plant in an MCZ which is a protected feature of the MCZ,
- S/he intentionally or recklessly takes anything form an MCZ which is or forms part of a protected feature of that MCZ, and
- S/he intentionally or recklessly destroys or damages any habitat or feature which is a protected feature of an MCZ.

This offence has both subjective and objective elements. A person is only guilty of the offence if s/he knows, or ought to have known, at the time of committing the act, that the feature to which the act relates is in or forms part of an MCZ; but it is immaterial whether the person knew or ought to have known that the feature was a protected feature of the MCZ.[234] This is a common-sense requirement: clearly, one might expect a member of the public to know that an area is a designated MCZ, but it is less likely that s/he will have consulted the MCZ designation and that s/he will therefore have a detailed knowledge of the conservation objectives and protected features specified for the zone. An objective element is also a constituent of the offence, in that it is necessary for the commission of the offence for the act in

[229] See s. 139(3): 'in this section contravene includes fail to comply'.

[230] S. 139(4) Marine and Coastal Access Act 2009.

[231] S. 142 Marine and Coastal Access Act 2009. The imposition of a fixed monetary penalty is subject to detailed procedures set out in s. 143 Marine and Coastal Access Act 2009, requiring the service of notice of intent offering him/her the opportunity to discharge liability by payment of a fixed monetary sum and giving prescribed information as to the offence alleged to have been committed, the period within which payment must be made if liability is to be discharged.

[232] See s. 140 Marine and Coastal Access Act 2009.

[233] S. 140(2) Marine and Coastal Access Act 2009.

[234] See s. 140(1)(b) and 140(3) Marine and Coastal Access Act 2009.

question to have 'significantly hindered', or that it 'may significantly hinder' the achievement of the conservation objectives for the MCZ.[235] Establishing these issues will require the presentation of specialist scientific evidence from, for example, the statutory Conservation Bodies.

There are a number of exceptions where liability will not apply. A public authority carrying out its functions in an MCZ will not be guilty of an offence, nor will an offence be committed if the act is carried out with an authorization or permit granted by a public authority under the terms of the Act.[236] There is also an exception from liability where an act that causes damage was necessary in the interests of national security, or for the prevention of crime, or for securing public health, or where it was necessary to secure the safety of a vessel aircraft or marine installation, or for the purpose of saving life.[237] The MCZ provision in the 2009 Act applies to the Crown, but no contravention by the Crown can give rise to criminal liability. In the event of the crown committing a contravention of the Act, the relevant public authorities can apply to the High Court (in England) or Court of Session (in Scotland) for an order declaring unlawful any act or omission of the Crown which constitutes a contravention of the 2009 Act.[238]

(g) Monitoring

The Secretary of State[239] must table a report to the relevant legislature by the end of 2012, and within a six-year period thereafter, detailing the extent to which the conservation objectives for each MCZ are being achieved and recommending any further steps that may in his opinion is necessary to achieve those objectives.[240] The statutory nature Conservation Body can be directed by the Secretary of State to carry out monitoring of MCZs in its area for this purpose.[241] These monitoring powers will be important post-designation to underpin the reporting function, and also to ensure that the network is delivering the conservation objectives for which each MCZ has been designated. The Science Advisory Panel recommended surveillance in reference areas, for example, in order to provide baselines that describe features present and their natural variability.[242] This will facilitate rigorous testing of the management measures within the wider MCZ within which the reference area is embedded to assess their effectiveness in delivering the conservation objectives for the conservation features of the zone.

235 S. 140(1)(c) Marine and Coastal Access Act 2009.

236 See s. 141(1)(a)–(c) Marine and Coastal Access Act 2009.

237 S. 141(1)(d)–(f).

238 See s. 145(2) Marine and Coastal Access Act 2009.

239 Or in Scotland and Wales the Scottish ministers and Welsh ministers, ie the 'appropriate authority'—see s. 116(5) Marine and Coastal Access Act 2009.

240 S. 124(2)(e) Marine and Coastal Access Act 2009.

241 S. 124(3) Marine and Coastal Access Act 2009.

242 Science Advisory Panel, Assessment of the Marine Conservation Zone Regional Projects Final Recommendations (15 November 2011) paras. 7.2 and 8.6.2.

Nature Conservation MPAs (Scotland)

The Marine (Scotland) Act 2010 makes provision for the Scottish ministers to designate Nature Conservation MPAs in Scotland. The 2010 Act applies to the 'Scottish marine protection area' (that is, the Scottish marine area)[243] excluding any waters upstream of the freshwater limit of estuarial waters.[244] The terms under which this may be done under Part 5 of the 2010 Act, and the conditions that can be imposed upon or restrict activities within a designated area, are broadly similar to those applicable under the legislation applicable in England and Wales and considered earlier. The Marine and Coastal Access Act 2009 provides for the Scottish ministers to designate MPAs for biodiversity protection in the offshore waters adjacent to Scotland:[245] the Marine (Scotland) Act 2010 complements this by providing for the designation of Nature Conservation MPAs within 12 nautical miles of the Scottish coast.[246]

A Nature Conservation MPA can be designated by the Scottish ministers for the purpose of conserving the marine flora and fauna or conserving the habitat of marine flora and fauna, or features of geological or geomorphological interest.[247] In considering whether it is desirable to designate an area as a Nature Conservation MPA, the Scottish ministers may have regard to any social or economic consequences of designation.[248] The MPA designation has a network focus, and the focus is to the functionality of the network across the UK marine area as a whole.[249] Accordingly, the objective of the designation is that the areas designated as Nature Conservation MPAs by the Scottish ministers, taken together with any areas designated as marine conservation zones under section 116 of the 2009 Act and any other relevant conservation sites in the UK marine area, together form a network which satisfies the conservation conditions set out in the Scottish legislation. These are[250] that the MPA network contributes to the conservation or improvement of the marine environment in the UK marine area as a whole, that the features which are protected by the sites contained in the network represent the range of features present in the UK marine area, and that the designation of sites contained in the network reflects the fact that the conservation of a feature may require the designation of more than one site.

Prior to the Scottish ministers making a formal designation order establishing a Nature Conservation MPA, public consultation is required.[251] Once a Nature Conservation MPA has been established, the Scottish legislation imposes similar duties to those imposed by the 2009 Act in MCZs in England and Wales. Thus

[243] S. 65(1) Marine (Scotland) Act 2010.
[244] S. 66 Marine (Scotland) Act 2010.
[245] Ss 116 and 117 Marine and Coastal Access Act 2009.
[246] S. 67 Marine (Scotland) Act 2010.
[247] S. 68(1) Marine (Scotland) Act 2010.
[248] S. 68(8) Marine (Scotland) Act 2010.
[249] S. 79(2) Marine (Scotland) Act 2010.
[250] See s. 78(3) Marine (Scotland) Act 2010.
[251] S. 75 Marine (Scotland) Act 2010.

there are statutory duties on public authorities to exercise their function so as to further the conservation objectives of the MPA,[252] and a duty to exercise their power in relation to decisions, such as marine licensing, so as to do so.[253] They have power to introduce restrictions on activities in an MPA through Marine Conservation Orders.[254] The 2010 Act is not prescriptive, but gives examples[255] of the types of provision that can be included in a marine conservation order. An order can include restrictions on the entry into, or movement activity or works in, the protected area by persons, animals, vessels (or by specified types of vessel) or by vehicles. It can also place restrictions on the anchoring of any vessel (or types of vessel) within the protected area. Importantly, restrictions can also be placed, and presumably will in most cases be placed, on the killing, taking, destruction, molestation, or disturbance of animals or plants of any description in the protected area. An order can also prohibit the removal of all or part of anything from the protected area, and can prohibit the depositing of anything or the undertaking of any act which may interfere with or damage the seabed in a protected area, or which may damage or disturb any object or otherwise cause harm to the protected area. Restrictions can be placed on the speed at which any vessel or vehicle may move in the protected area—or indeed outside the protected area if the movement might adversely impact upon the achievement of the stated nature conservation objectives for the MPA.

The 2010 Act places a duty on the Scottish ministers to assess the impact of any prohibition or restriction on human activity that is included in an order. The assessment must include not only an assessment of the impact of the order on the environment in the protected area and surrounding areas which may be exposed to the restricted activities, but also of the social and economic impacts of the restrictions in the order, with ministers placed under a duty to minimize adverse impacts insofar as is possible.[256] Marine Management Schemes for MPAs can be established by the public authorities acting on their own accord, either together or singly,[257] or acting under a direction from the Scottish ministers to establish one.[258]

Scottish Natural Heritage will have a major role in advising on the conservation objectives and their attainment in MPAs,[259] and can hold public authorities to account for decisions which in the opinion of SNH either fail to adhere to advice or guidance issued by SNH or fail to comply with the statutory duties imposed upon public authorities.[260]

[252] S. 82 Marine (Scotland) Act 2010.
[253] See s. 83 Marine (Scotland) Act 2010.
[254] S. 85 Marine (Scotland) Act 2010.
[255] These are set out in s. 86 Marine (Scotland) Act 2010.
[256] S. 91 Marine (Scotland) Act 2010.
[257] S. 99 Marine (Scotland) Act 2010.
[258] S. 102 Marine (Scotland) Act 2010.
[259] S. 80 Marine (Scotland) Act 2010.
[260] S. 84 Marine (Scotland) Act 2010.

A new body, Marine Scotland, a directorate of the Scottish Government, was established prior to the introduction of the 2010 Act to oversee the development and management of the MPA network and to exercise functions in connection with marine planning and licensing in Scotland. Marine Scotland combines the functions and resources of the former Scottish Government Marine Directorate, Fisheries Research Services, and the Scottish Fisheries Protection Agency. In order to advise Scottish ministers on the key strategies and business planning of Marine Scotland, and to ensure enhanced stakeholder involvement, a Marine Strategy Forum was established in 2009 to provide 'a cooperative base for an integrated strategic approach to the management, use, and protection of Scotland's seas and coasts by using cross-sector awareness and collaboration on marine issues'.[261]

The development of an MPA network is proceeding in parallel to that in England and Wales discussed earlier in this chapter, and in common with the latter this will involve extensive stakeholder consultation in the identification and selection of candidate MPAs. In 2010 the Scottish MPA Project—a partnership between Marine Scotland, SNH (territorial waters), JNCC (offshore waters), SEPA, Historic Scotland, and Marine Scotland Science, with the aim to identify and advise on nature conservation MPAs in Scottish waters, including offshore waters—started with initial survey work on specific target areas in order to identify PMFs; ie priority marine features. Scottish waters were divided into five search regions then further divided into 30 search locations. An initial gap analysis was carried out to identify whether existing MPAs (SACs, SPAs, and SSSIs) provided adequate protection for other priority features located within the area which were not the reason for the designation. This was to identify whether overlapping SACs, SPAs, and SSSIs with MPA designation would provide better protection for the important features within each area. MPA search features, identified by SNH and JNCC, 'represent species, habitats and natural features of conservation importance for which spatial measures are thought to be an appropriate conservation measure'.[262] A series of five workshops has been held in order to develop the suite of Nature Conservation MPAs in the Scottish marine area, with selection based upon the guidance to be found in Guidelines on MPA Selection.[263]

The Scottish Government strategy[264] for marine nature conservation sets out the Scottish government's aims and objectives for the marine environment and the timetable for delivering marine protected areas. Of note are the objectives of securing better access to data with the principle of collecting information once

[261] See Marine Strategy Forum Terms of Reference <http://www.scotland.gov.uk/Topics/marine/seamanagement/forum/Termsofref>.

[262] Scottish Government '*Marine Protected Areas in Scotland's Seas: Guidelines on the selection of MPAs and the development of the MPA network*' at 3, <http://www.scotland.gov.uk/Resource/Doc/295194/0114024.pdf>.

[263] *Marine Protected Areas in Scotland's Seas: Guidelines on the selection of MPAs and development of the MPA network* (Marine Scotland, JNCC and Scottish Natural Heritage, 2011) available at: <http://www.scotland.gov.uk/Resource/Doc/295194/0114024.pdf>. See Chapter 5 and Annex 1 which sets out Selection Guidelines for Nature Conservation MPAs.

[264] Marine Scotland, '*A Strategy for Marine Nature Conservation in Scotland's Seas*' Scottish Government (March 2011) <http://www.scotland.gov.uk/Resource/Doc/295194/0115590.pdf>.

but using it many times,[265] and reducing the reliance on the precautionary principle through better scientific research.[266] Focusing on short-term actions up until the end of 2012 and providing a framework for how Marine Scotland will work with partners on marine conservation issues to contribute to and deliver longer-term aims up until 2020, including a well-managed network of MPAs by 2016 and measures to achieve Good Environmental Status by 2020, the strategy adopts a three-pillar approach incorporating species conservation, site protection, and wider seas policies and measures to marine conservation.

A recommended list of priority marine features (also known as 'MPA search features') was published by Scottish National Heritage in April 2012.[267] This lists 19 habitats and 37 species for territorial waters, although identification of a priority marine feature will not necessarily result in the designation of MPA: a five-stage process is adopted in analysing locations and at stage 5 of this process, priority is given to those 'MPAs in terms of their contribution to the network at a national rather than regional level'.[268] The completed project aims to present the final report to Scottish ministers by the end of 2012, thereafter formal impact assessments for the areas identified and full public consultation on the proposals will commence.

265 Marine Scotland, '*A Strategy for Marine Nature Conservation in Scotland's Seas*' Scottish Government (March 2011) at 20.

266 Marine Scotland, '*A Strategy for Marine Nature Conservation in Scotland's Seas*' Scottish Government (March 2011) at 19.

267 SNH '*Recommended List of Priority Marine Features for Scottish Territorial Waters*' (2012) <http://www.snh.gov.uk/docs/B1064114.pdf>.

268 Marine Scotland, '*A Strategy for Marine Nature Conservation in Scotland's Seas*' Scottish Government (March 2011) <http://www.scotland.gov.uk/Resource/Doc/295194/0115590.pdf> para. 5.4 see Annex 1 for details of the five-stage process.

8

Property, Environment, and the Limits of Law

The central premise of this work has been that the role of property rights as a tool for resource allocation is fundamental to an understanding of the way in which the legal and economic instruments for promoting nature conservation work in practice, and to any assessment of their efficiency and effectiveness. The introductory explanation of the interaction between environmental regulation and property concepts offered in Chapter 1 was structured around the interaction between two property models: an entitlements model of property rights, and a resource allocation model.[1] These reflect the differing functions that property rights perform, in defining legally sanctioned rights to land and its produce, and as an allocative tool for defining the access to the land resource that the entitlement confers. The analysis offered in Chapter 1 focused on a functional analysis of property rights in relation to environmental regulation. To capture the full benefit of a property rights analysis of legal and economic instruments for nature conservation, it is, however, necessary to focus more closely on the resource allocation function of property rules. This chapter will develop an analysis grounded in a resource allocation model of property rights, and in doing so will seek to bring together key points made in the earlier chapters on habitat and species protection.

Property Rights and Nature Conservation

It is important to note at the outset that the functions of property entitlement and resource allocation rules are not mutually exclusive; they are interdependent, and in some respects overlap. A property entitlement rule will also fulfil an initial resource allocation function. Where land is freehold, for example, the owner will have relatively extensive land use privileges restrained principally by planning law and development control constraints. In the case of leasehold land, on the other hand, the landlord will commonly reserve minerals and game rights to himself and exclude them from the lease, thereby restricting the land resource available to the

[1] See Chapter 1, pp. 29ff. and Box 1.3.

tenant for economic exploitation. And in the case of common land, a grazier or other appropriator will have rights legally characterized as a profit à prendre (a limited right to take grass or other specific items of the land's produce, such as peat).[2] This will result in a complex allocation of the land resource to commoners, the owner of the soil (of unallocated residual resources) and others. The allocation of resources by common law property entitlement rules provides the starting point for an examination of the interaction between property rules and nature conservation law; a further reallocation of resource entitlements will often be implemented by legal and economic instruments external to the property entitlement rules defining the landholder's interest in the land. This may be done by environmental legislation restricting potentially damaging land uses, by 'soft law' instruments such as codes of practice, and by economic instruments to encourage land management for nature conservation. We considered numerous examples of the use of such instruments in Chapters 3, 4, and 6, especially in relation to the law of habitat protection. The *reallocation* of the resource entitlements initially determined by the general law, in order to promote the environmentally sensitive management of wildlife habitats, is indeed one of the principal objectives of nature conservation law.

A diagrammatic representation of the interaction of property entitlement rules, resource allocation rules, and environmental regulation is given in Box 8.1. Property entitlement rules determine the initial presumptive allocation of resources in land, conferring land use rights on the owner or occupier. The example given is simple; that of an owner (freehold) on the one hand and a tenant on the other. A more complex presumptive allocation of land use rights will apply in many cases; for example, where the land is subject to a trust, or where it is common land registered under the Commons Registration Act 1965 or Commons Act 2006.[3] The allocation of access to the land resource represented as 'A' in Box 8.1 indicates those land use rights that remain available for exchange or use by the landowner or tenant. This represents the residual resource allocation remaining to the freehold owner or tenant; that is, the presumptive allocation made by the relevant property entitlement rules applicable to the land tenure in question, minus those aspects of the land resource that have been reallocated by environmental legislation, or by legal and economic instruments.

The examples given in Box 8.1 are the reallocation of resources effected by the notification of land as an SSSI, by cross compliance under the rules of the single farm payment (CAP subsidy), and by development control law:

(a) Notification of land as an SSSI reallocates land use privileges to the state (B). This is effected by the service with the site notification of the list of operations likely to damage the conservation interest (OLDSIs), and which

[2] See *Besley v John* [2003] EWCA Civ 1737; *Dance v Savery* [2011] EWCA Civ 1250; and E. Cousins and R. Honey, *Gadsden on Commons and Greens* 2nd edn (Sweet and Maxwell, 2012) at paras. 2–02 to 2–015.

[3] See Box 8.2 for a similar examination of the resource allocation impacts of environmental legislation in relation to common land in England and Wales.

Box 8.1 Property Rights and Nature Conservation—a Resource Allocation Analysis

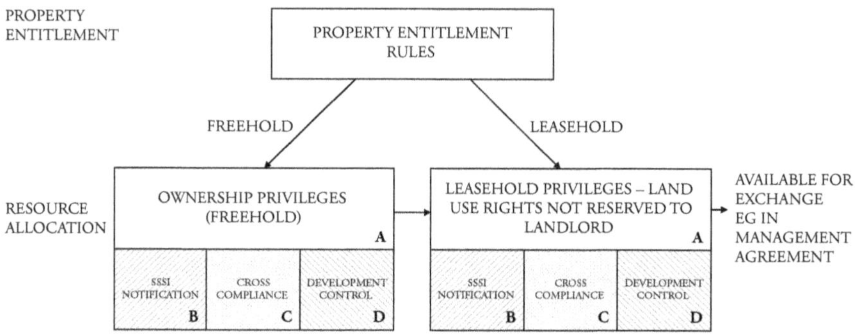

require the consent of the Conservation Body prior to being carried out.[4] The service of the list of OLDSIs has the effect of reallocating decision making about the stipulated operations to the state, represented by the Conservation Body, and an assessment of their potential environmental impacts on the protected features of the site will be carried out before a decision to approve is made; indeed, in the case of a European wildlife site, this is not only mandatory but the assessment must also comply with the requirements of the Habitats Directive.[5] If the land in question ceases to be an SSSI, this requirement will cease to apply and the property rights available to the landowner for exchange will accordingly be amplified.

(b) If land of high nature value is used for agriculture, and the occupier claims the single farm payment under the EU common agricultural policy, then he must comply with the cross compliance conditions that are a prerequisite for the receipt of payment (environmental conditionality) (C). In particular, he must comply with statutory management requirements and keep the land in good agricultural and environmental condition. These obligations are subsumed within property rights and must be adhered to without compensation. In this case, unlike (a), the relevant regulatory provisions[6] do not reallocate land use privileges to the state; they instead modify the property rights of the landowner if he opts to receive the single farm payment, and also restrict those land use practices for which compensation

[4] See s. 28E Wildlife and Countryside Act 1981, and Chapter 3, pp. 84ff.

[5] See Chapter 6, p. 222 and the Conservation of Habitats and Species Regulations 2010, reg. 21.

[6] The Agriculture (Cross Compliance) (No. 2) Regulations 2009, SI 2009/3365, reg. 3 and Schedule 1 (as amended by SI 2010/2941); Common Agricultural Policy Single Payment and Support Schemes (Cross Compliance)(Wales) Regulations 2004 SI 2004/3280 (W284), as amended, Schedule.

will be paid. If the landowner ceases to claim the single payment, the property rights available to him for exchange are amplified. Importantly, however, payments under agri-environment agreements funded by the rural development policy (such as entry-level or higher-level stewardship) are only payable for practice which goes beyond 'good agricultural practice', and this is the case whether or not the single farm payment is claimed by the farmer.

(c) Planning permission is required for building, engineering, or other operations in, over, or under land that constitute 'development', or for any material change of use of land.[7] Under the law of development control, therefore, decisions on resource use implicit in any operation requiring planning permission are reallocated to the local planning authority. And, as we have seen, special rules apply to applications for development consent in protected areas such as notified SSSIs or Special Areas of Conservation.[8] If planning permission is obtained on application,[9] the property rights available to the owner for exchange are correspondingly amplified.

The reallocation of land use privileges, as in scenarios A, B, and C, will be identical whether the land is tenanted, freehold, or subject to other types of property entitlement; for example, if it is common land. In principle, only the land use privileges represented by A in each case should be available for exchange in a land management agreement or a management scheme under which the landowner or occupier is paid to deliver environmental management to preserve or enhance the natural environment.

The utility of this model for analysing the efficiency and effectiveness of legal and economic instruments for nature conservation is readily apparent. The efficiency with which public resources are deployed to pay for nature conservation management in protected areas relies upon the effective integration of extant property rights with the terms of management agreements or other financial subventions; the statutory Conservation Bodies should only pay for conservation management that a landowner has land use privileges to perform, represented as 'A' in Box 8.1. Put another way, the efficient delivery of conservation management requires that the state pay only for property rights that are, as a matter of law, available for trade in an economic exchange such as a management agreement, and which also have value in the market place. In practice, effective integration often breaks down between (i) property rights (that is, entitlements), (ii) the legal instruments deployed in protected areas under environmental legislation, and (iii) economic instruments under which land use entitlements are modified to promote nature conservation. And integrative failure may be apparent between (i) and (ii), between (i) and (iii), or

[7] Town and Country Planning Act 1990, ss. 57 (requirement of planning permission) and 55 (definition of development).

[8] See Chapter 4, pp. 140ff. (SSSIs) and Chapter 6, pp. 225ff. (Special Areas of Conservation and Special Protection Areas).

[9] Or granted by the General Development Order (permitted development rights) or a special development order.

between (ii) and (iii). The following are indicative examples of integrative failure in each case.

In the first place, there may be a mismatch between the property entitlements of the occupier of land in a protected area and the reallocation of resources affected by a statutory designation such as an SSSI or SAC ((i) and (ii) considered earlier). The list of OLDSIs served on landowners in an SSSI will often be extensive, requiring consultation with the Conservation Body before a wide range of major land use operations can be initiated.[10] The OLDSIs will typically prohibit the removal of timber, peat, or turf, and in upland areas will also often prohibit changes in grazing numbers of livestock without prior consultation with the Conservation Body.[11] Where the land is farmed by a tenant, timber and game will commonly be reserved to the landlord by the tenancy; OLDSIs prohibiting the removal of timber will therefore be redundant if served on the tenant/occupier, and will depend for their efficacy upon service on the landowner. Similarly, if the SSSI comprises common land, the land use entitlements of common graziers will be reflected in the commons register. Lists of OLDSIs served on commoners in upland areas typically prohibit the removal of peat and turf, thus abrogating their registered entitlements to turbary and estovers. They also typically prohibit the supplementary feeding of livestock, and the release of wild, domestic or feral animals, plants, or seeds. These are redundant, inasmuch as they are not land use entitlements conferred on graziers by the common right of pasture or any other recognized category of common right; OLDSIs of this type should therefore be directed to the owner of the soil.[12] In cases where there is an absentee land owner—a surprisingly not uncommon scenario in the case of upland commons[13]—the list of OLDSIs does, however, provide an additional state-mediated mechanism to ensure that the limitations on common property rights are observed.

Secondly, there may be poor integration between the terms of a management agreement, under which payment is made for conservation management, and the occupier's land use privileges represented in property rights ((i) and (iii) considered earlier). Under the Environmentally Sensitive Areas programme, for example, management agreements in upland areas commonly prohibited the removal of timber, rushes, peat, and other land resources.[14] Where the occupier is a tenant, therefore, it was noted earlier that most of these matters fall outside his/her land use privileges

[10] See eg the OLDSIs in the site notification for the Elenydd SSSI in central Wales, which contains 28 OLDSIs requiring prior consultation with CCW: see further C. P. Rodgers, E. A. Winchester, A. Straughton, and M. Pieraccini, *Contested Common Land: environmental governance past and present* (Earthscan, 2010) at 152 ff.

[11] See for example Rodgers et al. (2010) at 103–104 (OLDSIs in Scafell Pike SSSI, Cumbria), at 129 (OLDSIs in the Ingleborough SSSI, North Yorkshire), and at 153 (OLDSIs in the Elenydd SSSI).

[12] See *Besley v John* [2003] EWCA Civ 1737 (supplementary livestock feeding not an incident of common right of pasture); Rodgers et al. (2010) at 104, 129, 153.

[13] An example is Scales Moor (CL 272) and Ingleton common (CL134) in North Yorkshire; see Rodgers et al. (2010) at 127.

[14] See eg the Environmentally Sensitive Areas (Lake District) Designation Order 1993, and (now) Environmentally Sensitive Areas (Stage II) Designation Order 2000, SI 2000/3050 1993; another example is the Environmentally Sensitive Areas (Cambrian Mountains) Designation Order 1987, SI 1987/2026.

Box 8.2 Environmental Management of Common Land—A Property Rights Analysis

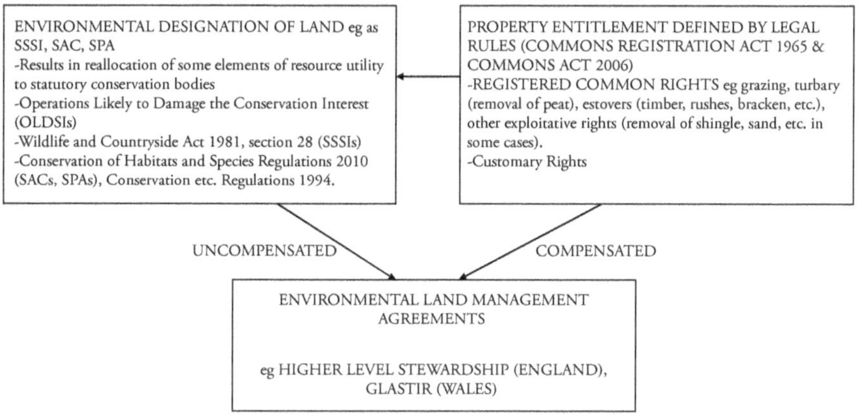

represented in property rights. The state is, in a case like this, effectively paying for an adjustment of land use rights that the other party to the agreement has no legal competence to deliver. The participation of the landlord in a management agreement is therefore necessary if a legally binding resolution that delivers the protection sought is to be achieved.

Finally, there may also be a lack of integration between the resource allocation effected by statutory instruments (such as the service of a list of OLDSIs in an SSSI) and the terms of a management agreement subsequently concluded to protect all or part of the site ((ii) and (iii) considered earlier). The list of OLDSIs in most SSSIs is, as noted earlier, often lengthy. In principle, the state should not deploy public resources to fund an agreement that delivers no more than adherence to the statutory list of OLDSIs, and the statutory mechanism will deliver a basic level of environmental protection without the payment of compensation.[15] In practice, however, there will usually be a negotiation between a landowner wishing to carry out OLDSIs and the Conservation Body, and this will commonly result in a negotiated solution under which a management agreement will be offered in return for positive land management.[16] The relationship between property rights and the statutory instruments for environmental management, and the (re)allocation of the land resource that they effect, is in this context central to the implementation of the 'partnership principle'

[15] For a comparison of the efficacy of the mechanism with the Environmentally Sensitive Areas programme, see M. Whitby and C. Saunders, 'Estimating the Supply of Conservation Goods in Britain: A Comparison of the Financial Efficiency of Two Policy Instruments' (1996) 72 *Land Economics* 313–25.

[16] Ie under the *Guidelines for Management Agreements and Other Matters* (DEFRA 2001), Chapter 4, p. 119. And see Rodgers and Bishop, *Management Agreements for Promoting Nature Conservation* (RICS, 1998), Ch. 3 and Figure 3 at p. 30.

of nature conservation law.[17] Compensation should not be paid under a management agreement simply for preventing the exercise of property rights in a manner that will damage the natural environment; this will be dealt with by the service of a list of OLDSIs and the adjustment of property rights that it reflects. Rather, public resource should be directed to funding management agreements that deliver positive management to improve or create natural habitats.[18] In other words, while the landowner's property entitlement remains unaffected, the manner in which the resource allocation that flows from that entitlement is exercised is adjusted by the agreement, and it is this adjustment in the manner in which the land resource is used that will be compensated under a management agreement.

Protected Areas Policy—Impact and Effectiveness

How effective has the state mediated approach to nature conservation, described in earlier chapters of this work, been? It can be argued that the designation of protected areas such as SSSIs delivers a basic level of protection, and that this can be delivered at a low transaction cost through the OLDSI mechanism, under which damaging land uses are prevented unless there is prior consultation with the Conservation Bodies.[19] Nevertheless, statistical evidence from the statutory Conservation Bodies reveals that a large proportion of SSSIs, SACs, and SPAs remain in poor conservation condition, with recurring damage to many protected sites from a variety of land use types. Agriculture, in particular, is responsible for a significant proportion of the extant damage to SSSIs. The most recent survey of SSSIs in England showed that only 37 per cent by area of the national suite of SSSIs was in favourable condition. Box 8.3 abstracts the four most prominent causes of unfavourable condition in English SSSIs, of which three are related to inappropriate agricultural land management. A similar picture emerges from the statistics for SSSI condition in Wales. The first review of SSSI condition in Wales, using the common standard monitoring methodology devised by the Joint Nature Conservation Committee,[20] was undertaken in 2003. This revealed that only 29 per cent of Welsh SSSIs by area were in favourable condition. In total 71 per cent of the Welsh SSSI network by area was in unfavourable condition, of which only 26 per cent by area was in an unfavourable but recovering condition; and 74 per cent of SSI features in unfavourable condition was found to be in a declining conservation condition.[21] A large proportion of these sites were recorded as affected by intensive agricultural land management, and in the case of

[17] As to which, see Chapter 1, p. 7.

[18] See further *Guidelines for Management Agreements and Other Matters* (DEFRA 2001), Chapter 4, pp. 119ff.

[19] See K. V. Last, 'Habitat Protection: Has the Wildlife and Countryside Act 1981 made a Difference?' (1999) 11 JEL 15–34.

[20] As to which, see Box 6.4 in Chapter 6, p. 239.

[21] See the SSSI condition summary for Wales, compiled in 2003 at: <http://www.ccgc.gov.uk/landscape–wildlife/protecting-our-landscape/special-landscapes–sites/protected-landscapes-and-sites/sssis/sssi–report/habitat-features.aspx>.

Box 8.3 Damage to Protected Wildlife Sites in England

Sites of Special Scientific Interest	Area in Favourable Conservation Condition	Area in Unfavourable Recovering Condition	Area in Unfavourable Condition No Change
	37.19%	59.46%	2.18%
Reasons for Adverse Condition	Number of Units	Area	% of unit area not in favourable condition
Inappropriate shrub control	632	5543.60 ha	15.28%
Undergrazimg	567	5247.15	14.46%
Overgrazing	252	4891.10	13.84%
Water pollution—agricultural run off	288	3930.82	10.84%

Source: Natural England SSSI condition summary as at 1 January 2012 <http://www.sssi.naturalengland.org.uk/Special/sssi/reportAction.cfm?Report = sdrt15&Category = N&Reference = 0>.
Reasons for adverse condition:
<http://www.sssi.naturalengland.org.uk/Special/sssi/reportAction.cfm?Report = sdrt17&Category = N&Reference = 0>.

upland peat mires sites were reported as in universally poor condition, usually due to the pressure of overgrazing and vegetation burning.[22]

The first national assessment of all UK protected sites using the Common Standards Monitoring methodology was published by the JNCC in 2006. This surveyed SSSIs, SACs and SPAs, and again revealed a large proportion of damage attributable to overgrazing and other inappropriate agricultural management issues.[23] These problems have informed calls for a new direction in public policy, and for a new approach to the promotion of biodiversity and the delivery of nature conservation. We will consider the latest developments in public policy in the next section.

A New Direction in Conservation Law and Policy?

The 2011 Natural Environment white paper[24] proposed fundamental changes in the way that England's natural environment is protected and managed. Rather than focus protection on specific natural habitats at a local geographic scale, it proposed a range of new measures based on the ecosystem approach; ie an approach premised

[22] <http://www.ccgc.gov.uk/landscape–wildlife/protecting-our-landscape/special-landscapes–sites/protected-landscapes-and-sites/sssis/sssi–report/habitat-features.aspx>.

[23] See Common Standards Monitoring for Designated Sites: first six-year report (JNCC 2006) available at: <http://jncc.defra.gov.uk/pdf/CSM_06summary.pdf>.

[24] *The Natural Choice: securing the value of nature,* Cm 8082, June 2011, available at: <http://www.defra.gov.uk/environment/natural/whitepaper/>.

on the need to maximize the benefits ('ecosystem services') we get from nature. The adoption of an ecosystem approach to the planning and implementation of policy to protect and promote biodiversity was a key element of the 1992 Convention of Biological Diversity, as we saw in Chapter 1.[25]

The development of these proposals for a new direction in nature conservation was informed by two important reports:

(i) In 2009 DEFRA commissioned a review of the ecological network in England to investigate whether the national suite of protected areas (SSSI, SACs, etc.) was sufficiently resilient to adapt to the challenges of climate change, and to investigate whether there was evidence that a more inter connected network might be more effective in protecting and promoting biodiversity for the future. The report, *Making Space for nature: a review of England's wildlife sites and ecological network* (the Lawton Report), was published in 2010.[26] This revealed major shortcomings in the current approach to nature conservation and recommended that a larger scale focus be adopted, at a landscape scale that made provision for the interconnection of protected areas by 'green corridors' and underpinned by an ecosystem approach. Its central conclusion was that 'there needs to be a step change in our approach to wildlife conservation, from trying to hang on to what we have to one of large scale habitat restoration and recreation underpinned by the re-establishment of ecological processes and ecosystem services for the benefits of both people and wildlife'.[27] Among key recommendations were the need to improve the quality of current protected habitats by better management, to increase the size of existing wildlife sites, enhance connections between sites by the provision of physical corridors or 'stepping stones', and to reduce the pressure on wildlife by improving the wider environment (outside protected areas such as SSSIs). Many of these recommendations informed the proposals in the subsequent Natural Environment white paper.

(ii) The first UK National Ecosystem Assessment ('NEA') was published in 2011.[28] Its key findings are set out in Box 8.4. Through its analysis of their changing status, the NEA identified broad habitats and ecosystem services where continuing pressures are causing deterioration in the benefits they provide. Of the range of ecosystem services provided by the eight broad aquatic and terrestrial habitat types in the UK[29] over 30 per cent have been

[25] See Chapter 1, pp. 9ff. and Box 1.1 defining ecosystem services.

[26] Lawton et al. (2010) *Making Space for Nature: a review of England's wildlife sites and ecological network,* available at: <http://www.defra.gov.uk/pubications/files/pb13428-newp-discussion-239710.pdf>.

[27] Lawton et al. (2010) at page ii.

[28] Available at: <http://uknea.unep-wcmc.org/Resources/tabid/82/Default.aspx>.

[29] The NEA assessed the status of the ecosystem services provided by the eight broad habitat types present in the UK: Mountains moorlands and heath; semi-natural grassland; enclosed farmland; woodland; freshwaters; urban; coastal margins; and marine habitats.

Box 8.4 The UK National Ecosystem Assessment 201—Key Findings[30]

How can we secure and improve the continued supply of ecosystem services?

- Contemporary society is less sustainable than it could be. Responding to the pressures to provide food, water, and energy security, while at the same time conserving biodiversity and adapting to rapid environmental change, will require getting the valuation right, creating functioning markets for ecosystem services, improving the use of our resources, and adopting new ways of managing those resources.
- No national-, regional-, or global-scale environmental issue (for example, air and water quality) has ever been successfully addressed without an appropriate enabling framework using a mix of regulations, technology, financial incentives, and behavioural changes. However, local initiatives have proved invaluable by instigating a range of local conservation activities and improving the delivery of some ecosystem services.
- Many of the recent improvements in ecosystem services and biodiversity conservation have happened as a result of effective regulation. These have been driven by various European Union policy directives such as the Rural Development Programme, and in particular by the European Union Common Agricultural Policy's agri-environment schemes, complemented by the Nature Directives and an increase in the area and condition of protected areas.
- In future, the management of ecosystem services will need to be resilient and adaptive to societal (for example, demographic), environmental (for example, climate change), and land use (for example, increased use of bio-energy) changes. Therefore, the underlying indirect and direct drivers of change must be considered.
- The transition to a more sustainable use of ecosystems and their services can be facilitated by taking a more integrated, rather than conventional sectoral, approach to their management, recognizing that some difficult trade-offs will have to be made between individual ecosystem services.
- Integration can be facilitated by taking a multi-functional approach adaptable enough to recognize the scale of response required, from local to global, and open and transparent enough to facilitate dialogue and collaboration between a wide range of different actors.
- Governments, the private sector, voluntary, and civil society at large all have key roles to play in the transition to a more sustainable use of ecosystems.

assessed as declining, often as a consequence of long-term declines in habitat extent or condition.[31]

[30] Source: *UK National Ecosystem Assessment—Synthesis of Key Findings* at p. 52. Available at: <http://uknea.unep-wcmc.org/Resources/tabid/82/Default.aspx>.

[31] For a tabular assessment of the overall importance of each of the broad habitat types in delivering ecosystem services, and the change in the flow of service they provide since 1990, see Figure 5 at p. 13 of the *Synthesis of Key Findings* available at: <http://uknea.unep-wcmc.org/Resources/tabid/82/Default.aspx>.

The proposals set out in the white paper itself mark out a new direction in the implementation of nature conservation policy, and will initiate a move away from a state-mediated approach towards one that seeks to facilitate greater involvement of the private sector in delivering habitat recreation and protection at a local scale. The targets which the new approach will seek to implement are ambitious:[32] to have 90 per cent of priority habitats in recovering or favourable condition by 2020, to achieve bigger and less fragmented areas for wildlife, and to achieve an increase of at least 200,000 hectares in the overall extent of priority habitats. The new strategy also aims to ensure that at least 50 per cent of SSSIs are in favourable condition by 2020.

The new approach, though radical, is still strongly premised on the existing partnership approach to the development and delivery of nature conservation.[33] Importantly, however, it seeks to radically shift the *balance* of responsibility and roles in the partnership between the public bodies who implement nature conservation policy and the private sector, including land managers who deliver habitat conservation and land management in practice. The measures outlined in the white paper will lead to the private sector playing a more prominent role in delivering nature conservation at a local level, and may envisage the role of the public bodies (the Conservation Bodies, local authorities, etc.) being reconfigured as primarily a facilitating one; public bodies will be given new tools and guidance to support local action for nature.[34] The existing legal framework of protected areas, and the legislation underpinning it,[35] will continue to play an important role in implementing public policy for the future; but the proposals in the white paper will lead to a much wider approach aimed at reversing the fragmentation of the natural environment, a key problem identified in the Lawton report.[36] The white paper proposed the development of a wider protected areas policy, in which five categories of area are identified, with different and complementary roles in restoring a healthy ecological network.[37] 'Core' wildlife areas containing rare or important habitats or ecosystem services will continue to be based upon SSSIs and other legally protected areas, as at present. The current approach to the identification and notification of SSSIs will be retained, but the policies supporting it will be strengthened, by identifying and protecting mosaics of small habitats, stepping stones, or corridors linking core sites and necessary for species movement between them, by identifying restoration areas where high nature value habitats can be (re)created to become the core areas of the future, and by the identification of buffer zones to protect core areas, stepping stones, and restoration areas from adverse impacts.

32 *The Natural Choice: securing the value of nature,* Cm 8082, June 2011, esp. at para. 2.9.

33 For the partnership approach, see Chapter 1, p. 7.

34 *The Natural Choice: securing the value of nature,* (n. 32) at para. 2.10.

35 Primarily the Wildlife and Countryside Act 1981, Part 2 (Chapter 3, pp. 68ff.) and the Conservation no Habitats and Species Regulations 2010 (Chapter 6, pp. 216ff.).

36 Lawton et al. (2010) *Making Space for nature: a review of England's wildlife sites and ecological network,* available at: <http://www.defra.gov.uk/pubications/files/pb13428-newp-discussion-239710.pdf>.

37 *The Natural Choice: securing the value of nature,* (n. 32) at para. 2.12. These are: core areas; stepping stones or corridors; restoration areas; buffer zones; and sustainable use areas.

The white paper also proposed identifying 'sustainable use areas' where there is a focus on the sustainable use of natural resources, to make the wider countryside more 'permeable' to wildlife and less hostile. Presumably this would include large areas of the farmed countryside, where agri-environment policy is already targeted (through schemes such as Higher Level and Entry Level Stewardship) to securing environmental benefits to wildlife through the promotion of environmentally friendly farming techniques. The white paper proposed, for example, that Natural England should work with stakeholders to investigate whether the Entry Level Stewardship scheme could be reconfigured to support the development of stepping stones, wildlife corridors, and buffer zones. It also proposes that Natural England should pilot an approach based on *outcomes*, such as measurable and tangible habitat improvements, and investigate the use of management agreements which include greater flexibility as to how these outcomes are achieved.[38]

Equally significant are proposed changes to the institutional arrangements for supporting nature conservation. As we have seen,[39] the implementation of nature conservation and the protection of wildlife is currently administered by a number of public bodies, notably the statutory Conservation Bodies (such as Natural England) and local government bodies, although private bodies such as the National Trust and the wildlife trusts also play an important role in practice (for example, in developing and managing nature reserves). The white paper proposed a shift in institutional responsibility for nature conservation to 'local nature partnerships' (LNPs).[40] An LNP may include representation from local authorities, from local businesses, statutory bodies (Natural England or the Environment Agency for example), civil society organizations, land owners and land managers, and members of the local community.[41] It is envisaged that there will eventually be around 50 LNPs across England. Local nature partnerships will complement the local enterprise partnerships (LEPs) established under the Localism Act 2011, and it is hoped that they will work together in the future to capture the value of nature and ecosystem services, and in so doing contribute to the growth of the 'green economy' that lies at the heart of the white paper's proposals. Support from central government will be provided in the form of an annual conference for local nature partnerships to share good practice and experience; space will be provided by DEFRA on its website; and an initial contribution of £1 million was made by DEFRA in 2011/12 to establish the first partnerships.[42] The white paper also proposed the establishment of a smaller number of 'Nature Improvement Areas' (NIAs). These will be ecological restoration zones in which partnerships of local

[38] Cf. the use of management agreements at present (Chapter 4, pp. 131 ff.) where the terms of agreements are focused on land management prescriptions and practice, rather than measuring the impact and outcomes to which these give rise.

[39] See Chapter 2, pp. 35 ff.

[40] See further Chapter 2, at pp. 61 ff.

[41] See *the Natural Choice: securing the value of nature* (see n. 31) at para. 2.18. On local nature partnerships generally see paras. 2.15–2.26.

[42] The first 41 were announced in July 2012: see <http://archive.defra.gov.uk/environment/natural/documents/lnp-list-20120717.pdf>.

people, local authorities, community groups, landowners, the private sector, and conservation organizations will work to 'restore and connect nature on a significant scale'.[43] The first 12 NIAs were announced in 2012, following a competition overseen by Natural England.[44]

The National Ecosystem Assessment identified land use change as one of the primary drivers of biodiversity loss in the UK. This can take many forms, from the introduction of intensive agricultural techniques to the approval of development projects that result in a loss or degradation of protected habitats. The white paper proposed the development of 'biodiversity offsetting', incorporating complementary habitat expansion or restoration elsewhere in development proposals that will have an adverse impact on wildlife and biodiversity.[45] The focus of offsetting would be development control, and especially the need to ensure that habitat loss is compensated when local planning authorities grant approval for new development projects with adverse biodiversity implications. This is not a new concept. It is used, for example, under the European Habitats Directive, where offsetting is mandatory where a development proposal is approved which will have a damaging impact on a Special Area of Conservation.[46] Similarly, the Environmental Liability Directive[47] requires an operator to undertake 'complementary' remediation when environmental damage to a protected area has occurred, and primary remediation does not fully rectify the damage and restore the site to its primary condition.[48] Complementary remediation can include creating a replacement habitat on another site where primary remediation of the damaged area is not fully possible.

The approach championed in the white paper would see an expansion of offsetting, implemented through development control law and the National Planning Framework established under the Localism Act 2011. The objective of an increased use of offsetting, as a strategic tool to be used in development control decision making, is that it will complement existing protected habitat designations, and ensure that arresting biodiversity loss is a central factor in planning for sustainable development. The approach will be piloted in several trial areas, and will be premised on a voluntary approach with the active cooperation of developers in putting forward offsetting proposals in applications for planning permission for new development. The use of planning obligations, under which developers enter into legally binding undertakings to deliver public benefits as an incident of

[43] *The Natural Choice* (see n. 32) para. 2.27.

[44] See: <http://www.defra.gov.uk/environment/natural/whitepaper/ nia/>.

[45] See the planning policy now set out in the *National Planning Policy Framework* (Department for Communities and Local Government, 2012) at paras. 116–118.

[46] Directive 92/43/EEC, Article 4(4). This is now implemented in England by the Conservation of Habitats and Species Regulations 2010, SI 2010/490, reg. 66. Chapter 6, p. 230.

[47] Directive 2004/35/CE of the European Parliament and of the Council on environmental liability with regard to the prevention and remedying of environmental liability, as amended by Directive 2006/21/EC of the European Parliament and of the Council of 15 March 2006.

[48] Directive 2004/35/EC, Articles 2 and 8. Guidance on equivalence is given in Annex II para. 1.2.2–1.3.3. Where possible the new habitat should be geographically linked to the damaged site (see Annex II para. 1.2.2. This is now implemented by Schedule 4 paras. 4(3) and 5(1) Environmental Damage (Prevention and Remediation) Regulations 2009, SI 2009/153 (England). See further Chapter 4, pp. 152ff.

planning permission,[49] is not uncommon already and can deliver complementary conservation management where a proposed development will inevitably incur habitat damage and loss.[50] Although planning policy guidance[51] encourages local planning bodies to use planning obligations to mitigate environmental damage, they are not legally required to do so. The approach in the White Paper would add a stronger strategic direction and focus to the use of the existing planning mechanisms (planning obligations and planning agreements) to compensate for damage to conservation features arising from development. The expansion in the use of planning obligations could also give legal enforceability to a wider range of innovative offsetting measures developed under the new policy.

Major problems of policy design and implementation will remain, however, if the concept is to be successfully integrated into development control law and planning procedures for the future. Not least of these will be the formulation of a clear set of guiding principles on what constitutes an acceptable 'offset' for the purposes of compensating for habitat and species loss. The Natural Environment White Paper gave little guidance on this,[52] save to stress the need to develop an approach based on the guiding principles set out in the Lawton Report.[53] The latter[54] set out nine guiding principles by reference to which an offset strategy should be developed and guided. The fundamental principle would be to ensure that offsets are only used as a last resort to compensate for unavoidable damage to habitats or species; development should be structured to avoid adverse impacts first, to mitigate impacts second, and to compensate (through offsets) adverse impacts as a last resort. Offsets should aim at a net gain in biodiversity, and be supported with mechanisms to deliver long-term habitat management (more than 25 years in some cases). And they should ideally be in place before development commences. The Lawton Report also stressed the need to identify an appropriate public authority to oversee the administration of the biodiversity offsets scheme, to verify the effectiveness of offset delivery, and to develop the evidence base needed for its successful operation, eg by refining the creation and restoration techniques used for some habitat types, for establishing multipliers for ensuring full compensation is achieved, and for setting rules for 'out of kind' offsetting where damage to one type of habitat is offset by providing a different habitat elsewhere.[55]

49 S. 106 Town and Country Planning Act 1990; s. 75 Town and Country Planning (Scotland) Act 1995.

50 See eg *WWF UK Ltd v Secretary of State for Scotland* (1999) Env LR 632 (mitigating design measures and monitoring of habitats following development of Cairngorm funicular railway to replace ski-lift facility); *R v Plymouth City Council ex parte Plymouth and South Devon Cooperative Society* (1994) 67 P&CR 78 (provision of future habitat conservation and a bird-viewing hide).

51 See the *National Planning Policy Framework* (Department for Communities and Local Government 2012) at para. 203 ff.

52 There is little guidance on these issues in the *National Planning Policy Framework* document either, above n. 51.

53 *The Natural Choice* (n. 32) para. 2.40.

54 See *Making Space for Nature* (Lawton et al. 2010) at para. 6.4.3.

55 See Lawton et al. (2010) at p. 88.

New Instruments—Conservation Covenants and Easements

The policy developments signalled in the 2011 Natural Environment White Paper are also representative of moves to 'privatize' nature conservation. This raises the further question of whether there may be scope for the greater use of conservation easements and other private law mechanisms for the delivery of nature conservation by landowners and private sector organizations. The thrust of the shift in policy, toward replacing a largely state mediated approach to nature conservation with a more participatory model based on local partnerships, naturally focuses attention on the potential for the development of new legal instruments that can create enforceable obligations to undertake conservation management. The use of conservation easements or covenants could, for example, create legally binding obligations entered into by private individuals and independent (non-public) bodies to manage land on a long-term basis for nature conservation. And the land, and habitats, to be protected by the easement would be decided by private individuals and not necessarily dictated by whether the land were in an SSSI or other statutory protected area. The use of easements and covenants is in some ways an extension of the type of approach currently pursued through the use of management agreements with public bodies, and discussed in earlier chapters.[56] Management agreements are, however, usually for fixed periods (for example 10 years in the case of Higher Level Stewardship agreements), whereas a conservation easement or covenant could endure indefinitely.

Conservation easements are widely used in some other common law jurisdictions, notably the USA, to underpin conservation obligations attached to privately owned land. Their use in England and Wales has, however, been restricted by the rules of property law applicable to the creation and subsequent enforcement of incorporeal hereditaments. English law has developed rules to prevent the creation of obligations attached to land which can endure indefinitely, and which can act as an impediment or restriction on the future transfer and use of the land in question. In the case of an easement, these are normally expressed by the rule[57] that there must be a dominant and a servient tenement; the easement will bind the servient tenement (the land over which it is created) and must be for the benefit of a specified area of other land (the 'dominant' tenement or estate in land). The easement must be connected with the enjoyment of, or for the benefit of, the dominant land in a manner recognized by law, and the dominant and servient landowners must be different persons.

The requirement of a dominant and servient tenement means that an easement to manage land for conservation purposes cannot normally be taken from its owner unless the beneficiary of the easement has other land that is to benefit from the

[56] See Reid, 'Possible New Approaches to Nature Conservation Law in the UK' (2011) 23 JEL 203–31, esp. at 211ff.

[57] See *Re Ellenborough Park* [1956] Ch 131, 140 (Danckwerts J.).

obligation that is created (ie the dominant land).[58] It is not, therefore, possible to create an easement 'in gross', one which does not benefit another piece of land.[59] The rationale for this rule is to prevent the servient owner creating obligations of indefinite duration that would, otherwise, act as a 'clog on the title' to the property that renders it unmarketable.[60] It nevertheless creates considerable difficulties for the creation of conservation easements. The promotion of conservation management on land with high nature value (the 'servient tenement') will rarely confer a direct benefit on other land nearby in the same way that, for example, the creation of a right of way over it for access to the dominant land would,[61] or the creation of a right to park vehicles on it might. The pursuit of nature conservation objectives is, moreover, more commonly viewed as a matter of public interest. As we saw in Chapter 1,[62] wild animals and birds are not 'owned' by the owner of the land on which they may be found. There is therefore an inherent difficulty in viewing an easement to manage land in a way that improves its biodiversity (for example if it is in a local nature reserve) as benefiting a plot of adjacent 'dominant' land *as land*. A further difficulty arises from the fact that English law views the role of the servient owner as essentially passive; an easement should not normally require the servient owner to spend money or undertake positive or onerous activities on the land burdened with the easement.[63] Yet this is, of course, exactly what a conservation easement will normally require him to do. The central problem, therefore, is that the rules of English property law outlined earlier, which are aimed at preventing the creation of indefinite and enduring obligations by way of easements, do not take into account considerations of wider public policy when determining the type of obligation that can be created in this way.

The rule against the creation of easements or covenants 'in gross' has been relaxed in the case of the National Trust, which has statutory power to take conservation easements and covenants for an indefinite or fixed period from a landowner, even though it has no land of its own in the immediate vicinity.[64] They can, moreover, enforce a covenant or easement against a successor in title of the owner of the servient land over which the easement or covenant subsists.[65] Easements, once created, can in principle endure indefinitely. In the case of a freehold covenant, however, the rules have historically been more restrictive, and

[58] *London and Blenheim Estates Ltd v Ladbroke Retail Parks Ltd* [1992]1 WLR 1278; [1994] 1 WLR 31.

[59] It is, however, possible to create a profit à prendre in gross. See *Bettinson v Langton* [2001] 3 All ER 417 (common right of pasturage). This can cause difficult problems for conservation management as the rights can be transferred without land: see *Contested Common Land: environmental governance past and present* (Rodgers et al. 2010) at 7, 177–80.

[60] K. Gray, *Elements of Land Law*, 5th edn (Oxford University Press, 2009), at 5.1.22.

[61] Eg *Borman v Griffith* [1930] 1 Ch. 493.

[62] See Chapter 1, pp. 2–4.

[63] See *Liverpool CC v Irwin* [1977] AC 256.

[64] S. 8 National Trust Act 1937. Chapter 2, p. 53.

[65] S. 8 National Trust Act 1937: '[The National Trust] shall have power to enforce such agreement or covenant against persons deriving title under him in the like manner and to the like extent as if the National Trust were possessed of or entitled to or interested in adjacent land and as if the agreement or covenant had been and had been expressed to be entered into for the benefit of that adjacent land.'

only restrictive (or negative) covenants will run with the land and bind the servient land over which the covenant subsists in the hands of a successive owner.[66] A positive freehold covenant,[67] for example to manage land in accordance with a scheme of conservation management, is not enforceable against successors to the owner of the servient land with whom it was originally concluded.[68]

Although the Law Commission has recommended that new covenants that create positive obligations should in future be enforceable as 'land obligations' against successive owners of land, its recommendations fell short of suggesting that such interests should be enforceable 'in gross'.[69] Positive land obligations would, under the Commission's proposals, only be enforceable if they create obligations to do or not to do something on the burdened land or its boundary, and only if they 'touch and concern' the dominant land that they are intended to benefit.[70] In the case of conservation covenants, therefore, the problems outlined earlier in relation to easements (the nature of the benefit required to satisfy this rule, for example) will remain problematic. The Law Commission has, however, separately recognized that there may be a case for the creation of a limited exception to the general rule for situations 'where a conservation objective would be met if an obligation to use, or not use, land in a particular way is enforceable against an owner of land despite the benefiting party having no neighbouring land'.[71] Its *Eleventh Programme of Law Reform* includes a project to investigate whether a new statutory interest in land should be created (a 'conservation covenant') that could be enforced by a particular body, or class of bodies, rather than by a neighbour with land that will benefit from the covenant. The project will review the piecemeal situations in which such interests can be created under the current law,[72] and investigate the feasibility of creating a new, more efficient, and more flexible system. The review will consider not only the identification of those conservation interests that are sufficiently important to bind land, but also how such interests would function and be enforced.[73]

[66] See *Tulk v Moxhay* (1848) 41 ER 1143.

[67] Positive leasehold covenants are, however, enforceable against assignees of a lease: the rule in *Spencer's case* (1583) 5 Co Rep 16a, 77 ER 72.

[68] The rule in *Keppel v Bailey* (1834) 39 ER 1042; *Austerberry v Corporation of Oldham* (1885) LR 29 ChD 750.

[69] See Law Commission Report 327, *Making Land Work: Easements, Covenants and Profits a Prendre* (2011), para. 5.69. And see clauses 1 and 5 of the Commission's draft Law of Property Bill to implement these proposals: Law Commission Report 327, Appendix A.

[70] See Law Commission Report 327 at para. 5.51: 'a "touch and concern" requirement is a robust control mechanism that prevents land being overburdened, even if it is vulnerable to the uncertainties of judicial interpretation at times. It acts as a filter, in limiting the range of enforceable covenants; it can therefore counter assertions that the enforceability of positive obligations would open the door to a wide range of unsuitable burdens.'

[71] Law Commission, *Eleventh Programme of Law Reform* (Law Com No. 330, 2011) at para. 2.8: available at <http://lawcommission.justice.gov.uk/docs/lc330_eleventh_programme.pdf>.

[72] Examples given by the Law Commission *Eleventh Programme of Law Reform* (n. 71) para. 2.10 include: s. 7(3) Natural Environment and Rural Communities Act 2006 (for which, see Chapter 4, pp. 115–16); reg. 16(4) Conservation of Habitats and Species Regulations 2010 SI 2010/490 (for which, see Chapter 4, p. 114); and the Countryside Act 1968 s. 15(4) (Chapter 4, pp. 112–13).These all relate to covenants taken in management agreements.

[73] See Law Commission *Eleventh Programme of Law Reform* (n. 71) at paras. 2.8–2.13. A report is to be produced by the end of 2014 with a Draft Bill.

The position in Scottish law has moved ahead of that in England and Wales, and is somewhat different.[74] Under the Title Conditions (Scotland) Act 2003, a 'conservation burden' can be created under which both positive and negative obligations can be enforced against successive owners of the land burdened. The law allows the enforcement of burdens by charities and other bodies who do not own nearby land that is benefited (that is, what in English law are referred to as rights 'in gross'). However, this is subject to restrictions that seek to address the concerns that, in England, have prevented the adoption of a similar solution. A conservation burden can be created for the purpose of preserving or protecting for the benefit of the public '. . . any special characteristics of the land (including . . . a special characteristic derived from the flora, fauna or general appearance of the land').[75] Concern over the impact of permitting the enforcement of positive obligations as rights in gross have been addressed by restricting the power to enter into conservation burdens to named public and Conservation Bodies; and in cases where the burden is created otherwise than by the Scottish Ministers or a Conservation Body, then the latter must consent to the creation of the burden in its favour before it can be registered.[76] This prevents the proliferation of conservation burdens and limits their application to responsible public and Conservation Bodies that have a clear focus to wildlife and/or landscape protection and the protection of the built environment in Scotland. The bodies recognized as 'Conservation Bodies' for this purpose, and permitted to conclude conservation burdens, include all the local authorities in Scotland and a further 15 public and private bodies including:[77] the National Trust for Scotland, the RSPB, the Woodland Trust, the John Muir Trust, the Landmark Trust, the Edinburgh World Heritage Trust, the Glasgow Building Preservation Trust, the Highland Buildings Preservation Trust, Plantlife (The Wild-Plant Conservation Charity), Scottish Natural Heritage and Solway Heritage. Once created, a conservation burden can only be assigned to another Conservation Body or to the Scottish ministers.[78] And if the Conservation Body holding the burden ceases to be approved under the relevant Scottish legislation,[79] then the conservation burden is extinguished.[80] Further safeguards apply in that a conservation burden must be registered, thus creating certainty as to the terms of the burden and its application to the burdened land (relevant, for example, where there

[74] See generally Reid, 'The Privatisation of Biodiversity? Possible New Approaches to Nature Conservation Law in the UK' (2011) 23 JEL 203, esp. at 212–14.The Scottish legislation was also considered by the Law Commission in England and Wales when evaluating the options for structuring positive obligations, and weighing the problems of avoiding some of the difficulties that this would engender: see Law Commission Report 327, *Making Land Work: Easements, Covenants and Profits a Prendre* (2011), paras. 5.32 ff.

[75] S. 38(1) Title Conditions (Scotland) Act 2003. And see the Scottish Law Commission, *Report on Real Burdens* (Scot Law Com No 181 (2000)) paras. 9.1 ff.

[76] S. 38(2) Title Conditions (Scotland) Act 2003.

[77] See s. 38(4) Title Conditions (Scotland) Act 2003 and the Title Conditions (Scotland) Act 2003 (Conservation Bodies) Order 2003, Schedule, SSI 2003/453.

[78] S. 39 Title Conditions (Scotland) Act 2003.

[79] Ie currently the Title Conditions (Scotland) Act 2003 (Conservation Bodies) Order 2003, Schedule, SSI 2003/453, as amended, or its successor.

[80] See s. 42 Title Conditions (Scotland) Act 2003.

is a later sale of the land). And a burden can be varied or discharged at any time by the Lands Tribunal.[81]

It will be obvious from the earlier discussion that, although the 2011 Natural Environment White Paper expresses a strong desire for a change in policy in England towards greater private sector involvement in nature conservation at the local level (for example, though local nature partnerships), the possibilities for underpinning this by the more extensive use of conservation easements and covenants is limited. In Scotland, the 2003 Act has addressed many of the issues that have prevented the adoption of a more wide ranging response in England and Wales. In both jurisdictions, however, the ultimate success of initiatives to develop greater participation by landowners and private bodies will depend upon the provision of appropriate tax and financial incentives to make it economically worthwhile to enter into long-term conservation burdens.

Property Rights and the Limits of Law?

Nature conservation law is ultimately concerned with regulating, and structuring, man's interactions and relationship with nature, and ensuring that adverse consequences of this interaction are minimized or corrected. We have seen that environmental regulation has inherent limitations as a medium for improving natural habitats and increasing the range and quality of biodiversity. In the case of terrestrial natural habitats this is reflected in the fact that law has to accept and work within structures of established property rights, and the resource allocation that these implement. The common law recognizes no inherent restriction on land use rights, and a constant theme throughout this work has been to stress the limitations that the need to accommodate property rights places upon the design and implementation of schemes to promote nature conservation and environmental stewardship, and on the manner in which nature conservation objectives are pursued in practice.

It is important to recognize, however, that property rights are themselves a social construct—the resource allocation that is recognized by society and implemented through legal norms enforced by the legal system. Lawyers often tend to view property rights as separate and distinct from legal rules. This is a fallacy, for as a social construct 'property' rights are themselves governed and shaped by legal rules. The analysis presented in Chapter 1 of this work categorized property rules into two broad groups, those that create and protect property entitlements, and those that perform a resource allocation role.[82] The landowner's rights are reflected in property entitlement rules, and these are defined by common law and (in some cases, for example some types of lease) by statute. The 'property entitlements' that

[81] See Part 9 s 90 ff, Title Conditions (Scotland) Act 2003. The Tribunal must have regard to, inter alia, the extent to which the burden confers benefit on the land to be benefited, or (if there is none) it must consider the extent to which the burden confers benefit on the public: ss. 98 and 100 (b) Title Conditions (Scotland) Act 2003.

[82] See Chapter 1, p. 28.

these rules legitmize are, however, just that: *entitlements*. There is little room in the common law notion of 'property' for the idea that the landowner must also assume environmental responsibilities with the bundle of rights conferred by landownership. There is a case to be made, however, for the recognition of a responsibility of environmental stewardship as an inherent attribute of property entitlements in English Law.[83]

Many of the problems and weaknesses of modern nature conservation law arise from the inevitable conflict that arises between the legal norms reflected in property entitlement rules, which grant to landowners unrestricted and extensive land use rights, and the impact of environmental regulation that seeks to restrict or mould property rights in order to promote a public interest goal in environmental protection. The legal instruments introduced by the environmental legislation considered in earlier chapters of this book are focused on altering the resource allocation represented by property rights; to modify access to, and the use of, the land resource where this is necessary to pursue a public policy objective in furthering nature conservation. Environmental legislation has not sought, however, to alter the fundamental paradigm underpinning property entitlements. A more radical approach would seek to resolve the tension between property entitlements and the implementation of environmental policy by combining reform of the basic constituents of property entitlement rules with an ongoing modification of property rights as tools of resource reallocation. In as much as property rights (including entitlement rules) are themselves a social construct reflected in legal norms, it remains open to both the courts and legislature to adapt property rights to incorporate a duty of environmental stewardship. A model for 'environmental' property rights would modify those property entitlements that currently confer a right to undertake environmentally damaging land use, and incorporate an explicit recognition of a basic responsibility of environmental stewardship as an integral component of property entitlement rules at common law.

What obligations would a duty of environmental stewardship impose, and how would they be determined? The stewardship component of property entitlements could be based upon a model reflecting a 'suitable for use' standard, not dissimilar to that already used in the law on contaminated land, where the legal standard for the cleanup of contaminated sites is dependent upon the use for which land has development consent.[84] Where land is registered for agricultural use in the Rural

[83] And in relation to conservation of the marine environment, it can be argued that the introduction of rights-based mechanisms such as licences and fish catch quotas captures an environmental stewardship responsibility: see *Property Rights and Natural Resources* (Barnes 2009), Ch. 9, and also Chapter 7, pp. 242–3.

[84] See DEFRA, *Environmental Protection Act: Part 2A- Contaminated Land Statutory Guidance* (2012) published at <http://www.defra.gov.uk/publications/files/pb13735cont-land-guidance.pdf>. This guidance replaced guidance issued by DEFRA in 2006, and elaborates on the suitable for use concept in terms that stress the need to minimize risk and harm, rather than make land suitable for its current use. But this is unlikely to make much difference to the application of the guidance in practice: see further E. Lees, 'The contaminated land regime–new guidance, and a new philosophy?' (2012) 14 Env L Rev 267–278, and passim E. Lees, 'Interpreting the contaminated land regime: should the polluter pay?' (2012) 14 Env L Rev 98–110.

Land Register, for example, the stewardship obligation might reflect the principles of sustainable agriculture incorporated in the principles of good agricultural practice and in the cross compliance requirements for the single payment scheme, eg the obligation to maintain land in good agricultural and environmental condition.[85] The principles of good agricultural practice are currently subsumed in property rights, but are not clothed with legal enforceability outside the confines of a voluntary agri-environment agreement.[86] Similarly, cross compliance will only impose enforceable land management obligations if a landowner is claiming the single farm payment. These mechanisms currently effect, therefore, a very limited reassignment of property rights.

The reform of property entitlement rules to incorporate a duty of environmental responsibility would have important consequences for the interrelationship of the property entitlement and resource allocation functions of property rights.[87] The formal expression of property entitlement rules as integral to estates and interests in land gives them primacy over adjustments in property rights implemented by economic instruments and by public law mechanisms. The property owner's entitlement will have priority unless his rights are adjusted by statute, or he chooses to reassign them in an economic exchange such as a land management agreement. And the primacy granted to the owner's property entitlement at common law will determine the payment of compensation for reassigning legally vested rights.

It follows that the reassignment of property rights by a management agreement is temporary and only endures for the lifetime of the contract. Similarly, adjusting property rights through the application of cross compliance imposes a transient measure of environmental regulation. The management rights traded in return for direct support payments or payments under a management agreement are automatically reassigned to the property owner on termination of the subsidy arrangement, or on termination of the agreement. Moreover, if the producer is willing to farm without subsidy the cross compliance technique is inapplicable. It can only be used to reassign private property rights if economic conditions are such that producers are dependent on subsidy for production, and are willing to trade elements of resource utility conferred by property entitlements in an interdependence arising from their participation in direct support arrangements within the CAP. The exposure of these mechanisms to fluctuations in the market for agricultural commodities may also increase the cost of the incentives necessary to encourage producers to join environmental management schemes. The use of conservation easements or covenants would provide a permanent or longer enduring reassignment of property rights, but as we have seen, the conditions for their extensive use do not exist in England, and while Scottish law makes more extensive provision for conservation 'burdens' the use of tax and other

[85] See the Agriculture (Cross Compliance) (No. 2) Regulations 2009, SI 2009/3365, reg. 3 and Schedule 1 (as amended by SI 2010/2941); Common Agricultural Policy Single Payment and Support Schemes (Cross Compliance)(Wales) Regulations 2004, SI 2004/3280 (W284), as amended, Schedule.

[86] See Chapter 4, pp. 129–30.

[87] See Chapter 1, p. 28 and Box 1.3 on pp. 30–31.

financial incentives to encourage landowner participation in conservation measures is currently underdeveloped.

The delivery of a basic level of environmental management for valuable wildlife habitats and for promoting biodiversity is a public policy objective that should not be exposed to the vagaries of the market.[88] Improvements in environmental resource management could be more effectively protected if cross compliance conditions applied irrespective of whether landowners claimed the single farm payment. The primacy of property entitlement rules also means that on termination of a management agreement the owner's resource utility rights will revert to the *status quo ante*, without necessarily protecting any environmental 'gain' secured at public expense by the agreement. Similarly, in a protected area (such as an SSSI or *Natura 2000* site) while those land use rights that are represented by notified OLDIs will be reassigned to the statutory Conservation Body,[89] the adjustment in property rights that this represents is far from permanent. If the site is subsequently de-notified, property rights will automatically be reallocated to the owner by operation of law and the *status quo ante* reinstated. There is currently no mechanism to prevent environmentally damaging land uses being reintroduced in an SSSI or SAC that has been de-notified unless they constitute development requiring planning permission, and no means to protect environmental improvements provided at public expense under management agreements in protected areas (other than through the site notification mechanism itself).

Modifying property entitlements to include a basic stewardship duty is unlikely to infringe the prohibition on uncompensated 'takings' of property in article 1 of the Protocol to the European Convention.[90] In SSSIs the restrictions on carrying out OLDSIs are currently uncompensated unless a management agreement is negotiated with Natural England. The stewardship obligation suggested here would be more limited than those currently applied in most SSSIs. It would support protected areas policy for SSSIs by ensuring a basic level of environmental management for the wider countryside, recognizing the interdependence of protected ecosystems and the importance of ecosystem facilities for the migration, sustenance and genetic exchange of protected species. This would also contribute to the wider objectives set out in the Natural Environment White Paper, which stressed the need to improve the environmental quality of sustainable use areas of the wider countryside and make it more permeable for wildlife.[91]

The legal order for agri-environment schemes under the common agricultural policy already assumes that standards of good agricultural practice are an integral element of property rights. This may be the case in some continental legal systems, but not in English law, where property entitlements are currently unqualified by

[88] For a survey of environmental regulation and property rights reform proposals in the context of rural land use see C. Rodgers, 'Property rights, land use and the rural environment: a case for reform' (2009) 26S *Land Use Policy* 134–41.

[89] Ie Scottish Natural Heritage, Natural England or the Countryside Council for Wales; see Box 8.1 p. 290.

[90] See Chapter 4, at pp. 120–121.

[91] Pp. 295ff.

duties of stewardship or good practice. The modification of property entitlements suggested earlier would remedy this. Furthermore, many of the statutory management standards applied through cross compliance are based on pre-existing legal obligations, for example, as to the protection of hedgerows, avoiding overgrazing, and compliance with land use restrictions in notified SSSIs.[92] The cross compliance mechanism supplies an additional enforcement tool (withdrawal of subsidy) to ensure regulatory compliance. Those that are not so based require a very basic level of management, eg in the case of land not in agricultural production a requirement to keep it in good environmental and agricultural condition by grazing rank vegetation once every five years.[93]

The reform of property entitlements to recognize a stewardship responsibility would assist in delivering a stable and effective environmental policy for the protection of wildlife habitats, while underpinning both agri-environmental initiatives and public policy for protected areas more effectively than the present property rights regime permits. It would effect a rebalancing of rights and interests away from the private benefit of the landowner and recognize the wider community interest in, and reliance upon, the sustainable management of land.[94] It would also underpin improvements in environmental management secured through publicly funded agri-environment schemes more effectively than the law at present allows. And, of course, the assumption of a level of good practice would provide a basis for evaluating incentive payments under management agreements more widely than at present, where the rules are limited to rural development payments and the single farm payment under the CAP. The property entitlements that could be traded in an economic exchange would be adjusted to reflect the new stewardship obligation implicit in property entitlements.

Property, Environment, and the Limits of Regulation

The sub title to this work is 'Property, Environment and the Limits of Law'. It was noted earlier that 'property' is itself a social construct, supported and shaped by a system of legal rules, which performs the function of governing access to, and control of, material resources. This is especially true of property *rules*, which are

[92] See the Agriculture (Cross Compliance) (No. 2) Regulations 2009, SI 2009/3365, reg. 3 and Schedule 1 (as amended by SI 2010/2941); (eg as to overgrazing, the protection of hedgerows) and the observance of SSSI notifications); and the Common Agricultural Policy Single Payment and Support Schemes (Cross Compliance)(Wales) Regulations 2004 SI 2004/3280 (W284), as amended, reg. 4 and Schedule. at para. 6 (overgrazing), paras. 11 and 12 (protection of hedgerows), para. 21 (observance of SSSI notifications).

[93] Agriculture (Cross Compliance) (No. 2) Regulations 2009, SI 2009/3365, reg. 3 and Schedule 1 (as amended by SI 2010/2941); reg. 3 and Schedule; Common Agricultural Policy Single Payment and Support Schemes (Cross Compliance)(Wales) Regulations 2004 SI 2004/3280 (W284), as amended, reg. 4 and Schedule para. 7.

[94] See W. Lucy and C. Mitchell, 'Replacing Private Property: The Case for Stewardship' (1996) 55 *Cambridge Law Journal* 566.

essentially social rules for solving the problem of conflicts over access to resources.[95] As a social construct, the law in its broadest sense is not itself subject to any inherent limitations in its potential relevance to the promotion and management of nature conservation. Rather than recognize the inherent limits of *the law* in promoting nature conservation, it might be more apposite in conclusion to reflect on the choice of legal instruments and regulatory approaches to nature conservation that have been deployed since 1949, and on their relative strengths and weaknesses.

The law has developed from a largely voluntary approach in the immediate post-war years to one based on a mixture of regulation and the voluntary participation by property owners in nature conservation—encapsulated in the 'partnership' approach underpinning modern nature conservation policy.[96] We saw earlier that this has met with very limited success.[97] Command and control regulatory techniques, in particular, have inherent limitations as a vehicle for fostering nature conservation and for promoting biodiversity. The legislation on protected areas has, since the Countryside and Rights of Way Act 2000, been based on a mixture of command and control regulation[98] combined with the use of consensual techniques implemented through state mediated land management agreements with payments for positive conservation management by landowners.[99] The inadequacy of the regulatory techniques deployed hitherto by public policy is clearly demonstrated by the relative failure of the Wildlife and Countryside Act 1981 to prevent the loss of, and deterioration in, protected wildlife habitats, despite successive amendment in 1985, 2000, and 2006 to strengthen its regulatory elements.[100] A more appropriate sub title for this work might therefore have been 'Property, Environment and the Limits of Regulation'.

The development of a new approach to nature conservation following the Lawton Review and the 2011 Natural Environment White Paper is premised on a clear recognition of the shortcoming of the current law, and of the need for a more radical approach that engenders as wide a participation as possible in delivering nature conservation. The reforms will not, however, impact directly upon pre-existing property rights or alter the allocation of material resources represented in property rights.[101] The central premise of this work has been that the role of property rights as a resource allocation tool is fundamental—both to an understanding of the way in which the legal and economic instruments for promoting

[95] See J. Waldron, 'What is Private Property?' (1985) 5 OJLS 313 at 318.

[96] See Chapter 1, p. 7.

[97] See pp. 295ff. and Box 8.2.

[98] Typified in the OLDSI mechanism under s. 28E Wildlife and Countryside Act 1981 as amended by Schedule 9 to the 2000 Act.

[99] Eg under the arrangements for payments in protected areas: see the *Guidelines on Management Agreement Payments and related matters* (DEFRA 2001) Chapter 4, pp. 119ff, and more widely through agri-environment agreements under higher-level and entry-level stewardship agreements in England and their equivalents in Wales and Scotland.

[100] See Chapter 1, at pp. 4–8.

[101] There will be some property rights implications of the new local nature partnership proposals, however: eg in relation to development control decisions where the right to develop land may be subject to greater local control under the provisions in the Localism Act 2011.

nature conservation work in practice, and to any assessment of their efficiency and effectiveness. This will remain the case. The measures outlined in the 2011 Natural Environment White Paper will, when fully implemented, make potentially radical changes to the administration of nature conservation law, and may deepen and widen the partnership on which it is based. The underlying property rights of those engaged in this wider partnership endeavour will be unaffected, however, and they will have to be accommodated within any new conservation initiatives to which the reforms give rise.

A more radical reform would consider changes to the constituent elements of property entitlements, and to the rules that shape them. There is no inherent reason why the property entitlements recognized at common law should not be remodelled to include environmental stewardship responsibilities of a basic nature as outlined earlier. This would also bridge the gap between *public law* mechanisms for environmental regulation and the common law concepts that shape *private* property rights in land.[102] Common law concepts focus on the commercial and exploitative rights granted by property rights—as seen, for example, in the rules for establishing the validity of conservation easements and covenants discussed earlier.[103] These are largely inappropriate for securing public policy objectives in land management.

The law of nature conservation has, accordingly, developed largely through the use of land use controls introduced using public law instruments; the designation of protected areas by public bodies acting under statutory powers is one example of the many that have been discussed in earlier chapters of this work, and the use of development control another. Remodelling property rights to incorporate into the property domain relevant public policy objectives for the conservation of natural habitats and species would bridge this gap. It would, at the same time, introduce a new obligation of environmental stewardship into the property domain as a constituent element of the bundle of rights represented by property in land. Clothing a new duty of environmental stewardship with enforceability as a *legal* control on damaging land use would, however, raise significant difficulties. Conferring 'horizontal' enforceability on a duty of environmental stewardship could be accomplished fairly easily through changes to the administrative arrangements for the supervision of (for example) CAP support payments to farmers and through changes in the rules governing the oversight of management in protected areas (such as SSSIs) by the statutory Conservation Bodies.[104] Creating duties that are subject to direct enforcement by public bodies or members of the public would, however, be a much more difficult and challenging matter.

[102] See the discussion of the dichotomy between private and public law responses to ecology and nature conservation in Chapter 1, pp. 25ff. and Box 1.3.

[103] Pp. 302ff.

[104] For example through changes in the Guidelines for Management Agreements and Other Matters in SSSIs (DEFRA 2001), for which, see Chapter 4, at p. 119.

Select Bibliography

Adams, W. M. (1986) *Nature's Place: conservation sites and countryside change* (London and Boston: Allen & Unwin).

Adams, W. M. (1997) *Future Nature; a vision for conservation* (London: Earthscan).

Arnold, C. A. (2002) 'The Reconstitution of Property: Property as a Web of Interests', 26 *Harvard Environmental Law Review*, 281–364.

Balanced Seas Marine Conservation Zone Project, (2011) Final Recommendations 7th September 2011. Available at: <http://www.balancedseas.org/page/national_mcz.html>.

Baldock, D. and Mitchell, K. (1995) *Cross Compliance within the Common Agricultural Policy: a review of options or landscape and nature conservation* (London: IEEP).

Ball, S. (1996) 'Reforming the Law of Habitat Protection', in C. Rodgers (ed.) *Nature Conservation and Countryside Law* (Cardiff: University of Wales Press).

Barnes, R. (2009) *Property Rights and Natural Resources* (Oxford: Hart Publishing).

Bergkamp, L. (2000) 'Allocating Unknown Risk: Liability for Environmental Damage Caused by Deliberately Released Genetically Modified Organisms' (Social Science Research Network). Available at SSRN: http://ssrn.com/abstract=223068.

Bergkamp, L. (2000) 'The Commission's White Paper on Environmental Liability: A Weak Case for an EC Strict Liability Regime', 9 *European Environmental Law Review*, 105–14.

Birnie P., Boyle A., and Redgewell C. (2009) *International Law and the Environment* 3rd edn (New York: Oxford University Press).

Bishop, K., Phillips, A., and Warren, L. (1997) 'Protected Areas for the Future; Models from the Past', 40 *Journal of Environmental Planning and Management*, 81–110.

Blackstone, W. (1792) *Commentaries* on the Laws of England, vol. II. Available at: <http://avalon.law.yale.edu/subject_menus/blackstone.asp>.

Bosselmann, K. (2008) *The Principle of Sustainability—Transforming Law and Governance* (Aldershot: Ashgate).

Brans, E. H. P. (2005) 'Liability for Damage to Public Natural Resources under the 2004 Environmental Liability Directive', 7 *Environmental Law Review*, 90–109.

Bromley, D. W. (1991) *Environment and Economy: property rights and public policy* (Oxford: Basil Blackwell).

Butler, J. (2007) *Interactions between ecological condition and the management of grazing rights on Eskdale Common in the Lake District National Park*, Msc Thesis, Newcastle University.

Cardwell, M. (2006) 'The Polluter Pays Principle in European Community Law and its Impact on UK Farmers', 59 *Oklahoma Law Review*, 89–113.

Cardwell, M. (2011) 'European Union Agricultural Policy and Practice: The New Challenge of Climate Change', 13 *Environmental Law Review*, 271–95.

Cardwell, M. and Rodgers, C. P. (2006) 'Reforming the WTO Legal Order for Agricultural Trade: Issues for European Rural Policy in the Doha Round', 55 *International and Comparative Law Quarterly*, 805–38.

Cardwell, M. N. (2004) *The European Model of Agriculture* (Oxford: Oxford University Press).

Churchill R. and Lowe, V. (1999) *The Law of the Sea* (Manchester: Manchester University Press).

Coase, R. H. (1960) 'The Problem of Social Cost', 3 *Journal of Law and Economics*, 1–69.

Coase, R. H. (1986) *The Firm, the Market and the Law* (Chicago, University of Chicago Press).

Colby, B. (1995) 'Bargaining over Agricultural Property Rights', 77 *American Journal of Agricultural Economics*, 1186–91.

Commission of the European Communities (2002) *Assessment of plans and projects significantly affecting Natura 2000 sites: methodological guidance on the provisions of Article 6 (3) and (4) of the Habitats Directive 92/43/EEC* (Luxembourg: Office for Official Publications of the European Communities 2002).

Countryside Council for Wales, *Enforcement on SSSIs*. Available at: <http://www.ccw.gov.uk/landscape—wildlife/protecting-our-landscape/special-landscapes—sites/protected-landscapes/sssis/sssi—report/enforcement-on-sssis.aspx?lang = en>.

Cox G. and Lowe P. (1983) 'Countryside Politics: goodbye to goodwill?', 54 *Politics Quarterly*, 268–82.

Coyle, S. and.Morrow, K. (2004) *Philosophical Foundations of Environmental Law* (Oxford: Hart Publishing).

Demerieux, M. (2001) 'Deriving Environmental Rights from the European Convention for the Protection of Human Rights and Fundamental Freedoms', 21 *Oxford Journal of Legal Studies*, 521.

Demsetz, H. (1967) 'Towards a Theory of Property Rights', [1967] 57 *American Economic Review*, 373–59.

Demsetz, H. (2002) 'Towards a Theory of Property Rights II: The Competition between Private and Collective Ownership', 31 *Journal of Legal Studies*, S653-S672.

Department of Business Innovation and Skills (2009) The *Code of Practice on Guidance on Regulation.* Available at: <http://www.bis.gov.uk/files/file53268.pdf>.

Department for Communities and Local Government (1999) *Environmental Impact Assessment,* Circular 02/1999. Available at: https://www.gov.uk/government/publications/environmental-impact-assessment-circular-02-1999

Department for Communities and Local Government (2000) *Tree Preservation Orders: A Guide to the Law and Good Practice.* Available at: <http://www.communities.gov.uk/documents/planningandbuilding/pdf/tposguide.pdf>.

Department for Communities and Local Government (2012) *National Planning Policy Framework for England.* Available at: <http://www.communities.gov.uk/documents/planningandbuilding/pdf/2116950.pdf>.

Department of Environment Food and Rural Affairs (1998) *The Protection of Field Boundaries—Statutory Controls* (FB 7(a)). Available at: <http://www.publications.parliament.uk/pa/cm199798/cmselect/cmenvtra/969/8072921.htm>, and <http://archive.defra.gov.uk/rural/documents/protected/sssi-code.pdf>.

Department of Environment Food and Rural Affairs (2001) *Guidelines on Management Agreement Payments and other related matters.* Available at: <http://archive.defra.gov.uk/rural/documents/protected/sssi-payments.pdf>.

Department of Environment Food and Rural Affairs (2003) *Sites of Special Scientific interest: Encouraging Positive Partnerships* (code of guidance).

Department of Environment Food and Rural Affairs Circular 01/2005 *Government Circular: Biodiversity and Geological Conservation—Statutory Obligations and their impact within the Planning System* (16 August 2005). Available at: <https://www.gov.uk/government/uploads/system/uploads/attachment_data/file/7692/147570.pdf>.

Department of Environment Food and Rural Affairs (2007) *Conserving BioDiversity: The UK Approach.* Available at: <http://jncc.defra.gov.uk/_ukbap/UKBAP_ConBio-UKApproach-2007.pdf>.

Department of Environment Food and Rural Affairs (2008) *Farming and the Environment: Final Report of Sir Don Curry's High Level Set Aside Group.* Available at: <http://archive.defra.gov.uk/foodfarm/policy/sustainfarmfood/documents/hlsag-report080722.pdf>.

Department of Environment Food and Rural Affairs (2010) *The Government's strategy for contributing to the delivery of a UK Network of Marine Protected Areas,* London: DEFRA. Available at: <http://archive.defra.gov.uk/environment/marine/documents/mpa-strategy100330.pdf>.

Department of Environment Food and Rural Affairs (2010) *Making Space for nature: a review of England's wildlife sites and ecological network* (The 'Lawton Review'). Available at: <http://www.defra.gov.uk/pubications/files/pb13428-newp-discussion-239710.pdf>.

Department of Environment Food and Rural Affairs (2011) Science Advisory Panel: *Assessment of the Marine Conservation Zone Regional Projects Final Recommendations* (15 November 2011). Available at: <http://www.defra.gov.uk/environment/marine/protect/mpa/mcz/sap/>.

Department of Environment Food and Rural Affairs (2011) *The Natural Choice—securing the value of nature.* Available at: <http://www.defra.gov.uk/environment/natural/whitepaper/>.

Department of Environment Food and Rural Affairs (2012) *An Overview of the Local Nature Partnership Role.* Available at: <http://www.archive.defra.gov.uk/environment/natural/documents/local-nature-partnerships-overview120402.pdf>.

Department of Environment Food and Rural Affairs (2012) *Current Local Nature Partnerships.* Available at: <http://archive.defra.gov.uk/environment/natural/documents/lnp-list-20120717.pdf>.

Department of Environment Food and Rural Affairs (2012) *UK Biodiversity Indicators in Your Pocket 2012.* Available at: <http://jncc.defra.gov.uk/pdf/BIYP_2012.pdf>.

Department of the Environment Transport and the Regions (1981) *Financial Guidelines for Management Agreements under the Wildlife and Countryside Act 1981.* DETR Circular 4/83.

Dwyer J., Baldock D., and Einschutz S. (2000) *Cross Compliance under the Common Agricultural Policy—a report for the Department of the Environment Transport and the Regions.* (London, Institute for European Environmental Policy).

Frazier, T. W. (1995) 'The Green Alternative to Classical Liberal Property Theory', 20 *Vermont Law Review,* 299–371.

Freyfogle, E. T. (1999) 'Land Ownership and the Level of Regulation: The Particulars of Owning', 25 *Ecology Law Quarterly*, 574–601.

Gillespie, A. (2007) *Protected Areas in International Environmental Law* (Leiden: BRILL).

Gray, K. and Gray, S. F. (1998) 'The Idea of Property in Land' pp. 15–51, in Bright, S. and Dewar, K. (eds) *Land Law: Themes and Perspectives* (Oxford: Oxford University Press).

Gray, K. and Gray, S. F. (1999) 'Private Property and Public Propriety' pp. 11–39, in J. McLean (ed.) *Property and the Constitution* (Oxford: Hart Publishing Ltd).

Gray, K. J. (1991) 'Property in Thin Air' 50 *Cambridge Law Journal*, 252–307.

Gray, K. J. and Gray, S. F. (2009) *Elements of Land Law* 5th edn (Oxford: Oxford University Press).

Grossman, M. R. (2011) 'Good Agricultural Practice in the US: Conservation and Climate', 13 *Environment Law Review*, 296–317.

Hardin, G. (1968) 'The Tragedy of the Commons', 162 *Science*, 1243–48.

Harris, J. W. (1996) *Property and Justice* (Oxford: Clarendon Press).

Holder, J. (1999) 'Hedgerows, Laws and Cultural Landscape' in Holder J. and McGillivray, D. (eds) *Locality and Identity: Environmental Issues in Law and Society* (Dartmouth: Ashgate Publishing).

Holder, J. (1999) 'Law and Landscape: The Legal Construction and Protection of Hedgerows', 62 *Modern Law Review*, 100–14.

Holder, J. (2004) 'Overriding Public Interest in Planning and Conservation Law' 16 *Journal of Environmental Law*, 377–407.

Honore, A. (1961) 'Ownership' in Guest (ed.) *Oxford Essays in Jurisprudence* (Oxford: Clarendon Press).

House of Commons (2011) *The Natural Choice: securing the value of nature,* Cm 8082, June 2011.

House of Commons Environment Food and Rural Affairs Committee (2007) *Implementation of the Environmental Liability Directive, Sixth report of Session 2006–07* (HC 694) London: Stationery Office.

House of Commons Select Committee on Environment Transport and Rural Affairs (1998) *Protection of Field Boundaries*, 13th Report of 1997–8 (HC 869, London: Stationery Office).

Howarth, W. and McGillivray, D. (2001) *Water Pollution and Water Quality Law* (Crayford Kent, Shaw & Sons).

Irish Sea Marine Conservation Zones Project, Final Report. Available at: <http://www.irishseaconservation.org.uk/MCZ-recommendations>.

Jack, B. (2001) 'Protecting the European Environment from the Community: the case of agriculture', 3 *Environmental Law Review*, 44–60.

Jack, B. (2009) *Agriculture and EU Environmental Law* (Farnham: Ashgate).

Joint Nature Conservation Committee (1989, revised 1992, 1995, 1996, 1997, 1998) *Guidelines for the Selection of Biological SSSIs* (JNCC: Peterborough,). Available at: <http://jncc.defra.gov.uk/pdf/sssi_ptA.pdf>.

Joint Nature Conservation Committee (1998) *Statement on Common Standards Monitoring,* (JNCC: Peterborough). Available at: <http://jncc.defra.gov.uk/page-2198>.

Joint Nature Conservation Committee (2006) Common Standards Monitoring for Designated Sites: first six year report (JNCC 2006), Available at: <http://jncc.defra.gov.uk/pdf/CSM_06summary.pdf>.

Joint Nature Conservation Committee, (2007) *Second Report by the United Kingdom under article 17 on the Implementation of the Habitats Directive from January 2001to December 2006*, (Peterborough: JNCC). Available at: <http:// www.jncc.gov.uk/article17>.

Joint Nature Conservation Committee (2011) *Geological Conservation Review.* Available at: <http://jncc.defra.gov.uk/default.aspx?page = 2947>.

Jones, P. J. S. (2006) 'Collective Action Problems Posed by No-Take Zones', 30 *Marine Policy*, 143–56.

Jones, P. J. S. (2009) 'Equity Justice and Power Issues raised by No-Take Marine Protected Area Proposals', 33 *Marine Policy*, 759–65.

Jones, P. J. S. (2012) 'Marine Protected Areas in the UK: challenges in combining top down and bottom up approaches to governance', 39 *Environmental Conservation*, 248–58.

Jones, P. J. S. and Burgess, J. (2005) 'Building Partnership Capacity for the Collaborative Management of Marine Protected Areas in the UK: A Preliminary Analysis', 77 *Journal of Environmental Management*, 227–43.

Joseph, P. A. (2003) 'The Environment, Property Rights and Public Choice Theory', 20 *NZULR*, 408.

Kramer, L. (2009) 'A Review of the European Commission's Opinions under Article 6(4) of the Habitats Directive', 21 *Journal of Environmental Law*, 59–85.

Last, K. (1999) 'Habitat Protection: Has the Wildlife and Countryside Act 1981 made a difference?', 11 *Journal of Environmental Law* 15–34

Last, K. (2000) 'Mechanism for Environmental Regulation—A Study of Habitat Conservation', 38–61 in A. Ross (ed.) *Environment and Regulation* (Hulme Papers on Public Policy Vol. 8) (Edinburgh: Edinburgh University Press).

Law Commission (2011) *Eleventh Programme of Law Reform* (Law Com. No. 330, 2011). Available at: <http://lawcommission.justice.gov.uk/docs/lc330_eleventh_programme.pdf>.

Law Commission (2011), *Making Land Work: Easements, Covenants and Profits a Prendre* (Law Com No. 327, 2011).

Lee, M. (2003) 'Regulatory Solutions for GMOs in Europe: the Problem of Liability', 12 *Journal of Environmental Law and Policy*, 311.

Lees, E. (2012) 'Interpreting the contaminated land regime: should the "polluter" pay?', 14 *Environmental Law Review*, 98–110.

Lees, E. (2012) 'The contaminated land regime- new guidance, and a new philosophy?',14 *Environmental Law Review*, 267–78.

Leopold, A. (1949) *A Sand County Almanac* (Oxford: Oxford University Press).

Livingstone, L., Rowan-Robinson, J., and Cunninghaw, R. (1990) *Management Agreements for Nature Conservation in Scotland* (Aberdeen, University of Aberdeen).

Lowe P., Cox, G., MacEwan, M., O'Riordan, T. and Winter, M. (1986) *Countryside Conflicts: the politics of farming, forestry and conservation* (Aldershot and Vermont: Gower Publishing).

Lucy, W. N. R. and Mitchell, C. (1996) 'Replacing Private Property: the Case for Stewardship', 55 *Cambridge Law Journal*, 566–600.

Macrory, R. (ed.) (2006) 'EC Law and Biodiversity' in *Reflections on 30 Years of EU Environmental Law: A High level of Protection?* (Groningen: Europa Law Publishing).

MacLean, J. (ed.) (1999) *Property and the Constitution* (Oxford: Hart Publishing).

Machin, G. (2004) 'Protecting Bird Habitat of European Importance—the view from Basses Corbieres', 6 *Environmental Law Review*, 174–89.

Metzger, M. B. (1976) 'Private Property and Environment Sanity', 5 *Ecology Law Quarterly*, 793–819.

Moore, V. (2012) *A Practical Approach to Planning Law* 12th edn (Oxford: Oxford University Press).

Mynors, C. (1999) 'Hedgerows, Biodiversity and Rupert Bear', in N. Herbert-Young (ed.) *Law, Policy and Development in the Rural Environment* (Cardiff: University of Wales Press).

Natural England (2008) *Regulatory Strategy*. Available at: <http://www.naturalengland.org.uk/images/natural-england-regulatorystrategy_tcm6-20560.pdf>.

Natural England (2008) *Sites of Special Scientific Interest (SSSI): a notification strategy for England.* Available at: <http://www.naturalengland.org.uk/Images/Notification%20strategy%20for%20web_tcm6-15235.pdf>.

Natural England (2008) *State of the Natural Environment.* Available at: <http://www.naturalengland.org.uk/Images/sone-section6.3_tcm6-4794.pdf>.

Natural England (2009) *A Hampton Implementation Review Report* (Department for Business Innovation and Skills and the Better Regulation Executive). Available at: <http://www.naturalengland.org.uk/images/natural-england-regulatorystrategy_tcm6-20560.pdf>.

Natural England (2009) *Agri-Environment Schemes in England: a review of results and effectiveness.* Available at: <http://www.naturalengland.org.uk/Images/AE-schemes09_tcm6-14969.pdf>.

Natural England (2010) *Lost Life—England's Lost and Threatened Species* (Natural England Research Report NE233: Peterborough).

Natural England (2011) *Annual Report on Natural England's Enforcement Activity 1 April 2010 to 31 March 2011.* Available at: <http://www.naturalengland.org.uk/Images/annual-report2010-11_tcm6-27479.pdf>.

Natural England (2011) *Enforcement Guidance.* Available at: <http://www.naturalengland.org.uk/Images/enforcement-guidance_tcm6-29091.pdf>.

Natural England (2011) *Higher Level Stewardship: Environmental Stewardship Handbook* 3rd edn (NE227). Available at: <http://publications.naturalengland.org.uk/publication/31047?category = 45001>.

Natural England (2011) *Protecting England's'Natural Treasures: Sites of Special Scientific Interest* (Natural England Research Report NE306: Peterborough). Available at: <http://publications.naturalengland.org.uk/publication/47003?category=20003>.

Natural England (2012) *Public Register—civil sanctions and prosecutions.* Available at: <http://www.naturalengland.org.uk/freedom_of_information/class6.aspx>.

Natural England and the Joint Nature Conservation Committee (2010) *The Marine Conservation Zone Project: Ecological Network Guidance.* (JNCC: Sheffield and Peterborough). Available at: <http://www.naturalengland.org.uk/ourwork/marine/mpa/mcz/guidanceandadvice.aspx>.

North Sea Marine Conservation Zone Project Final Report. Available at: <http://www.netgainmcz.org/docs/Net_Gain_Final_Rec_v1_1.pdf>.

Palmer, C. (1998) *Environmental Ethics and Process Thinking.* (Oxford: Clarendon Press).

Penner, J. (1998) 'The "Bundle of Rights" Picture of Property', 43 *UCLA Law Review*, 711–820.

Pigou, A. C. (1932) *The Economics of Welfare* 4th edn (London: Macmillan).

Potter, C. (1998) *Against the Grain: Agri Environmental Reform in the United States and the European Union.* (New York: CABI).

Purdue, M. (2004) 'The Human Rights Act, planning and proportionality', 6 *Environmental Law Review*, 161–73.

Raff, M. (1998) 'Environmental Obligations and the Western Liberal property Concept', 22 *Melbourne University Law Review*, 657–92.

Reid, C. (2011) 'The Privatisation of Biodiversity? Possible New Approaches to Nature Conservation Law in the UK', 23 *Journal of Environmental Law*, 203–31.

Reid, C. T. (2000) 'Devolution and the Environment' in A. Ross (ed.) *Environment and Regulation.* (Edinburgh: Edinburgh University Press).

Reid, C. T. (2009) *Nature Conservation Law* 3rd edn (Edinburgh: Thomson/W. Green).

Rodgers, C. (1996) 'Environmental Gain, Set-aside and the Implementation of EU Agricultural Reform in the United Kingdom' in C. P. Rodgers (ed.) *Nature Conservation and Countryside Law.* (Cardiff: University of Wales Press).

Rodgers, C. (2009) 'Property Rights, land use and the rural environment: a case for reform', 26S *Land Use Policy,* 134–41.

Rodgers, C. P. (1998) 'Reforming Property Rights for Nature Conservation' in P. Jackson and D. C. Wilde (eds) *Property Law: Current Issues and Debates* (Aldershot: Ashgate).

Rodgers, C. P. (2003) 'Agenda 2000, Land use and the Environment: Towards a Theory of Environmental Property Rights' in J. Holder and C. Harrison (eds) *Law and Geography* (Oxford, Oxford University Press).

Rodgers, C. P. (2008) *Agricultural Law* 3rd edn (Haywards Heath: Tottel Publishing Ltd).

Rodgers, C. P. (2009) 'Implementing the EC Environmental Liability Directive: GMOS and the Problem of Unknown Risk', in L. Bodiguel. and M. N. Cardwell (eds) *The Regulation of GMOs: Comparative Approaches* (Oxford: Oxford University Press).

Rodgers, C. P. (2009) 'Nature's Place? Property Rights, Property Rules and Environmental Stewardship', 68 *Cambridge Law Journal,* 550–74.

Rodgers, C. P. (2009) 'Rural Development Policy and Environmental Protection: Reorienting English Law for a multifunctional agriculture', 14 *Drake Journal of Agricultural Law*, 259.

Rodgers, C. and Bishop, J. (1998) *Management Agreements for Promoting Nature Conservation* (London; Royal Institution of Chartered Surveyors, RICS Research Reports).

Rodgers, C. P., Straughton, E. A., Winchester, A., and Pieraccini, M. (2010) *Contested Common Land: Environmental Governance Past and Present* (London: Earthscan).

Ross, A. (2008) 'Why legislate for Sustainable Development? An Examination of Sustainable Development Provisions in UK and Scottish Statutes', 20 *Journal of Environmental Law*, 35–68.

Ross, A. (2009) 'Modern interpretations of sustainable development', 36 *Journal of Law and Society*, 32–54.

Ross, A. and Rowan-Robinson, J. (1999) 'Behind Closed Doors: the use of agreements in the UK to protect the environment', 1 *Environment Law Review*, 82–94.

Scottish Government (2011) *Marine Protected Areas in Scotland's Seas: Guidelines on the selection of MPAs and development of the MPA network* (Marine Scotland, JNCC and Scottish Natural Heritage, 2011). Available at: <http://www.scotland.gov.uk/Resource/Doc/295194/0114024.pdf>.

Scottish Government (2011) Marine Scotland, (2011) '*A Strategy for Marine Nature Conservation in Scotland's Seas*' Scottish Government (March 2011). Available at: <http://www.scotland.gov.uk/Resource/Doc/295194/0115590.pdf>.

Scottish Natural Heritage (2012) *Recommended List of Priority Marine Features for Scottish Territorial Waters* (2012) Available at: <http://www.snh.gov.uk/docs/B1064114.pdf>.

Scottish Natural Heritage (2008) *SNH Guidance: Policy Guidance—Wildlife Crime.* Available at: <http://www.snh.gov.uk/docs/A328657.pdf>.

Shoard, M. (1997) *This Land is Our Land* (London, Gaia Books).

Swinbank, A. and Tranter, R. (2005) 'Decoupling EU Farm Support: Does the New Single Payment Scheme Fit within the Green Box?', 6 *Estey Centre Journal of International Law and Trade Policy*, 47–61.

UK National Ecosystem Assessment. Available at: <http://uknea.unep-wcmc.org/Resources/tabid/82/Default.aspx>.

Waldron, J. (1985) 'What is Private Property?', 5 *Oxford Journal of Legal Studies*, 313–49.

Warren, L. M. (1996) 'Law and Policy for Marine Protected Areas', Chapter 3 in C. P. Rodgers (ed.) *Nature Conservation and Countryside Law* (Cardiff: University of Wales Press).

Welsh Assembly Government (2003) *SSSI condition summary for Wales* Available at: <http://www.ccgc.gov.uk/landscape—wildlife/protecting-our-landscape/special-landscapes—sites/protected-landscapes-and-sites/sssis/sssi—report/habitat-features.aspx>.

Welsh Assembly Government (2010) *A Living Wales—a new framework for our environment, our countryside, our seas.* Available at: <http://wales.gov.uk/topics/environmentcountryside/consmanagement/nef/?land = eng>.

Whitby, M. (ed.) (1994) *Incentives for Countryside Management: the Case of Environmentally Sensitive Areas* (Oxford, Wallingford CABI).

Whitby, M. and Saunders, C. (1996) 'Estimating the Supply of Conservation Goods in Britain; A Comparison of the Financial Efficiency of Two Policy Instruments', 72 *Land Economics*, 313–25.

Winter, Michael (1996) *Rural Politics: policies for agriculture, forestry and the environment* (London: Routledge).

Woolf, Lord H., Jowell J., and Le Sueur, A. (2007) *De Smith's Judicial Review* 6th edn (London: Sweet & Maxwell).

Index